Named Entities Workshop: Shared Task on Transliteration 2009

(NEWS 2009)

Held at ACL-IJCNLP 2009

Singapore
7 August 2009

ISBN: 978-1-61738-457-8

Printed from e-media with permission by:

Curran Associates, Inc.
57 Morehouse Lane
Red Hook, NY 12571

proceedings.com

Some format issues inherent in the e-media version may also appear in this print version.

Printed by Curran Associates, Inc. (2010)

For permission requests, please contact the Association for Computational Linguistics at the address below.

Association for Computational Linguistics
209 N. Eighth Street
Stroudsburg, Pennsylvania 18360

Phone: 1-570-476-8006
Fax: 1-570-476-0860

acl@aclweb.org

Additional copies of this publication are available from:

Curran Associates, Inc.
57 Morehouse Lane
Red Hook, NY 12571 USA
Phone: 845-758-0400
Fax: 845-758-2634
Email: curran@proceedings.com
Web: www.proceedings.com

Preface

Named Entities play a significant role in Natural Language Processing and Information Retrieval. While identifying and analyzing named entities in a given natural language is a challenging research problem by itself, the phenomenal growth in the Internet user population, especially among the non-English speaking parts of the world, has extended this problem to the crosslingual arena. This is the specific research focus for the Named Entities WorkShop (NEWS), being held as a part of ACL-IJCNLP 2009 conference.

The purpose of the NEWS workshop is to bring together researchers across the world interested in identification, analysis, extraction, mining and transformation of named entities in monolingual or multilingual natural language text. Under such broad scope as above, many interesting specific research areas pertaining to the named entities are identified, such as, orthographic and phonetic characteristics, corpus analysis, unsupervised and supervised named entities extraction in monolingual or multilingual corpus, transliteration modelling, and evaluation methodologies, to name a few. 17 research papers were submitted, each of which was reviewed by at least 3 reviewers from the program committee. Finally, 9 papers were chosen for publication, covering main research areas, from named entities tagging and extraction, to computational phonology to machine transliteration of named entities. All accepted research papers are published in the workshop proceedings.

An important part of the NEWS workshop is the shared task on Machine Transliteration of named entities. Machine transliteration is a vibrant research area as witnessed by increasing number of publications over the last decade in the Computational Linguistics, Natural Language Processing (ACL, EACL, NAACL, IJCNLP, COLING, HLT, EMNLP, etc.), and Information Retrieval (SIGIR, ECIR, AIRS, etc.) conferences, and primarily in languages that use non-Latin based scripts. However, in spite of its popularity, no meaningful comparison could be possible between the research approaches, as the publications tended to be on different language pairs and different datasets, and on a variety of different metrics. For the first time, we organize a shared task as part of the NEWS workshop to provide a common evaluation platform for benchmarking and calibration of transliteration technologies.

We collected significantly large, hand-crafted parallel named entities corpora in 7 different languages from 6 language families, and made available as common dataset for the shared task. We defined 6 metrics that are language-independent, intuitive and computationally easy to compute. We published the details of the shared task and the training and development data six months ahead of the conference that attracted an overwhelming response from the research community. Totally 31 teams participated from around the world, including industry, government laboratories and academia. The approaches ranged from traditional unsupervised learning methods (such as, naive-Bayes, Phrasal SMT-based, Conditional Random Fields, etc.) to somewhat unique approaches (such as, sequence prediction models, to Minimum Description Length-based methods, etc.), combined with several model combinations for results re-ranking. While every team submitted *standard runs* that use only the data provided by the NEWS organizers, many teams also submitted *non-standard runs* where they were allowed to use any additional data or language specific modules. In total, about 190 task runs were submitted, covering most approaches comprehensively. A report of the shared task that summarizes all submissions and the original whitepaper are also included in the proceedings, and will be presented in the workshop. The participants in the shared task were asked to submit short system papers (4 pages each) describing their approach, and each of such papers was reviewed by at least two members of the program committee; 27 of them were finally are accepted to publish in the workshop proceedings.

NEWS 2009 is the first workshop that specifically addresses comprehensively all research avenues concerned with named entities, to the best of our knowledge. Also, the transliteration shared task is the first of its kind, to calibrate such large number of systems using common metrics on common language-specific datasets in a comprehensive set of language pairs.

We hope that NEWS 2009 would provide an exciting and productive forum for researchers working in this research area. The technical programme includes 9 research papers and 27 system papers to be presented in the workshop. Further, we are pleased to have invited Dr Kevin Knight to deliver a keynote speech in the workshop. Dr Knight is a well-known researcher in natural language processing, an Associate Professor at University of Southern California, and the Founder and Chief Scientist of Language Weaver, a human communication solutions company.

We wish to thank all the researchers for their research submission and the enthusiastic participation in the transliteration shared task. We wish to express our gratitude for the data providers (CJK Institute, Institute for Infocomm Research and Microsoft Research India) for the shared task. Finally, we thank all the programme committee members for reviewing the submissions in spite of the tight schedule.

Workshop Chairs

Haizhou Li, *Institute for Infocomm Research, Singapore*
A Kumaran, *Microsoft Research, India*

7 August 2009

Organizers

Chairs
Haizhou Li, *Institute for Infocomm Research, Singapore*
A Kumaran, *Microsoft Research, India*

Organizing Committee
Sanjeev Khudanpur, *Johns Hopkins University, USA*
Raghavendra Udupa, *Microsoft Research, India*
Min Zhang, *Institute for Infocomm Research, Singapore*
Monojit Choudhury, *Microsoft Research, India*

Program Committee
Kalika Bali, *Microsoft Research, India*
Rafael Banchs, *BarcelonaMedia, Spain*
Sivaji Bandyopadhyay, *University of Jadavpur, India*
Pushpak Bhattacharyya, *IIT-Bombay, India*
Monojit Choudhury, *Microsoft Research, India*
Marta Ruiz Costa-jussà, *UPC, Spain*
Gregory Grefenstette, *Exalead, France*
Sanjeev Khudanpur, *Johns Hopkins University, USA*
Kevin Knight, *University of Southern California/ISI, USA*
Greg Kondrak, *University of Alberta, Canada*
A Kumaran, *Microsoft Research, India*
Olivia Kwong, *City University, Hong Kong*
Gina-Anne Levow, *University of Chicago, USA*
Haizhou Li, *Institute for Infocomm Research, Singapore*
Raghavendra Udupa, *Microsoft Research, India*
Arul Menezes, *Microsoft Research, USA*
Jong-Hoon Oh, *NICT, Japan*
Vladimir Pervouchine, *Institute for Infocomm Research, Singapore*
Yan Qu, *Advertising.com, USA*
Sunita Sarawagi, *IIT-Bombay, India*
Sudeshna Sarkar, *IIT-Kharagpur, India*
Richard Sproat, *University of Illinois, Urbana-Champaign, USA*
Keh-Yih Su, *Behavior Design Corporation, Taiwan*
Raghavendra Udupa, *Microsoft Research, India*
Vasudeva Varma, *IIIT-Hyderabad, India*
Min Zhang, *Institute for Infocomm Research, Singapore*

Table of Contents

Conference Program

Friday, August 7, 2009

8:30–9:10 Opening Remarks

Overview of the Shared Tasks

Report of NEWS 2009 Machine Transliteration Shared Task
Haizhou Li, A Kumaran, Vladimir Pervouchine and Min Zhang

Keynote Speech

9:10–10:00 *Automata for Transliteration and Machine Translation*
Kevin Knight

10:00–10:30 Coffee Break

Session 1: Shared Task Paper Presentation

10:30–10:45 *DirecTL: a Language Independent Approach to Transliteration*
Sittichai Jiampojamarn, Aditya Bhargava, Qing Dou, Kenneth Dwyer and Grzegorz Kondrak

10:45–11:00 *Named Entity Transcription with Pair n-Gram Models*
Martin Jansche and Richard Sproat

11:00–11:15 *Machine Transliteration using Target-Language Grapheme and Phoneme: Multi-engine Transliteration Approach*
Jong-Hoon Oh, Kiyotaka Uchimoto and Kentaro Torisawa

11:15–11:30 *A Language-Independent Transliteration Schema Using Character Aligned Models at NEWS 2009*
Praneeth Shishtla, Surya Ganesh V, Sethuramalingam Subramaniam and Vasudeva Varma

11:30–11:45 *Experiences with English-Hindi, English-Tamil and English-Kannada Transliteration Tasks at NEWS 2009*
Manoj Kumar Chinnakotla and Om P. Damani

Friday, August 7, 2009 (continued)

12:00–13:50 Lunch Break

Session 2: Posters

13:50–15:30 Poster Presentation

Friday, August 7, 2009 (continued)

Friday, August 7, 2009 (continued)

Bridging Languages by SuperSense Entity Tagging
Davide Picca, Alfio Massimiliano Gliozzo and Simone Campora

Chinese-English Organization Name Translation Based on Correlative Expansion
Feiliang Ren, Muhua Zhu, Huizhen Wang and Jingbo Zhu

Name Matching between Roman and Chinese Scripts: Machine Complements Human
Ken Samuel, Alan Rubenstein, Sherri Condon and Alex Yeh

Analysis and Robust Extraction of Changing Named Entities
Masatoshi Tsuchiya, Shoko Endo and Seiichi Nakagawa

15:30–16:00 Coffee Break

Session 3: Research Paper Presentation

16:00–16:20 *Tag Confidence Measure for Semi-Automatically Updating Named Entity Recognition*
Kuniko Saito and Kenji Imamura

16:20–16:40 *A Hybrid Model for Urdu Hindi Transliteration*
Abbas Malik, Laurent Besacier, Christian Boitet and Pushpak Bhattacharyya

16:40–17:00 *Graphemic Approximation of Phonological Context for English-Chinese Transliteration*
Oi Yee Kwong

17:00–17:20 *Czech Named Entity Corpus and SVM-based Recognizer*
Jana Kravalova and Zdenek Zabokrtsky

17:20–17:40 *Voted NER System using Appropriate Unlabeled Data*
Asif Ekbal and Sivaji Bandyopadhyay

Report of NEWS 2009 Machine Transliteration Shared Task

Haizhou Li[†], **A Kumaran**[‡], **Vladimir Pervouchine**[†] **and Min Zhang**[†]

[†]Institute for Infocomm Research, A*STAR, Singapore 138632
{hli,vpervouchine,mzhang}@i2r.a-star.edu.sg

[‡]Multilingual Systems Research, Microsoft Research India
A.Kumaran@microsoft.com

Abstract

This report documents the details of the Machine Transliteration Shared Task conducted as a part of the Named Entities Workshop (NEWS), an ACL-IJCNLP 2009 workshop. The shared task features machine transliteration of proper names from English to a set of languages. This shared task has witnessed enthusiastic participation of 31 teams from all over the world, with diversity of participation for a given system and wide coverage for a given language pair (more than a dozen participants per language pair). Diverse transliteration methodologies are represented adequately in the shared task for a given language pair, thus underscoring the fact that the workshop may truly indicate the state of the art in machine transliteration in these language pairs. We measure and report 6 performance metrics on the submitted results. We believe that the shared task has successfully achieved the following objectives: (i) bringing together the community of researchers in the area of Machine Transliteration to focus on various research avenues, (ii) Calibrating systems on common corpora, using common metrics, thus creating a reasonable baseline for the state-of-the-art of transliteration systems, and (iii) providing a quantitative basis for meaningful comparison and analysis between various algorithmic approaches used in machine transliteration. We believe that the results of this shared task would uncover a host of interesting research problems, giving impetus to research in this significant research area.

1 Introduction

Names play a significant role in many Natural Language Processing (NLP) and Information Retrieval (IR) systems. They have a critical role in Cross Language Information Retrieval (CLIR) and Machine Translation (MT) systems as the systems' performances are shown to positively correlate with the correct conversion of names between the languages in several studies (Demner-Fushman and Oard, 2002; Mandl and Womser-Hacker, 2005; Hermjakob et al., 2008; Udupa et al., 2009). The traditional source for name equivalence, the bilingual dictionaries — whether handcrafted or statistical — offer only limited support as they do not have sufficient coverage of names. New names are introduced to the vocabulary of a language every day.

All of the above point to the critical need for robust Machine Transliteration technology and systems. This has attracted attention from the research community. Over the last decade scores of papers on Machine Transliteration have appeared in the top Computational Linguistics, Information Retrieval and Data Management conferences, exploring diverse algorithmic approaches in a wide variety of different languages (Knight and Graehl, 1998; Li et al., 2004; Zelenko and Aone, 2006; Sproat et al., 2006; Sherif and Kondrak, 2007; Hermjakob et al., 2008; Goldwasser and Roth, 2008; Goldberg and Elhadad, 2008; Klementiev and Roth, 2006). However, there has not been any coordinated effort in calibrating the state-of-the-art technical capabilities of machine transliteration: the studies explore different algorithmic approaches in different language pairs and report their performance in different metrics and tested on different corpora.

The overarching objective of this shared task is to drive the machine transliteration technology forward, to measure and baseline the state-of-the-

Proceedings of the 2009 Named Entities Workshop, ACL-IJCNLP 2009, pages 1–18,
Suntec, Singapore, 7 August 2009. ©2009 ACL and AFNLP

art and to provide a meaningful comparison between the most promising algorithmic approaches in order to stimulate the discussions among the researchers. The NLP community in Asia is especially interested in transliteration as several major Asian languages do not use Latin script in their native writing systems. The Named Entity Workshop (NEWS 2009) in ACL-IJCNLP 2009 in Singapore provides an ideal platform for the shared task to take off. This is precisely what we address in this shared task on machine transliteration that is conducted as a part of the Named Entity Workshop (NEWS-2009), an ACL-IJCNLP 2009 workshop.

The shared task aims at achieving the following objectives:

- Providing a forum to bring together the community of researchers in the area of Machine Transliteration to focus on various research avenues in this important research area.
- Calibrating systems on common hand-crafted corpora, using common metrics, in many different languages, thus creating a reasonable baseline for the state-of-the-art of transliteration systems.
- Analysing the results so that a reasonable comparison of different algorithmic approaches and their trade-offs (such as, transliteration quality vs. generality of approach across languages vs. training data size, etc.) may be explored.

We believe that a substantial part of what we have set out to achieve has been accomplished, and we present this report as a record of the task process, system participation and results and our findings. It is our hope that this reporting will generate lively discussions during the NEWS workshop and subsequent research in this important area.

This introduction outlines the purpose of the transliteration shared task conducted as a part of the NEWS workshop. Section 2 outlines the machine transliteration task and the corpora used and Section 3 discusses the metrics chosen for evaluation, along with the rationale for choosing them. Section 4 sketches the participation. Section 5 presents the results of the shared task and the analysis of the results. Section 6, summarises the queries and feedback we have received from the participants and Section 7 concludes, presenting some lessons learnt from the current edition of the shared task, and some ideas we want to pursue in the future plan for the Machine Transliteration tasks.

2 Transliteration Shared Task

In this section, we outline the definition of the task, the process followed and the rationale for the decisions.

2.1 "Transliteration": A definition

There exists several terms that are used interchangeably in the contemporary research literature for the conversion of names between two languages, such as, transliteration, transcription, and sometimes Romanisation, especially if Latin scripts are used for target strings (Halpern, 2007).

Our aim is not only at capturing the name conversion process from a source to a target language, but also at its ultimate utility for downstream applications, such as CLIR and MT. We have narrowed down to three specific requirements for the task, as follows: *"Transliteration is the conversion of a given name in the source language (a text string in the source writing system or orthography) to a name in the target language (another text string in the target writing system or orthography), such that the target language name is: (i) phonemically equivalent to the source name (ii) conforms to the phonology of the target language and (iii) matches the user intuition of the equivalent of the source language name in the target language."*

Given that the phoneme set of languages may not be exactly the same, the first requirement must be diluted to "close to", instead of "equivalent". The second requirement is needed to ensure that the target string is a valid string as per the target language phonology. The third requirement is introduced to produce what a normal user would expect (at least for the popular names), and in order to make it useful for downstream applications like MT or CLIR systems. Though the third requirement make systems produce target language strings that marginally violate the first or second requirements, it ensures that such transliteration system is of value to downstream systems. All the above requirements are implicitly enforced by the choice of name pairs used to define the training and test corpora in a given language pair. In cases where multiple equivalent target language names are possible for a source language name, we include all of them.

After much debate, we have also retained the task name as "transliteration", though our definition may be closest to the "popular transcription" (Halpern, 2007), due to the popularity of term "Machine Transliteration" among the language technology researchers.

2.2 Shared Task Description

The shared task is specified as development of machine transliteration systems in one or more of the specified language pairs. Each language pair of the shared task consists of a source and a target language, implicitly specifying the transliteration direction. Training and development data in each of the language pairs have been made available to all registered participants for developing a transliteration system for that specific language pair using any approach that they find appropriate.

At the evaluation time, a standard hand-crafted test set consisting of between 1,000 and 3,000 source names (approximately 10% of the training data size) have been released, on which the participants are required to produce a ranked list of transliteration candidates in the target language for each source name. The system output is tested against a reference set (which may include multiple correct transliterations for some source names), and the performance of a system is captured in multiple metrics (defined in Section 3), each designed to capture a specific performance dimension.

For every language pair every participant is required to submit one run (designated as a "standard" run) that uses only the data provided by the NEWS workshop organisers in that language pair, and no other data or linguistic resources. This standard run ensures parity between systems and enables meaningful comparison of performance of various algorithmic approaches in a given language pair. Participants are allowed to submit more runs (designated as "non-standard") for every language pair using either data beyond that provided by the shared task organisers or linguistic resources in a specific language, or both. This essentially may enable any participant to demonstrate the limits of performance of their system in a given language pair.

The shared task timelines provide adequate time for development, testing (approximately 2 months after the release of the training data) and the final result submission (5 days after the release of the test data).

2.3 Shared Task Corpora

We have had two specific constraints in selecting languages for the shared task: language diversity and data availability. To make the shared task interesting and to attract wider participation, it is important to ensure a reasonable variety among the languages in terms of linguistic diversity, orthography and geography. Clearly, the ability of procuring and distributing a reasonably large (approximately 10K paired names for training and testing together) hand-crafted corpora consisting primarily of paired names is critical for this process. At the end of the planning stage and after discussion with the data providers, we have chosen the set of 7 languages shown in Table 1 for the task (Li et al., 2004; Kumaran and Kellner, 2007; MSRI, 2009; CJKI, 2009).

For all of the languages chosen, we have been able to procure paired names data between English and the respective languages and were able to make them available to the participants. In addition, we have been able to procure a specific corpus of about 40K Romanised Japanese names and their Kanji counterparts, and the corresponding language pair (Japanese names from their Romanised form to Kanji) has been included as one of the task language pair.

It should be noted here that each corpus has a definite skew in its characteristics: the names in the Chinese, Japanese and Korean (CJK) language corpora are Western names; the Indic languages (Hindi, Kannada and Tamil) corpora consists of a mix of Indian and Western names. The Romanised Kanji to Kanji corpus consists only of native Japanese names. While such characteristics may have provided us an opportunity to specifically measure the performance for forward transliterations (in CJK) and backward transliterations (in Romanised Kanji), we do not highlight such fine distinctions in this edition.

Finally, it should be noted here that the corpora procured and released for NEWS 2009 represent perhaps the most diverse and largest corpora to be used for any common transliteration tasks today.

3 Evaluation Metrics and Rationale

The participants have been asked to submit results of one standard and up to four non-standard

Source language	Target language	Data Source	Data Size (No. source names) Training	Development	Testing	Task ID
English	Hindi	Microsoft Research India	9,975	974	1,000	EnHi
English	Tamil	Microsoft Research India	7,974	987	1,000	EnTa
English	Kannada	Microsoft Research India	7,990	968	1,000	EnKa
English	Russian	Microsoft Research India	5,977	943	1,000	EnRu
English	Chinese	Institute for Infocomm Research	31,961	2,896	2,896	EnCh
English	Korean Hangul	CJK Institute	4,785	987	989	EnKo
English	Japanese Katakana	CJK Institute	23,225	1,492	1,489	EnJa
Japanese name (in English)	Japanese Kanji	CJK Institute	6,785	1,500	1,500	JnJk

Table 1: Source and target languages for the shared task on transliteration.

runs. Each run contains a ranked list of up to 10 candidate transliterations for each source name. The submitted results are compared to the ground truth (reference transliterations) using 6 evaluation metrics capturing different aspects of transliteration performance. Since a name may have multiple correct transliterations, all these alternatives are treated equally in the evaluation, that is, any of these alternatives is considered as a correct transliteration, and all candidates matching any of the reference transliterations are accepted as correct ones.

The following notation is further assumed:

- N : Total number of names (source words) in the test set
- n_i : Number of reference transliterations for i-th name in the test set ($n_i \geq 1$)
- $r_{i,j}$: j-th reference transliteration for i-th name in the test set
- $c_{i,k}$: k-th candidate transliteration (system output) for i-th name in the test set ($1 \leq k \leq 10$)
- K_i : Number of candidate transliterations produced by a transliteration system

3.1 Word Accuracy in Top-1 (ACC)

Also known as Word Error Rate, it measures correctness of the first transliteration candidate in the candidate list produced by a transliteration system. $ACC = 1$ means that all top candidates are correct transliterations i.e. they match one of the references, and $ACC = 0$ means that none of the top candidates are correct.

$$ACC = \frac{1}{N}\sum_{i=1}^{N}\left\{\begin{array}{l} 1 \text{ if } \exists r_{i,j} : r_{i,j} = c_{i,1}; \\ 0 \text{ otherwise} \end{array}\right\} \quad (1)$$

3.2 Fuzziness in Top-1 (Mean F-score)

The mean F-score measures how different, on average, the top transliteration candidate is from its closest reference. F-score for each source word is a function of Precision and Recall and equals 1 when the top candidate matches one of the references, and 0 when there are no common characters between the candidate and any of the references.

Precision and Recall are calculated based on the length of the Longest Common Subsequence (LCS) between a candidate and a reference:

$$LCS(c,r) = \frac{1}{2}\left(|c| + |r| - ED(c,r)\right) \quad (2)$$

where ED is the edit distance and $|x|$ is the length of x. For example, the longest common subsequence between "abcd" and "afcde" is "acd" and its length is 3. The best matching reference, that is, the reference for which the edit distance has the minimum, is taken for calculation. If the best matching reference is given by

$$r_{i,m} = \arg\min_j \left(ED(c_{i,1}, r_{i,j})\right) \quad (3)$$

then Recall, Precision and F-score for i-th word are calculated as

$$R_i = \frac{LCS(c_{i,1}, r_{i,m})}{|r_{i,m}|} \quad (4)$$

$$P_i = \frac{LCS(c_{i,1}, r_{i,m})}{|c_{i,1}|} \quad (5)$$

$$F_i = 2\frac{R_i \times P_i}{R_i + P_i} \quad (6)$$

- The length is computed in distinct Unicode characters.
- No distinction is made on different character types of a language (e.g., vowel vs. consonants vs. combining diereses' etc.)

3.3 Mean Reciprocal Rank (MRR)

Measures traditional MRR *for any right answer* produced by the system, from among the candidates. $1/MRR$ tells approximately the average rank of the correct transliteration. MRR closer to 1 implies that the correct answer is mostly produced close to the top of the n-best lists.

$$RR_i = \left\{ \begin{array}{l} \min_j \frac{1}{j} \text{ if } \exists r_{i,j}, c_{i,k} : r_{i,j} = c_{i,k}; \\ 0 \text{ otherwise} \end{array} \right\} \quad (7)$$

$$MRR = \frac{1}{N} \sum_{i=1}^{N} RR_i \quad (8)$$

3.4 MAP$_{ref}$

Measures tightly the precision in the n-best candidates for i-th source name, for which reference transliterations are available. If all of the references are produced, then the MAP is 1. Let's denote the number of correct candidates for the i-th source word in k-best list as $num(i, k)$. MAP$_{ref}$ is then given by

$$MAP_{ref} = \frac{1}{N} \sum_{i}^{N} \frac{1}{n_i} \left(\sum_{k=1}^{n_i} num(i, k) \right) \quad (9)$$

3.5 MAP$_{10}$

MAP$_{10}$ measures the precision in the 10-best candidates for i-th source name provided by the candidate system. In general, the higher MAP$_{10}$ is, the better is the quality of the transliteration system in capturing the multiple references.

$$MAP_{10} = \frac{1}{N} \sum_{i=1}^{N} \frac{1}{10} \left(\sum_{k=1}^{10} num(i, k) \right) \quad (10)$$

3.6 MAP$_{sys}$

MAP$_{sys}$ measures the precision in the top K_i-best candidates produced by the system for i-th source name, for which n_i reference transliterations are available. This measure allows the systems to produce variable number of transliterations, based on their confidence in identifying and producing correct transliterations.

$$MAP_{sys} = \frac{1}{N} \sum_{i=1}^{N} \frac{1}{K_i} \left(\sum_{k=1}^{K_i} num(i, k) \right) \quad (11)$$

4 Participation in Shared Task

There have been 31 systems from around the world that participated in the shared task and submitted the transliteration results for a common test data, produced by their systems trained on the common training corpora.

A few teams have participated in all or almost all tasks (that is, language pairs); most others participated in 3 tasks on average. Each language pair has attracted on average around 13 teams. The participation details are shown in Table 3 and the demographics of the participating teams by country is shown in Figure 1.

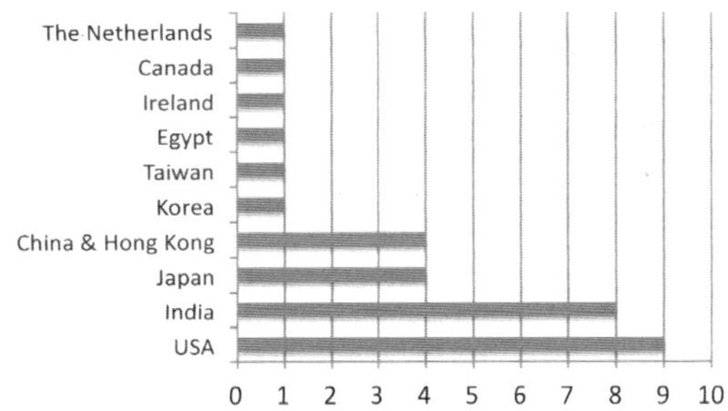

Figure 1: Participation by country.

Teams are required to submit at least one standard run for every task they participated in. In total 104 standard and 86 non-standard runs have been submitted. Table 2 shows the number of standard and non-standard runs submitted for each task. It is clear that the most "popular" tasks are transliteration from English to Hindi and from English to Chinese, attempted by 21 and 18 participants respectively. Overall, as can be noted from the results, each task has received significant participation.

5 Task Results and Analysis

5.1 Standard runs

The 8 individual plots in Figure 2 summarise (for each task) the results of standard runs via 3 measured metrics concerning output of at least one correct candidate per source word, namely, accuracy in top-1, F-score and Mean Reciprocal Rank (MRR). The plots in Figure 3 summarise (for each task) the results for 3 metrics on ranked ordered transliteration output of the systems, namely MAP$_{ref}$, MAP$_{10}$ and MAP$_{sys}$ metrics. All the results are presented numerically in Tables 8–11, for all evaluation metrics. These are the official

	English to Hindi	English to Tamil	English to Kannada	English to Russian	English to Chinese	English to Korean	English to Japanese Katakana	Japanese transliterated to Japanese Kanji
Language pair code	EnHi	EnTa	EnKa	EnRu	EnCh	EnKo	EnJa	JnJk
Standard runs	21	13	14	13	18	8	10	7
Non-standard runs	18	5	5	16	20	9	5	8

Table 2: Number of runs submitted for each task. Number of participants coincides with the number of standard runs submitted.

evaluation results published for this edition of the transliteration shared task. Note that two teams have updated their results (after fixing bugs in their systems) after the deadline; their results are identified specifically.

We find that two approaches to transliteration are most popular in the shared task submissions. One of these approaches is Phrase-based statistical machine transliteration (Finch and Sumita, 2008), an approach initially developed for machine translation (Koehn et al., 2003). Systems that adopted this approach are (Song, 2009; Haque et al., 2009; Noeman, 2009; Rama and Gali, 2009; Chinnakotla and Damani, 2009).[1] The other is Conditional Random Fields(Lafferty et al., 2001) (CRF), adopted by (Aramaki and Abekawa, 2009; Shishtla et al., 2009). With only a few exceptions, most implementations are based on approaches that are language-independent. Indeed, many of the participants fielded their systems on multiple languages, as can be seen from Table 3.

We also note that combination of several different models via re-ranking of their outputs (CRF, Maximum Entropy Model, Margin Infused Relaxed Algorithm) proves to be very successful (Oh et al., 2009); their system (reported as Team ID 6) produced the best or second-best transliteration performance consistently across all metrics, in all tasks, except Japanese back-transliteration. Examples of other model combinations are (Das et al., 2009).

At least two teams (reported as Team IDs 14 and 27) incorporate language origin detection in their system (Bose and Sarkar, 2009; Khapra and Bhattacharyya, 2009). The Indian language corpora contains names of both English and Indic origin. Khapra and Bhattacharyya (2009) demonstrate how much the transliteration performance can be improved when language of origin detection is employed, followed by a language-specific transliteration model for decoding.

Some systems merit specific mention as they adopt are rather unique approaches. Jiampojamarn et al. (2009) propose DirectTL discriminative sequence prediction model that is language-independent (reported as Team ID 7). Their transliteration accuracy is among the highest in several tasks (EnCh, EnHi and EnRu). Zelenko (2009) present an approach to the transliteration problem based on Minimum Description Length (MDL) principle. Freitag and Wang (2009) approach the problem of transliteration with bidirectional perceptron edit models.

Finally, in Figure 4 we present a plot where each point represents a standard run by a system, with different tasks marked with specific shape and colour. This plot gives a bird-eye-view of the system performances across two most uncorrelated evaluation metrics, namely accuracy in top-1 (ACC) and Mean F-score. Not surprisingly, we notice very high performance in terms of F-score for English to Russian transliteration task, likely because Russian orthography follows pronunciation very closely, except for characters like soft and hard signs that can hardly be recovered from English words.

We also observe that Japanese back-transliteration has proven to be much harder than other (forward-transliteration) tasks. In general, we note that a well-performing transliteration system performs well across all metrics. We are curious about the correlation between different metrics, and the results (specifically, the Spearman's rank correlation coefficient) are presented below:

- Accuracy in top-1 vs. F-score: 0.40
- Accuracy in top-1 vs. MRR: 0.97
- Accuracy in top-1 vs. MAP_{ref}: 0.997

[1] To maintain anonymity, papers of the teams that submitted anonymous results are not cited in this report.

- Accuracy in top-1 vs. MAP_{10}: 0.89
- Accuracy in top-1 vs. MAP_{sys}: 0.80

We find that F-score is the most uncorrelated metric: the Spearman's rank correlation coefficient between F-score and accuracy in top-1 is 0.40 and between F-score and MRR it is 0.44. This is likely because all metrics, except for F-score, are based on word accuracy, while F-score is based on word similarity allowing non-matching words to have scores well above 0.

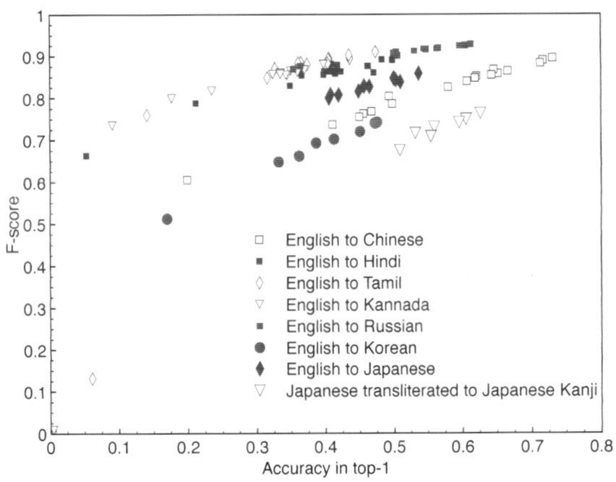

Figure 4: Accuracy in top-1 vs. F-score for different tasks.

5.2 Non-standard runs

For the non-standard runs there exist no restrictions for the teams on the use of more data or other linguistic resources. The purpose of non-standard runs is to see how accurate personal name transliteration can be, for a given language pair. The approaches used in non-standard runs are typical and may be summarised as follows:

- Dictionary lookup.
- Pronunciation dictionaries to convert words to their phonetic transcription.
- Additional corpora for training and dictionary lookup, such as LDC English-Chinese named entity list LDC2005T34 (Linguistic Data Consortium, 2005).
- Web search, and in particular, Wikipedia search. First, transliteration candidates are generated. Then a Web search is performed to see if any of the candidates appear in the search results. Based on the results, the candidates are re-ranked.

The results are shown in Tables 16–19. For English to Chinese and English to Russian transliteration tasks the accuracy in top-1 can go as high as 0.909 and 0.955 respectively when Web search is used to aid transliteration.

5.3 Post-evaluation

Two participants have found a bug in their system implementation and re-evaluated the results after the deadline. Their results are marked specifically in Tables 4–8 and 16.

6 Process Analysis and Fine-tuning

In this section we highlight some of the suggestions and feedback that we have received from the participants during the course of this shared task. While a few of them have been implemented in the current edition, many of these may be considered in the future editions of the shared task.

More or different languages There is quite a bit of interest in enhancing the list of language pairs short-listed. While we are constrained (in this edition) due to the availability of manually verified data, certainly more languages will be included in the future editions, as some specific data have already been promised for future editions.

Bidirectional transliteration Many participants express interest in transliterations into English; and this reflexive task will be added in the future editions. We believe it will encourage more participation as it will be easy to read and verify system output in English for those teams not familiar with the non-English side of the language.

Forward vs. backward transliteration There is quite a bit of interest expressed in specifically separating forward and backward transliteration tasks. However, such separation requires specific corpora with known origin for each name pair, and clearly we are constrained by the availability of corpora. When corpora is available, the task may be designated explicitly in future editions.

Number of standard runs The number of standard runs that may be submitted may be increased in the future editions, as many participants would like to submit many standard runs, trained with different parameters.

Errors in training and development corpora While we have taken all precautions in acquiring and creating the corpora, some errors still remain. We thank those who have sent us the errata. However, since the affected part is less than 0.5% of the data, we believe that the effect on final results is minimal. The errata will be made available to all participants.

7 Conclusions and Future Plans

We are pleased to report a comprehensive calibration and baselining of machine transliteration apporaches as most state-of-the-art machine transliteration techniques are represented in the shared task. The most popular techniques such as Phrase-Based Machine Transliteration (Koehn et al., 2003), and Conditional Random Fields (Lafferty et al., 2001) are inspired by recent progress in machine translation. As the standard runs are limited by the use of corpus, most of the systems are implemented under the direct orthographic mapping (DOM) framework (Li et al., 2004). While the standard runs allow us to conduct meaningful comparison across different algorithms, we recognise that the non-standard runs open up more opportunities for exploiting larger linguistic corpora. It is also noted that several systems have reported improved performance over any previously reported results on similar corpora.

NEWS 2009 Shared Task represents a successful debut of a community effort in driving machine transliteration techniques forward. The overwhelming responses in the first shared task also warrant continuation of such an effort in future ACL or IJCNLP events.

Acknowledgements

The organisers of the NEWS 2009 Shared Task would like to thank the Institute for Infocomm Research (Singapore), Microsoft Research India and CJK Institute (Japan) for providing the corpora and technical support. Without those, the Shared Task would not be possible. We thank those participants who identified errors in the data and sent us the errata. We want to thank Monojit Choudhury for his contribution to metrics defined for the shared task. We also want to thank the members of programme committee for their invaluable comments that improve the quality of the shared task papers. Finally, we wish to thank all the participants for their active participation that have made this first machine transliteration shared task a comprehensive one.

References

Eiji Aramaki and Takeshi Abekawa. 2009. Fast decoding and easy implementation: Transliteration as a sequential labeling. In *Proc. ACL/IJCNLP Named Entities Workshop Shared Task*.

Dipankar Bose and Sudeshna Sarkar. 2009. Learning multi character alignment rules and classification of training data for transliteration. In *Proc. ACL/IJCNLP Named Entities Workshop Shared Task*.

Manoj Kumar Chinnakotla and Om P. Damani. 2009. Experiences with English-Hindi, English-Tamil and English-Kannada transliteration tasks at NEWS 2009. In *Proc. ACL/IJCNLP Named Entities Workshop Shared Task*.

CJKI. 2009. CJK Institute. http://www.cjk.org/.

Amitava Das, Asif Ekbal, Tapabrata Mondal, and Sivaji Bandyopadhyay. 2009. English to Hindi machine transliteration system at NEWS 2009. In *Proc. ACL/IJCNLP Named Entities Workshop Shared Task*.

D. Demner-Fushman and D. W. Oard. 2002. The effect of bilingual term list size on dictionary-based cross-language information retrieval. In *Proc. 36-th Hawaii Int'l. Conf. System Sciences*, volume 4, page 108.2.

Andrew Finch and Eiichiro Sumita. 2008. Phrase-based machine transliteration. In *Proc. 3rd Int'l. Joint Conf NLP*, volume 1, Hyderabad, India, January.

Dayne Freitag and Zhiqiang Wang. 2009. Name transliteration with bidirectional perceptron edit models. In *Proc. ACL/IJCNLP Named Entities Workshop Shared Task*.

Yoav Goldberg and Michael Elhadad. 2008. Identification of transliterated foreign words in Hebrew script. In *Proc. CICLing*, volume LNCS 4919, pages 466–477.

Dan Goldwasser and Dan Roth. 2008. Transliteration as constrained optimization. In *Proc. EMNLP*, pages 353–362.

Jack Halpern. 2007. The challenges and pitfalls of Arabic romanization and arabization. In *Proc. Workshop on Comp. Approaches to Arabic Script-based Lang.*

Rejwanul Haque, Sandipan Dandapat, Ankit Kumar Srivastava, Sudip Kumar Naskar, and Andy Way. 2009. English-Hindi transliteration using context-informed PB-SMT. In *Proc. ACL/IJCNLP Named Entities Workshop Shared Task*.

Ulf Hermjakob, Kevin Knight, and Hal Daumé. 2008. Name translation in statistical machine translation: Learning when to transliterate. In *Proc. ACL*, Columbus, OH, USA, June.

Sittichai Jiampojamarn, Aditya Bhargava, Qing Dou, Kenneth Dwyer, and Grzegorz Kondrak. 2009. DirecTL: a language-independent approach to transliteration. In *Proc. ACL/IJCNLP Named Entities Workshop Shared Task*.

Mitesh Khapra and Pushpak Bhattacharyya. 2009. Improving transliteration accuracy using word-origin detection and lexicon lookup. In *Proc. ACL/IJCNLP Named Entities Workshop Shared Task*.

Alexandre Klementiev and Dan Roth. 2006. Weakly supervised named entity transliteration and discovery from multilingual comparable corpora. In *Proc. 21st Int'l Conf Computational Linguistics and 44th Annual Meeting of ACL*, pages 817–824, Sydney, Australia, July.

Kevin Knight and Jonathan Graehl. 1998. Machine transliteration. *Computational Linguistics*, 24(4).

P. Koehn, F. J. Och, and D. Marcu. 2003. Statistical phrase-based translation. In *Proc. HLT-NAACL*.

A Kumaran and T. Kellner. 2007. A generic framework for machine transliteration. In *Proc. SIGIR*, pages 721–722.

J. Lafferty, A. McCallum, and F. Pereira. 2001. Conditional random fields: Probabilistic models for segmenting and labeling sequence data. In *Proc. Int'l. Conf. Machine Learning*, pages 282–289.

Haizhou Li, Min Zhang, and Jian Su. 2004. A joint source-channel model for machine transliteration. In *Proc. 42nd ACL Annual Meeting*, pages 159–166, Barcelona, Spain.

Linguistic Data Consortium. 2005. LDC Chinese-English name entity lists LDC2005T34.

T. Mandl and C. Womser-Hacker. 2005. The effect of named entities on effectiveness in cross-language information retrieval evaluation. In *Proc. ACM Symp. Applied Comp.*, pages 1059–1064.

MSRI. 2009. Microsoft Research India. http://research.microsoft.com/india.

Sara Noeman. 2009. Language independent transliteration system using phrase based SMT approach on substring. In *Proc. ACL/IJCNLP Named Entities Workshop Shared Task*.

Jong-Hoon Oh, Kiyotaka Uchimoto, and Kentaro Torisawa. 2009. Machine transliteration with target-language grapheme and phoneme: Multi-engine transliteration approach. In *Proc. ACL/IJCNLP Named Entities Workshop Shared Task*.

Taraka Rama and Karthik Gali. 2009. Modeling machine transliteration as a phrase based statistical machine translation problem. In *Proc. ACL/IJCNLP Named Entities Workshop Shared Task*.

Tarek Sherif and Grzegorz Kondrak. 2007. Substring-based transliteration. In *Proc. 45th Annual Meeting of the ACL*, pages 944–951, Prague, Czech Republic, June.

Praneeth Shishtla, V Surya Ganesh, S Sethuramalingam, and Vasudeva Varma. 2009. A language-independent transliteration schema using character aligned models. In *Proc. ACL/IJCNLP Named Entities Workshop Shared Task.*

Yan Song. 2009. Name entities transliteration via improved statistical translation on character-level chunks. In *Proc. ACL/IJCNLP Named Entities Workshop Shared Task.*

Richard Sproat, Tao Tao, and ChengXiang Zhai. 2006. Named entity transliteration with comparable corpora. In *Proc. 21st Int'l Conf Computational Linguistics and 44th Annual Meeting of ACL*, pages 73–80, Sydney, Australia.

Raghavendra Udupa, K. Saravanan, Anton Bakalov, and Abhijit Bhole. 2009. "They are out there, if you know where to look": Mining transliterations of OOV query terms for cross-language information retrieval. In *LNCS: Advances in Information Retrieval*, volume 5478, pages 437–448. Springer Berlin / Heidelberg.

Dmitry Zelenko and Chinatsu Aone. 2006. Discriminative methods for transliteration. In *Proc. EMNLP*, pages 612–617, Sydney, Australia, July.

Dmitry Zelenko. 2009. Combining MDL transliteration training with discriminative modeling. In *Proc. ACL/IJCNLP Named Entities Workshop Shared Task.*

Team ID	Organisation	English to Hindi	English to Tamil	English to Kannada	English to Russian	English to Chinese	English to Korean	English to Japanese Katakana	Japanese transliterated to Japanese Kanji
		EnHi	EnTa	EnKa	EnRu	EnCh	EnKo	EnJa	JnJk
1	IIT Bombay	x	x	x					
2	Institution of Computational Linguistics Peking University					x			
3	University of Tokyo	x	x	x	x	x	x	x	
4*	University of Illinois, Urbana-Champaign				x	x			
5	IIT Bombay	x		x					
6	NICT	x	x	x	x	x	x	x	x
7	University of Alberta	x			x	x	x	x	x
8		x	x	x	x	x	x	x	x
9		x	x	x	x	x	x	x	x
10	Johns Hopkins University	x	x	x	x	x			
11		x	x	x					
12							x	x	
13	Jadavpur University	x							
14	IIIT Hyderabad	x							
15						x		x	x
16*	ARL-CACI	x							
17		x	x	x	x	x	x	x	x
18						x			
19*	Chaoyang University of Technology					x			
20	Pondicherry University	x	x	x					
21	Microsoft Research	x						x	
22	SRI International	x	x	x	x	x			
23	IBM Cairo TDC				x	x			
24	SRA	x	x	x	x	x	x	x	x
25	IIT Kharagpur	x	x	x					
26	Institute of Software Chinese Academy of Sciences					x			
27					x				
28	George Washington University					x			
29*		x							
30	Dublin City University	x							
31	IIIT	x	x	x	x	x			

Table 3: Participation of teams in different tasks. *Participants without a system paper.

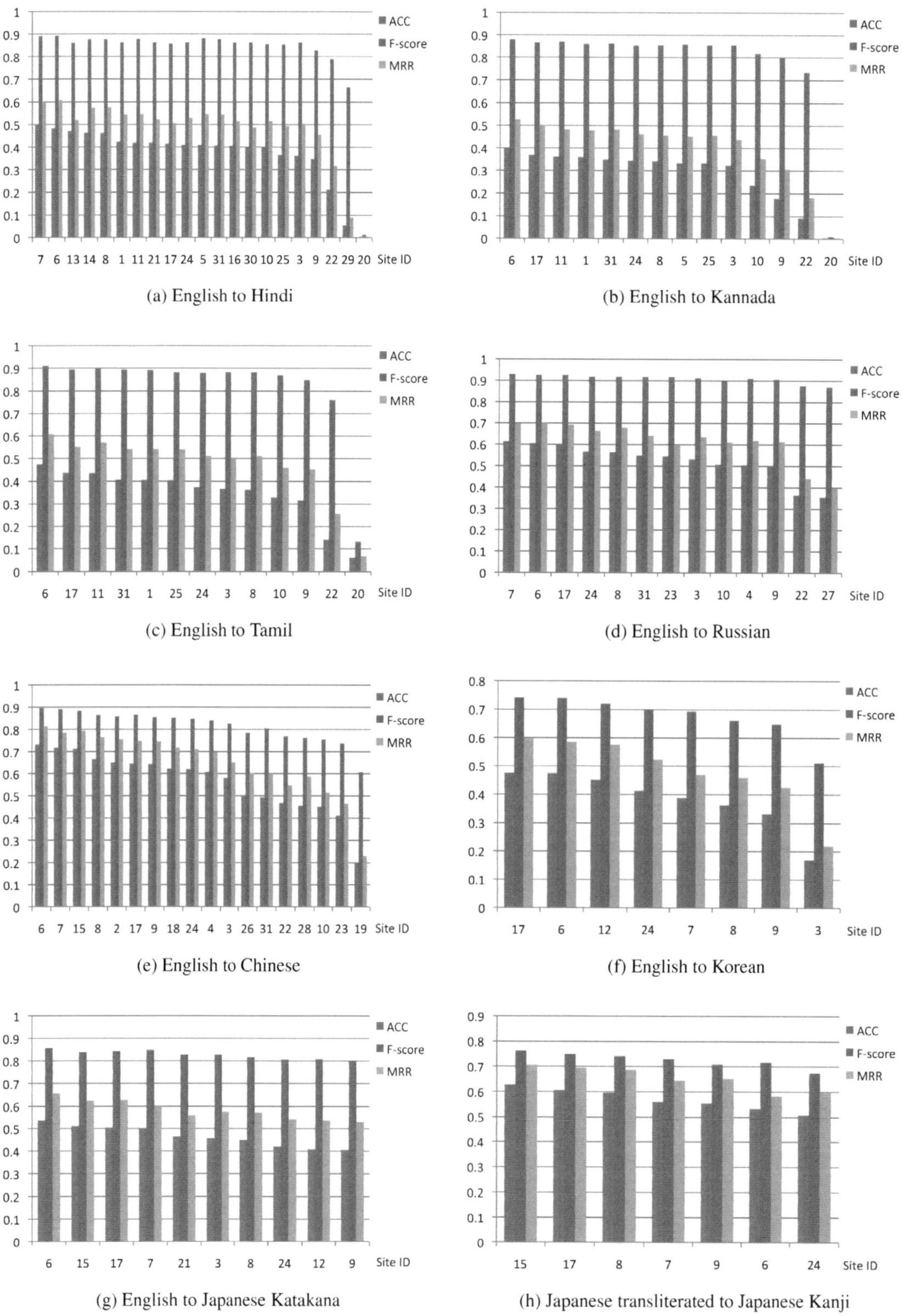

(a) English to Hindi

(b) English to Kannada

(c) English to Tamil

(d) English to Russian

(e) English to Chinese

(f) English to Korean

(g) English to Japanese Katakana

(h) Japanese transliterated to Japanese Kanji

Figure 2: Accuracy in top-1, F-score and MRR for standard runs.

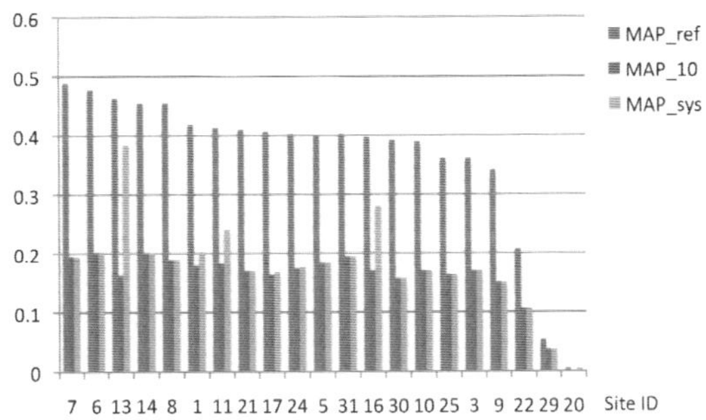

(a) English to Hindi

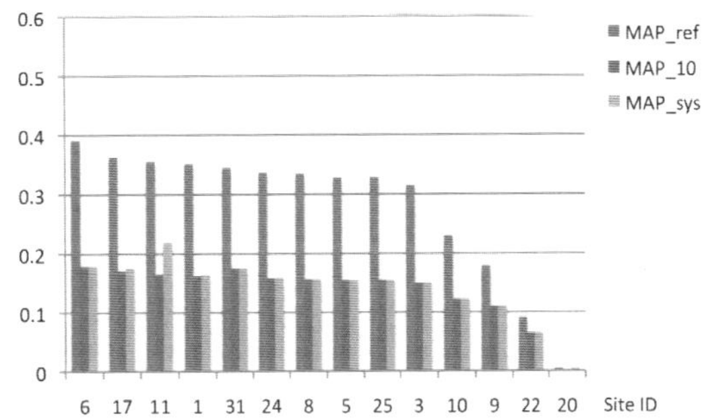

(b) English to Kannada

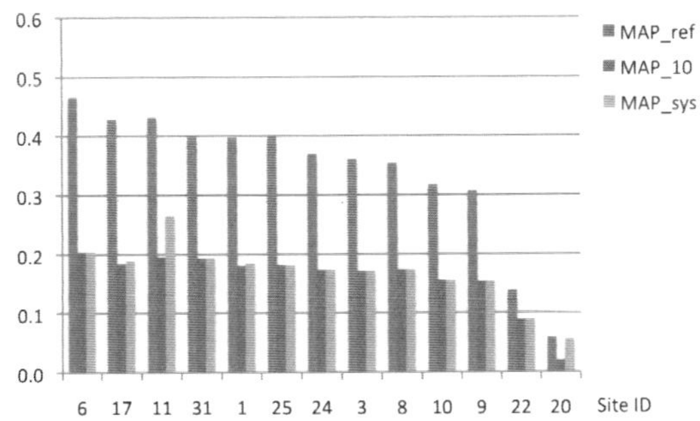

(c) English to Tamil

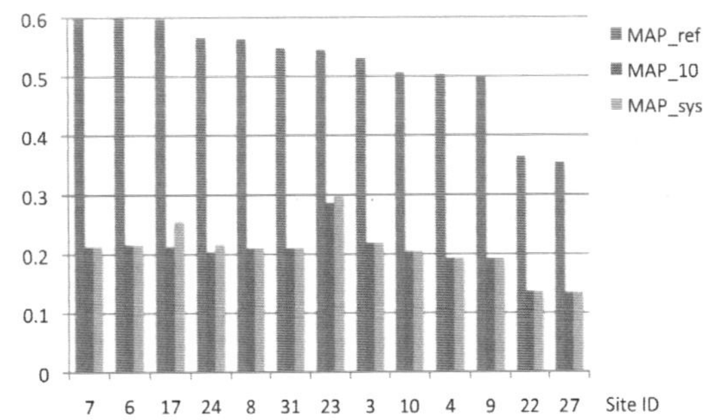

(d) English to Russian

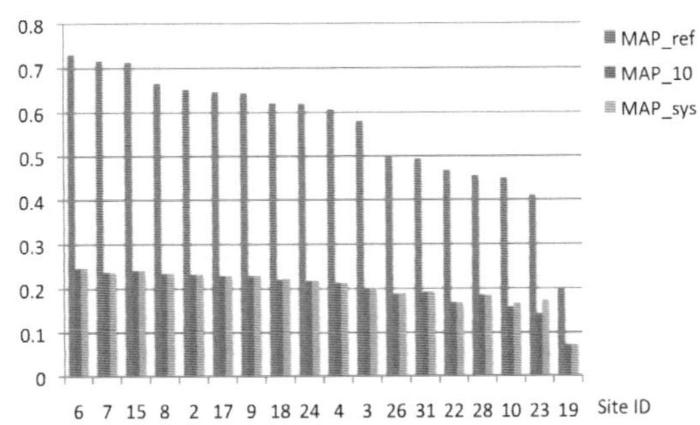

(e) English to Chinese

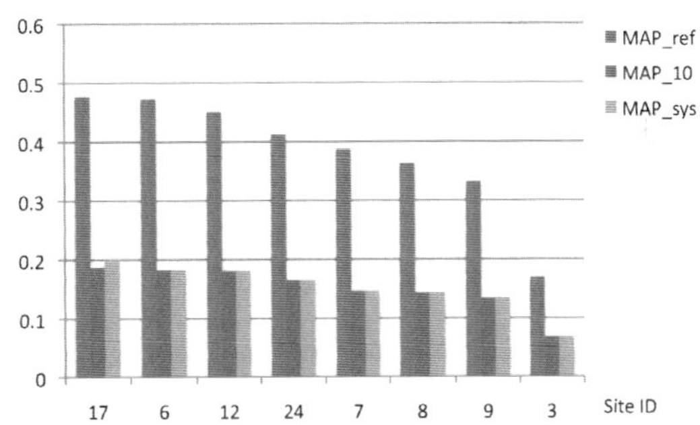

(f) English to Korean

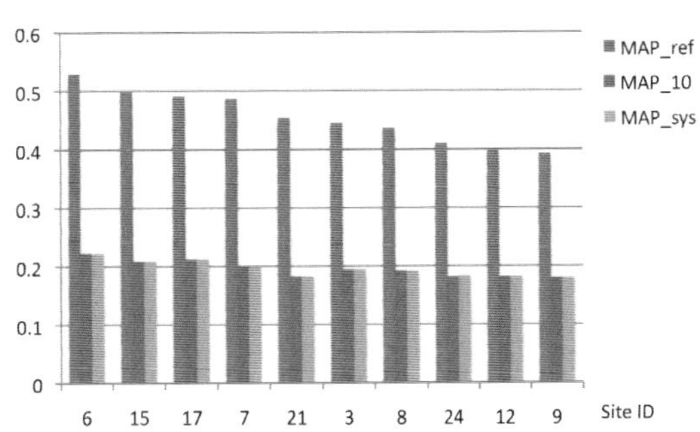

(g) English to Japanese Katakana

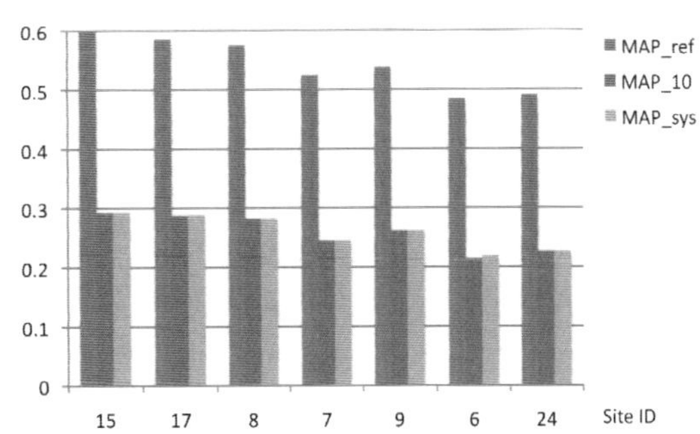

(h) Japanese transliterated to Japanese Kanji

Figure 3: MAP_{ref}, MAP_{10} and MAP_{sys} scores for standard runs.

Team ID	ACC	F-score	MRR	MAP_{ref}	MAP_{10}	MAP_{sys}	Organisation
7	0.498	0.890	0.603	0.488	0.195	0.195	University of Alberta
6	0.483	0.892	0.607	0.477	0.202	0.202	NICT
13	0.471	0.861	0.519	0.463	0.162	0.383	Jadavpur University
14	0.463	0.876	0.573	0.454	0.201	0.201	IIIT Hyderabad
8	0.462	0.876	0.576	0.454	0.189	0.189	
1	0.423	0.863	0.544	0.417	0.179	0.202	IIT Bombay
11	0.418	0.879	0.546	0.412	0.183	0.240	
21	0.418	0.864	0.522	0.409	0.170	0.170	Microsoft Research
17	0.415	0.858	0.505	0.406	0.164	0.168	
24	0.409	0.864	0.527	0.402	0.174	0.176	SRA
5	0.409	0.881	0.546	0.400	0.184	0.184	IIT Bombay
31	0.407	0.877	0.544	0.402	0.195	0.195	IIIT
16	0.406	0.863	0.514	0.397	0.170	0.280	ARL-CACI
30	0.399	0.863	0.488	0.392	0.157	0.157	Dublin City University
10	0.398	0.855	0.515	0.389	0.170	0.170	Johns Hopkins University
25	0.366	0.854	0.493	0.360	0.164	0.164	IIT Kharagpur
3	0.363	0.864	0.503	0.360	0.170	0.170	University of Tokyo
9	0.349	0.829	0.455	0.341	0.151	0.151	
22	0.212	0.788	0.317	0.207	0.106	0.106	SRI International
29	0.053	0.664	0.089	0.053	0.037	0.037	
20	0.004	0.012	0.004	0.004	0.001	0.004	Pondicherry University
21	0.466	0.881	0.567	0.457	0.183	0.183	Microsoft Research (post-evaluation)
22	0.465	0.886	0.567	0.458	0.185	0.185	SRI International (post-evaluation)

Table 4: Standard runs for English to Hindi task.

TeamID	ACC	F-score	MRR	MAP_{ref}	MAP_{10}	MAP_{sys}	Organisation
6	0.474	0.910	0.608	0.465	0.204	0.204	NICT
17	0.436	0.894	0.551	0.427	0.184	0.189	
11	0.435	0.902	0.572	0.430	0.195	0.265	
31	0.406	0.894	0.542	0.399	0.193	0.193	IIIT
1	0.405	0.892	0.542	0.397	0.181	0.184	IIT Bombay
25	0.404	0.883	0.539	0.398	0.182	0.182	IIT Kharagpur
24	0.374	0.880	0.512	0.369	0.174	0.174	SRA
3	0.365	0.884	0.504	0.360	0.172	0.172	University of Tokyo
8	0.361	0.883	0.510	0.354	0.174	0.174	
10	0.327	0.870	0.458	0.317	0.156	0.156	Johns Hopkins University
9	0.316	0.848	0.451	0.307	0.154	0.154	
22	0.141	0.760	0.256	0.139	0.090	0.090	SRI International
20	0.061	0.131	0.068	0.059	0.021	0.056	Pondicherry University
22	0.475	0.909	0.581	0.466	0.193	0.193	SRI International (post-evaluation)

Table 5: Standard runs for English to Tamil task.

Team ID	ACC	F-score	MRR	MAP_{ref}	MAP_{10}	MAP_{sys}	Organisation
6	0.398	0.880	0.526	0.391	0.178	0.178	NICT
17	0.370	0.867	0.499	0.362	0.170	0.175	
11	0.363	0.870	0.482	0.355	0.164	0.218	
1	0.360	0.861	0.479	0.351	0.161	0.164	IIT Bombay
31	0.350	0.864	0.482	0.344	0.175	0.175	IIIT
24	0.345	0.854	0.462	0.336	0.157	0.157	SRA
8	0.343	0.855	0.458	0.334	0.155	0.155	
5	0.335	0.859	0.453	0.327	0.154	0.154	IIT Bombay
25	0.335	0.856	0.457	0.328	0.154	0.154	IIT Kharagpur
3	0.324	0.856	0.438	0.315	0.148	0.148	University of Tokyo
10	0.235	0.817	0.353	0.229	0.121	0.121	Johns Hopkins University
9	0.177	0.799	0.307	0.178	0.109	0.109	
22	0.091	0.735	0.180	0.090	0.064	0.064	SRI International
20	0.004	0.009	0.004	0.004	0.001	0.004	Pondicherry University
22	0.396	0.874	0.494	0.385	0.161	0.161	SRI International (post-evaluation)

Table 6: Standard runs for English to Kannada task.

Team ID	ACC	F-score	MRR	MAP_{ref}	MAP_{10}	MAP_{sys}	Organisation
7	0.613	0.928	0.696	0.613	0.212	0.212	University of Alberta
6	0.605	0.926	0.701	0.605	0.215	0.215	NICT
17	0.597	0.925	0.691	0.597	0.212	0.255	
24	0.566	0.919	0.662	0.566	0.203	0.216	SRA
8	0.564	0.917	0.677	0.564	0.210	0.210	
31	0.548	0.916	0.640	0.548	0.210	0.210	IIIT
23	0.545	0.917	0.596	0.545	0.286	0.299	IBM Cairo TDC
3	0.531	0.912	0.635	0.531	0.219	0.219	University of Tokyo
10	0.506	0.901	0.609	0.506	0.204	0.204	Johns Hopkins University
4	0.504	0.909	0.618	0.504	0.193	0.193	University of Illinois, Urbana-Champaign
9	0.500	0.906	0.613	0.500	0.192	0.192	
22	0.364	0.876	0.440	0.364	0.136	0.136	SRI International
27	0.354	0.869	0.394	0.354	0.134	0.134	
22	0.609	0.928	0.686	0.609	0.209	0.209	SRI International (post-evaluation)

Table 7: Standard runs for English to Russian task.

Team ID	ACC	F-score	MRR	MAP_{ref}	MAP_{10}	MAP_{sys}	Organisation
6	0.731	0.895	0.812	0.731	0.246	0.246	NICT
7	0.717	0.890	0.785	0.717	0.237	0.237	University of Alberta
15	0.713	0.883	0.794	0.713	0.241	0.241	
8	0.666	0.864	0.765	0.666	0.234	0.234	
2	0.652	0.858	0.755	0.652	0.232	0.232	Institution of Computational Linguistics Peking University China
17	0.646	0.867	0.747	0.646	0.229	0.229	
9	0.643	0.854	0.745	0.643	0.228	0.229	
18	0.621	0.852	0.718	0.621	0.220	0.222	
24	0.619	0.847	0.711	0.619	0.217	0.217	SRA
4	0.607	0.840	0.695	0.607	0.213	0.213	University of Illinois, Urbana-Champaign
3	0.580	0.826	0.653	0.580	0.199	0.199	University of Tokyo
26	0.498	0.786	0.603	0.498	0.187	0.189	Institute of Software Chinese Academy of Sciences
31	0.493	0.804	0.600	0.493	0.192	0.192	IIIT
22	0.468	0.768	0.546	0.468	0.168	0.168	SRI International
28	0.456	0.763	0.587	0.456	0.185	0.185	George Washington University
10	0.450	0.755	0.514	0.450	0.157	0.166	Johns Hopkins University
23	0.411	0.737	0.464	0.411	0.141	0.173	IBM Cairo TDC
19	0.199	0.606	0.229	0.199	0.070	0.070	Chaoyang University of Technology
22	0.671	0.872	0.725	0.672	0.218	0.218	SRI International (post-evaluation)

Table 8: Standard runs for English to Chinese task.

Team ID	ACC	F-score	MRR	MAP_{ref}	MAP_{10}	MAP_{sys}	Organisation
17	0.476	0.742	0.596	0.477	0.187	0.199	
6	0.473	0.740	0.584	0.473	0.182	0.182	NICT
12	0.451	0.720	0.576	0.451	0.181	0.181	
24	0.413	0.702	0.524	0.412	0.165	0.165	SRA
7	0.387	0.693	0.469	0.387	0.146	0.146	University of Alberta
8	0.362	0.662	0.460	0.362	0.144	0.144	
9	0.332	0.648	0.425	0.331	0.134	0.135	
3	0.170	0.512	0.218	0.170	0.069	0.069	University of Tokyo

Table 9: Standard runs for English to Korean task.

Team ID	ACC	F-score	MRR	MAP_{ref}	MAP_{10}	MAP_{sys}	Organisation
6	0.537	0.858	0.657	0.529	0.223	0.223	NICT
15	0.510	0.838	0.624	0.498	0.209	0.209	
17	0.503	0.843	0.627	0.491	0.212	0.212	
7	0.500	0.847	0.604	0.487	0.199	0.199	University of Alberta
21	0.465	0.827	0.559	0.454	0.183	0.183	Microsoft Research
3	0.457	0.828	0.576	0.445	0.194	0.194	University of Tokyo
8	0.449	0.816	0.571	0.436	0.192	0.192	
24	0.420	0.807	0.541	0.410	0.182	0.184	SRA
12	0.408	0.808	0.537	0.398	0.182	0.182	
9	0.406	0.800	0.529	0.393	0.180	0.180	
21	0.469	0.834	0.567	0.454	0.186	0.186	Microsoft Research (post-evaluation)

Table 10: Standard runs for English to Japanese Katakana task.

Team ID	ACC	F-score	MRR	MAP_{ref}	MAP_{10}	MAP_{sys}	Organisation
15	0.627	0.763	0.706	0.605	0.292	0.292	
17	0.606	0.749	0.695	0.586	0.287	0.288	
8	0.596	0.741	0.687	0.575	0.282	0.282	
7	0.560	0.730	0.644	0.525	0.244	0.244	University of Alberta
9	0.555	0.708	0.653	0.538	0.261	0.261	
6	0.532	0.716	0.583	0.485	0.214	0.218	NICT
24	0.509	0.675	0.600	0.491	0.226	0.226	SRA

Table 11: Standard runs for Japanese Transliterated to Japanese Kanji task.

Team ID	ACC	F-score	MRR	MAP_{ref}	MAP_{10}	MAP_{sys}	Organisation
7	0.509	0.893	0.610	0.498	0.198	0.198	University of Alberta
1	0.487	0.873	0.594	0.481	0.195	0.229	IIT Bombay
6	0.475	0.893	0.601	0.469	0.200	0.200	NICT
6	0.469	0.884	0.581	0.464	0.192	0.193	NICT
6	0.455	0.888	0.575	0.448	0.191	0.191	NICT
5	0.448	0.885	0.570	0.439	0.190	0.190	IIT Bombay
6	0.443	0.879	0.555	0.437	0.184	0.191	NICT
17	0.424	0.862	0.513	0.415	0.166	0.174	
30	0.421	0.864	0.519	0.415	0.171	0.171	Dublin City University
30	0.420	0.867	0.519	0.413	0.170	0.170	Dublin City University
30	0.419	0.868	0.464	0.419	0.338	0.338	Dublin City University
16	0.407	0.862	0.528	0.399	0.175	0.289	ARL-CACI
16	0.407	0.862	0.528	0.399	0.175	0.289	ARL-CACI
30	0.407	0.856	0.507	0.399	0.168	0.168	Dublin City University
16	0.400	0.864	0.516	0.391	0.171	0.212	ARL-CACI
13	0.389	0.831	0.487	0.385	0.160	0.328	Jadavpur University
13	0.384	0.828	0.485	0.380	0.160	0.325	Jadavpur University
16	0.273	0.796	0.358	0.266	0.119	0.193	ARL-CACI

Table 12: Non-standard runs for English to Hindi task.

Team ID	ACC	F-score	MRR	MAP_{ref}	MAP_{10}	MAP_{sys}	Organisation
6	0.478	0.910	0.606	0.472	0.203	0.203	NICT
6	0.459	0.906	0.583	0.453	0.195	0.196	NICT
6	0.459	0.906	0.583	0.453	0.195	0.196	NICT
6	0.453	0.907	0.584	0.446	0.196	0.196	NICT
17	0.437	0.894	0.555	0.426	0.185	0.193	

Table 13: Non-standard runs for English to Tamil task.

Team ID	ACC	F-score	MRR	MAP_{ref}	MAP_{10}	MAP_{sys}	Organisation
6	0.399	0.881	0.522	0.391	0.176	0.176	NICT
6	0.386	0.877	0.503	0.379	0.169	0.169	NICT
6	0.380	0.869	0.488	0.370	0.163	0.163	NICT
17	0.374	0.868	0.502	0.366	0.170	0.176	
6	0.373	0.869	0.485	0.362	0.162	0.168	NICT

Table 14: Non-standard runs for English to Kannada task.

Team ID	ACC	F-score	MRR	MAP_{ref}	MAP_{10}	MAP_{sys}	Organisation
17	0.955	0.989	0.966	0.955	0.284	0.504	
17	0.609	0.928	0.701	0.609	0.214	0.263	
7	0.608	0.927	0.694	0.608	0.212	0.212	University of Alberta
7	0.607	0.927	0.690	0.607	0.211	0.211	University of Alberta
6	0.600	0.927	0.634	0.600	0.189	0.189	NICT
6	0.600	0.926	0.699	0.600	0.214	0.214	NICT
7	0.591	0.928	0.679	0.591	0.208	0.208	University of Alberta
6	0.561	0.918	0.595	0.561	0.178	0.182	NICT
6	0.557	0.920	0.596	0.557	0.179	0.233	NICT
23	0.545	0.917	0.618	0.545	0.188	0.206	IBM Cairo TDC
23	0.524	0.913	0.602	0.524	0.184	0.203	IBM Cairo TDC
23	0.524	0.913	0.579	0.524	0.277	0.291	IBM Cairo TDC
4	0.496	0.908	0.613	0.496	0.191	0.191	University of Illinois, Urbana-Champaign
27	0.338	0.872	0.408	0.338	0.128	0.128	
27	0.293	0.845	0.325	0.293	0.099	0.099	
27	0.162	0.849	0.298	0.162	0.188	0.188	

Table 15: Non-standard runs for English to Russian task.

Team ID	ACC	F-score	MRR	MAP_{ref}	MAP_{10}	MAP_{sys}	Organisation
17	0.909	0.960	0.933	0.909	0.276	0.276	
7	0.746	0.900	0.814	0.746	0.245	0.245	University of Alberta
7	0.734	0.895	0.807	0.734	0.244	0.244	University of Alberta
7	0.732	0.895	0.803	0.732	0.242	0.242	University of Alberta
6	0.731	0.894	0.812	0.731	0.246	0.246	NICT
6	0.715	0.890	0.741	0.715	0.220	0.231	NICT
6	0.699	0.884	0.729	0.699	0.216	0.232	NICT
6	0.684	0.873	0.711	0.684	0.211	0.211	NICT
22	0.663	0.867	0.754	0.663	0.230	0.230	SRI International
17	0.658	0.865	0.752	0.658	0.230	0.230	
18	0.587	0.834	0.665	0.587	0.203	0.330	
26	0.500	0.786	0.607	0.500	0.189	0.191	Institute of Software Chinese Academy of Sciences
22	0.487	0.787	0.622	0.487	0.196	0.196	SRI International
28	0.462	0.764	0.564	0.462	0.175	0.175	George Washington University
28	0.458	0.763	0.602	0.458	0.191	0.191	George Washington University
23	0.411	0.737	0.464	0.411	0.141	0.173	IBM Cairo TDC
19	0.279	0.668	0.351	0.279	0.110	0.110	Chaoyang University of Technology
28	0.058	0.353	0.269	0.058	0.101	0.101	George Washington University
28	0.050	0.359	0.260	0.050	0.098	0.098	George Washington University
4	0.001	0.249	0.001	0.001	0.000	0.000	University of Illinois, Urbana-Champaign
22	0.674	0.873	0.763	0.674	0.232	0.232	SRI International (post-evaluation)
22	0.500	0.793	0.636	0.500	0.200	0.200	SRI International (post-evaluation)

Table 16: Non-standard runs for English to Chinese task.

Team ID	ACC	F-score	MRR	MAP_{ref}	MAP_{10}	MAP_{sys}	Organisation
17	0.794	0.894	0.836	0.793	0.249	0.323	
12	0.785	0.887	0.840	0.785	0.252	0.441	
12	0.784	0.889	0.840	0.784	0.252	0.484	
12	0.781	0.885	0.839	0.781	0.252	0.460	
12	0.740	0.868	0.806	0.740	0.243	0.243	
6	0.461	0.737	0.576	0.461	0.180	0.180	NICT
6	0.457	0.734	0.506	0.457	0.153	0.153	NICT
6	0.447	0.718	0.493	0.447	0.149	0.149	NICT
6	0.369	0.679	0.406	0.369	0.123	0.123	NICT

Table 17: Non-standard runs for English to Korean task.

Team ID	ACC	F-score	MRR	MAP_{ref}	MAP_{10}	MAP_{sys}	Organisation
6	0.535	0.858	0.656	0.526	0.222	0.222	NICT
6	0.517	0.850	0.567	0.495	0.177	0.188	NICT
6	0.513	0.854	0.567	0.495	0.178	0.178	NICT
7	0.510	0.848	0.614	0.496	0.202	0.202	University of Alberta
6	0.500	0.842	0.547	0.480	0.170	0.196	NICT

Table 18: Non-standard runs for English to Japanese Katakana task.

Team ID	ACC	F-score	MRR	MAP_{ref}	MAP_{10}	MAP_{sys}	Organisation
17	0.717	0.818	0.784	0.691	0.319	0.319	
17	0.703	0.805	0.768	0.673	0.311	0.311	
17	0.698	0.805	0.774	0.676	0.317	0.317	
17	0.681	0.790	0.755	0.657	0.308	0.309	
6	0.525	0.713	0.607	0.503	0.248	0.249	NICT
6	0.525	0.712	0.606	0.502	0.248	0.248	NICT
6	0.523	0.712	0.572	0.479	0.211	0.213	NICT
6	0.517	0.705	0.603	0.496	0.248	0.249	NICT

Table 19: Non-standard runs for Japanese Transliterated to Japanese Kanji task.

Whitepaper of NEWS 2009 Machine Transliteration Shared Task*

Haizhou Li†, A Kumaran‡, Min Zhang† and Vladimir Pervouchine†

†Institute for Infocomm Research, A*STAR, Singapore 138632
{hli,mzhang,vpervouchine}@i2r.a-star.edu.sg

‡Multilingual Systems Research, Microsoft Research India
A.Kumaran@microsoft.com

Abstract

Transliteration is defined as phonetic translation of names across languages. Transliteration of Named Entities (NEs) is necessary in many applications, such as machine translation, corpus alignment, cross-language IR, information extraction and automatic lexicon acquisition. All such systems call for high-performance transliteration, which is the focus of the shared task in the NEWS 2009 workshop. The objective of the shared task is to promote machine transliteration research by providing a common benchmarking platform for the community to evaluate the state-of-the-art technologies.

1 Task Description

The task is to develop machine transliteration system in one or more of the specified language pairs being considered for the task. Each language pair consists of a source and a target language. The training and development data sets released for each language pair are to be used for developing a transliteration system in whatever way that the participants find appropriate. At the evaluation time, a test set of source names only would be released, on which the participants are expected to produce a ranked list of transliteration candidates in another language (i.e. n-best transliterations), and this will be evaluated using common metrics. For every language pair the participants must submit one run that uses only the data provided by the NEWS workshop organisers in a given language pair (designated as "standard" runs). Users may submit more runs ("non-standard") for each language pair that uses other data than those provided by the NEWS 2009 workshop; such runs would be evaluated and reported separately.

*http://www.acl-ijcnlp-2009.org/workshops/NEWS2009/

2 Important Dates

Research paper submission deadline	1 May 2009
Shared task	
Registration opens	16 Feb 2009
Registration closes	9 Apr 2009
Release Training/Development Data	16 Feb 2009
Release Test Data	10 Apr 2009
Results Submission Due	14 Apr 2009
Results Announcement	29 Apr 2009
Task (short) Papers Due	3 May 2009
For all submissions	
Acceptance Notification	1 Jun 2009
Camera-Ready Copy Deadline	7 Jun 2009
Workshop Date	7 Aug 2009

3 Participation

1. Registration (16 Feb 2009)
   (a) NEWS Shared Task opens for registration.
   (b) Prospective participants are to register to the NEWS Workshop homepage.
2. Training & Development Data (16 Feb 2009)
   (a) Registered participants are to obtain training and development data from the Shared Task organiser and/or the designated copyright owners of databases.
3. Evaluation Script (16 Mar 2009)
   (a) A sample test set and expected user output format are to be released.
   (b) An evaluation script, which runs on the above two, is to be released.
   (c) The participants must make sure that their output is produced in a way that the evaluation script may run and produce the expected output.

Proceedings of the 2009 Named Entities Workshop, ACL-IJCNLP 2009, pages 19–26,
Suntec, Singapore, 7 August 2009.

(d) The same script (with held out test data and the user outputs) would be used for final evaluation.

4. Test data (10 April 2009)

   (a) The test data would be released on 10 Apr 2009, and the participants have a maximum of 4 days to submit their results in the expected format.
   (b) Only 1 "standard" run must be submitted from every group on a given language pair; more "non-standard" runs (0 to 4) may be submitted. In total, maximum 5 runs (1 "standard" run plus up to 4 "non-standard" runs) can be submitted from each group on a registered language pair.
   (c) Any runs that are "non-standard" must be tagged as such.
   (d) The test set is a list of names in source language only. Every group will produce and submit a ranked list of transliteration candidates in another language for each given name in the test set. Please note that this shared task is a "transliteration generation" task, i.e., given a name in a source language one is supposed to generate one or more transliterations in a target language. It is not the task of "transliteration discovery", i.e., given a name in the source language and a set of names in the target language evaluate how to find the appropriate names from the target set that are transliterations of the given source name.

5. Results (29 April 2009)

   (a) On 29 April 2009, the evaluation results would be announced and will be made available on the Workshop website.
   (b) Note that only the scores (in respective metrics) of the participating systems on each language pairs would be published, and no explicit ranking of the participating systems would be published.
   (c) Note that this is a shared evaluation task and not a competition; the results are meant to be used to evaluate systems on common data set with common metrics, and not to rank the participating systems. While the participants can cite the performance of their systems (scores on metrics) from the workshop report, they should not use any ranking information in their publications.
   (d) Further, all participants should agree not to reveal identities of other participants in any of their publications unless you get permission from the other respective participants. If the participants want to remain anonymous in published results, they should inform the organisers (mzhang@i2r.a-star.edu.sg, a.kumaran@microsoft.com), at the time of registration. Note that the results of their systems would still be published, but with the participant identities masked. As a result, in this case, your organisation name will still appear in the web site as one of participants, but it is not linked explicitly with your results.

6. Short Papers on Task (3 May 2009)

   (a) Each submitting site is required to submit a 4-page system paper (short paper) for its submissions, including their approach, data used and the results on either test set or development set or by n-fold cross validation on training set.
   (b) All system short papers will be included in the proceedings. Selected short papers will be presented orally in the NEWS 2009 workshop. Reviewers' comments for all system short papers and the acceptance notification for the system short papers for oral presentation would be announced on 1 June 2009 together with that of other papers.
   (c) All registered participants are required to register and attend the workshop to introduce your work.
   (d) All paper submission and review will be managed electronically through https://www.softconf.com/acl-ijcnlp09/NEWS/.

4 Languages Involved

The tasks are to transliterate personal names or place names from a source to a target language as summarised in Table 1.

Source language	Target language	Data Owner	Approx. Data Size	Task ID
English	Chinese	Institute for Infocomm Research	30K	EnCh
English	Japanese Katakana	CJK Institute	25K	EnJa
English	Korean Hangul	CJK Institute	7K	EnKo
Japanese name (in English)	Japanese Kanji	CJK Institute	20K	JnJk
English	Hindi	Microsoft Research India	15K	EnHi
English	Tamil	Microsoft Research India	15K	EnTa
English	Kannada	Microsoft Research India	15K	EnKa
English	Russian	Microsoft Research India	10K	EnRu

Table 1: Source and target languages for the shared task on transliteration.

The names given in the training sets for Chinese, Japanese and Korean languages are Western names and their CJK transliterations; the Japanese Name (in English) → Japanese Kanji data set consists only of native Japanese names. The Indic data set (Hindi, Tamil, Kannada) consists of a mix of Indian and Western names.

English → Chinese
Timothy → 蒂莫西

English → Japanese Katakana
Harrington → ハリントン

English → Korean Hangul
Bennett → 베넷

Japanese name in English → Japanese Kanji
Akihiro → 秋宏

English → Hindi
San Francisco → सैन फ्रान्सिस्को

English → Tamil
London → லண்டன்

English → Kannada
Tokyo → ಟೋಕ್ಯೋ

English → Russian
Moscow → Москва

5 Standard Databases

Training Data (Parallel)
Paired names between source and target languages; size 5K – 40K.
Training Data is used for training a basic transliteration system.

Development Data (Parallel)
Paired names between source and target languages; size 1K – 2K.
Development Data is in addition to the Training data, which is used for system fine-tuning of parameters in case of need. Participants are allowed to use it as part of training data.

Testing Data
Source names only; size 1K – 3K.
This is a held-out set, which would be used for evaluating the quality of the transliterations.

1. Participants will need to obtain licenses from the respective copyright owners and/or agree to the terms and conditions of use that are given on the downloading website (Li et al., 2004; Kumaran and Kellner, 2007; MSRI, 2009; CJKI, 2009). NEWS 2009 will provide the contact details of each individual database. The data would be provided in Unicode UTF-8 encoding, in XML format; the results are expected to be submitted in XML format. The XML formats will be announced at the workshop website.

2. The data are provided in 3 sets as described above.

3. Name pairs are distributed as-is, as provided by the respective creators.
   (a) While the databases are mostly manually checked, there may be still inconsistency (that is, non-standard usage, region-specific usage, errors, etc.) or incompleteness (that is, not all right variations may be covered).
   (b) The participants may use any method to further clean up the data provided.
      i. If they are cleaned up manually, we appeal that such data be provided back to the organisers for redistribution to all the participating groups in that language pair; such sharing benefits all participants, and further

ensures that the evaluation provides normalisation with respect to data quality.

ii. If automatic cleanup were used, such cleanup would be considered a part of the system fielded, and hence not required to be shared with all participants.

4. We expect that the participants to use only the data (parallel names) provided by the Shared Task for transliteration task for a "standard" run to ensure a fair evaluation. One such run (using only the data provided by the shared task) is mandatory for all participants for a given language pair that they participate in.

5. If more data (either parallel names data or monolingual data) were used, then all such runs using extra data must be marked as "non-standard". For such "non-standard" runs, it is required to disclose the size and characteristics of the data used in the system paper.

6. A participant may submit a maximum of 5 runs for a given language pair (including the mandatory 1 "standard" run).

6 Paper Format

Paper submissions to NEWS 2009 should follow the ACL-IJCNLP-2009 paper submission policy, including paper format, blind review policy and title and author format convention. Full papers (research paper) are in two-column format without exceeding eight (8) pages of content plus one extra page for references and short papers (task paper) are also in two-column format without exceeding four (4) pages, including references. Submission must conform to the official ACL-IJCNLP-2009 style guidelines. For details, please refer to the website[2].

7 Evaluation Metrics

We plan to measure the quality of the transliteration task using the following 6 metrics. We accept up to 10 output candidates in a ranked list for each input entry.

Since a given source name may have multiple correct target transliterations, all these alternatives are treated equally in the evaluation. That is, any of these alternatives are considered as a correct transliteration, and the first correct transliteration in the ranked list is accepted as a correct hit.

The following notation is further assumed:

N : Total number of names (source words) in the test set

n_i : Number of reference transliterations for i-th name in the test set ($n_i \geq 1$)

$r_{i,j}$: j-th reference transliteration for i-th name in the test set

$c_{i,k}$: k-th candidate transliteration (system output) for i-th name in the test set ($1 \leq k \leq 10$)

K_i : Number of candidate transliterations produced by a transliteration system

1. Word Accuracy in Top-1 (ACC) Also known as Word Error Rate, it measures correctness of the first transliteration candidate in the candidate list produced by a transliteration system. $ACC = 1$ means that all top candidates are correct transliterations i.e. they match one of the references, and $ACC = 0$ means that none of the top candidates are correct.

$$ACC = \frac{1}{N} \sum_{i=1}^{N} \left\{ \begin{array}{l} 1 \text{ if } \exists r_{i,j} : r_{i,j} = c_{i,1}; \\ 0 \text{ otherwise} \end{array} \right\} \quad (1)$$

2. Fuzziness in Top-1 (Mean F-score) The mean F-score measures how different, on average, the top transliteration candidate is from its closest reference. F-score for each source word is a function of Precision and Recall and equals 1 when the top candidate matches one of the references, and 0 when there are no common characters between the candidate and any of the references.

Precision and Recall are calculated based on the length of the Longest Common Subsequence between a candidate and a reference:

$$LCS(c,r) = \frac{1}{2}\left(|c| + |r| - ED(c,r)\right) \quad (2)$$

where ED is the edit distance and $|x|$ is the length of x. For example, the longest common subsequence between "abcd" and "afcde" is "acd" and its length is 3. The best matching reference, that is, the reference for which the edit distance has the minimum, is taken for calculation. If the best matching reference is given by

$$r_{i,m} = \arg\min_{j} \left(ED(c_{i,1}, r_{i,j})\right) \quad (3)$$

[2]http://www.acl-ijcnlp-2009.org/main/authors/stylefiles/index.html

then Recall, Precision and F-score for i-th word are calculated as

$$R_i = \frac{LCS(c_{i,1}, r_{i,m})}{|r_{i,m}|} \quad (4)$$

$$P_i = \frac{LCS(c_{i,1}, r_{i,m})}{|c_{i,1}|} \quad (5)$$

$$F_i = 2\frac{R_i \times P_i}{R_i + P_i} \quad (6)$$

- The length is computed in distinct Unicode characters.
- No distinction is made on different character types of a language (e.g., vowel vs. consonants vs. combining diereses' etc.)

3. Mean Reciprocal Rank (MRR) Measures traditional MRR *for any right answer* produced by the system, from among the candidates. $1/MRR$ tells approximately the average rank of the correct transliteration. MRR closer to 1 implies that the correct answer is mostly produced close to the top of the n-best lists.

$$RR_i = \left\{ \begin{array}{l} \min_j \frac{1}{j} \text{ if } \exists r_{i,j}, c_{i,k} : r_{i,j} = c_{i,k}; \\ 0 \text{ otherwise} \end{array} \right\} \quad (7)$$

$$MRR = \frac{1}{N}\sum_{i=1}^{N} RR_i \quad (8)$$

4. MAP$_{ref}$ Measures tightly the precision in the n-best candidates for i-th source name, for which reference transliterations are available. If all of the references are produced, then the MAP is 1. Let's denote the number of correct candidates for the i-th source word in k-best list as $num(i,k)$. MAP$_{ref}$ is then given by

$$MAP_{ref} = \frac{1}{N}\sum_{i}^{N}\frac{1}{n_i}\left(\sum_{k=1}^{n_i} num(i,k)\right) \quad (9)$$

5. MAP$_{10}$ measures the precision in the 10-best candidates for i-th source name provided by the candidate system. In general, the higher MAP$_{10}$ is, the better is the quality of the transliteration system in capturing the multiple references. Note that the number of reference transliterations may be more or less than 10. If the number of reference transliterations is below 10, then MAP$_{10}$ can never be equal to 1. Only if the number of reference transliterations for every source word is at least 10, then MAP$_{10}$ could possibly be equal to 1.

$$MAP_{10} = \frac{1}{N}\sum_{i=1}^{N}\frac{1}{10}\left(\sum_{k=1}^{10} num(i,k)\right) \quad (10)$$

Note that in general MAP$_m$ measures the "goodness in m-best" candidate list. We use $m = 10$ because we have asked the systems to produce up to 10 candidates for every source name in the test set.

6. MAP$_{sys}$ Measures the precision in the top K_i-best candidates produced by the system for i-th source name, for which n_i reference transliterations are available. This measure allows the systems to produce variable number of transliterations, based on their confidence in identifying and producing correct transliterations. If all of the n_i references are produced in the top-n_i candidates (that is, $K_i = n_i$, and all of them are correct), then the MAP$_{sys}$ is 1.

$$MAP_{sys} = \frac{1}{N}\sum_{i=1}^{N}\frac{1}{K_i}\left(\sum_{k=1}^{K_i} num(i,k)\right) \quad (11)$$

8 Contact Us

If you have any questions about this share task and the database, please email to

Dr. Haizhou Li
Institute for Infocomm Research (I2R), A*STAR
1 Fusionopolis Way
#08-05 South Tower, Connexis
Singapore 138632
hli@i2r.a-star.edu.sg

Dr. A. Kumaran
Microsoft Research India
Scientia, 196/36, Sadashivnagar 2nd Main Road
Bangalore 560080 INDIA
a.kumaran@microsoft.com

Mr. Kurt Easterwood
The CJK Dictionary Institute (CJK Data)
Komine Building (3rd & 4th floors)
34-14, 2-chome, Tohoku, Niiza-shi
Saitama 352-0001 JAPAN
akurt@cjki.org

References

CJKI. 2009. CJK Institute. http://www.cjk.org/.

A Kumaran and T. Kellner. 2007. A generic framework for machine transliteration. In *Proc. SIGIR*, pages 721–722.

Haizhou Li, Min Zhang, and Jian Su. 2004. A joint source-channel model for machine transliteration. In *Proc. 42nd ACL Annual Meeting*, pages 159–166, Barcelona, Spain.

MSRI. 2009. Microsoft Research India. http://research.microsoft.com/india.

Appendix A: Training/Development Data

- File Naming Conventions:
  `NEWS09_train_XXYY_nnnn.xml`
  `NEWS09_dev_XXYY_nnnn.xml`
  `NEWS09_test_XXYY_nnnn.xml`
  - `XX`: Source Language
  - `YY`: Target Language
  - `nnnn`: size of parallel/monolingual names ("25K", "10000", etc)
- File formats:
  All data will be made available in XML formats (Figure 1).
- Data Encoding Formats:
  The data will be in Unicode UTF-8 encoding files without byte-order mark, and in the XML format specified.

Appendix B: Submission of Results

- File Naming Conventions:
  `NEWS09_result_XXYY_gggg_nn_descr.xml`
  - `XX`: Source Language
  - `YY`: Target Language
  - `gggg`: Group ID
  - `nn`: run ID. Note that run ID "1" stands for "standard" run where only the provided data are allowed to be used. Run ID "2–5" means "non-standard" run where additional data can be used.
  - `descr`: Description of the run.
- File formats:
  All data will be made available in XML formats (Figure 2).
- Data Encoding Formats:
  The results are expected to be submitted in UTF-8 encoded files without byte-order mark only, and in the XML format specified.

```
<?xml version="1.0" encoding="UTF-8"?>

<TransliterationCorpus
    CorpusID = "NEWS2009-Train-EnHi-25K"
    SourceLang = "English"
    TargetLang = "Hindi"
    CorpusType = "Train|Dev"
    CorpusSize = "25000"
    CorpusFormat = "UTF8">

    <Name ID=" 1" >
        <SourceName>eeeeee1</SourceName>
        <TargetName ID="1">hhhhhh1_1</TargetName>
    <TargetName ID="2">hhhhhh1_2</TargetName>
        ...
        <TargetName ID="n">hhhhhh1_n</TargetName>
    </Name>
    <Name ID=" 2" >
        <SourceName>eeeeee2</SourceName>
        <TargetName ID="1">hhhhhh2_1</TargetName>
        <TargetName ID="2">hhhhhh2_2</TargetName>
        ...
        <TargetName ID="m">hhhhhh2_m</TargetName>
    </Name>
    ...
    <!-- rest of the names to follow -->
    ...
</TransliterationCorpus>
```

Figure 1: File: NEWS2009_Train_EnHi_25K.xml

```
<?xml version="1.0" encoding="UTF-8"?>

<TransliterationTaskResults
    SourceLang = "English"
    TargetLang = "Hindi"
    GroupID = "Trans University"
    RunID = "1"
    RunType = "Standard"
    Comments = "HMM Run with params: alpha=0.8 beta=1.25">

    <Name ID="1">
        <SourceName>eeeeee1</SourceName>
        <TargetName ID="1">hhhhhh11</TargetName>
        <TargetName ID="2">hhhhhh12</TargetName>
        <TargetName ID="3">hhhhhh13</TargetName>
        ...
        <TargetName ID="10">hhhhhh110</TargetName>

        <!-- Participants to provide their
        top 10 candidate transliterations -->
    </Name>
    <Name ID="2">
        <SourceName>eeeeee2</SourceName>
        <TargetName ID="1">hhhhhh21</TargetName>
        <TargetName ID="2">hhhhhh22</TargetName>
        <TargetName ID="3">hhhhhh23</TargetName>
        ...
        <TargetName ID="10">hhhhhh110</TargetName>
        <!-- Participants to provide their
        top 10 candidate transliterations -->
    </Name>
    ...
    <!-- All names in test corpus to follow -->
    ...
</TransliterationTaskResults>
```

Figure 2: Example file: NEWS2009_EnHi_TUniv_01_StdRunHMMBased.xml

Automata for Transliteration and Machine Translation

Kevin Knight
Information Sciences Institute
University of Southern California
knight@isi.edu

Abstract

Automata theory, transliteration, and machine translation (MT) have an interesting and intertwined history.

Finite-state string automata theory became a powerful tool for speech and language after the introduction of the AT&T's FSM software. For example, string transducers can convert between word sequences and phoneme sequences, or between phoneme sequences and acoustic sequences; furthermore, these machines can be pipelined to attack complex problems like speech recognition. Likewise, n-gram models can be captured by finite-state acceptors, which can be reused across applications.

It is possible to mix, match, and compose transducers to flexibly solve all kinds of problems. One such problem is transliteration, which can be modeled as a pipeline of string transformations. MT has also been modeled with transducers, and descendants of the FSM toolkit are now used to implement phrase-based machine translation. Even speech recognizers and MT systems can themselves be composed to deliver speech-to-speech MT.

The main rub with finite-state string MT is word re-ordering. Tree transducers offer a natural mechanism to solve this problem, and they have recently been employed with some success.

In this talk, we will survey these ideas (and their origins), and we will finish with a discussion of how transliteration and MT can work together.

Proceedings of the 2009 Named Entities Workshop, ACL-IJCNLP 2009, page 27,
Suntec, Singapore, 7 August 2009.

DIRECTL: a Language-Independent Approach to Transliteration

Sittichai Jiampojamarn, Aditya Bhargava, Qing Dou, Kenneth Dwyer, Grzegorz Kondrak
Department of Computing Science
University of Alberta
Edmonton, AB, T6G 2E8, Canada
{sj,abhargava,qdou,dwyer,kondrak}@cs.ualberta.ca

Abstract

We present DIRECTL: an online discriminative sequence prediction model that employs a many-to-many alignment between target and source. Our system incorporates input segmentation, target character prediction, and sequence modeling in a unified dynamic programming framework. Experimental results suggest that DIRECTL is able to independently discover many of the language-specific regularities in the training data.

1 Introduction

In the transliteration task, it seems intuitively important to take into consideration the specifics of the languages in question. Of particular importance is the relative character length of the source and target names, which vary widely depending on whether languages employ alphabetic, syllabic, or ideographic scripts. On the other hand, faced with the reality of thousands of potential language pairs that involve transliteration, the idea of a language-independent approach is highly attractive.

In this paper, we present DIRECTL: a transliteration system that, in principle, can be applied to any language pair. DIRECTL treats the transliteration task as a sequence prediction problem: given an input sequence of characters in the source language, it produces the most likely sequence of characters in the target language. In Section 2, we discuss the alignment of character substrings in the source and target languages. Our transcription model, described in Section 3, is based on an online discriminative training algorithm that makes it possible to efficiently learn the weights of a large number of features. In Section 4, we provide details of alternative approaches that incorporate language-specific information. Finally, in Section 5 and 6, we compare the experimental results of DIRECTL with its variants that incorporate language-specific pre-processing, phonetic alignment, and manual data correction.

2 Transliteration alignment

In the transliteration task, training data consist of word pairs that map source language words to words in the target language. The matching between character substrings in the source word and target word is not explicitly provided. These hidden relationships are generally known as *alignments*. In this section, we describe an EM-based many-to-many alignment algorithm employed by DIRECTL. In Section 4, we discuss an alternative phonetic alignment method.

We apply an unsupervised many-to-many alignment algorithm (Jiampojamarn et al., 2007) to the transliteration task. The algorithm follows the expectation maximization (EM) paradigm. In the expectation step shown in Algorithm 1, partial counts γ of the possible substring alignments are collected from each word pair (x^T, y^V) in the training data; T and V represent the lengths of words x and y, respectively. The forward probability α is estimated by summing the probabilities of all possible sequences of substring pairings from left to right. The FORWARD-M2M procedure is similar to lines 5 through 12 of Algorithm 1, except that it uses Equation 1 on line 8, Equation 2 on line 12, and initializes $\alpha_{0,0} := 1$. Likewise, the backward probability β is estimated by summing the probabilities from right to left.

$$\alpha_{t,v} \mathrel{+}= \delta(x_{t-i+1}^{t}, \epsilon)\alpha_{t-i,v} \tag{1}$$

$$\alpha_{t,v} \mathrel{+}= \delta(x_{t-i+1}^{t}, y_{v-j+1}^{v})\alpha_{t-i,v-j} \tag{2}$$

The $maxX$ and $maxY$ variables specify the maximum length of substrings that are permitted when creating alignments. Also, for flexibility, we allow a substring in the source word to be aligned with a "null" letter (ϵ) in the target word.

Proceedings of the 2009 Named Entities Workshop, ACL-IJCNLP 2009, pages 28–31,
Suntec, Singapore, 7 August 2009. ©2009 ACL and AFNLP

Algorithm 1: Expectation-M2M alignment

Input: $x^T, y^V, maxX, maxY, \gamma$
Output: γ

$\alpha :=$ FORWARD-M2M $(x^T, y^V, maxX, maxY)$
$\beta :=$ BACKWARD-M2M $(x^T, y^V, maxX, maxY)$
if $(\alpha_{T,V} = 0)$ **then**
  return
for $t = 0 \dots T$, $v = 0 \dots V$ **do**
  if $(t > 0)$ **then**
    for $i = 1 \dots maxX$ **st** $t - i \geq 0$ **do**
      $\gamma(x_{t-i+1}^t, \epsilon) \mathrel{+}= \frac{\alpha_{t-i,v}\delta(x_{t-i+1}^t, \epsilon)\beta_{t,v}}{\alpha_{T,V}}$
  if $(v > 0 \wedge t > 0)$ **then**
    for $i = 1 \dots maxX$ **st** $t - i \geq 0$ **do**
      for $j = 1 \dots maxY$ **st** $v - j \geq 0$ **do**
        $\gamma(x_{t-i+1}^t, y_{v-j+1}^v) \mathrel{+}= \frac{\alpha_{t-i,v-j}\delta(x_{t-i+1}^t, y_{v-j+1}^v)\beta_{t,v}}{\alpha_{T,V}}$

In the maximization step, we normalize the partial counts γ to the alignment probability δ using the conditional probability distribution. The EM steps are repeated until the alignment probability δ converges. Finally, the most likely alignment for each word pair in the training data is computed with the standard Viterbi algorithm.

3 Discriminative training

We adapt the online discriminative training framework described in (Jiampojamarn et al., 2008) to the transliteration task. Once the training data has been aligned, we can hypothesize that the ith letter substring $x_i \in \mathbf{x}$ in a source language word is transliterated into the ith substring $y_i \in \mathbf{y}$ in the target language word. Each word pair is represented as a feature vector $\Phi(\mathbf{x}, \mathbf{y})$. Our feature vector consists of (1) n-gram context features, (2) HMM-like transition features, and (3) linear-chain features. The n-gram context features relate the letter evidence that surrounds each letter x_i to its output y_i. We include all n-grams that fit within a context window of size c. The c value is determined using a development set. The HMM-like transition features express the cohesion of the output $\mathbf{y}$ in the target language. We make a first order Markov assumption, so that these features are bigrams of the form (y_{i-1}, y_i). The linear-chain features are identical to the context features, except that y_i is replaced with a bi-gram (y_{i-1}, y_i).

Algorithm 2 trains a linear model in this feature space. The procedure makes k passes over the aligned training data. During each iteration, the model produces the n most likely output words $\hat{Y}_j$ in the target language for each input word $\mathbf{x}_j$ in the source language, based on the current parameters ψ. The values of k and n are determined using a development set. The model parameters are updated according to the correct output $\mathbf{y}_j$ and the predicted n-best outputs $\hat{Y}_j$, to make the model prefer the correct output over the incorrect ones. Specifically, the feature weight vector ψ is updated by using MIRA, the Margin Infused Relaxed Algorithm (Crammer and Singer, 2003). MIRA modifies the current weight vector ψ_o by finding the smallest changes such that the new weight vector ψ_n separates the correct and incorrect outputs by a margin of at least $\ell(\mathbf{y}, \hat{\mathbf{y}})$, the loss for a wrong prediction. We define this loss to be 0 if $\hat{\mathbf{y}} = \mathbf{y}$; otherwise it is $1 + d$, where d is the Levenshtein distance between $\mathbf{y}$ and $\hat{\mathbf{y}}$. The update operation is stated as a quadratic programming problem in Equation 3. We utilize a function from the SVM^{light} package (Joachims, 1999) to solve this optimization problem.

Algorithm 2: Online discriminative training

Input: Data $\{(\mathbf{x}_1, \mathbf{y}_1), (\mathbf{x}_2, \mathbf{y}_2), \dots, (\mathbf{x}_m, \mathbf{y}_m)\}$, number of iterations k, size of n-best list n
Output: Learned weights ψ

$\psi := \vec{0}$
for *k iterations* **do**
  for $j = 1 \dots m$ **do**
    $\hat{Y}_j = \{\hat{\mathbf{y}}_{j1}, \dots, \hat{\mathbf{y}}_{jn}\} = \arg\max_{\mathbf{y}}[\psi \cdot \Phi(\mathbf{x}_j, \mathbf{y})]$
    update ψ according to $\hat{Y}_j$ and $\mathbf{y}_j$
return ψ

$$\begin{aligned} &\min_{\psi_n} \parallel \psi_n - \psi_o \parallel \\ &\text{subject to } \forall \hat{\mathbf{y}} \in \hat{Y}: \\ &\psi_n \cdot (\Phi(\mathbf{x}, \mathbf{y}) - \Phi(\mathbf{x}, \hat{\mathbf{y}})) \geq \ell(\mathbf{y}, \hat{\mathbf{y}}) \end{aligned} \quad (3)$$

The $\arg\max$ operation is performed by an exact search algorithm based on a phrasal decoder (Zens and Ney, 2004). This decoder simultaneously finds the l most likely substrings of letters $\mathbf{x}$ that generate the most probable output $\mathbf{y}$, given the feature weight vector ψ and the input word x^T. The search algorithm is based on the following dynamic programming recurrence:

$$\begin{aligned} &Q(0, \$) = 0 \\ &Q(t, p) = \max_{\substack{p', p, \\ t - maxX \leq t' < t}} \{\psi \cdot \phi(x_{t'+1}^t, p', p) + Q(t', p')\} \\ &Q(T+1, \$) = \max_{p'} \{\psi \cdot \phi(\$, p', \$) + Q(T, p')\} \end{aligned}$$

To find the n-best predicted outputs, the table Q records the top n scores for each output substring that has the suffix p substring and is generated by the input letter substring x_1^t; here, p' is a sub-output generated during the previous step. The notation $\phi(x^t_{t'+1}, p', p)$ is a convenient way to describe the components of our feature vector $\Phi(\mathbf{x}, \mathbf{y})$. The n-best predicted outputs $\hat{Y}$ can be discovered by backtracking from the end of the table, which is denoted by $Q(T+1, \$)$.

4 Beyond DIRECTL

4.1 Intermediate phonetic representation

We experimented with converting the original Chinese characters to Pinyin as an intermediate representation. Pinyin is the most commonly known Romanization system for Standard Mandarin. Its alphabet contains the same 26 letters as English. Each Chinese character can be transcribed phonetically into Pinyin. Many resources for Pinyin conversion are available online.[1] A small percentage of Chinese characters have multiple pronunciations represented by different Pinyin representations. For those characters (about 30 characters in the transliteration data), we manually selected the pronunciations that are normally used for names. This preprocessing step significantly reduces the size of target symbols from 370 distinct Chinese characters to 26 Pinyin symbols which enables our system to produce better alignments.

In order to verify whether the addition of language-specific knowledge can improve the overall accuracy, we also designed intermediate representations for Russian and Japanese. We focused on symbols that modify the neighboring characters without producing phonetic output themselves: the two *yer* characters in Russian, and the long vowel and *sokuon* signs in Japanese. Those were combined with the neighboring characters, creating new "super-characters."

4.2 Phonetic alignment with ALINE

ALINE (Kondrak, 2000) is an algorithm that performs phonetically-informed alignment of two strings of phonemes. Since our task requires the alignment of characters representing different writing scripts, we need to first replace every character with a phoneme that is the most likely to be produced by that character.

We applied slightly different methods to the test languages. In converting the Cyrillic script into phonemes, we take advantage of the fact that the Russian orthography is largely phonemic, which makes it a relatively straightforward task. In Japanese, we replace each Katakana character with one or two phonemes using standard transcription tables. For the Latin script, we simply treat every letter as an IPA symbol (International Phonetic Association, 1999). The IPA contains a subset of 26 letter symbols that tend to correspond to the usual phonetic value that the letter represents in the Latin script. The Chinese characters are first converted to Pinyin, which is then handled in the same way as the Latin script.

Similar solutions could be engineered for other scripts. We observed that the transcriptions do not need to be very precise in order for ALINE to produce high quality alignments.

4.3 System combination

The combination of predictions produced by systems based on different principles may lead to improved prediction accuracy. We adopt the following combination algorithm. First, we rank the individual systems according to their top-1 accuracy on the development set. To obtain the top-1 prediction for each input word, we use simple voting, with ties broken according to the ranking of the systems. We generalize this approach to handle n-best lists by first ordering the candidate transliterations according to the highest rank assigned by any of the systems, and then similarly breaking ties by voting and system ranking.

5 Evaluation

In the context of the NEWS 2009 Machine Transliteration Shared Task (Li et al., 2009), we tested our system on six data sets: from English to Chinese (EnCh) (Li et al., 2004), Hindi (EnHi), Russian (EnRu) (Kumaran and Kellner, 2007), Japanese Katakana (EnJa), and Korean Hangul (EnKo); and from Japanese Name to Japanese Kanji (JnJk)[2]. We optimized the models' parameters by training on the training portion of the provided data and measuring performance on the development portion. For the final testing, we trained the models on all the available labeled data (training plus development data). For each data set, we converted any uppercase letters to lowercase. Our system outputs the top 10 candidate answers for each input word.

Table 1 reports the performance of our system on the development and final test sets, measured in terms of top-1 word accuracy (ACC). For certain language pairs, we tested variants of the base

[1]For example, http://www.chinesetopinyin.com/

[2]http://www.cjk.org/

Task	Model	Dev	Test
EnCh	DIRECTL	72.4	71.7
	INT(M2M)	73.9	73.4
	INT(ALINE)	73.8	73.2
	COMBINED	74.8	74.6
EnHi	DIRECTL	41.4	49.8
	DIRECTL+MC	42.3	50.9
EnJa	DIRECTL	49.9	50.0
	INT(M2M)*	49.6	49.2
	INT(ALINE)	48.3	51.0
	COMBINED*	50.6	50.5
EnKo	DIRECTL	36.7	38.7
EnRu	DIRECTL	80.2	61.3
	INT(M2M)	80.3	60.8
	INT(ALINE)	80.0	60.7
	COMBINED*	80.3	60.8
JnJk	DIRECTL	53.5	56.0

Table 1: Top-1 word accuracy on the development and test sets. The asterisk denotes the results obtained after the test reference sets were released.

system described in Section 4. DIRECTL refers to our language-independent model, which uses many-to-many alignments. The INT abbreviation denotes the models operating on the language-specific intermediate representations described in Section 4.1. The alignment algorithm (ALINE or M2M) is given in brackets.

In the EnHi set, many names consisted of multiple words: we assumed a one-to-one correspondence between consecutive English words and consecutive Hindi words. In Table 1, the results in the first row (DIRECTL) were obtained with an automatic cleanup script that replaced hyphens with spaces, deleted the remaining punctuation and numerical symbols, and removed 43 transliteration pairs with a disagreement between the number of source and target words. The results in the second row (DIRECTL+MC) were obtained when the cases with a disagreement were individually examined and corrected by a Hindi speaker.

We did not incorporate any external resources into the models presented in Table 1. In order to emphasize the performance of our language-independent approach, we consistently used the DIRECTL model for generating our "standard" runs on all six language pairs, regardless of its relative performance on the development sets.

6 Discussion

DIRECTL, our language-independent approach to transliteration achieves excellent results, especially on the EnCh, EnRu, and EnHi data sets, which represent a wide range of language pairs and writing scripts. Both the many-to-many and phonetic alignment algorithms produce high-quality alignments. The former can be applied directly to the training data without the need for an intermediate representation, while the latter does not require any training. Surprisingly, incorporation of language-specific intermediate representations does not consistently improve the performance of our system, which indicates that DIRECTL may be able to discover the structures implicit in the training data without additional guidance. The EnHi results suggest that manual cleaning of noisy data can yield noticeable gains in accuracy. On the other hand, a simple method of combining predictions from different systems produced clear improvement on the EnCh set, but mixed results on two other sets. More research on this issue is warranted.

Acknowledgments

This research was supported by the Alberta Ingenuity, Informatics Circle of Research Excellence (iCORE), and Natural Sciences of Engineering Research Council of Canada (NSERC).

References

Koby Crammer and Yoram Singer. 2003. Ultraconservative online algorithms for multiclass problems. *Journal of Machine Learning Research*, 3:951–991.

International Phonetic Association. 1999. *Handbook of the International Phonetic Association*. Cambridge University Press.

Sittichai Jiampojamarn, Grzegorz Kondrak, and Tarek Sherif. 2007. Applying many-to-many alignments and Hidden Markov Models to letter-to-phoneme conversion. In *Proc. HLT-NAACL*, pages 372–379.

Sittichai Jiampojamarn, Colin Cherry, and Grzegorz Kondrak. 2008. Joint processing and discriminative training for letter-to-phoneme conversion. In *Proc. ACL*, pages 905–913.

Thorsten Joachims. 1999. Making large-scale SVM learning practical. Advances in kernel methods: support vector learning, pages 169–184. MIT Press.

Grzegorz Kondrak. 2000. A new algorithm for the alignment of phonetic sequences. In *Proc. NAACL*, pages 288–295.

A. Kumaran and Tobias Kellner. 2007. A generic framework for machine transliteration. In *Proc. SIGIR*, pages 721–722.

Haizhou Li, Min Zhang, and Jian Su. 2004. A joint source channel model for machine transliteration. In *Proc. ACL*, pages 159–166.

Haizhou Li, A Kumaran, Min Zhang, and Vladimir Pervouchine. 2009. Whitepaper of NEWS 2009 machine transliteration shared task. In *Proc. ACL-IJCNLP Named Entities Workshop*.

Richard Zens and Hermann Ney. 2004. Improvements in phrase-based statistical machine translation. In *Proc. HLT-NAACL*, pages 257–264.

Named Entity Transcription with Pair n-Gram Models

Martin Jansche
Google Inc.
mjansche@google.com

Richard Sproat
Google Inc. and OHSU
rws@google.com

Abstract

We submitted results for each of the eight shared tasks. Except for Japanese name kanji restoration, which uses a noisy channel model, our Standard Run submissions were produced by generative long-range pair n-gram models, which we mostly augmented with publicly available data (either from LDC datasets or mined from Wikipedia) for the Non-Standard Runs.

1 Introduction

This paper describes the work that we did at Google, Inc. for the NEWS 2009 Machine Transliteration Shared Task (Li et al., 2009b; Li et al., 2009a). Except for the Japanese kanji task (which we describe below), all models were pair n-gram language models. Briefly, we took the training data, and ran an iterative alignment algorithm using a single-state weighted finite-state transducer (WFST). We then trained a language model on the input-output pairs of the alignment, which was then converted into a WFST encoding a joint model. For the Non-Standard runs, we use additional data from Wikipedia or from the LDC, except where noted below. In the few instances where we used data not available from Wikipedia or LDC, we will be happy to share them with other participants of this competition.

2 Korean

For Korean, we created a mapping between each Hangul glyph and its phonetic transcription in World-Bet (Hieronymus, 1993) based on the tables from Unitran (Yoon et al., 2007). Vowel-initial syllables were augmented with a "0" at the beginning of the syllable, to avoid spurious resyllabifications: *Abbott* should be 애버트, never 앱얼으. We also filtered the set of possible Hangul syllable combinations, since certain syllables are never used in transliterations, e.g. any with two consonants in the coda. The mapping between Hangul syllables and phonetic transcription was handled with a simple FST.

The main transliteration model for the Standard Run was a 10-gram pair language model trained on an alignment of English letters to Korean phonemes. All transliteration pairs observed in the training/development data were cached, and made available if those names should recur in the test data. We also submitted a Non-Standard Run with English/Korean pairs mined from Wikipedia. These were derived from the titles of corresponding interlinked English and Korean articles. Obviously not all such pairs are transliterations, so we filtered the raw list by predicting, for each English word, and using the trained transliteration model, what the ten most likely transliterations were in Korean; and then accepting any pair in Wikipedia where the string in Korean also occurred in the set of predicted transliterations. This resulted in 11,169 transliteration pairs. In addition a dictionary of 9,047 English and Korean transliteration pairs that we had obtained from another source was added. These pairs were added to the cache, and were also used to retrain the transliteration model, along with the provided data.

3 Indian Languages

For the Indian languages Hindi, Tamil and Kannada, the same basic approach as for Korean was used. We created a reversible map between Devanagari, Tamil or Kannada symbols and their phonemic values, using a modified version of Unitran. However, since Brahmi-derived scripts distinguish between diacritic and full vowel forms, in order to map back from phonemic transcription into the script form, it is necessary to know whether a vowel comes after a consonant or not, in order to select the correct form. These and other constraints were implemented with a simple hand-constructed WFST for each script.

The main transliteration model for the Standard Run was a 6-gram pair language model trained on an alignment of English letters to Hindi, Kannada

Proceedings of the 2009 Named Entities Workshop, ACL-IJCNLP 2009, pages 32–35,
Suntec, Singapore, 7 August 2009.

or Tamil phonemes in the training and development sets. At test time, this WFST was composed with the phoneme to letter WFST just described to produce a WFST that maps directly between English letters and Indian script forms. As with Korean, all observed transliteration pairs from the training/development data were cached, and made available if those names should recur in the test data. For each Indian language we also submitted a Non-Standard Run which included English/Devanagari, English/Tamil and English/Kannada pairs mined from Wikipedia, and filtered as described above for Korean. This resulted in 11,674 pairs for English/Hindi, 10,957 pairs for English/Tamil and 2,436 pairs for English/Kannada. These pairs were then added to the cache, and were also used to retrain the transliteration model, along with the provided data.

4 Russian

For Russian, we computed a direct letter/letter correspondences between the Latin representation of English and the Cyrillic representation of Russian words. This seemed to be a reasonable choice since Russian orthography is fairly phonemic, at least at an abstract level, and it was doubtful that any gain would be had from trying to model the pronunciation better. We note that many of the examples were, in fact, not English to begin with, but a variety of languages, including Polish and others, that happen to be written in the Latin script.

We used a 6-gram pair language model for the Standard Run. For the Non-Standard Runs we included: (for NSR1) a list of 3,687 English/Russian pairs mined from the Web; and (for NSR2), those, plus a set of 1,826 mined from Wikipedia and filtered as described above. In each case, the found pairs were put in the cache, and were used to retrain the language model.

5 Chinese

For Chinese, we built a direct stochastic model between strings of Latin characters representing the English names and strings of hanzi representing their Chinese transcription. It is well known (Zhang et al., 2004) that the direct approach produces significantly better transcription quality than indirect approaches based on intermediate pinyin or phoneme representations. This observation is consistent with our own experience during system development.

In our version of the direct approach, we first aligned the English letter strings with their corresponding Chinese hanzi strings using the same memoryless monotonic alignment model as before. We then built standard n-gram models over the alignments, which were then turned, for use at runtime, into weighted FSTs computing a mapping from English to Chinese.

The transcription model we chose for the Standard Run is a 6-gram language model over alignments, built with Kneser-Ney smoothing and a minimal amount of Seymore-Rosenfeld shrinking.

We submitted two Non-Standard Runs with additional names taken from the LDC Chinese/English Name Entity Lists v 1.0 (LDC2005T34). The only list from this collection we used was Propernames People EC, which contains 572,213 "English" names (in fact, names from many languages, all represented in the Latin alphabet) with one or more Chinese transcriptions for each name. Data of similar quality can be easily extracted from the Web as well. For the sake of reproducible results, we deliberately chose to work with a standard corpus. The LDC name lists have all of the problems that are usually associated with data extracted from the Web, including improbable entries, genuine mistakes, character substitutions, a variety of unspecified source languages, etc.

We removed names with symbols other than letters 'a' through 'z' from the list and divided it into a held-out portion, consisting of names that occur in the development or test data of the Shared Task, and a training portion, consisting of everything else, for a total of 622,187 unique English/Chinese name pairs. We then used the model from the Standard Run to predict multiple pronunciations for each of the names in the training portion of the LDC list and retained up to 5 pronunciations for each English name where the prediction from the Standard model agreed with a pronunciation found in the LDC list.

For our first Non-Standard Run, we trained a 7-gram language model based on the Shared Task training data (31,961 name pairs) plus an additional 95,576 name pairs from the intersection of the LDC list and the Standard model predictions. Since the selection of additional training data was, by design, very conservative, we got a small improvement over the Standard Run.

The reason for this cautious approach was that the additional LDC data did not match the provided training and development data very well, partly due to noise, partly due to different transcription conventions. For example, the Pinyin syllable *bó* is predominantly written as 博 in the LDC data, but 博 does not occur at all in the Shared Task training data:

Character	Occurrences	
	Train	LDC
博	0	13,110
伯	1,547	3,709

We normalized the LDC data (towards the transcription conventions implicit in the Shared Task data) by replacing hanzi for frequent Pinyin syllables with the predominant homophonous hanzi from the Shared Task data. This resembles a related approach to pronunciation extraction from the web (Ghoshal et al., 2009), where extraction validation and pronunciation normalization steps were found to be tremendously helpful, even necessary, when using web-derived pronunciations. One of the conclusions there was that extracted pronunciations should be used directly when available.

This is what we did in our second Non-Standard Run. We used the filtered and normalized LDC data as a static dictionary in which to look up the transcription of names in the test data. This is how the shared task problem would be solved in practice and it resulted in a huge gain in quality. Notice, however, that doing so is non-trivial, because of the data quality and data mismatch problems described above.

6 Japanese Katakana

The "English" to Japanese katakana task suffered from the usual problem that the Latin alphabet side covered many languages besides English. It thus became an exercise in guessing which one of many valid ways of pronouncing the Latin letter string would be chosen as the basis for the Japanese transcription. We toyed with the idea of building mixture models before deciding that this issue is more appropriate for a pronunciation modeling shared task. In the end, we built the same kinds of straightforward pair *n*-gram models as in the tasks described earlier.

For Japanese katakana we performed a similar kind of preprocessing as for the Indian languages: since it is possible (under minimal assumptions) to construct an isomorphism between katakana and Japanese phonemes, we chose to use phonemes as the main level of representation in our model. This is because Latin letters encode phonemes as opposed to syllables or morae (to a first approximation) and one pays a penalty (a loss of about 4% in accuracy on the development data) for constructing models that go from Latin letters directly to katakana.

For the Standard Run, we built a 5-gram model that maps from Latin letter strings to Japanese phoneme strings. The model used the same kind of Kneser-Ney smoothing and Seymore-Rosenfeld shrinking as before. In addition, we restrict the model to only produce well-formed Japanese phoneme strings, by composing it with an unweighted Japanese phonotactic model that enforces the basic syllable structure.

7 Japanese Name Kanji

It is important to note that the Japanese name kanji task is conceptually completely different from all of the other tasks. We argue that this conceptual difference must translate into a different modeling and system building approach.

The conceptual difference is this: In all other tasks, we're given well-formed "English" names. For the sake of argument, let's say that they are indeed just English names. These names have an English pronunciation which is then mapped to a corresponding Hindi or Korean pronunciation, and the resulting Hindi or Korean "words" (which do not look like ordinary Hindi or Korean words at all, except for superficially following the phonology of the target language) can be written down in Devanagari or Hangul. Information is lost when distinct English sounds get mapped to the same phonemes in the target language and when semantic information (such as the gender of the bearer of a name) is simply not transmitted across the phonetic channel that produces the approximation in the target language (transcription into Chinese is an exception in this regard). We call this *forward transcription* because we're projecting the original representation of a name onto an impoverished approximation.

In name kanji restoration, we're moving in the opposite direction. The most natural, information-rich form of a Japanese name is its kanji representation (ja-Hani). When this gets transcribed into rōmaji (ja-Latn), only the sound of the name is preserved. In this task, we're asked to recover the richer kanji form from the impoverished rōmaji form. This is the opposite of the forward transcription tasks and just begs to be described by a noisy channel model, which is exactly what we did.

The noisy channel model is a factored generative model that can be thought of as operating by drawing an item (kanji string) from a source model over the universe of Japanese names, and then, conditional on the kanji, generating the observation (rōmaji string) in a noisy, nondeterministic fashion, by drawing it at random from a channel model (in this case, basically a model of kanji readings).

To simplify things, we make the natural assumption that there is a latent segmentation of the rōmaji string into segments of one or more syllables and that each individual kanji in a name generates exactly one segment. For illustration, consider the example *abukawa* 虻川, which has three possible segmentations: *a+bukawa*, *abu+kawa*, and *abuka+wa*. Note that boundaries can fall into the middle of ambisyllabic long consonants, as in *matto* 松任.

Complicating this simple picture are several kinds of noise in the training data: First, Chinese pinyin mixed in with Japanese rōmaji, which we removed mostly automatically from the training and development data and for which we deliberately chose not to produce guesses in the submitted runs on the test data. Second, the seemingly arbitrary coalescence of certain vowel sequences. For example, *ōnuma* 大沼 and *onuma* 小沼 appear as *onuma*, and *kouda* 国府田 and *kōda* 幸田 appear as *koda* in the training data. Severe space limitations prevent us from going into further details here: we will however discuss the issues during our presentation at the workshop.

For the Standard Run, we built a trigram character language model on the kanji names (16,182 from the training data plus 3,539 from the development data, discarding pinyin names). We assume a zero-order channel model, where each kanji generates its portion of the rōmaji observation independent of its kanji or rōmaji context. We applied an EM algorithm to the parallel rōmaji/kanji data (19,684 items) in order to segment the rōmaji under the stated assumptions and train the channel model. We pruned the model by replacing the last EM step with a Viterbi step, resulting in faster runtime with no loss in quality. NSR 1 uses more than 100k additional names (kanji only, no additional parallel data) extracted from biographical articles in Wikipedia, as well as a list, found on the Web, of the 10,000 most common Japanese surnames. A total of 117,782 names were used to train a trigram source model. Everything else is identical to the Standard Run. NSR 2 is like NSR 1 but adds dictionary lookup. If we find the rōmaji name in a dictionary of 27,358 names extracted from Wikipedia and if a corresponding kanji name from the dictionary is among the top 10 hypotheses produced by the model, that hypothesis is promoted to the top (again, this performs better than using the extracted names blindly). NSR 3 is like NSR 1 but the channel model is trained on a total of 108,172 rōmaji/kanji pairs consisting of the training and development data plus data extracted from biographies in Wikipedia. Finally NSR 4 is like NSR 3 but adds the same kind of dictionary lookup as in NSR 2. Note that the biggest gains are due first to the richer source model in NSR 1 and second to the richer channel model in NSR 3. The improvements due to dictionary lookups in NSR 2 and 4 are small by comparison.

8 Results

Results for the runs are summarized below. "Rank" is rank in SR/NSR as appropriate:

	Run	ACC	F	Rank
en/ta	SR	0.436	0.894	2
	NSR1	0.437	0.894	5
ja-Latn/	SR	0.606	0.749	2
ja-Hani	NSR1	0.681	0.790	4
	NSR2	0.703	0.805	3
	NSR3	0.698	0.805	2
	NSR4	**0.717**	**0.818**	**1**
en/ru	SR	0.597	0.925	3
	NSR1	0.609	0.928	2
	NSR2	**0.955**	**0.989**	**1**
en/zh	SR	0.646	0.867	6
	NSR1	0.658	0.865	10
	NSR2	**0.909**	**0.960**	**1**
en/hi	SR	0.415	0.858	9
	NSR1	0.424	0.862	8
en/ko	**SR**	**0.476**	**0.742**	**1**
	NSR1	**0.794**	**0.894**	**1**
en/kn	SR	0.370	0.867	2
	NSR1	0.374	0.868	4
en/ja-Kana	SR	0.503	0.843	3
	NSR1	0.564	0.862	n/a

Acknowledgments

The authors acknowledge the use of the English-Chinese (EnCh) (Li et al., 2004), English-Japanese Katakana (EnJa), English-Korean Hangul (EnKo), Japanese Name (in English)-Japanese Kanji (JnJk) (`http://www.cjk.org`), and English-Hindi (EnHi), English-Tamil (EnTa), English-Kannada (EnKa), English-Russian (EnRu) (Kumaran and Kellner, 2007) corpora.

References

Arnab Ghoshal, Martin Jansche, Sanjeev Khudanpur, Michael Riley, and Morgan E. Ulinksi. 2009. Web-derived pronunciations. In *ICASSP*.

James L. Hieronymus. 1993. ASCII phonetic symbols for the world's languages: Worldbet. AT&T Bell Laboratories, technical memorandum.

A. Kumaran and Tobias Kellner. 2007. A generic framework for machine transliteration. In *SIGIR--30*.

Haizhou Li, Min Zhang, and Jian Su. 2004. A joint source channel model for machine transliteration. In *ACL-42*.

Haizhou Li, A. Kumaran, Vladimir Pervouchine, and Min Zhang. 2009a. Report on NEWS 2009 machine transliteration shared task. In *ACL-IJCNLP 2009 Named Entities Workshop*, Singapore.

Haizhou Li, A. Kumaran, Min Zhang, and Vladimir Pervouchine. 2009b. Whitepaper of NEWS 2009 machine transliteration shared task. In *ACL-IJCNLP 2009 Named Entities Workshop*, Singapore.

Su-Youn Yoon, Kyoung-Young Kim, and Richard Sproat. 2007. Multilingual transliteration using feature based phonetic method. In *ACL*.

Min Zhang, Haizhou Li, and Jian Su. 2004. Direct orthographical mapping for machine transliteration. In *COLING*.

Machine Transliteration using Target-Language Grapheme and Phoneme: Multi-engine Transliteration Approach

Jong-Hoon Oh, Kiyotaka Uchimoto, and Kentaro Torisawa
Language Infrastructure Group, MASTAR Project,
National Institute of Information and Communications Technology (NICT)
3-5 Hikaridai Seika-cho, Soraku-gun, Kyoto 619-0289 Japan
{rovellia,uchimoto,torisawa}@nict.go.jp

Abstract

This paper describes our approach to "NEWS 2009 Machine Transliteration Shared Task." We built multiple transliteration engines based on different combinations of two transliteration models and three machine learning algorithms. Then, the outputs from these transliteration engines were combined using re-ranking functions. Our method was applied to all language pairs in "NEWS 2009 Machine Transliteration Shared Task." The official results of our standard runs were ranked the best for four language pairs and the second best for three language pairs.

1 Outline

This paper describes our approach to "NEWS 2009 Machine Transliteration Shared Task." Our approach was based on two transliteration models – **TM-G** (**T**ransliteration **m**odel based on target-language **G**raphemes) and **TM-GP** (**T**ransliteration **m**odel based on target-language **G**raphemes and **P**honemes). The difference between the two models lies in whether or not a machine transliteration process depends on target-language phonemes. TM-G directly converts source-language graphemes into target-language graphemes, while TM-GP first transforms source language graphemes into target-language phonemes and then target-language phonemes coupled with their corresponding source-language graphemes are converted into target-language graphemes. We used three different machine learning algorithms (conditional random fields (CRFs), margin infused relaxed algorithm (MIRA), and maximum entropy model (MEM)) (Berger et al., 1996; Crammer and Singer, 2003; Lafferty et al., 2001) for building multiple machine transliteration engines. We attempted to improve the transliteration quality by combining the outputs of different machine transliteration engines operating on the same input. Our approach was applied to all language pairs in "NEWS 2009 Machine Transliteration Shared Task." The official results of our approach were ranked as the best for four language pairs and the second best for three language pairs (Li et al., 2009a).

2 Transliteration Model

Let **S** be a source-language word and **T** be a target-language transliteration of **S**. **T** is represented in two ways – T_G, a sequence of target-language graphemes, and T_P, a sequence of target-language phonemes. Here, a target-language grapheme is defined as a target-language character. We regard consonant and vowel parts in the romanized form of a target language grapheme as a target-language phoneme. Then **TM-G** and **TM-GP** are formulated as Eq (1) and (2), respectively.

$$P_{TM-G}(T|S) = P(T_G|S) \quad (1)$$

$$P_{TM-GP}(T|S) = \sum_{\forall T_P} P(T_P|S) \times P(T_G|T_P, S) \quad (2)$$

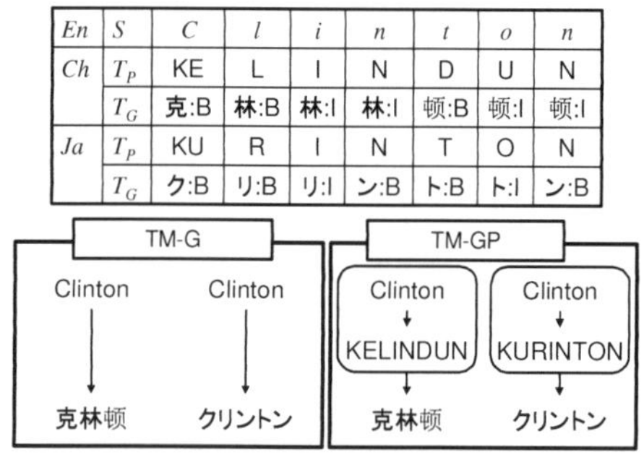

Figure 1: Illustration of the two transliteration models

Proceedings of the 2009 Named Entities Workshop, ACL-IJCNLP 2009, pages 36–39,
Suntec, Singapore, 7 August 2009.

Figure 1 illustrates the two transliteration models with examples, *Clinton* and its Chinese and Japanese transliterations. Target language graphemes are represented in terms of the BIO notation. This makes it easier to represent many-to-one correspondence between target language phoneme and grapheme.

3 Machine Learning Algorithms

A machine transliteration problem can be converted into a sequential labeling problem, where each source-language grapheme is tagged with its corresponding target-language grapheme. This section briefly describes the machine learning algorithms used for building multiple transliteration engines.

3.1 Maximum Entropy Model

Machine transliteration based on the maximum entropy model was described in detail in Oh et al. (2006) along with comprehensive evaluation of its performance. We used the same way as that proposed by Oh et al. (2006), thus its full description is not presented here.

3.2 Conditional Random Fields (CRFs)

CRFs, a statistical sequence modeling framework, was first introduced by Lafferty et al. (2001). CRFs has been used for sequential labeling problems such as text chunking and named entity recognition (McCallum and Li, 2003). CRF++[1] was used in our experiment.

3.3 Margin Infused Relaxed Algorithm

The Margin Infused Relaxed Algorithm (MIRA) has been introduced by Crammer and Singer (2003) for large-margin multi-class classification. Kruengkrai et al. (2008) proposed a discriminative model for joint Chinese segmentation and POS tagging, where MIRA was used as their machine learning algorithm. We used the same model for our machine transliteration, exactly joint syllabication[2] and transliteration.

3.4 Features

We used the following features within the ± 3 context window[3] for the above mentioned three machine learning algorithms.

- Left-three and right-three source-language graphemes (or syllables)
- Left-three and right-three target-language phonemes
- Target-language graphemes assigned to the previous three source-language graphemes (or syllables)

4 Multi-engine Transliteration

4.1 Individual Transliteration Engine

The main aim of the multi-engine transliteration approach is to combine the outputs of multiple engines so that the final output is better in quality than the output of each individual engine. We designed four transliteration engines using different combinations of source-language transliteration units, transliteration models, and machine learning algorithms as listed in Table 1. We named four transliteration engines as CRF-G, MEM-G, MEM-GP, and MIRA-G. Here, the prefixes represent applied machine learning algorithms (maximum entropy model (MEM), CRFs, and MIRA), while G and GP in the suffix represent the transliteration models, **TM-G** and **TM-GP**, respectively. Each individual engine produces 30-best transliterations for a given source-language word.

	Source-language transliteration unit	
	Grapheme	Syllable
TM-G	ME-G, CRF-G	MIRA-G
TM-GP	ME-GP	N/A

Table 1: Design strategy for multiple transliteration engines

4.2 Combining Methodology

We combined the outputs of multiple transliteration engines by means of a re-ranking function, $g(x)$. Let X be a set of transliterations generated by multiple transliteration engines for source-language word s and ref be a reference transliteration of s. A re-ranking function is defined as Eq. (3), where it ranks ref in X higher and the others lower (Oh and Isahara, 2007).

$$g(x) : X \rightarrow \{r : r\ is\ ordering\ of\ x \in X\} \quad (3)$$

We designed two types of re-ranking functions by using the rank of each individual engine and machine learning algorithm.

[1] Available at `http://crfpp.sourceforge.net/`

[2] A syllable in English is defined as a sequence of English grapheme corresponding to one target-language grapheme.

[3] The unit of context window is source-language grapheme or syllable.

4.2.1 Re-ranking Based on the Rank of Individual Engines

Two re-ranking functions based on the rank of each individual engine, g_{rank} and $g_{Fscore}(x)$, are used for combining the outputs of multiple transliteration engines. Let X be a set of outputs of N transliteration engines for the same input. $g_{rank}(x)$ re-ranks $x \in X$ in the manner shown in Eq. (4), where $Rank_i(x)$ is the position of x in the n-best list generated by the ith transliteration engine. $g_{rank}(x)$ can be interpreted as the average rank of x over outputs of each individual engine. If x is not in the n-best list of the ith transliteration engine, $\frac{1}{Rank_i(x)} = 0$.

$$g_{rank}(x) = \frac{1}{N} \sum_{i=1}^{N} \frac{1}{Rank_i(x)} \quad (4)$$

$g_{Fscore}(x)$ is based on $g_{rank}(x)$ and the F-score measure, which is one of the evaluation metrics in the "NEWS 2009 Machine Transliteration Shared Task" (Li et al., 2009b). We considered the top three outputs of each individual engine as reference transliterations and defined them as *virtual reference transliterations*. We calculated the F-score measure between the virtual reference transliteration and each output of multiple transliteration engines. $g_{Fscore}(x)$ is defined by Eq. (5), where VRef is a set of virtual reference transliterations, and $F_{score}(vr, x)$ is a function that restores the F-score measure between vr and x.

$$g_{Fscore}(x) = g_{rank}(x) \times MF(x) \quad (5)$$
$$MF(x) = \frac{1}{|VRef|} \sum_{vr \in VRef} F_{score}(vr, x)$$

Since the F-score measure is calculated in terms of string similarity, x gets a high score from $g_{MF}(x)$ when it is orthographically similar to virtual reference transliterations.

4.2.2 Re-ranking based on Machine Learning Algorithm

We used the maximum entropy model for learning re-ranking function $g_{ME}(x)$. Let ref be a reference transliteration of source-language word s, $feature(x)$ be a feature vector of $x \in X$, and $y \in \{ref, wrong\}$ be the training label for x. $g_{ME}(x)$ assigns a probability to $x \in X$ as shown in Eq. (6).

$$g_{ME}(x) = P(ref|feature(x)) \quad (6)$$

A feature vector of x is composed of

- $\langle g_{rank}(x), g_{Fscore}(x), \frac{1}{Rank_i(x)}, P(T|S) \rangle$

where $\frac{1}{Rank_i(x)}$ and $P(T|S)$ of each individual engine are used as a feature.

We estimated $P(ref|feature(x))$ by using the development data.

5 Our Results

5.1 Individual Engine

	CRF-G	MEM-G	MEM-GP	MIRA-G
EnCh	0.628	0.686	**0.715**	0.684
EnHi	0.455	**0.469**	**0.469**	0.412
EnJa	0.514	0.517	**0.519**	0.490
EnKa	**0.386**	0.380	0.380	0.338
EnKo	**0.460**	0.438	0.447	0.367
EnRu	**0.600**	0.561	0.566	0.568
EnTa	0.453	**0.459**	**0.459**	0.412
JnJk	N/A	0.532	N/A	**0.571**

Table 2: ACC of individual engines on the test data

Table 2 presents ACC[4] of individual transliteration engines, which was applied to all language pairs in "NEWS 2009 Machine Transliteration Shared Task" (Li et al., 2004; Kumaran and Kellner, 2007; The CJK Dictionary Institute, 2009). CRF-G was the best transliteration engine in EnKa, EnKo, and EnRu. Owing to the high training costs of CRFs, we trained CRF-G in EnCh with a very small number of iterations[5]. Hence, the performance of CRF-G was poorer than that of the other engines in EnCh. MEM-GP was the best transliteration engine in EnCh, EnHi, EnJa, and EnTa. These results indicate that joint use of source language graphemes and target language phonemes were very useful for improving performance. MIRA-G was sensitive to the training data size, because it was based on joint syllabication and transliteration. Therefore, the performance of MIRA-G was relatively better in EnCh and EnJa, whose training data size is bigger than other language pairs. CRF-G could not be applied to JnJk, mainly due to too long training time. Further, MEM-GP could not be applied to JnJk, because transliteration in JnJk can be regarded as conversion of target language phonemes to target language graphemes. MEM-G and MIRA-G were

[4]Word accuracy in Top-1 (Li et al., 2009b)

[5]We applied over 100 iterations to other language pairs but only 30 iterations to EnCh.

applied to JnJk and MIRA-G showed the best performance in JnJK.[6]

5.2 Combining Multiple Engines

	g_{rank}	g_{Fscore}	g_{ME}	I-BEST
EnCh	0.730	**0.731**	**0.731**	0.715
EnHi	0.481	0.475	**0.483**	0.469
EnJa	0.535	0.535	**0.537**	0.519
EnKa	0.393	**0.399**	0.398	0.386
EnKo	0.461	0.444	**0.473**	0.460
EnRu	0.602	**0.605**	0.600	0.600
EnTa	0.470	**0.478**	0.474	0.459
JnJk	**0.597**	0.593	0.590	0.571

Table 3: Multi-engine transliteration results on the test data: the underlined figures are our official result

Table 3 presents the ACC of our multi-engine transliteration approach and that of the best individual engine (I-BEST) in each language pair. g_{ME} gave the best performance in EnCh, EnHi, EnJa, and EnKo, while g_{Fscore} did in EnCh, EnKa, EnRu, and EnTa. Comparison between the best individual transliteration engine and our multi-engine transliteration showed that g_{rank} and g_{ME} consistently showed better performance except in EnRu, while g_{Fscore} showed the poorer performance in EnKo. The results to be submitted as "the standard run" were selected among the results listed in Table 3 by using cross-validation on the development data. We submitted the results of g_{ME} as the standard run to "NEWS 2009 Machine Transliteration Shared Task" for the six language pairs in Table 3, while the result of g_{Fscore} is submitted as the standard run for EnRu. The official results of our standard runs were ranked the best for EnCh, EnJa, EnKa, and EnTa, and the second best for EnHi, EnKo, and EnRu (Li et al., 2009a).

6 Conclusion

In conclusion, we have applied multi-engine transliteration approach to "NEWS 2009 Machine Transliteration Shared Task." We built multiple transliteration engines based on different combinations of transliteration models and machine learning algorithms. We showed that the transliteration model, which is based on target language graphemes and phonemes, and our multi-engine transliteration approach are effective, regardless of the nature of the language pairs.

[6]We submitted the results of MEM-G as a standard run for JnJk because we had only one transliteration engine for JnJK before the submission deadline of the NEWS 2009 machine transliteration shared task.

References

A. L. Berger, S. D. Pietra, and V. J. D. Pietra. 1996. A maximum entropy approach to natural language processing. *Computational Linguistics*, 22(1):39–71.

Koby Crammer and Yoram Singer. 2003. Ultraconservative online algorithms for multiclass problems. *Journal of Machine Learning Research*, 3:951–991.

Canasai Kruengkrai, Jun'ichi Kazama, Kiyotaka Uchimoto, Kentaro Torisawa, and Hitoshi Isahara. 2008. A discriminative hybrid model for joint Chinese word segmentation and pos tagging. In *Proc. of The 11th Oriental COCOSDA Workshop*.

A. Kumaran and Tobias Kellner. 2007. A generic framework for machine transliteration. In *Proc. of SIGIR '07*, pages 721–722.

John Lafferty, Andrew McCallum, and Fernando Pereira. 2001. Conditional random fields: Probabilistic models for segmenting and labeling sequence data. In *Proc. of ICML01*, pages 282–289.

Haizhou Li, Min Zhang, and Su Jian. 2004. A joint source-channel model for machine transliteration. In *Proc. of ACL '04*, pages 160–167.

Haizhou Li, A Kumaran, Vladimir Pervouchine, and Min Zhang. 2009a. Report on NEWS 2009 machine transliteration shared task. In *Proc. of ACL-IJCNLP 2009 Named Entities Workshop*.

Haizhou Li, A Kumaran, Min Zhang, and Vladimir Pervouchine. 2009b. Whitepaper of NEWS 2009 machine transliteration shared task. In *Proc. of ACL-IJCNLP 2009 Named Entities Workshop*.

Andrew McCallum and Wei Li. 2003. Early results for named entity recognition with conditional random fields, feature induction and web-enhanced lexicons. In *Proc. of CoNLL '03*, pages 188–191.

Jong-Hoon Oh and Hitoshi Isahara. 2007. Machine transliteration using multiple transliteration engines and hypothesis re-ranking. In *Proc. of the 11th Machine Translation Summit*, pages 353–360.

Jong-Hoon Oh, Key-Sun Choi, and Hitoshi Isahara. 2006. A comparison of different machine transliteration models. *Journal of Artificial Intelligence Research (JAIR)*, 27:119–151.

The CJK Dictionary Institute. 2009. http://www.cjk.org.

A Language-Independent Transliteration Schema Using Character Aligned Models At NEWS 2009

Praneeth Shishtla, Surya Ganesh V, Sethuramalingam Subramaniam, Vasudeva Varma
Language Technologies Research Centre,
IIIT-Hyderabad, India
praneethms@students.iiit.ac.in
{suryag,sethu}@research.iiit.ac.in, vv@iiit.ac.in

Abstract

In this paper we present a statistical transliteration technique that is language independent. This technique uses statistical alignment models and Conditional Random Fields (CRF). Statistical alignment models maximizes the probability of the observed (source, target) word pairs using the expectation maximization algorithm and then the character level alignments are set to maximum posterior predictions of the model. CRF has efficient training and decoding processes which is conditioned on both source and target languages and produces globally optimal solution.

1 Introduction

A significant portion of out-of-vocabulary (OOV) words in machine translation systems, information extraction and cross language retrieval models are named entities (NEs). If the languages are written in different scripts, these named entities must be transliterated. Transliteration is defined as the process of obtaining the phonetic translation of names across languages. A source language word can have more than one valid transliteration in the target language. In areas like Cross Language Information Retrieval (CLIR), it is important to generate all possible transliterations of a Named Entity.

Most current transliteration systems use a generative model for transliteration such as freely available GIZA++[1] (Och and Ney , 2000), an implementation of the IBM alignment models (Brown et al., 1993) and HMM alignment model. These systems use GIZA++ to get character level alignments from word aligned data. The transliteration system (Nasreen and Larkey , 2003) is built by counting up the alignments and converting the counts to conditional probabilities.

In this paper, we describe our participation in *NEWS 2009 Machine Transliteration Shared Task* (Li et al., 2009). We present a simple statistical, language independent technique which uses statistical alignment models and Conditional Random Fields (CRFs) (Hanna , 2004). Using this technique a desired number of transliterations are generated for a given word.

2 Previous work

One of the works on Transliteration is done by Arababi et al. (Arababi et. al., 1994). They model forward transliteration through a combination of neural net and expert systems. Work in the field of Indian Language CLIR was done by Jaleel and Larkey (Larkey et al., 2003). They did this based on their work in English-Arabic transliteration for CLIR (Nasreen and Larkey , 2003). Their approach was based on HMM using GIZA++ (Och and Ney , 2000). Prior work in Arabic-English transliteration for machine translation purpose was done by Arababi (Arbabi et al., 1994). They developed a hybrid neural network and knowledge-based system to generate multiple English spellings for Arabic person names. Knight and Graehl (Knight and Graehl , 1997) developed a five stage statistical model to do back transliteration, that is, recover the original English name from its transliteration into Japanese Katakana. Stalls and Knight (Stalls and Knight , 1998) adapted this approach for back transliteration from Arabic to English of English names. Al-Onaizan and Knight (Onaizan and Knight , 2002) have produced a simpler Arabic/English transliterator and evaluates how well their system can match a source spelling. Their work includes an

[1] http://www.fjoch.com/GIZA++.html

Proceedings of the 2009 Named Entities Workshop, ACL-IJCNLP 2009, pages 40–43,
Suntec, Singapore, 7 August 2009.

evaluation of the transliterations in terms of their reasonableness according to human judges. None of these studies measures their performance on a retrieval task or on other NLP tasks. Fujii and Ishikawa (Fujii and Ishikawa , 2001) describe a transliteration system for English-Japanese CLIR that requires some linguistic knowledge. They evaluate the effectiveness of their system on an English-Japanese CLIR task.

3 Problem Description

The problem can be stated formally as a sequence labeling problem from one language alphabet to other. Consider a source language word $x_1x_2..x_i..x_N$ where each x_i is treated as a word in the observation sequence. Let the equivalent target language orthography of the same word be $y_1y_2..y_i..y_N$ where each y_i is treated as a label in the label sequence. The task here is to generate a valid target language word (label sequence) for the source language word (observation sequence).

x_1 ———————— y_1
x_2 ———————— y_2
. ———————— .
. ———————— .
. ———————— .
x_N ———————— y_N

Here the valid target language alphabet (y_i) for a source language alphabet (x_i) in the input source language word may depend on various factors like

1. The source language alphabet in the input word.
2. The context (alphabets) surrounding source language alphabet (x_i) in the input word.
3. The context (alphabets) surrounding target language alphabet (y_i) in the desired output word.

4 Transliteration using alignment models and CRF

Our approach for transliteration is divided into two phases. The first phase induces character alignments over a word-aligned bilingual corpus, and the second phase uses some statistics over the alignments to transliterate the source language word and generate the desired number of target language words. The selected statistical model for transliteration is based on a combination of statistical alignment models and CRF. The alignment models maximize the probability of the observed (source, target) word pairs using the expectation maximization algorithm. After the maximization process is complete, the character level alignments are set to maximum posterior predictions of the model. This alignment is used to get character level alignment of source and target language words. From the character level alignment obtained we compare each source language character to a word and its corresponding target language character to a label. Conditional random fields (CRFs) are a probabilistic framework for labeling and segmenting sequential data. We use CRF to generate target language word (similar to label sequence) from source language word (similar to observation sequence). CRFs are undirected graphical models which define a conditional distribution over a label sequence given an observation sequence. We define CRFs as conditional probability distributions $P(Y|X)$ of target language words given source language words. The probability of a particular target language word Y given source language word X is the normalized product of potential functions each of the form

$$e^{(\sum_j \lambda_j t_j(Y_{i-1},Y_i,X,i))+(\sum_k \mu_k s_k(Y_i,X,i))}$$

where $t_j(Y_{i-1}, Y_i, X, i)$ is a transition feature function of the entire source language word and the target language characters at positions i and $i-1$ in the target language word; $s_k(Y_i, X, i)$ is a state feature function of the target language word at position i and the source language word; and λ_j and μ_k are parameters to be estimated from training data.

$$F_j(Y,X) = \sum_{i=1}^{n} f_j(Y_{i-1}, Y_i, X, i)$$

where each $f_j(Y_{i-1}, Y_i, X, i)$ is either a state function $s(Y_{i-1}, Y_i, X, i)$ or a transition function $t(Y_{i-1}, Y_i, X, i)$. This allows the probability of a target language word Y given a source language word X to be written as

$$P(Y|X,\lambda) = (\frac{1}{Z(X)})e^{(\sum \lambda_j F_j(Y,X))}$$

$Z(X)$ is a normalization factor.

5 Our Transliteration system

The whole model has three important phases. Two of them are off-line processes and the other is a on-line process. The two off-line phases are preprocessing the parallel corpora and training the model using CRF++[2] (Lafferty et al., 2001). CRF++ is a simple, customizable, and open source implementation of Conditional Random Fields (CRFs) for segmenting/labeling sequential data. The on-line phase involves generating desired number of target language transliterations (UTF-8 encoded) for the given English input word. In our case, the source is always an English word. The same system is used for every language pair which makes it a language independent. The target languages consist of Chinese, Hindi, Kannada Tamil and Russian words.

5.1 Preprocessing

The training file is converted into a format required by CRF++. The sequence of steps in preprocessing are

1. Both source and target language words were prefixed with a begin symbol B and suffixed with an end symbol E which correspond to start and end states. English words were converted to lower case.

2. The training words were segmented in to unigrams and the source-target word pairs were aligned using GIZA++ (IBM model1, HMM alignment model, IBM model3 and IBM model4).

3. The alignment consist of $NULLs$ on source language i.e., a target language unigram is aligned to $NULL$ on the source language. These $NULLs$ are problematic during on-line phase (as positions of $NULLs$ are unknown). So, these $NULLs$ are removed by appending the target language unigram to the unigram of its previous alignment. For example, the following alignment,

$$k - K$$

$$NULL - A$$

transforms to -

$$k - KA$$

So, in the final alignment, the source side always contains unigrams and the target side might contain ngrams which depends on alphabet size of the languages. These three steps are performed to get the character level alignment for each source and target language training words.

4. This final alignment is transformed to training format as required by CRF++ to work. In the training format, a source language unigram aligned to a target language ngram is called a token. Each token must be represented in one line, with the columns separated by white space (spaces or tabular characters). Each token should have equal number of columns.

5.2 Training Phase

The preprocessing phase converts the corpus into CRF++ input file format. This file is used to train the CRF model. The training requires a template file which specifies the features to be selected by the model. The training is done using Limited memory Broyden-Fletcher-Goldfarb-Shannon method (L-BFGS) (Liu and Nocedal, 1989) which uses quasi-newton algorithm for large scale numerical optimization problem. We used English characters as features for our model and a window size of 5.

5.3 Transliteration

For a language pair, the list of English words that need to be transliterated is taken. These words are converted into CRF++ test file format and transliterated using the trained model which gives the top n probable English words. CRF++ uses forward Viterbi and backward A* search whose combination produces the exact n-best results. This process is repeated for all the five language pairs.

6 Results

In this section, we present the results of our participation in the NEWS-2009 shared task. We conducted our experiments on five language pairs namely English-Chinese (Li et al., 2004), English-{Hindi, Kannada, Tamil, Russian} (Kumaran and Kellner , 2007). As specified in *NEWS 2009 Machine Transliteration Shared Task* (Li et al., 2009), we submitted our standard runs on all the five language pairs. Table 1 shows the results of our system.

[2]http://crfpp.sourceforge.net/

Language Pair	Accuracy in top-1	Mean F-score	MRR	MAP_{ref}	MAP_{10}	MAP_{sys}
English-Tamil	0.406	0.894	0.542	0.399	0.193	0.193
English-Hindi	0.407	0.877	0.544	0.402	0.195	0.195
English-Russian	0.548	0.916	0.640	0.548	0.210	0.210
English-Chinese	0.493	0.804	0.600	0.493	0.192	0.192
English-Kannada	0.350	0.864	0.482	0.344	0.175	0.175

Table 1: Transliteration results for the language pairs

7 Conclusion

In this paper, we have described our transliteration system build on a discriminative model using CRF and statistical alignment models. As mentioned earlier, our system is language independent and works on any language pair provided parallel word lists are available for training in the particular language pair. The main advantage of our system is that we use no language-specific heuristics in any of our modules and hence it is extensible to any language-pair with least effort.

References

A. Kumaran, Tobias Kellner. 2007. *A generic framework for machine transliteration, Proc. of the 30th SIGIR.*

A. L. Berger. 1997. *The improved iterative scaling algorithm: A gentle introduction.*

Arbabi, M. and Fischthal, S. M. and Cheng, V. C. and Bart, E. 1994. *Algorithms for Arabic name transliteration, IBM Journal of Research And Development.*

Al-Onaizan Y, Knight K. 2002. *Machine translation of names in Arabic text. Proceedings of the ACL conference workshop on computational approaches to Semitic languages.*

Arababi Mansur, Scott M. Fischthal, Vincent C. Cheng, and Elizabeth Bar. 1994. *Algorithms for Arabic name transliteration. IBM Journal of research and Development.*

D. C. Liu and J. Nocedal. 1989. *On the limited memory BFGS method for large-scale optimization, Math. Programming 45 (1989), pp. 503–528.*

Fujii Atsushi and Tetsuya Ishikawa. 2001. *Japanese/English Cross-Language Information Retrieval: Exploration of Query Translation and Transliteration. Computers and the Humanities, Vol.35, No.4, pp.389-420.*

H. M. Wallach. 2002. *Efficient training of conditional random fields. Masters thesis, University of Edinburgh.*

Hanna M. Wallach. 2004. *Conditional Random Fields: An Introduction.*

Haizhou Li, A Kumaran, Min Zhang, Vladimir Pervouchine. 2009. *Whitepaper of NEWS 2009 Machine Transliteration Shared Task. Proceedings of ACL-IJCNLP 2009 Named Entities Workshop (NEWS 2009), Singapore.*

Haizhou Li, A Kumaran, Vladimir Pervouchine, Min Zhang. 2009. *Report on NEWS 2009 Machine Transliteration Shared Task. Proceedings of ACL-IJCNLP 2009 Named Entities Workshop (NEWS 2009), Singapore.*

Haizhou Li, Min Zhang, Jian Su. 2004. *A joint source channel model for machine transliteration. Proc. of the 42nd ACL.*

J. Darroch and D. Ratcliff. 1972. *Generalized iterative scaling for log-linear models. The Annals of Mathematical Statistics, 43:14701480.*

J. Lafferty, A. McCallum, and F. Pereira. 2001. *Conditional random fields: Probabilistic models for segmenting and labeling sequence data. In Proc. of ICML, pp.282-289.*

Knight Kevin and Graehl Jonathan. 1997. *Machine transliteration. In Proceedings of the 35th Annual Meeting of the Association for Computational Linguistics, pp. 128-135. Morgan Kaufmann.*

Larkey, Connell,AbdulJaleel. 2003. *Hindi CLIR in Thirty Days.*

Nasreen Abdul Jaleel and Leah S. Larkey. 2003. *Statistical Transliteration for English-Arabic Cross Language Information Retrieval.*

Och Franz Josef and Hermann Ney. 2000. *Improved Statistical Alignment Models. Proc. of the 38th Annual Meeting of the Association for Computational Linguistics, pp. 440-447, Hong Kong, China.*

P. F. Brown, S. A. Della Pietra, and R. L. Mercer. 1993. *The mathematics of statistical machine translation: Parameter estimation. Computational Linguistics, 19(2):263-311.*

Phil Blunsom and Trevor Cohn. 2006. *Discriminative Word Alignment with Conditional Random Fields.*

Stalls Bonnie Glover and Kevin Knight. 1998. *Translating names and technical terms in Arabic text.*

Experiences with English-Hindi, English-Tamil and English-Kannada Transliteration Tasks at NEWS 2009

Manoj Kumar Chinnakotla and **Om P. Damani**
Department of Computer Science and Engineering,
IIT Bombay,
Mumbai, India
{manoj,damani}@cse.iitb.ac.in

Abstract

We use a Phrase-Based Statistical Machine Translation approach to Transliteration where the words are replaced by characters and sentences by words. We employ the standard SMT tools like GIZA++ for learning alignments and Moses for learning the phrase tables and decoding. Besides tuning the standard SMT parameters, we focus on tuning the Character Sequence Model (CSM) related parameters like order of the CSM, weight assigned to CSM during decoding and corpus used for CSM estimation. Our results show that paying sufficient attention to CSM pays off in terms of increased transliteration accuracies.

1 Introduction

Transliteration of Named-Entities (NEs) is an important problem that affects the accuracy of many NLP applications like Cross Lingual Search and Machine Translation. *Transliteration* is defined as the process of automatically mapping a given grapheme sequence in the source language to a grapheme sequence in the target language such that it preserves the pronunciation of the original source word. A *Grapheme* refers to the unit of written language which expresses a phoneme in the language. Multiple alphabets could be used to express a grapheme. For example, *sh* is considered a single grapheme expressing the phoneme */SH/*. For phonetic orthography like Devanagari, each grapheme corresponds to a unique phoneme. However, for English, a grapheme like *c* may map to multiple phonemes */S/,/K/*. An example of transliteration is mapping the Devanagari grapheme sequence प्रिन्स हैरी to its phonetically equivalent grapheme sequence *Prince Harry* in English.

This paper discusses our transliteration approach taken for the NEWS 2009 Machine Transliteration Shared Task [Li et al.2009b, Li et al.2009a]. We model the transliteration problem as a Phrased-Based Machine Translation problem. Later, using the development set, we tune the various parameters of the system like order of the Character Sequence Model (CSM), typically called language model, weight assigned to CSM during decoding and corpus used to estimate the CSM. Our results show that paying sufficient attention to the CSM pays off in terms of improved accuracies.

2 Phrase-Based SMT Approach to Transliteration

In the Phrase-Based SMT Approach to Transliteration [Sherif and Kondrak2007, Huang2005], the words are replaced by characters and sentences are replaced by words. The corresponding noisy channel model formulation where a given english word **e** is to be transliterated into a foreign word **h**, is given as:

$$\begin{aligned} h^* &= \operatorname*{argmax}_h Pr(h|e) \\ &= \operatorname*{argmax}_h Pr(e|h) \cdot Pr(h) \qquad (1) \end{aligned}$$

In Equation 1, $Pr(e|h)$ is known as the *translation model* which gives the probability that the character sequence h could be transliterated to e and $Pr(h)$ is known as the *character sequence model* typically called language model which gives the probability that the character sequence h forms a valid word in the target language.

Proceedings of the 2009 Named Entities Workshop, ACL-IJCNLP 2009, pages 44–47,
Suntec, Singapore, 7 August 2009.

Task	Run	Optimal Parameter Set	Accuracy in top-1	Mean F-score	MRR	MAPref	MAP10	MAPsys
English-Hindi	Standard	LM Order: 5, LM Weight: 0.6	0.47	0.86	0.58	0.47	0.18	0.20
English-Hindi	Non-standard	LM Order: 5, LM Weight: 0.6	0.52	0.87	0.62	0.52	0.19	0.21
English-Tamil	Standard	LM Order: 5, LM Weight: 0.3	0.45	0.88	0.56	0.45	0.18	0.18
English-Kannada	Standard	LM Order: 5, LM Weight: 0.3	0.44	0.87	0.55	0.44	0.17	0.18

Figure 1: NEWS 2009 Development Set Results

Task	Run	Accuracy in top-1	Mean F-score	MRR	MAPref	MAP10	MAPsys
English-Hindi	Standard	0.42	0.86	0.54	0.42	0.18	0.20
English-Hindi	Non-standard	0.49	0.87	0.59	0.48	0.20	0.23
English-Tamil	Standard	0.41	0.89	0.54	0.40	0.18	0.18
English-Kannada	Standard	0.36	0.86	0.48	0.35	0.16	0.16

Figure 2: NEWS 2009 Test Set Results

Given the parallel training data pairs, we preprocessed the source (English) and target (Hindi, Tamil and Kannada) strings into character sequences. We then ran the GIZA++ [Och and Ney2003] aligner with default options to obtain the character-level alignments. For alignment, except for Hindi, we used single character-level units without any segmentation. In case of Hindi, we did a simple segmentation where we added the halant character (U094D) to the previous Hindi character. Moses Toolkit [Hoang et al.2007] was then used to learn the phrase-tables for English-Hindi, English-Tamil and English-Kannada. We also learnt the character sequence models on the target language training words using the SRILM toolkit [Stolcke2002]. Given a new English word, we split the word into sequence of characters and run the Moses decoder with the phrase-table of target language obtained above to get the transliterated word. We ran Moses with the *DISTINCT* option to obtain the top *k* distinct transliterated options.

2.1 Moses Parameter Tuning

The Moses decoder computes the cost of each translation as a product of probability costs of four models: a) translation model b) language model c) distortion model and d) word penalty as shown in Equation 2. The distortion model controls the cost of re-ordering phrases (transliteration units) in a given sentence (word) and the word penalty model controls the length of the final translation. The parameters λ_T, λ_{CSM}, λ_D and λ_W control the relative importance given to each of the above models.

Task	Run	Baseline Model (LM Order N=3)	Best Run	% Improvement
English-Hindi	Standard	0.4	0.42	5.00
English-Hindi	Non-standard	0.37	0.49	32.43
English-Tamil	Standard	0.39	0.45	15.38
English-Kannada	Standard	0.36	0.36	0.00

Figure 3: Improvements Obtained over Baseline on Test Set due to Language Model Tuning

$$Pr(h|e) = Pr_T(e|h)^{\lambda_T} \cdot Pr_{CSM}(h)^{\lambda_{CSM}} \cdot Pr_D(h,e)^{\lambda_D} \cdot \omega^{length(h) \cdot \lambda_W} \quad (2)$$

Since no re-ordering of phrases is required during translation task, we assign a zero weight to λ_D. Similarly, we varied the word penalty factor λ_W between $\{-1, 0, +1\}$ and found that it achieves maximum accuracy at 0. All the above tuning was done with a trigram CSM and default weight (0.5) in Moses for λ_T.

2.2 Improving CSM Performance

In addition to the above mentioned parameters, we varied the order of the CSM and the monolingual corpus used to estimate the CSM. For each task, we started with a trigram CSM as mentioned above and tuned both the order of the CSM and λ_{CSM} on the development set. The optimal set of parameters and the development set results are shown in Figure 1. In addition, we use a monolingual Hindi corpus of around 0.4 million documents called Guruji corpus. We extracted the 2.6 million unique words from the above corpus and trained a CSM on that. This CSM which was learnt on the monolingual Hindi corpus was used for the non-standard Hindi run. We repeat the above procedure of tuning the order of CSM and λ_{CSM} and find the optimal set of parameters for the non-standard run on the development set.

3 Results and Discussion

The details of the NEWS 2009 dataset for Hindi, Kannada and Tamil are given in [Li et al.2009a, Kumaran and Kellner2007]. The final results of our system on the test set are shown in Figure 2. Figure 3 shows the improvements obtained on test set by tuning the CSM parameters. The trigram CSM model used along with the optimal Moses parameter set tuned on development set was taken as baseline for the above experiments. The results show that a major improvement (32.43%) was obtained in the non-standard run where the monolingual Hindi corpus was used to learn the CSM. Because of the use of monolingual Hindi corpus in the non-standard run, the transliteration accuracy improved by 22.5% when compared to the standard run. The improvements (15.38%) obtained in Tamil are also significant. However, the improvement in Hindi standard run was not significant. In Kannada, there was no improvement due to tuning of LM parameters. This needs further investigation.

The above results clearly highlight the importance of improving CSM accuracy since it helps in improving the transliteration accuracy. Moreover, improving the CSM accuracy only requires monolingual language resources which are easy to obtain when compared to parallel transliteration training data.

4 Conclusion

We presented the transliteration system which we used for our participation in the NEWS 2009 Machine Transliteration Shared Task on Transliteration. We took a Phrase-Based SMT approach to transliteration where words are replaced by characters and sentences by words. In addition to the standard SMT parameters, we tuned the CSM related parameters like order of the CSM, weight assigned to CSM and corpus used to estimate the CSM. Our results show that improving the accuracy of CSM pays off in terms of improved transliteration accuracies.

Acknowledgements

We would like to thank the Indian search-engine company Guruji (`http://www.guruji.com`) for providing us the Hindi web content which was used to train the language model for our non-standard Hindi runs.

References

Hieu Hoang, Alexandra Birch, Chris Callison-burch, Richard Zens, Rwth Aachen, Alexandra Constantin, Marcello Federico, Nicola Bertoldi, Chris Dyer, Brooke Cowan, Wade Shen, Christine Moran, and Ondej Bojar. 2007. Moses: Open Source Toolkit for Statistical Machine Translation. In *In Proceedings of ACL, Demonstration Session*, pages 177–180.

Fei Huang. 2005. Cluster-specific Named Entity Transliteration. In *HLT '05: Proceedings of the conference on Human Language Technology and Empirical Methods in Natural Language Processing*, pages 435–442, Morristown, NJ, USA. Association for Computational Linguistics.

A. Kumaran and Tobias Kellner. 2007. A Generic Framework for Machine Transliteration. In *SIGIR '07: Proceedings of the 30th annual international ACM SIGIR conference on Research and development in information retrieval*, pages 721–722, New York, NY, USA. ACM.

Haizhou Li, A Kumaran, Vladimir Pervouchine, and Min Zhang. 2009a. Report on NEWS 2009 Machine Transliteration Shared Task. In *Proceedings of ACL-IJCNLP 2009 Named Entities Workshop (NEWS 2009)*.

Haizhou Li, A Kumaran, Min Zhang, and Vladimir Pervouchine. 2009b. Whitepaper of NEWS 2009 Machine Transliteration Shared Task. In *Proceedings of ACL-IJCNLP 2009 Named Entities Workshop (NEWS 2009)*.

Franz Josef Och and Hermann Ney. 2003. A Systematic Comparison of Various Statistical Alignment Models. *Computational Linguistics*, 29(1):19–51.

Tarek Sherif and Grzegorz Kondrak. 2007. Substring-Based Transliteration. In *In Proceedings of ACL 2007*. The Association for Computer Linguistics.

Andreas Stolcke. 2002. SRILM - An Extensible Language Modeling Toolkit. In *In Proceedings of Intl. Conf. on Spoken Language Processing*.

Testing and Performance Evaluation of Machine Transliteration System for Tamil Language

Kommaluri Vijayanand[1, 2]*, Inampudi Ramesh Babu[1, 3], Poonguzhali Sandiran[1, 2]
(1) Department of Computer Science and Engineering,
(2) Pondicherry University, Puducherry - 605 014, India.
(3) Acharya Nagarjuna University, Nagarjuna Nagar - 522 510, India.
kvixs@yahoo.co.in, rinampudi@yahoo.com, poon_8724@yahoo.com

Abstract

Machine Translation (MT) is a science fiction that was converted into reality with the enormous contributions from the MT research community. We cannot expect any text without Named Entities (NE). Such NEs are crucial in deciding the quality of MT. NEs are to be recognized from the text and transliterated accordingly into the target language in order to ensure the quality of MT. In the present paper we present various technical issues encountered during handling the shared task of NE transliteration for Tamil.

1 Introduction

Out of several underlying issues relating to Machine Translation (MT) against the dependence on the human editors, Named Entity Recognition (NER) play a pivotal role. When a MT system is developed and executed, majority of the initial test cases are bound to fail, when the system attempt to translate the names, acronyms etc. Special attention is required to handle such cases where in NER and transliteration task play a pivot role (Vijayanand and Subramanian, 2006).

We had participated in the shared task towards the languages English to Tamil, English to Hindi and English to Kannada after receiving the reference corpora which consists of 1000 names for each language pair (Li et al., 2009b). Though we committed responsibility for the three language pairs viz., English to Tamil, English to Kannada and English to Hindi, we mainly concentrated on the English to Tamil language pair. The Tamil Machine Transliteration System shall be available for demonstration during the workshop.

The present transliteration system is implemented using JDK 1.6.0 for transliterating the Named Entities in Tamil language from the source names in English. The character combination in English such as *A, Aa, I, ee, u, oo, ai, o, ou,* forms vowels in Tamil. Similarly the characters *k, ng, ch, t,* etc., form consonants and the characters *ka, nga, cha* etc., form compound characters. One single character in English produce different pronunciations and for each pronunciation, there exists a separate character. For example in the words *Madura* and *Ramya* the sound of *a* is different when *a* is suffixed with *r* and *y*. Similarly, the character *n* has different pronunciations depending upon the suffix. For example in the words *Sanchit, Pannu, Nandini, Jahangir* the character *n* has different pronunciations depending upon the suffix. We need to identify and consider these criteria when we transliterate the words from the languages English to Tamil. Thus the present system takes into account all such cases and generate the possible transliterations for the data given by the shared task (Li et al., 2009a).

The paper is organized in such a way that, we enumerate various rules that are formulated and deployed in favor of segmentation are explained with suitable examples in section 2. The technical details regarding the system design is presented in the section 3. The results generated by the system and the evaluation of the transliterations that are carried out using different kinds of data are explained in the section 4, followed by the section 5 that concludes the papers with the overall remarks and future work.

2 Segmentation Rules

Every word is a combination of characters and transforms its sound based on the characters that surrounds it as described in the previous section. During transliteration it is quite important to identify the break points with in the word to pronounce

†Research Scholar at Acharya Nagarjuna University, India and Visiting Scholar of Université Joseph Fourier (Grenoble 1), Grenoble, France.

Proceedings of the 2009 Named Entities Workshop, ACL-IJCNLP 2009, pages 48–51,
Suntec, Singapore, 7 August 2009.

the given word correctly. Towards enforcing such constraint we had devised and employed various rules towards segmentation based on the phonetic conversions. They are enumerated as follows :

1. If the second index to the current index of the word is *a*, *e*, *I* or *u*, then it is considered to be one individual segment.
2. If the second index to the current index of the word is *h* and the third index to the current index of the word is *a*, *e*, *I*, *o* or *u*, then it is considered as one segment.
3. If the second and third index to the current index of the word is *a*, *e*, *I*, *o* or *u* and if it is same character i.e., *aa*,*ee*, *oo*, then it is considered as one segment.
4. If the second index to the current index of the word is *a*, *o* and the third index to the current index of the word is *e* or *u*, then it is considered as one segment.
5. If the second and third index to the current index of the word does not satisfy any of the above four conditions then the current index of the word is considered to be as one segment.

Based on these rules the partition algorithm was sketched and implemented in favor of partitioning the word. The partitioning algorithm is applied only for the named entities and explained with the following example.

Let us consider a word *Chandrachur*, the present system navigate through five steps for segmenting this word as listed below :

1. The word is fragmented as Cha | ndrachur

   Initially the system parse from the initial character *c* and checks the second index. It recognizes that the second index is *h*. Then it reads the third index according to the rule number 2. It then recognizes that the third index is *a*. So the system partitions up to that third index and consider it as one segment.

2. Further segmentation : Cha | n | drachur

   Now the system starts from the fourth index and consider that index as the current index. It continues checking the fifth index. As it does not satisfy any of the rules, it partitions the fourth index from the source word and consider it as one segment.

3. Cha | n | d | rachur

   In the third step checking starts from the fifth index and now it is considered to be the current index. Then it checks the sixth index. Since, it does not satisfy any of the rules, the system partitions the fifth index from the source name and it is considered as one segment.

4. Cha | n | d | ra | chur

   Now the system starts from the sixth index and consider this to be the current index. It checks the seventh index, after recognizing the presence of *a*, then it checks whether the eighth index is *a*, *e* or *u*, as per the rule 3 and rule 4. As it does not satisfy with those rules, the system partitions from sixth index to seventh index as one segment.

5. Cha | n | d | ra | chu | r

   Finally checking starts from the eighth index which is treated as the current index and the system checks the ninth index. The ninth index consists of *h*. Thus, checks the tenth index for the presence of *a*, *e*, *I*, *o* or *u* according to the rule 2 and satisfies with that rule. Thus, the system partitions from eighth index to tenth index as one segment and the eleventh index become one segment.

Similarly, for the word *Manikkam* the system applies the partitioning algorithm and segment the word as shown below :

1. Ma | nikkam
2. Ma | ni | kkam
3. Ma | ni | k | kam
4. Ma | ni | k | ka | m

3 The System Design

The system was designed in such a way that it produces four to six transliterations for a given word in English. We stored all the possible combinations of characters in English and its corresponding Tamil characters in a database and created an interface to read the test file. The system is facilitated to browse the test file using the file handling technique which was designed applying the logical concepts. Consonants in English when combined with vowels in English to form compound words in Tamil. Compound words have many forms for a single combination.

The present system extract the source names and store them in an array list. These source names are retrieved from an array list sequentially and stored in a string variable for further processing. The value of the string is parsed character wise and check for the existence of a vowel or *h*, in the next two positions to its index i.e., for each character the next two characters are checked, if there exists vowels or *h*, then these characters are extracted up to that index and stored in another string variable. Other wise only that variable is stored and compared with the database that contain Tamil characters, for each combination of characters that are present in English. Thereafter each index in an array list of each transliteration will be combined with each index in another array list of transliterated letter combination, stored in another variable. This process will continue until the system encounter the end of each array list. After getting all the combinations, these combinations are stored in an array list and it is written to the file.

It is to be noted that only one source name is assigned to the string variable at a time. After getting the target name of that source name, the next source name is retrieved from an array list. After retrieving the source name it is passed to the next module for segmentation. The segments formed are stored in an array list. Then these target characters for each segment is retrieved from the database and stored in a separate list. There after the values in an array list are merged appropriately and stored in an array list.

4 Results and Evaluation

This section describes briefly about the results and evaluation conducted and present the results. We had employed various techniques and algorithms as explained in previous sections, to select the appropriate transliterated word that matches the source name from the n-best candidate list using six metrics.

4.1 Results

The result file consists of source name with its ID and the ranked list of target names. The target names are generated along with the source names, after being processed by the system. The source names are the names given in the test file. The target names are the names that are generated by the system. The target names are ranked according to their ID's. The target names are Unicode characters in Tamil. After applying various techniques we produce the result file. It is worth stating that the result file is generated in the XML format using UTF-8 encoding schema.

The present system transliterates for 1000 source names and generates up to six best candidate lists (Target names). We conducted testing for the given data towards transliterations. The first transliteration present in the four best candidate lists are considered to be the correct hit. The evaluation is carried out using Python. These six metrics are implemented in python. The metrics are as follows :

1. Word Accuracy in Top-1 (ACC)
2. Mean F-Score
3. Mean Reciprocal Rank (MRR)
4. MAP ref
5. MAP_10
6. MAP sys

MAP refers to the Mean Average Precision. Python is preferred because it is an excellent programming language, easy to understand, dynamic and truly object oriented.

4.2 Evaluation

The Result file and the Test file in XML format and the python script developed with six metrics reads the above mentioned files. Execution of the script requires Python interpreter. The Result file is the one generated by the Transliteration System and the test file is created manually with a single transliteration for each source name and testing is conducted. As part of the shared task (Kumaran and Kellner, 2007) evaluation was done by running the system and thus 6 metrics are displayed as output, with each metric given the value 0 or 1. These metrics declare the performance of the system. The max-candidates argument in the script is assigned 10 (max-candidates=10). It is also changed according to target names provided. The output of the evaluation of our Transliteration System are as follows :

1. Word Accuracy in Top-1 (ACC) : The ACC of our system is 0.403974,
2. Mean F-Score : The Mean F-Score of our system is 0.865840.
3. MRR = The Mean Reciprocal rank of our system is 0.449227.
4. MAP ref : The MAP ref of the system is 0.390545.

5. MAP 10 ; The MAP_10 value of the system is 0.240066.
6. MAP sys : The MAP sys of the system is 0.369840.

The output that was generated by our system is presented in appendix.

5 Conclusions

After working with the experiment that was carried out for evaluating the metrics, we conclude that the accuracy in top-1 score of our system is 0.061. The reason could be that the accurate transliteration is not generated in the top scored transliteration. We could improve the performance of the present system by involving all the possible transliterations. With the initial test results are very low when compared to Urdu to Hindi transliteration system (M. G. et al., 2008), yields 97.12% and Hindi to Urdu delivers 97.88% of accuracy and NER system favor of the Bengali language which had demonstrated the evaluation results with a precision of 80.12% (Ekbal and Bandyopadhyay, 2008).

After participating in the shared task we had tested the transliteration system thoroughly by applying various techniques as explained in the present paper. So far we had carried out the transliteration for six named entity candidates. In future we would like to extend the task for transliteration candidates unto twenty. Thus the named entity transliteration task that is being carried out would be a solution for the long standing research problem in handling the named entities that is quite common in speech and text machine translation.

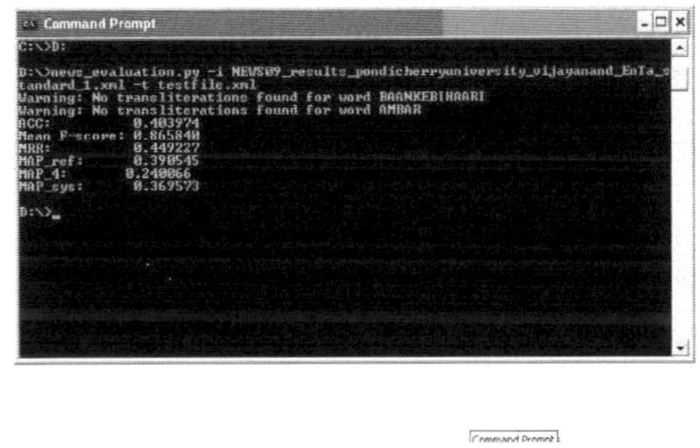

FIG. 1 – Screenshot of Evaluation Result.

Acknowledgments

I am thankful to the anonymous referees for their valuable advices towards improving this paper. I am thankful to my students Kanickairaj Caroline, Dhivya Moorthy and Kothandapani Selvi for rendering their service and cooperation in fulfilling this task. I extend my gratitude to all the elders for their support and encouragement.

References

Asif Ekbal and Sivaji Bandyopadhyay. 2008. Named entity recognition using support vector machine : A language independent approach. *International Journal of Computer Systems Science and Engineering*, 4(2) :155–170.

A. Kumaran and Tobias Kellner. 2007. A generic framework for machine transliteration. In *30th Annual ACM SIGIR Conference*, Amsterdam.

Hauzhou Li, A Kumaran, Vladimir Pervouchine, and Min Zhang. 2009a. Report on news 2009 machine transliteration shared task. In *Proceedings of the ACL-IJCNLP 2009 Named Entities Workshop (NEWS 2009)*, Singapore.

Hauzhou Li, A Kumaran, Min Zhang, and Vladimir Pervouchine. 2009b. White paper of news 2009 machine transliteration shared task. In *Proceedings of the ACL-IJCNLP 2009 Named Entities Workshop (NEWS 2009)*, Singapore.

Abbas Malik M. G., Christian Boitet, and Pushpak Bhattacharyya. 2008. Hindi urdu machine transliteration using finite state transducers. In *Proceedings of the 22nd International Conference on Computational Linguistics (COLING 2008)*, Manchester.

Kommaluri Vijayanand and Ramalingam Subramanian. 2006. Anuvadini : An automatic example-based machine translation system for bengali into assamese and oriya. In *Proceedings of the First National Symposium on Modeling and Shallow Parsing of Indian Languages (MSPIL-06)*, IIT Bombay, India.

Transliteration by Bidirectional Statistical Machine Translation

Andrew Finch
NICT
2-2-2 Hikaridai
Keihanna Science City
619-0288 JAPAN
andrew.finch@nict.go.jp

Eiichiro Sumita
NICT
2-2-2 Hikaridai
Keihanna Science City
619-0288 JAPAN
eiichiro.sumita@nict.go.jp

Abstract

The system presented in this paper uses phrase-based statistical machine translation (SMT) techniques to directly transliterate between all language pairs in this shared task. The technique makes no language specific assumptions, uses no dictionaries or explicit phonetic information. The translation process transforms sequences of tokens in the source language directly into to sequences of tokens in the target. All language pairs were transliterated by applying this technique in a single unified manner. The machine translation system used was a system comprised of two phrase-based SMT decoders. The first generated from the first token of the target to the last. The second system generated the target from last to first. Our results show that if only one of these decoding strategies is to be chosen, the optimal choice depends on the languages involved, and that in general a combination of the two approaches is able to outperform either approach.

1 Introduction

It is possible to couch the task of machine transliteration as a task of machine translation. Both processes involve the transformation of sequences of tokens in one language into sequences of tokens in another language. The principle differences between the machine translation and language translation are:

- Transliteration does not normally require the re-ordering of tokens that are generated in the target
- The number of types (the vocabulary size) in both source and target languages is considerably less for the transliteration task

We take a statistical machine translation paradigm (Brown at al., 1991) as the basis for our systems. The work in this paper is related to the work of (Finch and Sumita, 2008) who also use SMT directly to transliterate.

We view the task of machine transliteration as a process of machine translation at the character level (Donoual and LePage, 2006). We use state of the art phrase-based statistical machine translation systems (Koehn et al., 2003) to perform the transliteration. By adopting this approach we were able to build systems for all of the language pairs in the shared task using precisely the same procedures. No modeling of the phonetics of either source or target language (Knight and Graehl, 1997) was necessary, since the approach is simply a direct transformation of sequences of tokens in the source language into sequences of tokens in the target.

2 Overview

Our approach differs from the approach of (Finch and Sumita, 2008) in that we decode bidirectional. In a typical statistical machine translation system the sequence of target tokens is generated in a left-to-right manner, by left-to-right here we mean the target sequence is generated from the first token to its last. During the generation process the models (in particular the target language model) are able to refer to only the target tokens that have already been generated. In our approach, by using decoders that decode in both directions we are able to exploit context to the left and to the right of target tokens being generated. Furthermore, we expect our system to gain because it is a combination of two different MT systems that are performing the same task.

3 Experimental Conditions

In our experiments we used an in-house phrase-based statistical machine translation decoder called CleopATRa. This decoder operates on exactly the same principles as the publicly available MOSES decoder (Koehn et al., 2003). Like MOSES we utilize a future cost in our calculations. Our decoder was modified to be able to run two instances of the decoder at the same

Proceedings of the 2009 Named Entities Workshop, ACL-IJCNLP 2009, pages 52–56,
Suntec, Singapore, 7 August 2009.

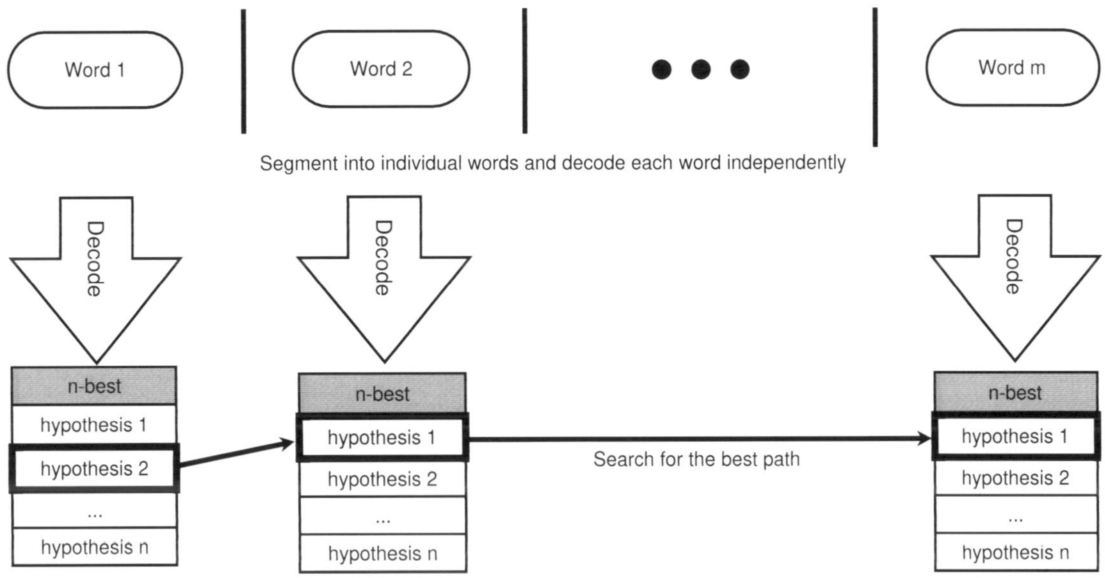

Figure 1: The decoding process for multi-word sequences

time. One instance decoding from left-to-right the other decoding from right-to-left. The hypotheses being combined by linearly interpolating the scores from both decoders at the end of the decoding process. In addition, the decoders were constrained decode in a monotone manner. That is, they were not allowed to re-order the phrases during decoding. The decoders were also configured to produce a list of unique sequences of tokens in their n-best lists. During SMT decoding it is possible to derive the same sequence of tokens in multiple ways. Multiply occurring sequences of this form were combined into a single hypothesis in the n-best list by summing their scores.

3.1 Pre-processing

In order to reduce data sparseness issues we took the decision to work with data in only its lowercase form. The only target language with case information was Russian. During the parameter tuning phase (where output translations are compared against a set of references) we restored the case for Russian by simply capitalizing the first character of each word.

We chose not to perform any tokenization for any of the language pairs in the shared task. We chose this approach for several reasons:

- It allowed us to have a single unified approach for all language pairs
- It was in the spirit of the evaluation, as it did not require specialist knowledge outside of the supplied corpora
- It enabled us to handle the Chinese names that occurred in the Japanese Romaji-Japanese Kanji task

However we believe that a more effective approach for Japanese-Kanji task may have been to re-tokenize the alphabetic characters into kana (for example transforming "k a" into the kana consonant vowel pair "ka") since these are the basic building blocks of the Japanese language.

3.2 Training

For the final submission, all systems were trained on the union of the training data and development data. It was felt that the training set was sufficiently small that the inclusion of the development data into the training set would yield a reasonable boost in performance by increasing the coverage of the language model and phrase table. The language models and translation models were therefore built from all the data, and the log-linear weights used to combine the models of the systems were tuned using systems trained only on the training data. The development data in this case being held-out. It was assumed that these parameters would perform well in the systems trained on the combined development/training corpora.

3.3 Parameter Tuning

The SMT systems were tuned using the minimum error rate training procedure introduced in (Och, 2003). For convenience, we used BLEU as a proxy for the various metrics used in the shared task evaluation. The BLEU score is

	En-Ch	En-Ja	En-Ko	En-Ru	Jn-Jk
After tuning	0.908	0.772	0.622	0.914	0.769
Before tuning	0.871	0.635	0.543	0.832	0.737

Table 1: The effect on 1-best accuracy by tuning with respect to BLEU score

commonly used to evaluate the performance of machine translation systems and is a function of the geometric mean of *n*-gram precision. Table 1 shows the effect of tuning for BLEU on the ACC (1-best accuracy) scores for several languages. Improvements in the BLEU score also gave improvements in ACC. Tuning to maximize the BLEU score gave improvements for all language pairs and in all of the evaluation metrics used in this shared task. Nonetheless, it is reasonable to assume that one would be able to improve the performance in a particular evaluation metric by doing minimum error rate training specifically for that metric.

3.3.1 Multi-word sequences

The data for some languages (for example Hindi) contained some multi-word sequences. These posed a challenge for our approach, and gave us the following alternatives:

- Introduce a <space> token into the sequence, and treat it as one long character sequence to transliterate; or
- Segment the word sequences into individual words and transliterate these independently, combining the n-best hypothesis lists for all the individual words in the sequence into a single output sequence.

We adopted both approaches for the training of our systems. For those multi-word sequences where the number of words in the source and target matched, the latter approach was taken. For those where the numbers of source and target words differed, the former approach was taken. The decoding process for multi-word sequences is shown in Figure 1. This approach was only used during the parameter tuning on the development set, and in experiments to evaluate the system performance on development data since no multi-word sequences occurred in the test data.

During recombination, the score for the target word sequence was calculated as the product of the scores of each hypothesis for each word. Therefore a search over all combinations of hypotheses was required. In almost all cases we were able to perform a full search. For the rare long word sequences in the data, a beam search strategy was adopted.

3.3.2 Bidirectional Decoding

In SMT it is usual to decode generating the target sequence in order from the first token to the last token (we refer to this as left-to-right decoding, as this is the usual term for this, even though it may be confusing as some languages are naturally written from right-to-left). Since the decoding process is symmetrical, it is also possible to reverse the decoding process, generating from the end of the target sequence to the start (we will refer to this as right-to-left decoding). This reverse decoding is counter-intuitive since language is generated in a left-to-right manner by humans (by definition), however, in pilot experiments on language translation, we found that the best decoding strategy varies depending on the languages involved. The analogue of this observation was observed in our transliteration results (Table 1). For some language pairs, a left-to-right decoding strategy performed better, and for other language pairs the right-to-left strategy was preferable.

Our pilot experiments also showed that combining the hypotheses from both decoding processes almost always gave better results that the best of either left-to-right or right-to-left decoding. We observe a similar effect in the experiments presented here, although our results here are less consistent. This is possibly due to the differences in the size of the data sets used for the experiments. The data used in the experiments here being an order of magnitude smaller.

4 Results

The results of our experiments are shown in Table 1. These results are from a closed evaluation on development data. Only the training data were used to build the system's models, the development data being used to tune the log-linear weights for the translation engines' models and for evaluation. We show results for the case of equal interpolation weights of the left-to-right and right-to-left decoders. For the final submis-

Language	Decoding Strategy	ACC	Mean F-score	MRR	MAP_ref	MAP_10	MAP_sys
En-Ch	$\Rightarrow$	0.908	0.972	0.908	0.266	0.266	0.908
	$\Leftarrow$	0.914	0.974	0.914	0.268	0.268	0.914
	$\Leftrightarrow$	0.915	0.974	0.915	0.268	0.268	0.915
En-Hi	$\Rightarrow$	0.788	0.969	0.788	0.231	0.231	0.788
	$\Leftarrow$	0.785	0.968	0.785	0.230	0.230	0.785
	$\Leftrightarrow$	0.790	0.970	0.790	0.231	0.231	0.790
En-Ja	$\Rightarrow$	0.773	0.950	0.793	0.251	0.251	0.776
	$\Leftarrow$	0.767	0.948	0.785	0.249	0.249	0.768
	$\Leftrightarrow$	0.769	0.949	0.789	0.250	0.250	0.771
En-Ka	$\Rightarrow$	0.682	0.954	0.684	0.202	0.202	0.683
	$\Leftarrow$	0.660	0.953	0.661	0.195	0.195	0.660
	$\Leftrightarrow$	0.674	0.955	0.675	0.199	0.199	0.674
En-Ko	$\Rightarrow$	0.622	0.850	0.623	0.183	0.183	0.622
	$\Leftarrow$	0.620	0.851	0.621	0.182	0.182	0.619
	$\Leftrightarrow$	0.627	0.853	0.628	0.184	0.184	0.626
En-Ru	$\Rightarrow$	0.915	0.982	0.915	0.268	0.268	0.915
	$\Leftarrow$	0.921	0.983	0.921	0.270	0.270	0.921
	$\Leftrightarrow$	0.922	0.983	0.922	0.270	0.270	0.922
En-Ta	$\Rightarrow$	0.731	0.963	0.732	0.216	0.216	0.731
	$\Leftarrow$	0.734	0.962	0.735	0.217	0.217	0.735
	$\Leftrightarrow$	0.748	0.965	0.749	0.221	0.221	0.749
Jn-Jk	$\Rightarrow$	0.769	0.869	0.797	0.301	0.301	0.766
	$\Leftarrow$	0.766	0.862	0.792	0.299	0.299	0.761
	$\Leftrightarrow$	0.772	0.867	0.799	0.300	0.300	0.767

Table 2: Results showing the peformance of three decoding strategies with respect to the evaluation metrics used for the shared task. Here $\Rightarrow$ denotes left-to-right decoding, $\Leftarrow$ denotes right-to-left decoding and $\Leftrightarrow$ denotes bidirectional decoding.

Key to Language Acronyms: En = English, Ch = Chinese, Hi = Hindi, Ja = Japanese Katakana, Ka = Kannada, Ko = Korean, Ru = Russian, Ta = Tamil, Jn = Japanese Romaji, Jk = Japanese Kanji.

sion these weights were tuned on the development data. The bidirectional performance was the best strategy for all but En-Ja and En-Ka in terms of ACC. This varies for other metrics but in general the bidirectional system most often gave the highest performance.

5 Conclusion

Our results show the performance of state of the art phrase-based machine translation techniques on the task of transliteration. We show that it is reasonable to use the BLEU score to tune the system, and that bidirectional decoding can improve performance. In future work we would like to consider more tightly coupling the decoders, introducing monotonicity into the alignment process, and adding contextual features into the translation models.

Acknowledgements

The results presented in this paper draw on the following data sets. For Chinese-English, Li et al., 2004. For Japanese-English, Korean-English, and Japanese(romaji)-Japanese(kanji), the reader is referred to the CJK website: http://www.cjk.org. For Hindi-English, Tamil-English, Kannada-English and Russian-English the data sets originated from the work of Kuraman and Kellner, 2007.

References

Peter Brown, S. Della Pietra, V. Della Pietra, and R. Mercer (1991). The mathematics of statistical machine translation: parameter estimation. *Computational Linguistics*, 19(2), 263-311.

Etienne Denoual and Yves Lepage. 2006. The character as an appropriate unit of processing for non-segmenting languages, *Proceedings of the 12th Annual Meeting of The Association of NLP*, pp. 731-734.

Kevin Knight and Jonathan Graehl. 1997. Machine Transliteration. *Proceedings of the Thirty-Fifth Annual Meeting of the Association for Computational Linguistics and Eighth Conference of the European Chapter of the Association for Computational Linguistics*, pp. 128-135, Somerset, New Jersey.

Philipp Koehn, Franz Josef Och, and Daniel Marcu. 2003. Statistical Phrase-Based Translation. *In Proceedings of the Human Language Technology Conference 2003 (HLT-NAACL 2003)*, Edmonton, Canada.

Franz Josef Och, "Minimum error rate training for statistical machine translation," *Proceedings of the ACL*, 2003.

Kumaran A., Kellner T., "A generic framework for machine transliteration", *Proc. of the 30th SIGIR*, 2007

Haizhou Li, Min Zhang, Jian Su, English-Chinese (EnCh): "A joint source channel model for machine transliteration", *Proc. of the 42nd ACL*, 2004.

Transliteration of Name Entity via Improved Statistical Translation on Character Sequences

Yan Song Chunyu Kit Xiao Chen
Department of Chinese, Translation and Linguistics
City University of Hong Kong
83 Tat Chee Ave., Kowloon, Hong Kong
Email: {yansong, ctckit}@cityu.edu.hk, cxiao2@student.cityu.edu.hk

Abstract

Transliteration of given parallel name entities can be formulated as a phrase-based statistical machine translation (SMT) process, via its routine procedure comprising training, optimization and decoding. In this paper, we present our approach to transliterating name entities using the log-linear phrase-based SMT on character sequences. Our proposed work improves the translation by using bidirectional models, plus some heuristic guidance integrated in the decoding process. Our evaluated results indicate that this approach performs well in all standard runs in the NEWS2009 Machine Transliteration Shared Task.

1 Introduction

To transliterate a foreign name into a target language, a direct instrument is to make use of existing rules for converting text to syllabus, or at least a phoneme base to support such transformation. Following this path, the well developed noisy channel model used for transliteration usually set an intermediate layer to represent the source and target names by phonemes or phonetic tags (Knight and Graehl, 1998; Virga and Khudanpur, 2003; Gao et al., 2004). Having been studied extensively though, the phonemes-based approaches cannot break its performance ceiling for two reasons (Li et al., 2004): (1) Language-dependent phoneme representation is not easy to obtain; (2) The phonemic representation to source and target names usually causes error spread.

Several approaches have been proposed for direct use of parallel texts for performance enhancement (Li et al., 2004; Li et al., 2007; Goldwasser and Roth, 2008). There is no straightforward mean for grouping characters or letters in the source or target language into better transliteration units for a better correspondence. There is no consistent deterministic mapping between two languages either, especially when they belong to different language families, such as English and Chinese. Usually, a single character in a source name is not enough to form a phonetic pattern in a target name. Thus a better way to model transliteration is to map character sequences between source and target name entities. The mapping is actually an alignment process. If a certain quantity of bilingual transliterated entities are available for training, it is a straight-forward idea to tackle this transliteration problem with a mature framework such as phrase-based SMT. It can be considered a general statistical translation task if the character sequences involved are treated like phrases.

In so doing, however, a few points need to be highlighted. Firstly, only parallel data are required for generating transliteration outputs via SMT, and this SMT translation process can be easily integrated as a component into a general-purpose SMT system. Secondly, on character sequences, the mapping between source and target name entities can be performed on even larger units. Consequently, contextual information can be exploited to facilitate the alignment, for a string can be used as a context for every one of its own characters. It is reasonable to expect such relevant information to produce more precisely statistical results for finding corresponding transliterations. Thirdly, transliteration as a monotonic word ordering transformation problem allows the alignment to be performed monotonously from the beginning to the end of a text. Thus its decoding is easy to perform as its search space shrinks this way, for re-ordering is considered not to be involved, in contrast to the general SMT process.

This paper is intended to present our work on applying phrased-based SMT technologies to tackle transliteration. The following sections will report how we have carried out our experiments

Proceedings of the 2009 Named Entities Workshop, ACL-IJCNLP 2009, pages 57–60,
Suntec, Singapore, 7 August 2009.

for the NEWS2009 task (Li et al., 2009) and present the experimented results.

2 Transliteration as SMT

In order to transliterate effectively via a phrase based SMT process for our transliteration task, we opt for the log-linear framework (Och and Ney, 2002), a straight-forward architecture to have several feature models integrated together as

$$P(t|s) = \frac{exp[\sum_{i=1}^{n} \lambda_i h_i(s,t)]}{\sum_t exp[\sum_{i=1}^{n} \lambda_i h_i(s,t)]} \quad (1)$$

Then the transliteration task is to find the proper source and corresponding target chunks to maximize $P(t|s)$ as

$$t = \underset{t}{\text{argmax}}\, P(t|s) \quad (2)$$

In (1), $h_i(s,t)$ is a feature model formulated as a probability functions on a pair of source and target texts in logarithmic form, and λ_i is a parameter to optimize its contribution. The two most important models in this framework are the translation model (i.e., the transliteration model in our case), and the target language model. The former is defined as

$$h_i(s,t) = \log p(s,t) \quad (3)$$

where $p(s,t)$ is $p(s|t)$ or $p(t|s)$ according to the direction of training corresponding phrases. (Och and Ney, 2002) show that $p(t|s)$ gives a result comparable to $p(s|t)$, as in the source-channel framework. (Gao et al., 2004) also confirm on transliteration that the direct model with $p(t|s)$ performs well while working on the phonemic level. For our task, we have tested these choices for $p(s,t)$ on all our development data, arriving at a similar result. However, we opt to use both $p(s|t)$ and $p(t|s)$ if they give similar transliteration quality in some language pairs. Thus we take $p(t|s)$ for our primary transliteration model for searching candidate corresponding character sequences, and $p(s|t)$ as a supplement.

In addition to the translation model feature, another feature for the language model can be described as

$$h_i(s,t) = \log p(t) \quad (4)$$

Usually the n-gram language model is used for its effectiveness and simplicity.

2.1 Training

For the purpose of modeling the training data, the characters from both the source and target name entities for training are split up for alignment, and then phrase extraction is conducted to find the mapping pairs of character sequence.

The alignment is performed by expectation-maximization (EM) iterations in the IBM model-4 SMT training using the GIZA++ toolkit[1]. In some runs, however, e.g., English to Chinese and English to Korean transliteration, the character number of the source text is always more than that of the target text, the training conducted only on characters may lead to many abnormal fertilities and then affect the character sequence alignment later. To alleviate this, a pre-processing step before GIZA++ training applies unsupervised learning to identify many frequently co-occurring characters as fixed patterns in the source texts, including all available training, development and testing data. All possible tokens of the source names are considered.

Afterwards, the extraction and probability estimation of corresponding sequences of characters or pre-processed small tokens aligned in the prior step is performed by 'diag-growth-final' (Koehn et al., 2003), with maximum length 10, which is tuned on development data, for both the source-to-target and the target-to-source character alignment. Then two transliteration models, namely $p(t|s)$ and $p(s|t)$, are generated by such extraction for each transliteration run.

Another component involved in the training is an n-gram language model. We set $n = 3$ and have it trained with the available data of the target language in question.

2.2 Optimization

Using the development sets for the NEWS2009 task, a minimum error rate training (MERT) (Och, 2003) is applied to tune the parameters for the corresponding feature models in (1). The training is performed with regard to the mean F-score, which is also called fuzziness in top-1, measuring on average how different the top transliteration candidate is from its closest reference. It is worth noting that a high mean F-score indicates a high accuracy of top candidates, thus a high mean reciprocal rank (MRR), which is used to quantify the overall performance of transliteration.

[1] http://code.google.com/p/giza-pp/

Table 1: Comparison: baseline v.s. optimized performance on EnCh and EnRu development sets.

		λ_1[a]	λ_2	λ_3	Mean F	MRR
EnCh[b]	B[c]	1	1	1	0.803	0.654
	O	2.38	0.33	0.29	0.837	0.709
EnRu	B	1	1	1	0.845	0.485
	O	2.52	0.27	0.21	0.927	0.687

[a] The subscripts 1, 2 and 3 refer to the two transliteration models $p(t|s)$ and $p(s|t)$ and another language model respectively, and normalized as $\sum_{i=1}^{3} \lambda_i = 3$.
[b] EnCh stands for English to Chinese run and EnRu for English to Russian run.
[c] B stands for baseline configuration and O for optimized case.

As shown in Table 1, the optimization of the three major models leads to a significant performance improvement, especially when training data is limited, such as the EnRu run, only 5977 entries of name entities are provided for training. And, it is also found that the optimized feature weights for other language pairs are similar to these for the two runs as shown in the table above[2].

Note for the optimization of the parameters, that only the training data is used for construction of models. For the test, both the training and the development sets are used for training.

2.3 Decoding

The trained source-to-target and target-to-source transliteration models are integrated with the language model as given in (1) for our decoding. We implement a beam-search decoder to deal with these multiple transliteration models, which takes both the forward- and backward-directional aligned character sequences as factors to contribute to the transliteration probability. Considering the monotonic transformation order, the decoding is performed sequentially from the beginning to the end of a source text. No re-ordering is needed for such transliteration. As the search space is restricted in this way, the accuracy of matching possible transliteration pairs is not affected when the decoding is maintained at a faster speed than that for ordinary translation. In addition, another heuristic condition is also used to guide this monotonic decoding. For those target character sequences found in the training data, their positions in a name entity can help the decoding to find better corresponding transliterations, for some texts appear more frequently at the beginning of a name entity and others at the end. We use the probabilities for all aligned target character sequences in different positions, and exploit the data as an auxiliary feature model for the generation. Finally, all possible target candidates are generated by (2) for source names.

[2] Interestingly, the first model contributes much more than others. It can achieve a comparable result even without model 2 and 3, according to our experiments.

Table 3: Numbers of name entities in NEWS2009 training data[6].

EnCh	34857	EnHi	10990
EnJa	29811	EnTa	9031
EnKo	5838	EnKa	9040
JnJk	19891	EnRu	6920

3 Evaluation Results

For NEWS2009, we participated in all 8 standard runs of transliteration task, namely, EnCh (Li et al., 2004), EnJa, EnKo, JnJk[3], EnHi, EnTa, EnKa and EnRu (Kumaran and Kellner, 2007). Ten best candidates generated for each source name are submitted for each run. The transliteration performance is evaluated by the official script[4], using six metrics[5]. The official evaluation results for our system are presented in Table 2.

The effectiveness of our approach is revealed by the fact that many of our Mean F-scores are above 0.8 for various tasks. These high scores suggest that our top candidates are close to the given references. Besides, it is also interesting to look into how well the desired targets are generated under a certain recall rate, by examining if the best answers are among the ten candidates produced for each source name. If the recall rate goes far beyond MRR, it can be a reliable indication that the desired targets are found for most source names, but just not put at the top of the ten-best. From the last column in Table 2, we can see a great chance to improve our performance, especially for EnCh, JnJk and EnRu runs.

[3] http://www.cjk.org

[4] https://translit.i2r.a-star.edu.sg/news2009/evaluation/

[5] The six metrics are Word Accuracy in Top-1 (ACC), Fuzziness in Top-1 (Mean F-score), Mean Reciprocal Rank (MRR), Precision in the n-best candidates (Map_ref), Precesion in the 10-best candidates (Map_10) and Precision in the system produced candidates (Map_sys).

[6] Note that in some of the runs, when a source name has multiple corresponding target names, the numbers are calculated according to the total target names in both the training and development data.

Table 2: Evaluation result of NEWS2009 task.

Task	Source	Target	ACC	Mean F	MRR	Map_ref	Map_10	Map_sys	Recall
EnCh	English	Chinese	0.643	0.854	0.745	0.643	0.228	0.229	0.917
EnJa	English	Katakana	0.406	0.800	0.529	0.393	0.180	0.180	0.786
EnKo	English	Hangul	0.332	0.648	0.425	0.331	0.134	0.135	0.609
JnJk	Japanese	Kanji	0.555	0.708	0.653	0.538	0.261	0.261	0.852
EnHi	English	Hindi	0.349	0.829	0.455	0.341	0.151	0.151	0.681
EnTa	English	Tamil	0.316	0.848	0.451	0.307	0.154	0.154	0.724
EnKa	English	Kannada	0.177	0.799	0.307	0.178	0.109	0.109	0.576
EnRu	English	Russian	0.500	0.906	0.613	0.500	0.192	0.192	0.828

But still, since SMT is a data-driven approach, the amount of training data could affect the transliteration results significantly. Table 3 shows the training data size in our task. It gives a hint on the connections between the performance, especially Mean F-score, and the data size. In spite of the low ACC, EnKa test has a Mean F-score close to other two runs, namely EnHi and EnTa, of similar data size. For EnRu test, although the training data is limited, the highest Mean F-score is achieved thanks to the nice correspondence between English and Russian characters.

4 Conclusion

In this paper we have presented our recent work to apply the phrase-based SMT technology to name entity transliteration on character sequences. For training, the alignment is carried out on characters and on those frequently co-occurring character sequences identified by unsupervised learning. The extraction of bi-directional corresponding source and target sequence pairs is then performed for the construction of our transliteration models. In decoding, a beam search decoder is applied to generate transliteration candidates using both the source-to-target and target-to-source transliteration models, the target language model and some heuristic guidance integrated. The MERT is applied to tune the optimum feature weights for these models. Finally, ten best candidates are submitted for each source name. The experimental results confirm that our approach is effective and robust in the eight runs of the NEWS2009 transliteration task.

Acknowledgments

The research described in this paper was supported by City University of Hong Kong through the Strategic Research Grants (SRG) 7002267 and 7002388.

References

W. Gao, K. F. Wong, and W. Lam. 2004. Improving transliteration with precise alignment of phoneme chunks and using context features. In *Proceedings of AIRS-2004*.

Dan Goldwasser and Dan Roth. 2008. Transliteration as constrained optimization. In *Proceedings of EMNLP-2008*, pages 353–362, Honolulu, USA, October.

Kevin Knight and Jonathan Graehl. 1998. Machine transliteration. *Computational Linguistics*, 24(4):599–612.

Philipp Koehn, Franz Josef Och, and Daniel Marcu. 2003. Pharaoh: A beam search decoder for phrase-base statistical machine translation models. In *Proceedings of the 6th AMTA*, Edomonton, Canada.

A Kumaran and Tobias Kellner. 2007. A generic framework for machine transliteration. In *Proceedings of the 30th SIGIR*.

Haizhou Li, Min Zhang, and Jian Su. 2004. A joint source-channel model for machine transliteration. In *Proceedings of ACL-04*, pages 159–166, Barcelona, Spain, July.

Haizhou Li, Khe Chai Sim, Jin-Shea Kuo, and Minghui Dong. 2007. Semantic transliteration of personal names. In *Proceedings of ACL-07*, pages 120–127, Prague, Czech Republic, June.

Haizhou Li, A Kumaran, Vladimir Pervouchine, and Min Zhang. 2009. Report on news 2009 machine transliteration shared task. In *Proceedings of ACL-IJCNLP 2009 Named Entities Workshop*, Singapore.

Franz Josef Och and Hermann Ney. 2002. Discriminative training and maximum entropy models for statistical machine translation. In *Proceedings of ACL-02*, pages 295–302, Philadelphia, USA, July.

Franz Josef Och. 2003. Minimum error rate training in statistical machine translation. In *Proceedings of ACL-03*, pages 160–167, Sapporo, Japan, July.

Paola Virga and Sanjeev Khudanpur. 2003. Transliteration of proper names in cross-lingual information retrieval. In *Proceedings of the ACL 2003 Workshop on Multilingual and Mixed-language Named Entity Recognition*, pages 57–64, Sapporo, Japan, July.

Learning Multi Character Alignment Rules and Classification of training data for Transliteration

Dipankar Bose
Dept. of Computer Science and Engg.
Indian Institute of Technology
Kharagpur, West Bengal
India - 721302
dipankarcsiit@gmail.com

Sudeshna Sarkar
Dept. of Computer Science and Engg.
Indian Institute of Technology
Kharagpur, West Bengal
India - 721302
shudeshna@gmail.com

Abstract

We address the issues of transliteration between Indian languages and English, especially for named entities. We use an EM algorithm to learn the alignment between the languages. We find that there are lot of ambiguities in the rules mapping the characters in the source language to the corresponding characters in the target language. Some of these ambiguities can be handled by capturing context by learning multi-character based alignments and use of character n-gram models. We observed that a word in the source script may have actually originated from different languages. Instead of learning one model for the language pair, we propose that one may use multiple models and a classifier to decide which model to use. A contribution of this work is that the models and classifiers are learned in a completely unsupervised manner. Using our system we were able to get quite accurate transliteration models.

1 Introduction

Transliteration is the practice of transcribing a word or text written in one writing system into another writing system which may have a different script (wikipedia [1]). The rules are often quite ambiguous, and they are often related with the pronunciation of the word.

Many applications like Machine Translation (MT), Cross Language Information Retrieval (CLIR), Question Answering (QA) require transliteration of named entities, which are the major component of out-of-vocabulary (OOV) words, and they are most often transliterated and not translated, in any cross language system. For example ,'Europe' is transliterated as 'iuropa' and 'Michael' transliterates to 'maaikela' in Bengali.[2]

In this paper we develop a scheme of transliteration, which captures context by creating a dictionary of multi-character transliteration rules. We have tested our system for English and several Indian languages. For Indian Languages, we have an additional preprocessor which enhances the performance.

2 Related Work

Brown et al. (1993) have come up with their revolutionary IBM alignment models, and the Giza++ (Och and Ney, 2000) is a well appreciated implementation which work with parallel data in two languages. Though originally designed for machine translation, the package can as well be used for transliteration, where the alignment is between the characters in the languages. Moses further enhances the accuracy by using phrase based decoding, which can capture context. We have Moses[3] as our baseline system.

Li et al. (2004) have pointed out the problems of using language information. Apart from the difficulty of collecting the language information, they pointed out that, although written in the same script, the origin of the source names may vary widely. For example French and English names may vary a lot. But it is difficult to collect information for each and every language. They came up with a joint source chan-

[1] http://www.wikipedia.org

[2] above Bengali words are scripted using ITrans, instead of traditional Bengali script.

[3] http://www.statmt.org/moses/

Proceedings of the 2009 Named Entities Workshop, ACL-IJCNLP 2009, pages 61–64,
Suntec, Singapore, 7 August 2009. ©2009 ACL and AFNLP

nel model, to transliterate foreign names to Chinese, Korean, and Japanese, which uses, direct orthographic mapping (DOM), between two different languages, to find out how the source and target words can be generated simultaneously. Ekbal et al. (2006) also used this model for English-Bengali Transliteration. Ganesh et al. (2008) used Hidden Markov Model (HMM) alignment and Conditional Random Field (CRF), a discriminative model together. Surana et al. (2008) used fuzzy string matching algorithms to identify the origin of the source word, and then apply rules of transliteration accordingly. However the classifier makes use of labeled training data, which is often not available.

3 Issues

Transliteration is ambiguous. Firstly, the transliteration rules depend on the context. For example, 'a' in English may transliterate to 'a' or 'A' in Hindi, but 'aa' almost definitely maps to 'A'. Secondly, there can be multiple transliterations of the same source word. For example 'abhijIta' may transliterate to 'abhijit' and 'abhijeet' as well. Thirdly, the transliteration rules also vary, depending on the origin of the word. For example, when considering Hindi to English transliteration the English characters used vary depending on whether the word originated from Arabic or from Sanskrit. We elaborate more on this in the section on classification of corpus.

4 Approach

Our method is primarily based on IBM models used in machine translation based on the EM algorithm. But before we move on to the IBM models, we first preprocess the training data. Other than marking the 'Start' and 'End', for each of the parallel words, we can do further preprocessing if any of the scripts is Indian. All Indian language scripts consist of a set of consonants and vowels. Independent vowels and their corresponding diacritic markers (Matra) are considered as the same character in the standard analysis of words into their constituent characters (varna vishleshhana). Unlike ITrans, Unicode assigns different codes to them. We found in our experiment that treating them as one, improves the accuracy of the system. Our preprocessor thus transforms Unicode data to ITrans format. We have seen that preprocessor improves the accuracy by around 10-15%.

After preprocessing, we align the letters using the expectation maximization (EM) algorithm of IBM model 1, using the parallel corpus of named entities as input. We use only the IBM model 1; the subsequent models are omitted since in transliteration we need not consider the re-ordering of letters. Both Unicode and transliterated text are in phonetic order, and re-ordering of letters are rarely observed. As an output of the EM learner we get a table of translation probabilities TP, of source letters to target letters. If, s_i and t_j are source and target letters, $\forall s_i, t_j, TP_{s_i,t_j} \in [0, 1]$, denotes the corresponding translation probability. For example after EM learning, the values of $TP_{bha,v}$ and $TP_{bha,b}$ will be much more than $TP_{bha,k}$, since 'bha' rarely transliterates to 'k'.

4.1 Learning Phrase Mappings

We now move on to capture context. For each word in the parallel data, we compute an alignment array, A_e, where $e \in [0, E]$, and I and E are the corresponding lengths of the words in Indian and English script respectively. So, we have, $\forall e \in [0, E], A_e \in [0, I]$. Following is an example: Let, source word be: Start s_1 s_2 s_3 End, target word be: Start t_1 t_2 t_3 t_4 End, and Alignment array be: 0 1 1 2 3 4. This means that s_1 maps to t_1 and t_2; s_2 maps to t_3 and so on. We further enforce $A_{e_1} \leq A_{e_2}$ *iff* $e_1 \leq e_2$, since we neglect re-ordering of letters. The aim is to figure out null mappings, filter out noises in the TP-table, and finally create a phrase to phrase mapped dictionary. Using the TP-table values, we propose an iterative algorithm to find the alignment array A. $W_L[i]$ denotes the ith letter of a word in language 'L'. Initially $A_i = 0$ if $i = 0$, $A_i = I - 1$ if $i < E$, otherwise $A_i = I$. The first and last characters are always the 'Start' and 'End' tags, in all the words.

Initially letters are allowed a larger window to fit to. After each iteration, the window size decreases and thus the margins are made more stringent. Using iterations we are being less greedy in deciding the alignment, so that noises in the TP-table are filtered out. Finally after 5 iterations, we freeze the alignment array. It may happen that $\exists i \in [0, I]$, such that $\forall j \in [0, E], A_j \neq i$. It means that the letter, $W_{Ind}[i]$ maps to 'null' in this case, and thus it is a 'Schwa' character.

4.2 Scoring the alignment

In spite of all our attempts, it may happen that the words are not well aligned; the reason may be a

Algorithm 1 Method to compute Alignment

```
for window = 5 to 1 do
  for e = 1 to E − 1 do
    left = Max(1, A_{e−1} − window + 1)
    right = Min(I, A_{e+1} + window)
    A_e = s : s ∈ [left, right] such that
    TP_{W_Ind[s],W_Eng[e]} × (1 − |s/I − e/E|)
    is maximum
  end for
  for e = 1 to E − 1 do
    if ¬(A_{e−1} ≤ A_e ≤ A_{e+1}) then
      {try to smooth out anomalies}
      A_e = (A_{e−1} + A_{e+1})/2
    end if
  end for
end for
```

deficiency in the Algorithm 1, or a badly transliterated parallel word as input. For example the training data may contain 'mississippi river' transliterated to Bengali as 'misisipi nadI'. In this case we see that the second word is translated and not transliterated. Retaining this in the training set will introduce noise in the model. There may also be typographical errors also. We have developed a filtering mechanism, so that we can eliminate these words, otherwise we will end up learning spurious mappings. We find the score of an alignment,
$SA = \sum_{e=1}^{N-1}(TP_{W_{Ind}[A_e],W_{Eng}[e]} \times (1 - |A_e/I - e/E|)$.
We were trying to maximize SA under certain constraints in algorithm 1. The value of SA is an estimate of how good our alignment is. Next we set thresholds to distinguish between different "Classes" of alignments.

4.3 Classifying the training corpus

The training corpus may consist of words from varied origins. Though they are written in the same script, pronunciation varies widely. For example Urdu origin names like Farooque (pharUka), Razzaq (rajjAka) tend to replace 'q' in place of 'ka', but Hindi names like Latika (latika), Nakul (nakula), tend to replace 'k' for 'ka'. Unlike Surana et al. (2008) who extracted 5-gram models from labeled data in different languages, we propose Algorithm 2, to classify the parallel corpus into groups, which does not need any labeled data. We define, Classes $C_1, C_2, ..., C_N$, where C_i consists of a set of parallel words $< I_j, E_j >$, (I_j, E_j being the jth word in Indian and English language, in the training corpus), such that the alignment score of the word pairs, lie between the predefined thresholds, th_{i+1} and th_i. Let us assume that C_1 is initialized with the parallel training corpus from input.

Algorithm 2 Classify the Corpus

```
for i = 1 to N do
  Set threshold, th_i for Class C_i: th_i ≤ th_{i−1}
  while size of Class C_i does not decrease do
    Compute TP-table using IBM model 1. on C_i
    for each parallel word pair < I_j, E_j > in C_i do
      Compute Alignment using Algorithm 1.
      Compute Score of Alignment, SA.
      if Score < th_i then
        {Move the word pair to the next class}
        C_{i+1} = C_{i+1} ∪ < I_j, E_j >
        C_i = C_i \ < I_j, E_j >
      end if
    end for
  end while{move on to next Class}
end for
```

We continuously discard word pairs from a class until there is no word pair to be discarded. We use IBM Model 1 to re-learn the TP-table, on the latest content of the class. Since the poor word pairs have been removed, learning the TP-table afresh, helps in improving the TP_{s_i,t_j} values. It helps in removing the bad word pairs yet left, in the subsequent iterations. It is to be noted that C_N consists of word pairs, which are of no use, and we discard them completely. We had 5 useful classes, and the thresholds of C_1 to C_5 were 0.4, 0.35, 0.3, 0.25, 0.2 respectively. In each class, for each word pair, we extract all possible ngrams on Indian language side and collect their corresponding English characters, using the alignment array. We keep frequency counts of these ngram mappings, and use this score in decoding. We use a language model, which uses Good Turing smoothing technique. We have used greedy beam search based decoder.

All that remains is to guess the class of an unknown word. Given a test word, in source script we calculate probability P_i of it being in class, C_i, based on ngram similarities. The decoders of each of the classes returns a list of feasible transliteration candidates along with their 'local scores'

Language	Accuracy in Top1	Mean F-Score	MRR	MAP_{ref}	MAP_{10}	MAP_{sys}
En2Ta	0.404	0.883	0.539	0.398	0.182	0.182
En2Hi	0.366	0.854	0.493	0.360	0.164	0.164
En2Ka	0.335	0.856	0.457	0.328	0.154	0.154

Table 1: Transliteration Accuracies. En2Ta: English to Tamil, En2Hi: English to Hindi, En2Ka: English to Kannada

(score according to that class), We denote the local score of a candidate from Class C_i as $LS[C_i]$. We calculate the global score, GS for each candidate, using $GS = \sum_{i=1}^{N-1}(LS[C_i] \times P_i)$. The candidates are sorted in decreasing order of their global scores and top 'K' of them produced as output.

5 Results

We have evaluated our system, against datasets with Hindi, Tamil, Kannada and English parallel named entities (Kumaran and Kellner, 2007). The results are in Table 1. The data consists of named entities from varied origins: almost all Indian languages and English. We combined the training and development sets to create the new training set. There are about 9000 parallel words in the training sets and 1000 words for testing.

Algorithm 2 classifies the training corpus, into 5 sets of corpus. Following are some details after classifying the Tamil-English dataset. Corpus 1, consists of Sanskrit derived words mostly; they get perfectly aligned and Schwa deletions rarely occur; Ex: Keena, Asiya, Nehra, Hemaraaj, Vijendra. This corpus contains 2167 words. Corpus 2 also is mostly comprised of Sanskrit derived words and also English words which easily align; like Wilton, Natesh, Raghu, Gerry, Achintya, Amaanat. Schwa deletions does occur, and hence the alignment scores are a little low. Size of this corpus is 2168.

Corpus 3 consists more of Urdu origin and English words, which are not fit for the normal transliteration rules. The corpus consists of words like Tarzan, Anoife, Sevier, Zahid Fazal, Floriane, where letters like 'q', 'zz', 'y' are more likely than 'k', 'j', 'i' respectively. The size of Corpus 3 is 1835. Corpus 4 & 5 consists largely of English origin words, like Lucky number, Ian Healy, Cleavant, Fort Vancouver, Virginia Reel, Bundesverdienstkreuz. These words need completely different set of rules, and moreover if these words were in any other class, it would corrupt their learning rules. Size of these corpora are 1234 and 1455 respectively.

6 Conclusion

Our system is robust in the sense that it can filter out noise in the training corpus, can handle words of different origins by classifying them into different classes. Our classifying algorithm improves the accuracy, but we believe that there is scope of further improvement and we are working on it.

References

Asif Ekbal, Sudip Kumar Naskar, Sivaji Bandyopadhyay. 2006. *A modified joint source-channel model for transliteration.* Proceedings of the COLING/ACL on Main conference poster sessions.Sydney, Australia.

Harshit Surana and A. K. Singh 2008. *A More Discerning and Adaptable Multilingual Transliteration Mechanism for Indian Languages.* The Third International Joint Conference on Natural Language Processing (IJCNLP). Hyderabad, India.

Kumaran A. and Kellner Tobias. 2007. A generic framework for machine transliteration *SIGIR '07: Proceedings of the 30th annual international ACM SIGIR conference on Research and development in information retrieval*, pages 721–722.

Li Haizhou, Zhang Min, Su Jian. 2004. *A joint source-channel model for machine transliteration.* Proceedings of the 42nd Annual Meeting on Association for Computational Linguistics. Barcelona, Spain.

Och Franz Josef and Hermann Ney. 2000. *Improved Statistical Alignment Models.* Proc. of the 38th Annual Meeting of the Association for Computational Linguistics, pp. 440-447, Hong Kong, China.

Peter F. Brown, Vincent J. Delta Pietra, Stephen A. Delta Pietra and Robert L. Mercer. 1993. *The mathematics of statistical machine translation: parameter estimation.* MIT Press Cambridge, MA, USA.

Surya Ganesh, Sree Harsha, Prasad Pingali, Vasudeva Verma. 2008. *Statistical Transliteration for Cross Language Information Retrieval using HMM alignment model and CRF.* CLIA-2008, 2nd International workshop on Cross Language Information Access, 3rd International Joint Conference on Natural Language Processing (IJCNLP 2008), January 7-12, 2008, Hyderabad, India.

Fast decoding and Easy Implementation: Transliteration as Sequential Labeling

Eiji ARAMAKI
The University of Tokyo
eiji.aramaki@gmail.com

Takeshi ABEKAWWA
National Institute of Informatics
abekawa@nii.ac.jp

Abstract

Although most of previous transliteration methods are based on a generative model, this paper presents a discriminative transliteration model using conditional random fields. We regard character(s) as a kind of label, which enables us to consider a transliteration process as a sequential labeling process. This approach has two advantages: (1) fast decoding and (2) easy implementation. Experimental results yielded competitive performance, demonstrating the feasibility of the proposed approach.

1 Introduction

To date, most transliteration methods have relied on a generative model which resembles a statistical machine translation (SMT) model. Although the generative approach has appealing feasibility, it usually suffers from parameter settings, length biases and decoding time.

We assume a transliteration process as a kind of sequential labeling that is widely employed for various tasks, such as Named Entity Recognition (NER), part-of-speech (POS) labeling, and so on. Figure 1 shows a lattice of both the transliteration and POS labeling. As shown in that figure, both tasks share a similar work frame: (1) an input sequence is decomposed into several segments; then (2) each segments produces a label. Although the label represents a POS in POS labeling, it represents a character (or a character sequence) in the transliteration task.

The proposed approach entails three risks.

1. **Numerous Label Variation**: Although POS requires only 10–20 labels at most, a transliteration process requires numerous labels. In fact, Japanese katakana requires more than 260 labels in the following experiment (we consider combinations of characters as a label). Such a huge label set might require extremely heavy calculation.

2. **No Gold Standard Data**: We build the gold standard label from character alignment using GIZA++ [1]. Of course, such gold standard data contain alignment errors, which might decrease labeling performance.

3. **No Language Model**: The proposed approach cannot incorporate the target language model.

In spite of the disadvantages listed above, the proposed method offers two strong advantages.

1. **Fast Decoding**: Decoding (more precisely labeling) is extremely fast (0.12–0.58 s/input). Such rapid decoding is useful for various applications, for example, a query expansion for a search engine and so on [2].

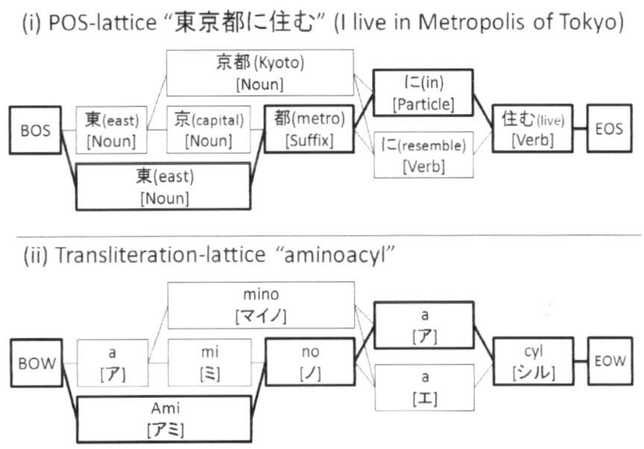

Figure 1: (i) Part-of-Speech Lattice and (ii) Transliteration Lattice.

[1] http://www.fjoch.com/GIZA++.html

[2] A fast transliteration demonstration is available at the web site; http://akebia.hcc.h.u-tokyo.ac.jp/NEWS/

Proceedings of the 2009 Named Entities Workshop, ACL-IJCNLP 2009, pages 65–68,
Suntec, Singapore, 7 August 2009. ©2009 ACL and AFNLP

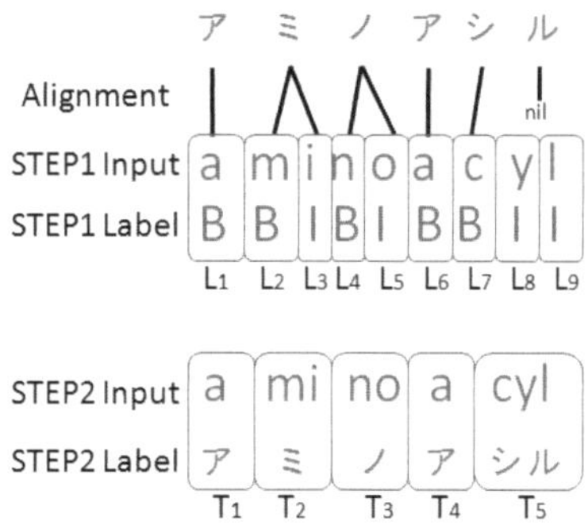

Figure 2: Conversion from Training set to Gold Standard Labels

2. **Easy Implementation**: Because sequential labeling is a traditional research topic, various algorithms and tools are available. Using them, we can easily realize various transliteration systems in any language pairs.

The experimental results empirically demonstrate that the proposed method is competitive in several language directions (e.g. English–Chinese).

2 Method

We developed a two-stage labeling system. First, an input term is decomposed into several segments (STEP1). Next, each segmentation produces symbol(s) (STEP2).

2.1 STEP1: Chunking

For a given noun phrase, consisting n characters, the system gave a label ($L_1 ... L_n$) that represents segmentations.

The segmentation is expressed as two types of labels (label B and I), where B signifies a beginning of the segmentation, and I signifies the end of segmentation. This representation is similar to the IOB representation, which is used in Named Entity Recognition (NER) or chunking.

For label prediction, we used Conditional Random Fields (CRFs), which is a state-of-the-art labeling algorithm. We regard a source character itself as a CRF feature. The window size is three (the current character and previous/next character).

2.2 STEP2: Symbol production

Next, the system estimates labels ($T_1 ... T_m$) for each segmentation, where m is the number of segmentations (the number of B labels in STEP1). The label of this step directly represents a target language character(s). The method of building a gold standard label is described in the next subsection.

Like STEP1, we use CRFs, and regard source characters as a feature (window size=3).

Table 1: Corpora and Sizes

Notation	Language	Train	Test
EN-CH	English–Chinese	31,961	2,896
EN-JA	English–Japanese	27,993	1,489
EN-KO	English–Korean	4,840	989
EN-HI	English–Hindi	10,014	1,000
EN-TA	English–Tamil	8,037	1,000
EN-KA	English–Kannada	8,065	1,000
EN-RU	English–Russian	5,977	1,000

* EN-CH is provided by (Li et al., 2004); EN-TA, EN-KA, EN-HI and EN-RU are from (Kumaran and Kellner, 2007); EN-JA and EN-KO are from `http://www.cjk.org/`.

2.3 Conversion from Alignment to Labels

First, character alignment is estimated using GIZA++ as shown at the top of Fig. 2. The alignment direction is a target- language-to-English, assuming that n English characters correspond to a target language character.

The STEP1 label is generated for each English character. If the alignment is 1:1, we give the character a B label. If the alignment is $n:1$, we assign the first character a B label, and give the others I. Note that we regard null alignment as a continuance of the last segmentation (I).

The STEP2 label is generated for each English segmentation (B or $BI*$). If a segmentation corresponds to two or more characters in the target side, we regard the entire sequence as a label (see T_5 in Fig. 2).

3 Experiments

3.1 Corpus, Evaluation, and Setting

To evaluate the performance of our system, we used a training-set and test-set provided by NEWS[3](Table 1).

We used the following six metrics (Table 2) using 10 output candidates. A white paper[4] presents the detailed definitions. For learning, we used CRF++[5] with standard parameters (f=20, c=.5).

[3]http://www.acl-ijcnlp-2009.org/workshops/NEWS2009/
[4]https://translit.i2r.a-star.edu.sg/news2009/whitepaper/
[5]http://crfpp.sourceforge.net/

Table 3: Results in Test-set

	ACC	$Mean_F$	MRR	MAP_{ref}	MAP_{10}	MAP_{sys}
EN–CH	0.580	0.826	0.653	0.580	0.199	0.199
EN–RU	0.531	0.912	0.635	0.531	0.219	0.219
EN–JA	0.457	0.828	0.576	0.445	0.194	0.194
EN–TA	0.365	0.884	0.504	0.360	0.172	0.172
EN–HI	0.363	0.864	0.503	0.360	0.170	0.170
EN–KA	0.324	0.856	0.438	0.315	0.148	0.148
EN–KO	0.170	0.512	0.218	0.170	0.069	0.069

Table 2: Evaluation Metrics

ACC	Word Accuracy in Top 1.
Mean$_F$	The $mean_F$ measures the fuzzy accuracy that is defined by the edit distance and Longest Common Subsequence (LCS).
MRR	Mean Reciprocal Rank. 1/MRR tells approximately the average rank of the correct transliteration.
MAP$_{ref}$	Measures the precision in the n−best candidates tightly for each reference.
MAP$_{10}$	Measures the precision in the 10-best candidates.
MAP$_{sys}$	Measures the precision in the top K_i-best candidates produced by the system.

3.2 Results and Discussion

Table 3 presents the performance. As shown in the table, a significant difference was found between languages (from low (0.17) to high (0.58)).

The high accuracy results(EN-CH or EN-RU) are competitive with other systems (the middle rank among the NEWS participating systems). However, several language results (such as EN-KO) were found to have poor performance.

We investigated the difference between high-performance languages and the others. Table 4 shows the training/test times and the number of labels. As shown in the table, wide divergence is apparent in the number of labels. For example, although EN–KO requires numerous labels (536 labels), EN–RU needs only 131 labels. This divergence roughly corresponds to both training-time and accuracy as follows: (1) EN–KO requires long training time (11 minutes) which gave poor performance (0.17 ACC), and (2) EN–RU requires short training (only 26.3 seconds) which gave high performance (0.53 ACC). This suggests that if the number of labels is small, we successfully convert transliteration into a sequential labeling task.

The test time seemed to have no relation to

Table 4: Average Test time, Training Time, and the number of labels (label variation).

Language	Test	Train	# of labels
EN–KO	0.436s	11m09.5s	536
EN–CH	0.201s	6m18.9s	283
EN–JA	0.247s	4m44.3s	269
EN–KA	0.190s	2m26.6s	231
EN–HI	0.302s	1m55.6s	268
EN–TA	0.124s	1m32.9s	207
EN–RU	0.580s	0m26.3s	131

* Test time is the average labeling time for an input. Training time is the average training time for 1000 labels.

both training time and performance. To investigate what gave effects on test time is a subject for our future work.

4 Related Works

Most previous transliteration studies have relied on a generative model resembling the IBM model(Brown et al., 1993). This approach is applicable to various languages: for Japanese (Goto et al., 2004; Knight and Graehl, 1998), Korean(Oh and Choi, 2002; Oh and Choi, 2005; Oh and Isahara, 2007), Arabic(Stalls and Knight, 1998; Sherif and Kondrak, 2007), Chinese(Li et al., 2007), and Persian(Karimi et al., 2007). As described previously, the proposed discriminative approach differs from them.

Another perspective is that of how to represent transliteration phenomena. Methods can be classified into three main types: (1) grapheme-based (Li et al., 2004), (2) phoneme-based (Knight and Graehl, 1998), and (3) combinations of these methods (hybrid-model(Bilac and Tanaka, 2004), and a correspondence-based model(Oh and Choi, 2002; Oh and Choi, 2005) re-ranking model (Oh and Isahara, 2007)). Our proposed method employs a grapheme-based approach. Employing phonemes is a challenge reserved for future studies.

Aramaki et al. (2008) proposed a discriminative transliteration approach using Support Vector Machines (SVMs). However, their goal, which is to judge whether two terms come from the same English words or not, differs from this paper goal.

5 Conclusions

This paper presents a discriminative transliteration model using a sequential labeling technique. Experimental results yielded competitive performance, demonstrating the feasibility of the proposed approach. In the future, how to incorporate more rich information, such as language model and phoneme, is remaining problem. We believe this task conversion, from generation to sequential labeling, can be useful for several practical applications.

ACKNOWLEDGMENT

Part of this research is supported by Japanese Grant-in-Aid for Scientific Research (A) Number:20680006.

References

Eiji Aramaki, Takeshi Imai, Kengo Miyo, and Kazuhiko Ohe. 2008. Orthographic disambiguation incorporating transliterated probability. In *Proceedings of International Joint Conference on Natural Language Processing (IJCNLP2008)*, pages 48–55.

Slaven Bilac and Hozumi Tanaka. 2004. A hybrid back-transliteration system for Japanese. In *Proceedings of The 20th International Conference on Computational Linguistics (COLING2004)*, pages 597–603.

Peter F. Brown, Stephen A. Della Pietra, Vi cent J. Della Pietra, and Robert L. Mercer. 1993. The mathematics of statistical machine translation: Parameter estimation. *Computational Linguistics*, 19(2).

Isao Goto, Naoto Kato, Terumasa Ehara, and Hideki Tanaka. 2004. Back transliteration from Japanese to English using target English context. In *Proceedings of The 20th International Conference on Computational Linguistics (COLING2004)*, pages 827–833.

Sarvnaz Karimi, Falk Scholer, and Andrew Turpin. 2007. Collapsed consonant and vowel models: New approaches for English-Persian transliteration and back-transliteration. In *Proceedings of the Annual Meeting of the Association of Computational Linguistics (ACL2007)*, pages 648–655.

Kevin Knight and Jonathan Graehl. 1998. Machine transliteration. *Computational Linguistics*, 24(4):599–612.

A. Kumaran and Tobias Kellner. 2007. A generic framework for machine transliteration. In *SIGIR '07: Proceedings of the 30th annual international ACM SIGIR conference on Research and development in information retrieval*, pages 721–722.

Haizhou Li, Min Zhang, and Jian Su. 2004. A joint source-channel model for machine transliteration. In *Proceedings of the Meeting of the Association for Computational Linguistics (ACL2004)*, pages 159–166.

Haizhou Li, Khe Chai Sim, Jin-Shea Kuo, and Minghui Dong. 2007. Semantic transliteration of personal names. In *Proceedings of the Annual Meeting of the Association of Computational Linguistics (ACL2007)*, pages 120–127.

Jong-Hoon Oh and Key-Sun Choi. 2002. An English-Korean transliteration model using pronunciation and contextual rules. In *Proceedings of The 19th International Conference on Computational Linguistics (COLING2002)*, pages 758–764.

Jong-Hoon Oh and Key-Sun Choi. 2005. An ensemble of grapheme and phoneme for machine transliteration. In *Proceedings of Second International Joint Conference on Natural Language Processing (IJCNLP2005)*, pages 450–461.

Jong-Hoon Oh and Hitoshi Isahara. 2007. Machine transliteration using multiple transliteration engines and hypothesis re-ranking. In *Proceedings of MT Summit XI*, pages 353–360.

Tarek Sherif and Grzegorz Kondrak. 2007. Substring-based transliteration. In *Proceedings of the 45th Annual Meeting of the Association of Computational Linguistics (ACL2007)*, pages 944–951.

Bonnie Glover Stalls and Kevin Knight. 1998. Translating names and technical terms in arabic text. In *Proceedings of The International Conference on Computational Linguistics and the 36th Annual Meeting of the Association of Computational Linguistics (COLING-ACL1998) Workshop on Computational Approaches to Semitic Languages*.

NEWS 2009 Machine Transliteration Shared Task System Description: Transliteration with Letter-to-Phoneme Technology

Colin Cherry and **Hisami Suzuki**
Microsoft Research
One Microsoft Way
Redmond, WA, 98052
{colinc,hisamis}@microsoft.com

Abstract

We interpret the problem of transliterating English named entities into Hindi or Japanese Katakana as a variant of the letter-to-phoneme (L2P) subtask of text-to-speech processing. Therefore, we apply a re-implementation of a state-of-the-art, discriminative L2P system (Jiampojamarn et al., 2008) to the problem, without further modification. In doing so, we hope to provide a baseline for the NEWS 2009 Machine Transliteration Shared Task (Li et al., 2009), indicating how much can be achieved without transliteration-specific technology. This paper briefly summarizes the original work and our reimplementation. We also describe a bug in our submitted implementation, and provide updated results on the development and test sets.

1 Introduction

Transliteration occurs when a word is borrowed into a language with a different character set from its language of origin. The word is transcribed into the new character set in a manner that maintains phonetic correspondence.

When attempting to automate machine transliteration, modeling the channel that transforms source language characters into transliterated target language characters is a key component to good performance. Since the primary signal followed by human transliterators is phonetic correspondence, it makes sense that a letter-to-phoneme (L2P) transcription engine would perform well at this task. Of course, transliteration is often framed within the larger problems of translation and bilingual named entity co-reference, making available a number of other interesting features, such as target lexicons (Knight and Graehl, 1998), distributional similarity (Bilac and Tanaka, 2005), or the dates of an entity's mentions in the news (Klementiev and Roth, 2006). However, this task's focus on generation has isolated the character-level component, which makes L2P technology a near-ideal match. For our submission, we re-implement the L2P approach described by Jiampojamarn et al. (2008) as faithfully as possible, and apply it unmodified to the transliteration shared task for the English-to-Hindi (Kumaran and Kellner, 2007) and English-to-Japanese Katakana[1] tests.

2 Approach

2.1 Summary of L2P approach

The core of the L2P transduction engine is the dynamic programming algorithm for monotone phrasal decoding (Zens and Ney, 2004). The main feature of this algorithm is its capability to transduce many consecutive characters with a single operation. This algorithm is used to conduct a search for a max-weight derivation according to a linear model with indicator features. A sample derivation is shown in Figure 1.

There are two main categories of features: context and transition features, which follow the first two feature templates described by Jiampojamarn et al. (2008). Context features are centered around a transduction operation. These features include an indicator for the operation itself, which is then conjoined with indicators for all n-grams of source context within a fixed window of the operation. Transition features are Markov or n-gram features. They ensure that the produced target string makes sense as a character sequence, and are represented as indicators on the presence of target n-grams. The feature templates have two main parameters, the size S of the character window from which source context features are drawn, and the maximum length T of target n-gram indicators. We fit these parameters using grid search over 1-best

[1]Provided by http://www.cjk.org

Proceedings of the 2009 Named Entities Workshop, ACL-IJCNLP 2009, pages 69–71,
Suntec, Singapore, 7 August 2009. ©2009 ACL and AFNLP

ame → アメ , ri → リ , can → カン

Figure 1: Example derivation transforming "American" into "アメリカン".

accuracy on the provided development sets.

The engine's features are trained using the structured perceptron (Collins, 2002). Jiampojamarn et al. (2008) show strong improvements in the L2P domain using MIRA in place of the perceptron update; unfortunately, we did not implement a k-best MIRA update due to time constraints. In our implementation, no special consideration was given to the availability of multiple correct answers in the training data; we always pick the first reference transliteration and treat it as the only correct answer. Investigating the use of all correct answers would be an obvious next step to improve the system.

2.2 Major differences in implementation

Our system made two alternate design decisions (we do not claim improvements) over those made by (Jiampojamarn et al., 2008), mostly based on the availability of software. First, we employed a beam of 40 candidates in our decoder, to enable efficient use of large language model contexts. This is put to good use in the Hindi task, where we found n-gram indicators of length up to $n = 6$ provided optimal development performance.

Second, we employed an alternate character aligner to create our training derivations. This aligner is similar to recent non-compositional phrasal word-alignment models (Zhang et al., 2008), limited so it can only produce monotone character alignments. The aligner creates substring alignments, without insertion or deletion operators. As such, an aligned transliteration pair also serves as a transliteration derivation. We employed a maximum substring length of 3.

The training data was heuristically cleaned after alignment. Any derivation found by the aligner that uses an operation occurring fewer than 3 times throughout the entire training set was eliminated. This reduced training set sizes to 8,511 pairs for English-Hindi and 20,306 pairs for English-Katakana.

Table 1: Development and test 1-best accuracies, as reported by the official evaluation tool

System / Test set	With Bug	Fixed
Hindi Dev	36.7	39.6
Hindi Test	41.8	46.6
Katakana Dev	46.0	47.1
Katakana Test	46.6	46.9

3 The Bug

The submitted version of our system had a bug in its transition features: instead of generating an indicator for every possible n-gram in the generated target sequence, it generated n-grams over target substrings, defined by the operations used during transduction. Consider, for example, the derivation shown in Figure 1, which generates "アメリカン". With buggy trigram transition features, the final operation would produce the single indicator [メリ|カン], instead of the two character-level trigrams [メリ|カ] and [リカ|ン]. This leads to problems with data sparsity, which we had not noticed on unrelated experiments with larger training data. We report results both with the **bug** and with **fixed** transition features. We do so to emphasize the importance of a fine-grained language discriminative language model, as opposed to one which operates on a substring level.

4 Development

Development consisted of performing a parameter grid search over S and T for each language pair's development set. All combinations of $S = 0 \ldots 4$ and $T = 0 \ldots 7$ were tested for each language pair. Based on these experiments, we selected (for the fixed version), values of $S = 2$, $T = 6$ for English-Hindi, and $S = 4$, $T = 3$ for English-Katakana.

5 Results

The results of our internal experiments with the official evaluation tool are shown in Table 1. We report 1-best accuracy on both development and test sets, with both the buggy and fixed versions of our system. As one can see, the bug makes less of an impact in the English-Katakana setting, where more training data is available.

6 Conclusion

We have demonstrated that an automatic letter-to-phoneme transducer performs fairly well on this transliteration shared task, with no language-specific or transliteration-specific modifications. Instead, we simply considered Hindi or Katakana to be an alternate encoding for English phonemes. In the future, we would like to investigate proper use of multiple reference answers during perceptron training.

Acknowledgments

We would like to thank the NEWS 2009 Machine Transliteration Shared Task organizers for creating this venue for comparing transliteration methods. We would also like to thank Chris Quirk for providing us with his alignment software.

References

Slaven Bilac and Hozumi Tanaka. 2005. Extracting transliteration pairs from comparable corpora. In *Proceedings of the Annual Meeting of the Natural Language Processing Society*, Japan.

Michael Collins. 2002. Discriminative training methods for hidden markov models: Theory and experiments with perceptron algorithms. In *EMNLP*.

Sittichai Jiampojamarn, Colin Cherry, and Grzegorz Kondrak. 2008. Joint processing and discriminative training for letter-to-phoneme conversion. In *ACL*, pages 905–913, Columbus, Ohio, June.

Alexandre Klementiev and Dan Roth. 2006. Named entity transliteration and discovery from multilingual comparable corpora. In *HLT-NAACL*, pages 82–88, New York City, USA, June.

Kevin Knight and Jonathan Graehl. 1998. Machine transliteration. *Computational Linguistics*, 24(4):599–612.

A. Kumaran and Tobias Kellner. 2007. A generic framework for machine transliteration. In *Proc. of the 30th SIGIR*.

Haizhou Li, A. Kumaran, Vladimir Pervouchine, and Min Zhang. 2009. Report on NEWS 2009 machine transliteration shared task. In *Proceedings of ACL-IJCNLP 2009 Named Entities Workshop (NEWS 2009)*, Singapore.

Richard Zens and Hermann Ney. 2004. Improvements in phrase-based statistical machine translation. In *HLT-NAACL*, pages 257–264, Boston, USA, May.

Hao Zhang, Chris Quirk, Robert C. Moore, and Daniel Gildea. 2008. Bayesian learning of non-compositional phrases with synchronous parsing. In *ACL*, pages 97–105, Columbus, Ohio, June.

Combining a Two-step Conditional Random Field Model and a Joint Source Channel Model for Machine Transliteration

Dong Yang, Paul Dixon, Yi-Cheng Pan, Tasuku Oonishi
Masanobu Nakamura and Sadaoki Furui
Department of Computer Science
Tokyo Institute of Techonology
{raymond,dixonp,thomas,oonishi,masa,furui}@furui.cs.titech.ac.jp

Abstract

This paper describes our system for "NEWS 2009 Machine Transliteration Shared Task" (NEWS 2009). We only participated in the standard run, which is a direct orthographical mapping (DOP) between two languages without using any intermediate phonemic mapping. We propose a new two-step conditional random field (CRF) model for DOP machine transliteration, in which the first CRF segments a source word into chunks and the second CRF maps the chunks to a word in the target language. The two-step CRF model obtains a slightly lower top-1 accuracy when compared to a state-of-the-art n-gram joint source-channel model. The combination of the CRF model with the joint source-channel leads to improvements in all the tasks. The official result of our system in the NEWS 2009 shared task confirms the effectiveness of our system; where we achieved 0.627 top-1 accuracy for Japanese transliterated to Japanese Kanji(JJ), 0.713 for English-to-Chinese(E2C) and 0.510 for English-to-Japanese Katakana(E2J) .

1 Introduction

With the increasing demand for machine translation, the out-of-vocabulary (OOV) problem caused by named entities is becoming more serious.

The translation of named entities from an alphabetic language (like English, French and Spanish) to a non-alphabetic language (like Chinese and Japanese) is usually performed through transliteration, which tries to preserve the pronunciation in the source language.

For example, in Japanese, foreign words imported from other languages are usually written in a special syllabary called *Katakana*; in Chinese, foreign words accepted to Chinese are always written by Chinese characters; examples are given in Figure 1.

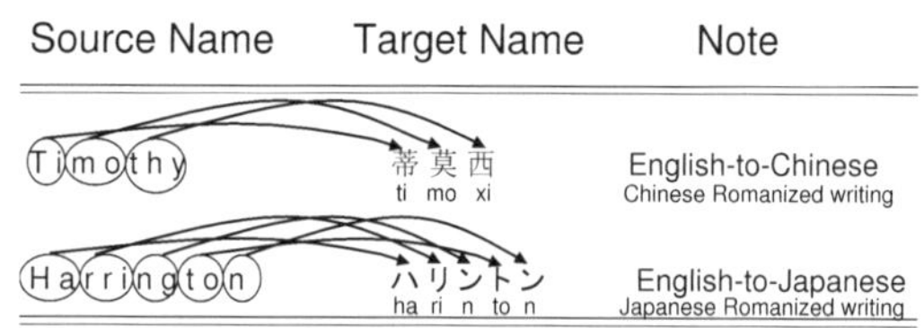

Figure 1: Transliteration examples

An intuitive transliteration method is to first convert a source word into phonemes, then find the corresponding phonemes in the target language, and finally convert to the target language's writing system (Knight and Graehl, 1998; Oh et al., 2006). One major limitation of this method is that the named entities are usually OOVs with diverse origins and this makes the grapheme-to-phoneme conversion very difficult.

DOP is gaining more attention in the transliteration research community which is also the standard evaluation of NEWS 2009.

The source channel and joint source-channel models (Li et al., 2004) have been proposed for DOP, which try to model $P(T|S)$ and $P(T,S)$ respectively, where T and S denotes the words in the target and source languages. (Ekbal et al., 2006) modified the joint source-channel model to incorporate different context information into the model for the Indian languages. Here we propose a two-step CRF model for transliteration, and the idea is to make use of the discriminative ability of CRF. For example, in E2C transliteration, the first step is to segment an English name into alphabet chunks and after this step the number of Chinese characters is decided. The second step is to perform a context-dependent mapping from each English chunk into one Chinese character. Figure 1 shows that this method is applicable to many other

Proceedings of the 2009 Named Entities Workshop, ACL-IJCNLP 2009, pages 72–75,
Suntec, Singapore, 7 August 2009. ©2009 ACL and AFNLP

transliteration tasks including E2C and E2J.

Our CRF method and the n-gram joint source-channel model use different information in predicting the corresponding Chinese characters and therefore in combination better results are expected. We interpolate the two models linearly and use this as our final system for NEWS 2009. The rest of the paper is organized as follows: Section 2 introduces our system in detail including the alignment and decoding modules, Section 3 explains our experiments and finally Section 4 describes conclusions and future work.

2 System Description

Our system starts from a joint source channel alignment to train the CRF segmenter. The CRF is used to re-segment and align the training data, and from this alignment we create a Weighted Finite State Transducer (WFST) based n-gram joint source-channel decoder and a CRF E2C converter. The following subsections explain the structure of our system shown in Figure 2.

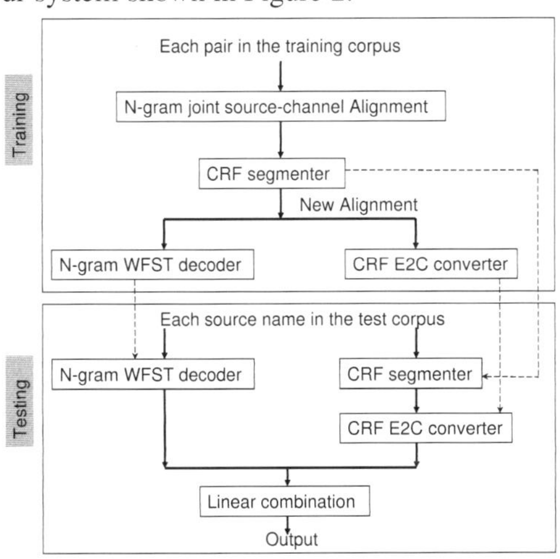

Figure 2: System structure

2.1 Theoretical background

2.1.1 Joint source channel model

The source channel model represents the conditional probability of target names given a source name $P(T|S)$. The joint source channel model calculates how the source words and target names are generated simultaneously (Li et al., 2004):

$$\begin{aligned} & P(S,T) = P(s_1, s_2, ..., s_k, t_1, t_2, ..., t_k) \\ = \; & P(<s,t>_1, <s,t>_2, ..., <s,t>_k) \\ = \; & \prod_{k=1}^{K} P(<s,t>_k \mid <s,t>_1^{k-1}) \end{aligned} \quad (1)$$

where, $S = (s_1, s_2, ..., s_k)$ and $T = (t_1, t_2, ..., t_k)$.

2.1.2 CRF

A CRF (Lafferty et al., 2001) is an undirected graphical model which assigns a probability to a label sequence $L = l_1 l_2 \ldots l_T$, given an input sequence $C = c_1 c_2 \ldots c_T$,

$$P(L|C) = \frac{1}{Z(C)} exp(\sum_{t=1}^{T} \sum_{k} \lambda_k f_k(l_t, l_{t-1}, C, t)) \quad (2)$$

For the kth feature, f_k denotes the feature function and λ_k is the parameter which controls the weighting. $Z(C)$ is a normalization term that ensure the distribution sums to one. CRF training is usually performed through the L-BFGS algorithm (Wallach, 2002) and decoding is performed by Viterbi algorithm (Viterbi, 1967). In this paper, we use an open source toolkit "crf++"[1].

2.2 N-gram joint source-channel alignment

To calculate the probability in Equation 1, the training corpus needs to be aligned first. We use the Expectation-Maximization(EM) algorithm to optimize the alignment A between the source S and target T pairs, that is:

$$\widetilde{A} = \arg\max_{A} P(S, T, A) \quad (3)$$

The procedure is summarized as follows:

1. Initialize a random alignment
2. E-step: update n-gram probability
3. M-step: apply the n-gram model to realign each entry in corpus
4. Go to step 2 until the alignment converges

2.3 CRF alignment & segmentation

The performance of EM algorithm is often affected by the initialization. Fortunately, we can correct mis-alignments by using the discriminative ability of the CRF. The alignment problem is converted into a tagging problem that doesn't require the use of the target words at all. Figure 3 is an example of a segmentation and alignment, where the labels B and N indicate whether the character is in the starting position of the chunk or not.

In the CRF method the feature function describes a co-occurrence relation, and it is formally

[1] crfpp.sourceforge.net

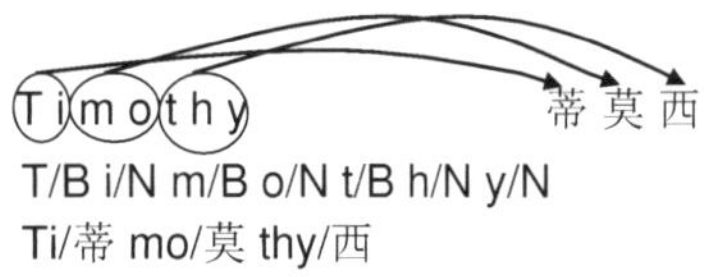

Figure 3: An example of the CRF segmenter format and E2C converter

defined as $f_k(l_t, l_{t-1}, C, t)$ (Eq. 2). f_k is usually a binary function, and takes the value 1 when both observation c_t and transition $l_{t-1} \rightarrow l_t$ are observed. In our segmentation tool, we use the following features

- 1. Unigram features: $C_{-2}, C_{-1}, C_0, C_1, C_2$
- 2. Bigram features:$C_{-1}C_0, C_0C_1$

Here, C_0 is the current character, C_{-1} and C_1 denote the previous and next characters and C_{-2} and C_2 are the characters two positions to the left and right of C_0.

In the alignment process, we use the CRF segmenter to split each English word into chunks. Sometimes a problem occurs in which the number of chunks in the segmented output will not be equal to the number of Chinese characters. In such cases our solution is to choose from the n-best list the top scoring segmentation which contains the correct number of chunks.

In the testing process, we use the segmenter in the similar way, but only take top-1 output segmented English chunks for use in the following CRF E2C conversion.

2.4 CRF E2C converter

Similar to the CRF segmenter, the CRF E2C converter has the format shown in Figure 3. For this CRF, we use the following features:

- 1. Unigram features: C_{-1}, C_0, C_1
- 2. Bigram features:$C_{-1}C_0, C_0C_1$

where C represents the English chunks and the subscript notation is the same as the CRF segmenter.

2.5 N-gram WFST decoder for joint source channel model

Our decoding approach makes use of WFSTs to represent the models and simplify the development by utilizing standard operations such as composition and shortest path algorithms.

After the alignments are generated, the first step is to build a *corpus* to train the transliteration WFST. Each aligned word is converted to a sequence of transliteration alignment pairs $\langle s,t\rangle_1, \langle s,t\rangle_2, ... \langle s,t\rangle_k$, where each s can be a chunk of one or more characters and t is assumed to be a single character. Each of the pairs is treated as a word and the entire set of alignments is used to train an n-gram language model. In these evaluations we used the MITLM toolkit (Hsu and Glass, 2008) to build a trigram model with modified Kneser-Ney smoothing.

We then use the procedure described in (Caseiro et al., 2002) and convert the n-gram to a weighted acceptor representation where each input label belongs to the set of transliteration alignment pairs. Next the pairs labels are broken down into the input and output parts and the acceptor is converted to a transducer M. To allow transliteration from a sequence of individual characters, a second WFST T is constructed. T has a single state and for each s a path is added to allow a mapping from the string of individual characters.

To perform the actual transliteration, the input word is converted to an acceptor I which has one arc for each of the characters in the word. I is then combined with T and M according to $O = I \circ T \circ M$ where $\circ$ denotes the composition operator. The n–best paths are extracted from O by projecting the output, removing the epsilon labels and applying the n-shortest paths algorithm with determinization from the OpenFst Toolkit(Allauzen et al., 2007).

2.6 Linear combination

We notice that there is a significant difference between the correct answers of the n-gram WFST and CRF decoders. The reason may be due to the different information utilized in the two decoding methods. Since their performance levels are similar, the overall performance is expected to be improved by the combination. From the CRF we compute the probability $P_{CRF}(T|S)$ and from the list of scores output from the n-gram decoder we calculate the conditional probability of $P_{n-gram}(T|S)$. These are used in our combination method according to:

$$P(T|S) = \lambda P_{CRF}(T|S) + (1-\lambda) P_{n-gram}(T|S) \quad (4)$$

where λ denotes the interpolation weight (0.3 in this paper).

3 Experiments

We use the training and development sets of NEWS 2009 data in our experiments as detailed in Table 1[2]. There are several measure metrics in the shared task and due to limited space in this paper we provide the results for top-1 accuracy.

Task	Training data size	Test data size
E2C	31961	2896
E2J	23808	1509

Table 1: Corpus introduction

Task	n-gram+CRF Alignment		interpolation
	WFST	CRF	
E2C	70.3	67.3	71.5
E2J	44.9	44.8	46.7

Table 2: Top-1 accuracies(%)

The results are listed in Table 2. For E2C task the top-1 accuracy of the joint source-channel model is 70.3% and 67.3% for the two-step CRF model. After combining the two results together the top-1 accuracy increases to 71.5% corresponding to a 1.2% absolute improvement over the state-of-the-art joint source-channel model. Similarly, we get 1.8% absolute improvement for E2J task.

4 Conclusions and future work

In this paper we have presented our new hybrid method for machine transliteration which combines a new two-step CRF model with a state-of-the-art joint source-channel model. In comparison to the joint source-channel model the combination approach achieved 1.2% and 1.8% absolute improvements for E2C and E2J task respectively.

In the first step of the CRF method we only use the top-1 segmentation, which may propagate transliteration errors to the following step. In future work we would like to optimize the 2-step CRF jointly. Currently, we are also investigating minimum classification error (MCE) discriminant training as a method to further improve the joint source channel model.

[2]For the JJ task the submitted results are only based on the joint source channel model. Unfortunately, we were unable to submit a combination result because the training time for the CRF was too long.

Acknowledgments

The corpora used in this paper are from "NEWS 2009 Machine Transliteration Shared Task" (Li et al., 2004; CJK, website)

References

Kevin Knight and Jonathan Graehl. 1998. *Machine Transliteration*, 1998 Association for Computational Linguistics.

Li Haizhou, Zhang Min and Su Jian. 2004. *A joint source-channel model for machine transliteration*, 2004 Proceedings of the 42nd Annual Meeting on Association for Computational Linguistics.

Asif Ekbal, Sudip Kumar Naskar and Sivaji Bandyopadhyay. 2006. *A modified joint source-channel model for transliteration*, Proceedings of the COLING/ACL, pages 191-198.

Jong-Hoon Oh, Key-Sun Choi and Hitoshi Isahara. 2006. *A comparison of different machine transliteration models* , Journal of Artificial Intelligence Research, 27, pages 119-151.

John Lafferty, Andrew McCallum, and Fernando Pereira 2001. *Conditional Random Fields: Probabilistic Models for Segmenting and Labeling Sequence Data.*, Proceedings of International Conference on Machine Learning, 2001, pages 282-289.

Hanna Wallach 2002. *Efficient Training of Conditional Random Fields*. M. Thesis, University of Edinburgh, 2002.

Andrew J. Viterbi 1967. *Error Bounds for Convolutional Codes and an Asymptotically Optimum Decoding Algorithm.* IEEE Transactions on Information Theory, Volume IT-13, 1967,pages 260-269.

Bo-June Hsu and James Glass 2008. *Iterative Language Model Estimation: Efficient Data Structure & Algorithms*. Proceedings Interspeech, pages 841-844.

Diamantino Caseiro, Isabel Trancosoo, Luis Oliveira and Ceu Viana 2002. *Grapheme-to-phone using finite state transducers*. Proceedings 2002 IEEE Workshop on Speech Synthesis.

Cyril Allauzen, Michael Riley, Johan Schalkwyk, Wojciech Skut and Mehryar Mohri 2002. *OpenFst: A General and Efficient Weighted Finite-State Transducer Library*. Proceedings of the Ninth International Conference on Implementation and Application of Automata, (CIAA 2007), pages 11-23.

http://www.cjk.org

Phonological Context Approximation and Homophone Treatment for NEWS 2009 English-Chinese Transliteration Shared Task

Oi Yee Kwong
Department of Chinese, Translation and Linguistics
City University of Hong Kong
Tat Chee Avenue, Kowloon, Hong Kong
Olivia.Kwong@cityu.edu.hk

Abstract

This paper describes our systems participating in the NEWS 2009 Machine Transliteration Shared Task. Two runs were submitted for the English-Chinese track. The system for the standard run is based on graphemic approximation of local phonological context. The one for the non-standard run is based on parallel modelling of sound and tone patterns for treating homophones in Chinese. Official results show that both systems stand in the mid range amongst all participating systems.

1 Introduction

This paper describes our systems participating in the English-Chinese track of the NEWS 2009 Machine Transliteration Shared Task.

The apparently free combination of Chinese characters in names is not entirely ungoverned. There are no more than a few hundred Chinese characters which are used in names. Moreover, beyond linguistic and phonetic properties, many social and cognitive factors are simultaneously influencing the naming process and superimposing on the surface graphemic correspondence.

Our systems in the standard and non-standard runs aim at addressing two issues in English-Chinese forward transliteration (referred to as *E2C* hereafter), namely graphemic ambiguity and homophones in Chinese respectively.

By graphemic ambiguity, we refer to the multiple mappings between English segments and Chinese segments. For example, the English segment "ty" could be rendered as 蒂 *di4* as in Christy 克里斯蒂 *ke4-li3-si1-di4*, or 太 *tai4* as in Style 斯太尔 *si1-tai4-er3*[1]. Although direct orthographic mapping (e.g. Li *et al.*, 2004) has been shown to work even more effectively than phoneme-based methods (e.g. Virga and Khudanpur, 2003), it is observed that phonological context plays an important role in resolving graphemic ambiguity. In the absence of an explicit phonemic representation of the source names, our GAP system, to be described in Section 4.1, attempts to approximate the local phonological context for a given segment by means of surface graphemic properties.

An English name could be acceptably transliterated in various ways, e.g. 希拉里 *xi1-la1-li3*, 希拉利 *xi1-la1-li4*, 希拉莉 *xi1-la1-li4*, as well as 希拉蕊 *xi1-la1-rui3* are all possible transliterations for Hilary. Homophones are abundant in Chinese, as evident from the first three alternatives above. However, conventional transliteration models often rely heavily on the distribution of the training data, which might preclude infrequent but similarly acceptable transliteration candidates. Also, Chinese is a typical tonal language. The sound-tone combination is important in names. Names which sound "nice" are often preferred to those which sound "monotonous". Our SoToP system to be described in Section 4.2 thus attempts to model sound and tone patterns in parallel, to deal with homophones more reasonably despite possible skewed prior distributions.

Related work will be briefly reviewed in Section 2, and the datasets will be described in Section 3. The systems for both runs and their performance will be reported in Section 4, followed by future work and conclusion in Section 5.

2 Related Work

There are basically two categories of work on machine transliteration. First, various alignment models are used for acquiring transliteration

[1] The transcriptions in this paper are in Hanyu Pinyin.

Proceedings of the 2009 Named Entities Workshop, ACL-IJCNLP 2009, pages 76–79,
Suntec, Singapore, 7 August 2009. ©2009 ACL and AFNLP

lexicons from parallel corpora and other resources (e.g. Kuo and Li, 2008). Second, statistical models are built for transliteration. These models could be phoneme-based (e.g. Knight and Graehl, 1998), grapheme-based (e.g. Li *et al.*, 2004), hybrid (Oh and Choi, 2005), or based on phonetic (e.g. Tao *et al.*, 2006) and semantic (e.g. Li *et al.*, 2007) features.

The core of our systems is based on Li *et al.*'s (2004) Joint Source-Channel Model under the direct orthographic mapping framework, which skips the middle phonemic representation in conventional phoneme-based methods and models the segmentation and alignment preferences by means of contextual n-grams of the transliteration segment pairs (or token pairs in their terminology). A bigram model under their framework is thus as follows:

$$\begin{aligned} P(E,C) &= P(e_1,e_2,\ldots,e_k,c_1,c_2,\ldots,c_k) \\ &= P(<e_1,c_1>,<e_2,c_2>,\ldots,<e_k,c_k>) \\ &\approx \prod_{k=1}^{K} P(<e_k,c_k>|<e_{k-1},c_{k-1}>) \end{aligned}$$

where E refers to the English source name and C refers to the transliterated Chinese name. With K segments aligned between E and C, e_k and c_k refer to the kth English segment and its corresponding Chinese segment respectively.

3 Datasets

The current study used the English-Chinese (EnCh) data provided by the shared task organisers. There are 31,961 English-Chinese name pairs in the training set, 2,896 English-Chinese name pairs in the development set, and another 2,896 English names in the test set. The Chinese transliterations basically correspond to Mandarin Chinese pronunciations of the English names, as used by media in Mainland China (Xinhua News Agency, 1992).

The training and development data were manually cleaned up and aligned with respect to the correspondence between English segments and Chinese segments, e.g. Aa/l/to 阿/尔/托, and the pronunciations for the Chinese characters were automatically looked up.

Based on all the unique English segments resulting from manual alignment, all possible segmentations of a test name were first obtained, and they were then ranked using a probabilistic score computed by:

$$Score(S) \approx \prod_{k=1}^{K} P(s_k \mid lc(s_{k-1}))\, P(s_k \mid fc(s_{k+1}))$$

where S is a segmentation sequence with K segments, s_k is the kth segment in S, $lc(s_{k-1})$ is the last character of segment s_{k-1} and $fc(s_{k+1})$ is the first character of segment s_{k+1}.

4 System Description

4.1 Standard Run – GAP

Our system for the standard run is called GAP, which stands for Graphemic Approximation of Phonological context.

Although direct orthographic mapping has been shown to be an effective method, it is nevertheless observed that phonological context significantly contributes to the resolution of some graphemic ambiguity. For example, the English segment "le" was found to correspond to as many as 15 Chinese segments in the data, including 利 *li4*, 勒 *le4*, 历 *li4*, 尔 *er3*, 莱 *lai2*, 里 *li3*, etc. When "le" appears at the end of a name, all but a few cases are rendered as 尔 *er3*, e.g. Dale 戴尔 *dai4-er3* and Dipasquale 迪帕斯奎尔 *di2-pa4-si1-kui2-er3*. This is especially true when the previous character is "a". On the contrary, when "le" appears at the end of a name following an "r", it is more often rendered as 利 *li4* instead, e.g. Berle 伯利 *bo2-li4*. On the other hand, "le" at the beginning of name is often rendered as 勒 *le4* or 莱 *lai2*, e.g. Lepke 莱普克 *lai2-pu3-ke4*, except when it is followed by the vowel "o", where it is then often transliterated as 利 *li4*, e.g. Leonor 利奥诺 *li4-ao4-nuo4*. Such observation thus indicates two important points for *E2C*. First, the phonological context is useful as English graphemic segments could be ambiguous in terms of pronunciation, and the actual pronunciation often determines which Chinese segment is to be used. Second, local contexts on both sides are important as they indicate the environment in which the segment is embedded, which might affect the way it is pronounced.

GAP thus attempts to approximate local phonological context by means of surface graphemic properties, making use of bigrams in both directions. Since the phonological environment might be sufficiently represented by a neighbouring phoneme instead of a whole syllable, we approximate the phonological context with one character on both sides of a given English segment, irrespective of their corresponding Chinese segments. Using single characters on both sides could also ensure that a small and consistent parameter space is maintained. Hence, weighting the context on both sides equally, GAP assigns a score *Score(E,C)* to a transliteration candidate with *K* segment pairs as follows:

$$\prod_{k=1}^{K} P(<e_k, c_k> | lc(e_{k-1}))\, P(<e_k, c_k> | fc(e_{k+1}))$$

where $<e_k,c_k>$ is the *k*th English-Chinese segment pair, $lc(e_{k-1})$ is the last character of segment e_{k-1} and $fc(e_{k+1})$ is the first character of segment e_{k+1}.

Taking the top 3 segmentation candidates, the transliteration candidates were generated by looking up the grapheme pairs obtained from manual alignment with frequency $f \geq 3$. If there is no grapheme pair above the threshold, all pairs below the threshold would be considered. All combinations obtained were then subject to ranking with *Score(E,C)* above.

4.2 Non-standard Run – SoToP

The homophone problem is notorious in Chinese. As far as personal name transliteration is concerned, unless there are standardised principles prescribed, the "correctness" of transliterated names is not clear-cut at all. As a tonal language, how a combination of characters sounds is also important in naming. As in the example given in Section 1, one cannot really say any of the transliterations for Hilary is "right" or "wrong", but perhaps only "better" or "worse". Hence naming is more of an art than a science, and automatic transliteration should avoid over-reliance on the training data and thus missing unlikely but good alternative candidates.

Our system for the non-standard run, SoToP, thus aims at addressing this cognitive or perceptual aspect of transliteration beyond its linguistic and phonetic properties. Instead of direct orthographic mapping, we use a Sound model (SoM) and a Tone model (ToM) in Parallel. The SoToP architecture is shown in Figure 1.

SoM basically assembles the homophones and captures the sound patterns in terms of a grapheme-phoneme mapping. The operation of SoM is like GAP above, except that the $<e_k,c_k>$ pairs are replaced by $<e_k,so_k>$ pairs, where so_k refers to the phonetic transcription in Hanyu Pinyin (without tone) for the *k*th Chinese segment in a candidate.

ToM, on the other hand, captures the tone patterns of transliteration, irrespective of the sound and the character choice. Although English does not have tones, the intonation and stress of a syllable may prompt for the usage of a Chinese character of a certain tone. Chinese, on the other hand, is a tonal language. The tone patterns are more cognitive in nature, as some combinations may just sound awkward for no apparent reason. Moreover, some sound-tone combinations might result in undesirable homophones, which are also avoided in names in general. The operation of ToM is also like GAP, except that the $<e_k,c_k>$ pairs are replaced by $<e_k,to_k>$ pairs, where to_k refers to the tone for the *k*th Chinese segment in a candidate.

The Candidate Generator combines the top *M* candidates from ToM and top *N* candidates from SoM to generate character combinations by looking up a pronunciation table. The lookup table lists the homophones for each sound-tone combination found in the data. In the current study, both *M* and *N* were set to 3. The generated candidates were then ranked by a simple bigram model based on the bigram probabilities of the Chinese segments.

4.3 System Testing

The two systems were tested on the NEWS development data, containing 2,896 English names. System performance was measured by the following evaluation metrics: Word Accuracy in Top-1 (ACC), Fuzziness in Top-1 (Mean F-score), Mean Reciprocal Rank (MRR), MAP_{ref}, MAP_{10}, and MAP_{sys}. Detailed description of these metrics can be found in the NEWS shared task whitepaper (Li *et al*., 2009).

Table 1 shows the system testing results on the development data. The standard run, GAP, in general gives better results than the non-standard run, SoToP. One possible reason is apart from the source name segmentation step, SoToP has more steps allowing error propagation as the mapping was done separately with sound and tone, whereas GAP directly maps English segments to Chinese segments at the graphemic level.

Metric	GAP	SoToP
ACC	0.645	0.597
Mean F-score	0.860	0.836
MRR	0.732	0.674
MAP_{ref}	0.645	0.597
MAP_{10}	0.223	0.206
MAP_{sys}	0.225	0.335

Table 1. System Testing Results

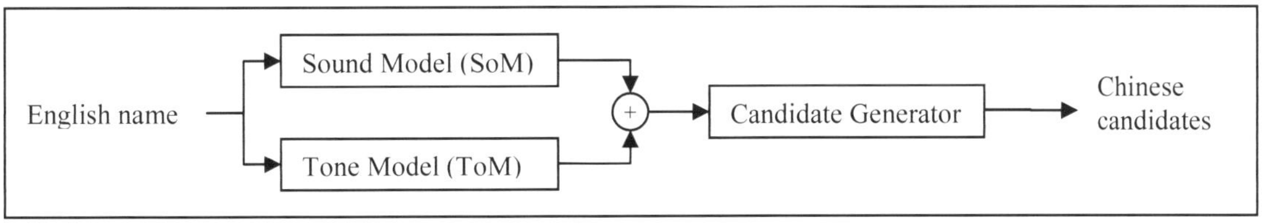

Figure 1. The SoToP Architecture for *E2C* Transliteration

4.4 Official Results

The two systems were trained on both the training data and development data together, and run on the test data. The official results are shown in Table 2. The performance of the two systems is in the mid range amongst all participating systems, including standard and non-standard runs. Despite the shortcoming and lower performance of SoToP, modelling the sound and tone patterns has its merits for handling homophones. For example, the expected transliteration for Mcgiveran, 麦吉弗伦 *mai4-ji2-fu2-lun2*, was ranked 6th by GAP but 1st by SoToP. The segment "ve" is much more likely rendered as 夫 *fu1* than as 弗 *fu2*, but ToM in SoToP was able to capture the preferred tone pattern 4-2-2-2 in this case.

Metric	GAP	SoToP
ACC	0.621	0.587
Mean F-score	0.852	0.834
MRR	0.718	0.665
MAP_{ref}	0.621	0.587
MAP_{10}	0.220	0.203
MAP_{sys}	0.222	0.330

Table 2. Official Results on Test Data

5 Future Work and Conclusion

Thus we have reported on the two systems participating in the NEWS shared task. The standard run, GAP, relies on direct orthographic mapping and approximates local phonological context with neighbouring graphemes to help resolve graphemic ambiguity. The non-standard run, SoToP, attempts to address the homophone issues in Chinese, by modelling the sound and tone patterns in parallel, and subsequently combining them to generate transliteration candidates. In general GAP gives better results than SoToP, while both are in the mid range amongst all participating systems. Future work includes more error analysis and improving the accuracy of individual steps to minimise error propagation. The possible combination of the two methods is also worth further investigation.

Acknowledgements

The work described in this paper was substantially supported by a grant from City University of Hong Kong (Project No. 7002203).

References

Knight, K. and Graehl, J. (1998) Machine Transliteration. *Computational Linguistics, 24(4)*:599-612.

Kuo, J-S. and Li, H. (2008) Mining Transliterations from Web Query Results: An Incremental Approach. In *Proceedings of SIGHAN-6*, Hyderabad, India, pp.16-23.

Li, H., Zhang, M. and Su, J. (2004) A Joint Source-Channel Model for Machine Transliteration. In *Proceedings of the 42nd Annual Meeting of ACL*, Barcelona, Spain, pp.159-166.

Li, H., Sim, K.C., Kuo, J-S. and Dong, M. (2007) Semantic Transliteration of Personal Names. In *Proceedings of 45th Annual Meeting of ACL*, Prague, Czech Republic, pp.120-127.

Li, H., Kumaran, A., Zhang, M. and Pervouchine, V. (2009) Whitepaper of NEWS 2009 Machine Transliteration Shared Task. In *Proceedings of ACL-IJCNLP 2009 Named Entities Workshop (NEWS 2009)*, Singapore.

Oh, J-H. and Choi, K-S. (2005) An Ensemble of Grapheme and Phoneme for Machine Transliteration. In R. Dale *et al.* (Eds.), *Natural Language Processing – IJCNLP 2005*. Springer, LNAI Vol. 3651, pp.451-461.

Tao, T., Yoon, S-Y., Fister, A., Sproat, R. and Zhai, C. (2006) Unsupervised Named Entity Transliteration Using Temporal and Phonetic Correlation. In *Proceedings of EMNLP 2006*, Sydney, Australia, pp.250-257.

Virga, P. and Khudanpur, S. (2003) Transliteration of Proper Names in Cross-lingual Information Retrieval. In *Proceedings of the ACL2003 Workshop on Multilingual and Mixed-language Named Entity Recognition*.

Xinhua News Agency. (1992) *Chinese Transliteration of Foreign Personal Names*. The Commercial Press.

English to Hindi Machine Transliteration System at NEWS 2009

Amitava Das, Asif Ekbal, Tapabrata Mandal and Sivaji Bandyopadhyay
Computer Science and Engineering Department
Jadavpur University, Kolkata-700032, India
amitava.research@gmail.com, asif.ekbal@gmail.com, tapabratamondal@gmail.com, sivaji_cse_ju@yahoo.com

Abstract

This paper reports about our work in the NEWS 2009 Machine Transliteration Shared Task held as part of ACL-IJCNLP 2009. We submitted one standard run and two non-standard runs for English to Hindi transliteration. The modified joint source-channel model has been used along with a number of alternatives. The system has been trained on the NEWS 2009 Machine Transliteration Shared Task datasets. For standard run, the system demonstrated an accuracy of 0.471 and the mean F-Score of 0.861. The non-standard runs yielded the accuracy and mean F-scores of 0.389 and 0.831 respectively in the first one and 0.384 and 0.828 respectively in the second one. The non-standard runs resulted in substantially worse performance than the standard run. The reasons for this are the ranking algorithm used for the output and the types of tokens present in the test set.

1 Introduction

Technical terms and named entities (NEs) constitute the bulk of the Out Of Vocabulary (OOV) words. Named entities are usually not found in bilingual dictionaries and are very generative in nature. Proper identification, classification and translation of Named entities (NEs) are very important in many Natural Language Processing (NLP) applications. Translation of NEs involves both translation and transliteration. Transliteration is the method of translating into another language by expressing the original foreign word using characters of the target language preserving the pronunciation in their source language. Thus, the central problem in transliteration is predicting the pronunciation of the original word. Transliteration between two languages that use the same set of alphabets is trivial: the word is left as it is. However, for languages those use different alphabet sets the names must be transliterated or rendered in the target language alphabets. Transliteration of NEs is necessary in many applications, such as machine translation, corpus alignment, cross-language Information Retrieval, information extraction and automatic lexicon acquisition. In the literature, a number of transliteration algorithms are available involving English (Li et al., 2004; Vigra and Khudanpur, 2003; Goto et al., 2003), European languages (Marino et al., 2005) and some of the Asian languages, namely Chinese (Li et al., 2004; Vigra and Khudanpur, 2003), Japanese (Goto et al., 2003; Knight and Graehl, 1998), Korean (Jung et al., 2000) and Arabic (Al-Onaizan and Knight, 2002a; Al-Onaizan and Knight, 2002c). Recently, some works have been initiated involving Indian languages (Ekbal et al., 2006; Ekbal et al., 2007; Surana and Singh, 2008).

2 Machine Transliteration Systems

Three transliteration models have been used that can generate the Hindi transliteration from an English named entity (NE). An English NE is divided into Transliteration Units (TUs) with patterns C*V*, where C represents a consonant and V represents a vowel. The Hindi NE is divided into TUs with patterns C+M?, where C represents a consonant or a vowel or a conjunct and M represents the vowel modifier or matra. The TUs are the lexical units for machine transliteration. The system considers the English and Hindi contextual information in the form of collocated TUs simultaneously to calculate the plausibility of transliteration from each English TU to various Hindi candidate TUs and chooses the one with maximum probability. This is equivalent to choosing the most appropriate sense of a word in the source language to identify its representation in the target language. The system learns the mappings automatically from the bilingual NEWS training set being guided by lin-

Proceedings of the 2009 Named Entities Workshop, ACL-IJCNLP 2009, pages 80–83,
Suntec, Singapore, 7 August 2009.

guistic features/knowledge. The system considers the linguistic knowledge in the form of conjuncts and/or diphthongs in English and their possible transliteration in Hindi. The output of the mapping process is a decision-list classifier with collocated TUs in the source language and their equivalent TUs in collocation in the target language along with the probability of each decision obtained from the training set. Linguistic knowledge is used in order to make the number of TUs in both the source and target sides equal. A Direct example base has been maintained that contains the bilingual training examples that do not result in the equal number of TUs in both the source and target sides during alignment. The Direct example base is checked first during machine transliteration of the input English word. If no match is obtained, the system uses direct orthographic mapping by identifying the equivalent Hindi TU for each English TU in the input and then placing the Hindi TUs in order. The transliteration models are described below in which S and T denotes the source and the target words respectively:

- Model A

This is essentially the joint source-channel model (Hazhiou et al., 2004) where the previous TUs with reference to the current TUs in both the source (s) and the target sides (t) are considered as the context.

$$P(S \mid T) = \prod_{k=1}^{K} P(<s,t>_k \mid <s,t>_{k-1})$$

$$S \rightarrow T(S) = \arg\max_T \{P(T) \times P(S \mid T)\}$$

- Model B

This is basically the trigram model where the previous and the next source TUs are considered as the context.

$$P(S \mid T) = \prod_{k=1}^{K} P(<s,t>_k \mid s_{k-1}, s_{k+1})$$

$$S \rightarrow T(S) = \arg\max_T \{P(T) \times P(S \mid T)\}$$

- Model C

In this model, the previous and the next TUs in the source and the previous target TU are considered as the context. This is the improved modified joint source-channel model.

$$P(S \mid T) = \prod_{k=1}^{K} P(<s,t>_k \mid <s,t>_{k-1,}\ s_{k+1})$$

$$S \rightarrow T(S) = \arg\max_T \{P(T) \times P(S \mid T)\}$$

For NE transliteration, P(*T*), i.e., the probability of transliteration in the target language, is calculated from a English-Hindi bilingual database of approximately 961,890 English person names, collected from the web[1]. If, *T* is not found in the dictionary, then a very small value is assigned to P(*T*). These models have been desribed in details in Ekbal et al. (2007).

- Post-Processing

Depending upon the nature of errors involved in the results, we have devised a set of transliteration rules. A few rules have been devised to produce more spelling variations. Some examples are given below.

Spelling variation rules

`Badlapur` बदलापुर | वदलापुर

`Shree | Shri` श्री

3 Experimental Results

We have trained our transliteration models using the English-Hindi datasets obtained from the NEWS 2009 Machine Transliteration Shared Task (Li et al., 2009). A brief statistics of the datasets are presented in Table 1. Out of 9975 English-Hindi parallel examples in the training set, 4009 are multi-words. During training, we have split these multi-words into collections of single word transliterations. It was observed that the number of tokens in the source and target sides mismatched in 22 multi-words and these cases were not considered further. Following are some examples:

`Paris Charles de Gaulle` पेरिस रॉसे चार्ल्स डे ग्यूले

`South Arlington Church of Christ` साउथ अर्लिंग्टन

In the training set, some multi-words were partly translated and not transliterated. Such examples were dropped from the training set. Finally, the training set consists of 15905 single word English-Hindi parallel examples.

[1]http://www.eci.gov.in/DevForum/Fullname.asp

Set	Number of examples
Training	9975
Development	974
Test	1000

Table 1. Statistics of Dataset

The output of the modified joint source-channel model is given more priority during output ranking followed by the trigram and the joint source-channel model. During testing, the *Direct example base* is searched first to find the transliteration. Experimental results on the development set yielded the accuracy of 0.442 and mean F-score of 0.829. Depending upon the nature of errors involved in the results, we have devised a set of transliteration rules. The use of these transliteration rules increased the accuracy and mean F-score values up to 0.489 and 0.881 respectively.

The system has been evaluated for the test set and the detailed reports are available in Li et al. (2009). There are 88.88% unknown examples in the test set. We submitted one standard run in which the outputs are provided for the modified joint source-channel model (Model C), trigram model (Model B) and joint source-channel model (Model A). The same ranking procedure (i.e., Model C, Model B and Model A) has been followed as that of the development set. The output of each transliteration model has been post-processed with the set of transliteration rules. For each word, three different outputs are provided in a ranked order. If the outputs of any two models are same for any word then only two outputs are provided for that particular word. Post-processing rules generate more number of possible transliteration output. Evaluation results of the standard run are shown in Table 2.

Parameters	Accuracy
Accuracy in top-1	0.471
Mean F-score	0.861
Mean Reciprocal Rank (MRR)	0.519
Mean Average Precision ($MAP)_{ref}$	0.463
MAP_{10}	0.162
MAP_{sys}	0.383

Table 2. Results of the standard run

The results of the two non-standard runs are presented in Table 3 and Table 4 respectively.

Parameters	Accuracy
Accuracy in top-1	0.389
Mean F-score	0.831
Mean Reciprocal Rank (MRR)	0.487
Mean Average Precision ($MAP)_{ref}$	0.385
MAP_{10}	0.16
MAP_{sys}	0.328

Table 3. Results of the non-standard run 1

Parameters	Accuracy
Accuracy in top-1	0.384
Mean F-score	0.823
Mean Reciprocal Rank (MRR)	0.485
Mean Average Precision ($MAP)_{ref}$	0.380
MAP_{10}	0.16
MAP_{sys}	0.325

Table 4. Results of the non-standard run2

In both the non-standard runs, we have used an English-Hindi bilingual database of approximately 961, 890 examples that have been collected from the web[2]. This database contains the (frequency) of the corresponding English-Hindi name pair. Along with the outputs of three models, the output obtained from this bilingual database has been also provided for each English word. In the first non-standard run, only the most frequent transliteration has been considered. But, in the second non-standard run all the possible transliteration have been considered. It is to be noted that in these two non-standard runs, the transliterations obtained from the bilingual database have been kept first in the ranking. Results of the tables show quite similar performance in both the runs. But the non-standard runs resulted in substantially worse performance than the standard run. The reasons for this are the ranking algorithm used for the output and the types of tokens present in the test set. The additional da-

[2]http://www.eci.gov.in/DevForum/Fullname.asp

taset used for the non-standard runs is mainly census data consisting of only Indian person names. The NEWS 2009 Machine Transliteration Shared Task training set is well distributed with foreign names (Ex. Sweden, Warren), common nouns (Mahfuz, Darshanaa) and a few non named entities. Hence the training set for the non-standard runs was biased towards the Indian person name transliteration pattern. Additional training set was quite larger (961, 890) than the shared task training set (9,975). Actually outputs of non-standard runs have more alternative transliteration outputs than the standard set. That means non-standard sets are superset of standard set. Our observation is that the ranking algorithm used for the output and biased training are the main reasons for the worse performance of the non-standard runs.

4 Conclusion

This paper reports about our works as part of the NEWS 2009 Machine Transliteration Shared Task. We have used the modified joint source-channel model along with two other alternatives to generate the Hindi transliteration from an English word (to generate more spelling variations of Hindi names). We have also devised some post-processing rules to remove the errors. During standard run, we have obtained the word accuracy of 0.471 and mean F-score of 0.831. In non-standard rune, we have used a bilingual database obtained from the web. The non-standard runs yielded the word accuracy and mean F-score values of 0.389 and 0.831 respectively in the first run and 0.384 and 0.823 respectively in the second run.

References

Al-Onaizan, Y. and Knight, K. 2002a. Named Entity Translation: Extended Abstract. In *Proceedings of the Human Language Technology Conference,* 122– 124.

Al-Onaizan, Y. and Knight, K. 2002b. Translating Named Entities using Monolingual and Bilingual Resources. In *Proceedings of the 40th Annual Meeting of the ACL*, 400–408, USA.

Ekbal, A. Naskar, S. and Bandyopadhyay, S. 2007. Named Entity Transliteration. *International Journal of Computer Processing of Oriental Languages (IJCPOL)*, Volume (20:4), 289-310, World Scientific Publishing Company, Singapore.

Ekbal, A., Naskar, S. and Bandyopadhyay, S. 2006. A Modified Joint Source Channel Model for Transliteration. In *Proceedings of the COLING-ACL 2006*, 191-198, Australia.

Goto, I., Kato, N., Uratani, N. and Ehara, T. 2003. Transliteration Considering Context Information based on the Maximum Entropy Method. In *Proceeding of the MT-Summit IX*, 125–132, New Orleans, USA.

Jung, Sung Young , Sung Lim Hong and Eunok Paek. 2000. An English to Korean Transliteration Model of Extended Markov Window. In *Proceedings of International Conference on Computational Linguistics (COLING 2000)*, 383-389.

Knight, K. and Graehl, J. 1998. Machine Transliteration, *Computational Linguistics,* Volume (24:4), 599–612.

Kumaran, A. and Tobias Kellner. 2007. A generic framework for machine transliteration. In *Proc. of the 30th SIGIR.*

Li, Haizhou, A Kumaran, Min Zhang and Vladimir Pervouchine. 2009. Whitepaper of NEWS 2009 Machine Transliteration Shared Task. In *Proceedings of ACL-IJCNLP 2009 Named Entities Workshop (NEWS 2009)*, Singapore.

Li, Haizhou, A Kumaran, Vladimir Pervouchine and Min Zhang. 2009. Report on NEWS 2009 Machine Transliteration Shared Task. In *Proceedings of ACL-IJCNLP 2009 amed Entities Workshop (NEWS 2009)*, Singapore.

Li, Haizhou, Min Zhang and Su Jian. 2004. A Joint Source-Channel Model for Machine Transliteration. In *Proceedings of the 42nd Annual Meeting of the ACL*, 159-166. Spain.

Marino, J. B., R. Banchs, J. M. Crego, A. de Gispert, P. Lambert, J. A. Fonollosa and M. Ruiz. 2005. Bilingual n-gram Statistical Machine Translation. In *Proceedings of the MT-Summit X*, 275–282.

Surana, Harshit, and Singh, Anil Kumar. 2008. A More Discerning and Adaptable Multilingual Transliteration Mechanism for Indian Languages. In *Proceedings of the 3rd International Joint Conference on Natural Language Processing (IJCNLP-08)*, 64-71, India.

Vigra, Paola and Khudanpur, S. 2003. Transliteration of Proper Names in Cross-Lingual Information Retrieval. In *Proceedings of the ACL 2003 Workshop on Multilingual and Mixed-Language Named Entity Recognition*, 57–60.

Improving transliteration accuracy using word-origin detection and lexicon lookup

Mitesh M. Khapra
IIT Bombay
miteshk@cse.iitb.ac.in

Pushpak Bhattacharyya
IIT Bombay
pb@cse.iitb.ac.in

Abstract

We propose a framework for transliteration which uses (i) a word-origin detection engine (*pre-processing*) (ii) a CRF based transliteration engine and (iii) a re-ranking model based on lexicon-lookup (*post-processing*). The results obtained for *English-Hindi* and *English-Kannada* transliteration show that the pre-processing and post-processing modules improve the top-1 accuracy by 7.1%.

1 Introduction

Machine transliteration is the method of automatically converting Out-Of-Vocabulary (OOV) words in one language to their phonetic equivalents in another language. An attempt is made to retain the original pronunciation of the source word to as great an extent as allowed by the orthographic and phonological rules of the target language. This is not a great challenge for language pairs like Hindi-Marathi which have very similar alphabetic and phonetic sets. However, the problem becomes non-trivial for language pairs like English-Hindi and English-Kannada which have reasonably different alphabet sets and sound systems.

Machine transliteration find its application in *Cross-Lingual Information Retrieval (CLIR)* and *Machine Translation (MT)*. In CLIR, machine transliteration can help in translating the OOV terms like proper names and technical terms which frequently appear in the source language queries (*e.g.* Jaipur in "Jaipur palace"). Similarly it can help improve the performance of MT by translating proper names and technical terms which are not present in the translation dictionary.

Current models for transliteration can be classified as *grapheme-based models*, *phoneme-based models* and *hybrid models*. Grapheme-based models like source channel model (Lee and Choi, 1998), Maximum Entropy Model (Goto et al., 2003), Conditional Random Fields (Veeravalli et al., 2008) and Decision Trees (Kang and Choi, 2000) treat transliteration as an orthographic process and try to map the source graphemes directly to the target graphemes. Phoneme based models like the ones based on Weighted Finite State Transducers (WFST) (Knight and Graehl, 1997) and extended Markov window (Jung et al., 2000) treat transliteration as a phonetic process rather than an orthographic process. Under this framework, transliteration is treated as a conversion from source grapheme to source phoneme followed by a conversion from source phoneme to target grapheme. Hybrid models either use a combination of a grapheme based model and a phoneme based model (Stalls and Knight, 1998) or capture the correspondence between source graphemes and source phonemes to produce target language graphemes (Oh and Choi, 2002).

Combining any of the above transliteration engines with pre-processing modules like word-origin detection (Oh and Choi, 2002) and/or post-processing modules like re-ranking using clues from monolingual resources (Al-Onaizan and Knight, 2002) can enhance the performance of the system. We propose such a framework which uses (i) language model based word-origin detection (ii) CRF based transliteration engine and (iii) a re-ranking model based on lexicon lookup on the target language (Hindi and Kannada in our case).

The roadmap of the paper is as follows. In section 2 we describe the 3 components of the proposed framework. In section 3 we present the results for English-Hindi and English-Kannada transliteration on the datasets (Kumaran and Kellner, 2007) released for NEWS 2009 Machine Transliteration Shared Task[1](Haizhou et al., 2009). Section 4 concludes the paper.

[1]https://translit.i2r.a-star.edu.sg/news2009/

Proceedings of the 2009 Named Entities Workshop, ACL-IJCNLP 2009, pages 84–87,
Suntec, Singapore, 7 August 2009. ©2009 ACL and AFNLP

2 Proposed framework for Transliteration

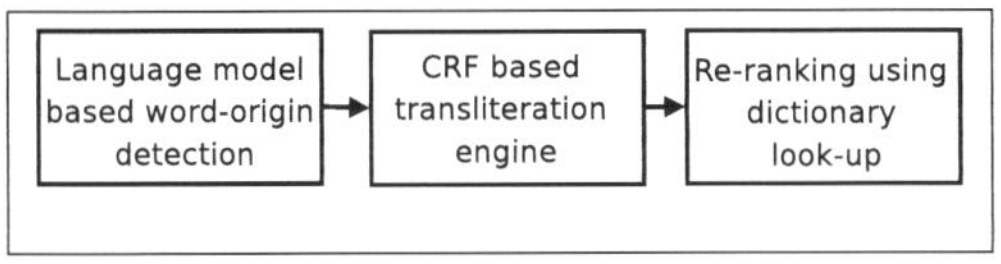

Figure 1: Proposed framework for transliteration.

2.1 Word Origin Detection

To emphasize the importance of Word Origin Detection we consider the example of letter *'d'*. When *'d'* appears in a name of Western origin (*e.g. Daniel, Durban*) and is not followed by the letter *'h'*, it invariably gets transliterated as Hindi letter ड, whereas, if it appears in a name of Indic origin (*e.g. Indore, Jharkhand*) then it is equally likely to be transliterated as द or ड. This shows that the decision is influenced by the origin of the word. The Indic dataset (Hindi, Kannada, and Tamil) for the Shared Task consisted of a mix of Indic and Western names. We therefore felt the need of training separate models for words of Indic origin and words of Western origin.

For this we needed to separate the words in the training data based on their origin. We first manually classified 3000 words from the training set into words of Indic origin and Western origin. These words were used as seed input for the bootstrapping algorithm described below:

1. Build two n-gram language models: one for the already classified names of Indic origin and another for the names of Western origin. Here, by n-gram we mean n-character obtained by splitting the words into a sequence of characters.

2. Split each of the remaining words into a sequence of characters and find the probability of this sequence using the two language models constructed in step 1.

3. If the probability of a word (i.e. a sequence of characters) is higher in the Indic language model than in the Western language model then classify it as Indic word else classify it as Western word.

4. Repeat steps 1-3 till all words have been classified.

Thus, we classified the entire training set into words of Indic origin and words of Western origin. The two language models (one for words of Indic origin and another for words of Western origin) thus obtained were then used to classify the test data using steps 2 and 3 of the above algorithm. Manual verification showed that this method was able to determine the origin of the words in the test data with an accuracy of 97%.

2.2 CRF based transliteration engine

Conditional Random Fields (Lafferty et al., 2001) are undirected graphical models used for labeling sequential data. Under this model, the conditional probability distribution of the target word given the source word is given by,

$$P(Y|X;\lambda) = \frac{1}{Z(X)} \cdot e^{\sum_{t=1}^{T} \sum_{k=1}^{K} \lambda_k f_k(Y_{t-1}, Y_t, X, t)} \quad (1)$$

where,

$$\begin{aligned} X &= source\ word\ (English) \\ Y &= target\ word\ (Hindi, Kannada) \\ T &= length\ of\ source\ word\ (English) \\ K &= number\ of\ features \\ \lambda_k &= feature\ weight \\ Z(X) &= normalization\ constant \end{aligned}$$

CRF++[2] which is an open source implementation of CRF was used for training and decoding. GIZA++ (Och and Ney, 2000), which is a freely available implementation of the IBM alignment models (Brown et al., 1993) was used to get character level alignments for English-Hindi word pairs in the training data. Under this alignment, each character in the English word is aligned to zero or more characters in the corresponding Hindi word. The following features are then generated using this character-aligned data (here e_i and h_i are the characters at position i of the source word and target word respectively):

- h_i and e_j such that $i-2 \leq j \leq i+2$
- h_i and source character bigrams ($\{e_{i-1}, e_i\}$ or $\{e_i, e_{i+1}\}$)
- h_i and source character trigrams ($\{e_{i-2}, e_{i-1}, e_i\}$ or $\{e_{i-1}, e_i, e_{i+1}\}$ or $\{e_i, e_{i+1}, e_{i+2}\}$)

[2] http://crfpp.sourceforge.net/

- h_i, h_{i-1} and e_j such that $i-2 \leq j \leq i+2$
- h_i, h_{i-1} and source character bigrams
- h_i, h_{i-1} and source character trigrams

Two separate models were trained: one for the words of Indic origin and another for the words of Western origin. At the time of testing, the words were first classified as Indic origin words and Western origin words using the classifier described in section 2.1. The top-10 transliterations for each word were then generated using the correct CRF model depending on the origin of the word.

2.3 Re-ranking using lexicon lookup

Since the dataset for the Shared Task contains words of Indic origin there is a possibility that the correct transliteration of some of these words may be found in a Hindi lexicon. Such a lexicon containing 90677 unique words was constructed by extracting words from the Hindi Wordnet[3]. If a candidate transliteration generated by the CRF engine is found in this lexicon then its rank is increased and it is moved towards the top of the list. If multiple outputs are found in the lexicon then all such outputs are moved towards the top of the list and the relative ranking of these outputs remains the same as that assigned by the CRF engine. For example, if the 4th and 6th candidate generated by the CRF engine are found in the lexicon then these two candidates will be moved to positions 1 and 2 respectively. We admit that this way of moving candidates to the top of the list is adhoc. Ideally, if the lexicon also stored the frequency of each word then the candidates could be re-ranked using these frequencies. But unfortunately the lexicon does not store such frequency counts.

3 Results

The system was tested for English-Hindi and English-Kannada transliteration using the dataset (Kumaran and Kellner, 2007) released for NEWS 2009 Machine Transliteration Shared Task. We submitted one standard run and one non-standard run for the English-Hindi task and one standard run for the English-Kannada task. The re-ranking module was used only for the non-standard run as it uses resources (lexicon) other than those provided for the task. We did not have a lexicon for Kannada so were not able to apply the re-ranking module for English-Kannada task. The performance of the system was evaluated using 6 measures, *viz.*, Word Accuracy in Top-1 (ACC), Fuzziness in Top-1 (Mean F-score), Mean Reciprocal Rank (MRR), MAP_{ref}, MAP_{10} and MAP_{sys}. Please refer to the white paper of NEWS 2009 Machine Transliteration Shared Task (Haizhou et al., 2009) for more details of these measures.

Table 1 and Table 2 report the results[4] for English-Hindi and English-Kannada transliteration respectively. For English-Hindi we report 3 results: (i) without any pre-processing (word-origin detection) or post-processing (re-ranking) (ii) with pre-processing but no post-processing and (iii) with both pre-processing and post-processing. The results clearly show that the addition of these modules boosts the performance. The use of word-origin detection boosts the top-1 accuracy by around 0.9% and the use of lexicon lookup based re-ranking boosts the accuracy by another 6.2%. Thus, together these two modules give an increment of 7.1% in the accuracy. Corresponding improvements are also seen in the other 5 metrics.

4 Conclusion

We presented a framework for transliteration which uses (i) a word-origin detection engine (*pre-processing*) (ii) a CRF based transliteration engine and (iii) a re-ranking model based on lexicon-lookup (*post-processing*). The results show that this kind of pre-processing and post-processing helps to boost the performance of the transliteration engine. The re-ranking using lexicon lookup is slightly adhoc as ideally the re-ranking should take into account the frequency of the words in the lexicon. Since such frequency counts are not available it would be useful to find the web counts for each transliteration candidate using a search engine and use these web counts to re-rank the candidates.

[3] http://www.cfilt.iitb.ac.in/wordnet/webhwn

[4] Please note that the results reported in this paper are better than the results we submitted to the shared task. This improvement was due to the correction of an error in the template file given as input to CRF++.

Method	ACC	Mean F-score	MRR	MAP_{ref}	MAP_{10}	MAP_{sys}
CRF Engine *(no word origin detection, no re-ranking)*	0.408	0.878	0.534	0.403	0.188	0.188
CRF Engine + Word-Origin detection (no re-ranking) **Standard run**	0.417	0.877	0.546	0.409	0.192	0.192
CRF Engine + Word-Origin detection + Re-ranking **Non-Standard run**	**0.479**	**0.884**	**0.588**	**0.475**	**0.208**	**0.208**

Table 1: Results for English-Kannada transliteration.

Method	Accuracy (top1)	Mean F-score	MRR	MAP_{ref}	MAP_{10}	MAP_{sys}
CRF Engine + Word-Origin detection (no re-ranking) **Standard run**	0.335	0.859	0.453	0.327	0.154	0.154

Table 2: Results for English-Kannada transliteration.

References

B. J. Kang and K. S. Choi 2000. *Automatic transliteration and back-transliteration by decision tree learning*. Proceedings of the 2nd International Conference on Language Resources and Evaluation, 1135-1411.

Bonnie Glover Stalls and Kevin Knight 1998. *Translating Names and Technical Terms in Arabic Text.* Proceedings of COLING/ACL Workshop on Computational Approaches to Semitic Languages, 34-41.

Haizhou Li, A Kumaran, Min Zhang, Vladimir Pervouchine 2009. *Whitepaper of NEWS 2009 Machine Transliteration Shared Task.* Proceedings of ACL-IJCNLP 2009 Named Entities Workshop (NEWS 2009).

I. Goto and N. Kato and N. Uratani and T. Ehara 2003. *Transliteration considering context information based on the maximum entropy method.* Proceedings of MT-Summit IX, 125132.

J. S. Lee and K. S. Choi. 1998. *English to Korean statistical transliteration for information retrieval.* Computer Processing of Oriental Languages, 17-37.

John Lafferty, Andrew McCallum, Fernando Pereira 2001. *Conditional Random Fields: Probabilistic Models for Segmenting and Labeling Sequence Data.* In Proceedings of the Eighteenth International Conference on Machine Learning.

Jong-hoon Oh and Key-sun Choi 2002. *An English-Korean Transliteration Model Using Pronunciation and Contextual Rules.* Proceedings of the 19th International Conference on Computational Linguistics (COLING), 758-764.

Kevin Knight and Jonathan Graehl 1997. *Machine transliteration.* Computational Linguistics, 128-135.

Kumaran, A. and Kellner, Tobias 2007. *A generic framework for machine transliteration.* SIGIR '07: Proceedings of the 30th annual international ACM SIGIR conference on Research and development in information retrieval, 721-722.

Och Franz Josef and Hermann Ney 2000. *Improved Statistical Alignment Models.* Proc. of the 38th Annual Meeting of the Association for Computational Linguistics, pp. 440-447

P. F. Brown, S. A. Della Pietra, and R. L. Mercer 1993. *The mathematics of statistical machine translation: Parameter estimation.* Computational Linguistics, 19(2):263-311.

Sung Young Jung and SungLim Hong and Eunok Paek 2000. *An English to Korean transliteration model of extended Markov window.* Proceedings of the 18th conference on Computational linguistics, 383-389.

Suryaganesh Veeravalli and Sreeharsha Yella and Prasad Pingali and Vasudeva Varma 2008. *Statistical Transliteration for Cross Language Information Retrieval using HMM alignment model and CRF.* Proceedings of the 2nd workshop on Cross Lingual Information Access (CLIA) Addressing the Information Need of Multilingual Societies.

Yaser Al-Onaizan and Kevin Knight 2001. *Translating named entities using monolingual and bilingual resources.* ACL '02: Proceedings of the 40th Annual Meeting on Association for Computational Linguistics, 400-408.

A Noisy Channel Model for Grapheme-based Machine Transliteration

Yuxiang Jia, Danqing Zhu, Shiwen Yu
Institute of Computational Linguistics, Peking University, Beijing, China
Key Laboratory of Computational Linguistics, Ministry of Education, China
{yxjia,zhudanqing,yusw}@pku.edu.cn

Abstract

Machine transliteration is an important Natural Language Processing task. This paper proposes a Noisy Channel Model for Grapheme-based machine transliteration. Moses, a phrase-based Statistical Machine Translation tool, is employed for the implementation of the system. Experiments are carried out on the NEWS 2009 Machine Transliteration Shared Task English-Chinese track. English-Chinese back transliteration is studied as well.

1 Introduction

Transliteration is defined as phonetic translation of names across languages. Transliteration of Named Entities is necessary in many applications, such as machine translation, corpus alignment, cross-language information retrieval, information extraction and automatic lexicon acquisition.

The transliteration modeling approaches can be classified into phoneme-based, grapheme-based and hybrid approach of phoneme and grapheme.

Many previous studies are devoted to the phoneme-based approach (Knight and Graehl, 1998; Virga and Khudanpur, 2003). Suppose that E is an English name and C is its Chinese transliteration. The phoneme-based approach first converts E into an intermediate phonemic representation p, and then converts p into its Chinese counterpart C. The idea is to transform both source and target names into comparable phonemes so that the phonetic similarity between two names can be measured easily.

The grapheme-based approach has also attracted much attention (Li et al., 2004). It treats the transliteration as a statistical machine translation problem under monotonic constraint. The idea is to obtain the bilingual orthographical correspondence directly to reduce the possible errors introduced in multiple conversions.

The hybrid approach attempts to utilize both phoneme and grapheme information for transliteration. (Oh and Choi, 2006) proposed a way to fuse both phoneme and grapheme features into a single learning process.

The rest of this paper is organized as follows. Section 2 briefly describes the noisy channel model for machine transliteration. Section 3 introduces the model's implementation details. Experiments and analysis are given in section 4. Conclusions and future work are discussed in section 5.

2 Noisy Channel Model

Machine transliteration can be regarded as a noisy channel problem. Take the English-Chinese transliteration as an example. An English name E is considered as the output of the noisy channel with its Chinese transliteration C as the input. The transliteration process is as follows. The language model generates a Chinese name C, and the transliteration model converts C into its back-transliteration E. The channel decoder is used to find $\hat{C}$ that is the most likely to the word C that gives rise to E. $\hat{C}$ is the result transliteration of E.

The process can be formulated with equation 1.

$$\hat{C} = \arg\max_{C} P(C \mid E) = \arg\max_{C} \frac{P(C)P(E \mid C)}{P(E)} \quad (1)$$

Since $P(E)$ is constant for the given E, we can rewrite equation 1 as follows:

$$\hat{C} = \arg\max_{C} P(C)P(E \mid C) \quad (2)$$

The language model $P(C)$ is simplified as n-gram model of Chinese characters and is trained with a Chinese name corpus. The transliteration model $P(E|C)$ is estimated from a parallel corpus of English names and their Chinese transliterations. The channel decoder combines the lan-

Proceedings of the 2009 Named Entities Workshop, ACL-IJCNLP 2009, pages 88–91,
Suntec, Singapore, 7 August 2009.

guage model and transliteration model to generate Chinese transliterations for given English names.

3 Implementation

Moses (Koehn et al., 2007), a phrase-based statistical machine translation tool, is leveraged to implement the noisy channel model for grapheme-based machine transliteration without reordering process (Matthews, 2007). Figure 1 is an illustration of the phrase alignment result in machine transliteration of the name pairs "Clinton" and "克林顿", where characters are as words and combinations of characters are as phrases.

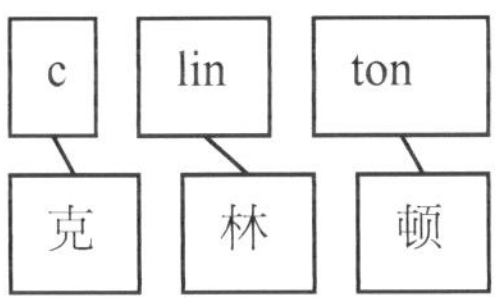

Figure 1. Example phrase alignment

A collection of tools are used by Moses. SRILM is used to build statistical language models. GIZA++ is used to perform word alignments over parallel corpora. Mert is used for weight optimization. It includes several improvements to the basic training method including randomized initial conditions and permuted model order and dynamic parameter range expansion or restriction. Bleu, an automatic machine translation evaluation metric, is used during Mert optimization. Moses' beam-search decoding algorithm is an efficient search algorithm that quickly finds the highest probability translation among the exponential number of choices.

Moses automatically trains translation models for any language pairs with only a collection of parallel corpora. The parallel transliteration corpora need to be preprocessed at first. English names need to be lowercased. Both English names and Chinese transliterations are space delimited. Samples of preprocessed input are shown in figure 2.

a a b y e	奥 比
a a g a a r d	埃 格 德
a a l l i b o n e	阿 利 本
a a l t o	阿 尔 托
a a m o d t	阿 莫 特

Figure 2. Sample preprocessed name pairs

4 Experiments

This section describes the data sets, experimental setup, experiment results and analysis.

4.1 Data Sets

The training set contains 31961 paired names between English and Chinese. The development set has 2896 pairs. 2896 English names are given to test the English-Chinese transliteration performance.

Some statistics on the training data are shown in table 1. All the English-Chinese transliteration pairs are distinct. English names are unique while some English names may share the same Chinese transliteration. So the total number of unique Chinese names is less than that of English names. The Chinese characters composing the Chinese transliterations are limited, where there are only 370 unique characters in the 25033 Chinese names. Supposing that the name length is computed as the number of characters it contains, the average length of English names is about twice that of Chinese names. Name length is useful when considering the order of the character n-gram language model.

#unique transliteration pairs	31961
#unique English names	31961
#unique Chinese names	25033
#unique Chinese characters	370
Average number of English characters per name	6.8231
Average number of Chinese characters per name	3.1665
Maximum number of English characters per name	15
Maximum number of Chinese characters per name	7

Table 1. Training data statistics

4.2 Experimental setup

Both English-Chinese forward transliteration and back transliteration are studied. The process can be divided into four steps: language model building, transliteration model training, weight tuning, and decoding. When building language model, data smoothing techniques Kneser-Ney and interpolate are employed. In transliteration model training step, the alignment heuristic is grow-diag-final, while other parameters are default settings. Tuning parameters are all defaults. When decoding, the parameter distortion-limit is set to 0, meaning that no reordering operation is needed. The system outputs the 10-best distinct transliterations.

The whole training set is used for language model building and transliteration model training. The development set is used for weight tuning and system testing.

4.3 Evaluation Metrics

The following 6 metrics are used to measure the quality of the transliteration results (Li et al., 2009a): Word Accuracy in Top-1 (ACC), Fuzziness in Top-1 (Mean F-score), Mean Reciprocal Rank (MRR), MAP_{ref}, MAP_{10}, and MAP_{sys}.

In the data of English-Chinese transliteration track, each source name only has one reference transliteration. Systems are required to output the 10-best unique transliterations for every source name. Thus, MAP_{ref} equals ACC, and MAP_{sys} is the same or very close to MAP_{10}. So we only choose ACC, Mean F-score, MRR, and MAP_{10} to show the system performance.

4.4 Results

The language model n-gram order is an important factor impacting transliteration performance, so we experiment on both forward and back transliteration tasks with increasing n-gram order, trying to find the order giving the best performance. Here the development set is used for testing.

Figure 3 and 4 show the results of forward and back transliteration respectively, where the performances become steady when the order reaches 6 and 11. The orders with the best performance in all metrics for forward and back transliteration are 2 and 5, which may relate to the average length of Chinese and English names.

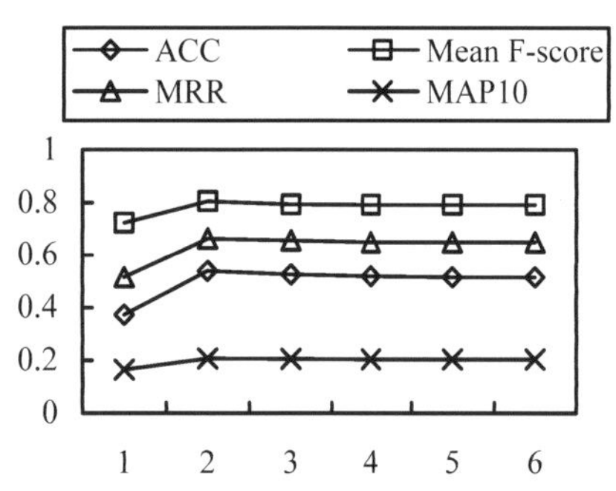

Figure 3. E2C language model n-gram (forward)

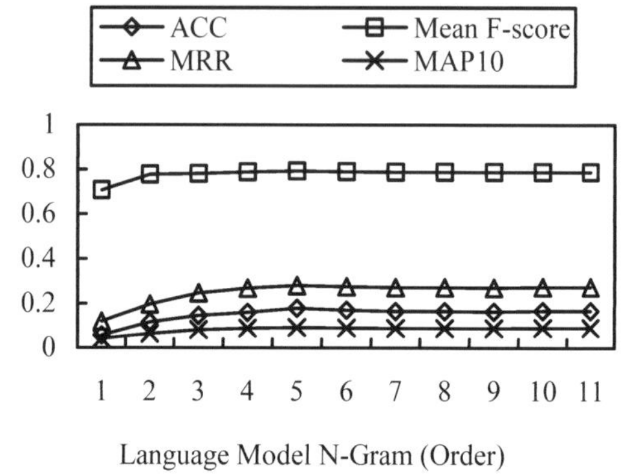

Figure 4. E2C language model n-gram (back)

Weights generated in the training step can be optimized through the tuning process. The development set, 2896 name pairs, is divided into 4 equal parts, 1 for testing and other 3 for tuning. We take the best settings as the baseline, and increase tuning size by 1 part at one time. Table 2 and 3 show the tuning results of forward and back transliteration, where the best results are boldfaced. Tuning set size of 0 refers to the best settings before tuning. Performances get improved after tuning, among which the ACC of forward transliteration gets improved by over 11%. The forward transliteration performance gets improved steadily with the increase of tuning set size, while the back transliteration performance peaks at tuning set size of 2.

Tuning size	ACC	Mean F-score	MRR	MAP_{10}
0	0.543	0.797	0.669	0.209
1	0.645	0.851	0.752	0.231
2	0.645	0.850	0.749	0.230
3	**0.655**	**0.854**	**0.758**	**0.233**

Table 2. E2C tuning performance (forward)

Tuning size	ACC	Mean F-score	MRR	MAP_{10}
0	0.166	0.790	0.278	0.092
1	0.181	0.801	0.306	0.102
2	**0.190**	**0.806**	**0.314**	**0.104**
3	0.187	0.801	0.312	0.104

Table 3. E2C tuning performance (back)

Table 2 shows that forward transliteration performance gets improved with the increase of tuning set size, so we use the whole development set as the tuning set to tune the final system and the final official results from the shared task report (Li et al., 2009b) are shown in table 4.

ACC	Mean F-score	MRR	MAP_{ref}	MAP_{10}	MAP_{sys}
0.652	0.858	0.755	0.652	0.232	0.232

Table 4. The final official results of E2C forward

Experiments show that forward transliteration has better performance than back transliteration. One reason may be that on average English name is longer than Chinese name, thus need more data to train a good character level language model. Another reason is that some information is lost during transliteration which can not be recovered in back transliteration. One more very important reason is as follows. Typically in back transliteration, you have only one correct reference transliteration, and therefore, a wide coverage word level language model is very useful. Without it, back transliteration may have a poor performance.

5 Conclusions and future work

This paper proposes a Noisy Channel Model for grapheme-based machine transliteration. The phrase-based statistical machine translation tool, Moses, is leveraged for system implementation. We participate in the NEWS 2009 Machine Transliteration Shared Task English-Chinese track. English-Chinese back transliteration is also studied. This model is language independent and can be applied to transliteration of any language pairs.

To improve system performance, extensive error analyses will be made in the future and methods will be proposed according to different error types. We will pay much attention to back transliteration for its seemingly greater difficulty and explore relations between forward and back transliteration to seek a strategy solving the two simultaneously.

Acknowledgements

The authors are grateful to the organizers of the NEWS 2009 Machine Transliteration Shared Task for their hard work to provide such a good research platform. The work in this paper is supported by a grant from the National Basic Research Program of China (No.2004CB318102) and a grant from the National Natural Science Foundation of China (No.60773173).

References

K. Knight and J. Graehl. 1998. Machine Transliteration. Computational Linguistics, Vol. 24, No. 4, pp. 599-612.

P. Virga and S. Khudanpur. 2003. Transliteration of Proper Names in Cross-lingual Information Retrieval. In Proceedings of the ACL Workshop on Multi-lingual Named Entity Recognition 2003.

H.Z. Li, M. Zhang and J. Su. 2004. A Joint Source Channel Model for Machine Transliteration. In Proceedings of the 42nd ACL, pp. 159-166.

J.H. Oh and K.S. Choi. 2006. An Ensemble of Transliteration Models for Information Retrieval. In Information Processing and Management, Vol. 42, pp. 980-1002.

P. Koehn, H. Hoang, A. Birch, C. Callison-Burch, M. Federico, N. Bertoldi, B. Cowan, W. Shen, C. Moran, R. Zens, C. Dyer, O. Bojar, A. Constantin and E. Herbst. 2007. Moses: Open Source Toolkit for Statistical Machine Translation. In Proceedings of the 45th ACL Companion Volume of the Demo and Poster Sessions, pp. 177-180.

D. Matthews. 2007. Machine Transliteration of Proper Names. Master thesis. University of Edinburgh.

H.Z. Li, A. Kumaran, M. Zhang and V. Pervouchine. 2009a. Whitepaper of NEWS 2009 Machine Transliteration Shared Task. In Proceedings of ACL-IJCNLP 2009 Named Entities Workshop (NEWS 2009), Singapore.

H.Z. Li, A. Kumaran, V. Pervouchine and M. Zhang. 2009b. Report on NEWS 2009 Machine Transliteration Shared Task. In Proceedings of ACL-IJCNLP 2009 Named Entities Workshop (NEWS 2009), Singapore.

Substring-based Transliteration with Conditional Random Fields

Sravana Reddy and **Sonjia Waxmonsky**
Department of Computer Science
The University of Chicago
Chicago, IL 60637
{sravana, wax}@cs.uchicago.edu

Abstract

Motivated by phrase-based translation research, we present a transliteration system where characters are grouped into substrings to be mapped atomically into the target language. We show how this substring representation can be incorporated into a Conditional Random Field model that uses local context and phonemic information.

1 Introduction

We present a transliteration system that is motivated by research in phrase-based machine translation. In particular, we borrow the concept of *phrases*, which are groups of words that are translated as a unit. These phrases correspond to multi-character *substrings* in our transliteration task. That is, source and target language strings are treated not as sequences of characters but as sequences of non-overlapping substrings.

We model transliteration as a *sequential labeling task* where substring tokens in the source language are labeled with tokens in the target language. This is done using Conditional Random Fields (CRFs), which are undirected graphical models that maximize the posterior probabilities of the label sequence given the input sequence. We use as features both *local contexts* and *phonemic information* acquired from an English pronunciation dictionary.

2 The Transliteration Process

Our transliteration system has the following steps:

1. **Pre-processing** of the target language.
2. **Substring alphabet generation** for both the source and target. This step also generates training data for the CRFs in Step 3 and 4.
3. **CRF training** on aligned data from Step 2.
4. **Substring segmentation and transliteration** of source language input.

Our training and test data consists of three sets – English to Hindi, English to Kannada, and English to Tamil (Kumaran and Kellner, 2007) – from the NEWS 2009 Machine Transliteration Shared Task (Li et al., 2009).

2.1 Step 1: Pre-Processing

The written words of Hindi, Tamil, and Kannada correspond almost perfectly to their phonological forms, with each character mapping to a phoneme. The only exception to this arises from the implicit vowel (which may be a schwa /ə/ or a central vowel /ɐ/) that is inserted after consonants that are not followed by the *halanta* or 'killer stroke'. Hence, any mappings of an English vowel to a target language schwa will not be reflected in the alignment of the named entity pair.

To minimize misalignments of target language strings with the English strings during training, we convert the Indic abugida strings to an internal phonemic representation. The conversion maps each unicode character to its corresponding phonemic character and inserts a single symbol (representing the schwa/central vowel) after all consonants that are not followed by the *halanta*.

These phoneme sequences are used as the internal representation of Indic character strings for all later steps in our system. Once transliteration is complete, the phonemic symbols are converted back to unicode by reversing the above process.

2.2 Step 2: Substring alphabet generation

Our decision to use substrings in the transliteration task is motivated by the differences in orthography and phonology between the target and source languages, which prevent trivial one-to-one character level alignment. We first discuss the cause of the poor character alignment between English and the

Proceedings of the 2009 Named Entities Workshop, ACL-IJCNLP 2009, pages 92–95,
Suntec, Singapore, 7 August 2009.

Indic languages, and then describe how we transform the input into substring representation.

English uses several digraphs for phonemes that are represented by single characters in Indic scripts, which are either part of standard orthographic convention (*oo*, *ch*, etc.), or necessitated by the lack of a single phoneme that approximates an Indic one (as in the case of aspirated consonants). Conversely, English sometimes uses a single character for a biphone (such as *x* for /ks/, or *u* for /ju/ as in *museum*), which is represented by two characters in the target languages. In certain cases, a digraph in English is transliterated to a digraph in the target, as a result of metathesis (*le* → /əl/, in words like *temple*). Further, all three target languages often insert vowels between English consonant clusters; for instance, Hindi inserts a schwa between *s* and *p* in 'transport', transliterated as ʈrɑnsəporʈ (ट्रांसपोर्ट).

To handle these cases, we borrow the concept of *phrases* from machine translation (Och and Ney, 2004), where groups of words are translated as a unit. In the case of transliteration, the 'phrases' are commonly occurring *substrings* – sequences of characters – in one language that map to a character or a substring in the other. We use the term 'substrings' after a previous work (Sherif and Kondrak, 2007) that employs it in a noisy channel transliteration system. Zhao et al. (2007) also use substrings (which they call 'blocks') in a bi-stream HMM.

We bootstrap the induction of substrings by aligning all named entity pairs in the training data, using the GIZA++ toolkit (Och and Ney, 2003). The toolkit performs *unidirectional one-to-many* alignments, meaning that a single symbol in its source string can be aligned to *at most one* symbol in its target. In order to induce many-to-many alignments, GIZA++ is run on the data in both directions (source language to target language and target language to source), and the bidirectional alignment of a named entity pair is taken to be the union of the alignments in each direction. Any inserted characters (maps within the alignment where the source or target character is *null*) are combined with the preceding character within the string. For example, the initial bidirectional alignment of *shivlal* → ʃivəlɑl (शिवलाल) contains the maps [*sh* → ʃ, *i* → i, *v* → v, *null* → ə, *l* → l, *a* → ɑ, and *l* → l]. The *null* → ə map is combined with the preceding map to give *v* → və, and hence a one-to-one alignment.

Multicharacter units formed by bidirectional alignments are added to source and target alphabets. The above example would add the substrings 'sh' to the source alphabet, and və to the target. Very low frequency substrings in both languages are removed, giving the final substring alphabets of single and multicharacter tokens. These alphabets (summarized in Table 1) are used as the token set for the CRF in Step 3.

We now transform our training data into a substring-based representation. The original named entity pairs are replaced by their bidirectional one-to-one alignments described earlier. For example, the ⟨*s h i v l a l*⟩ → ⟨ʃ i v ə l ɑ l⟩ training pair is replaced by ⟨*sh i v l a l*⟩ → ⟨ʃ i və l ɑ l⟩. A few (less than 3%) of the pairs are *not* aligned one-to-one, since their bidirectional alignments contain low-frequency substrings that have not been included in the alphabet.[1] These pairs are removed from the training data, since only one-to-one alignments can be handled by the CRF.

2.3 Step 3: CRF transliteration

With the transformed training data in hand, we can now train a CRF sequential model that uses substrings rather than characters as the basic token unit. The CRF algorithm is chosen for its ability to handle non-independent features of the source language input sequence. We use the open-source CRF++ software package (Kudo, 2005).

Ganesh et al. (2008) also apply a CRF to the transliteration task (Hindi to English) but with different alignment methods than those presented here. In particular, multicharacter substrings are only used as tokens on the target (English) side, and a null token is used to account for deletion.

We train our CRF using unigram, bigram, and trigram features over the source substrings, as well as pronunciation information described in §2.3.1. Table 2 describes these feature sets.

2.3.1 Phonetic information

Since the CRF model allows us to incorporate non-independent features, we add pronunciation data as a token-level feature. Doing so allows the CRF to use phonetic information for local decision-making. Word pronunciations were obtained from

[1] Note that if we did not filter out any of the substrings, every pair would be aligned one-to-one.

Target Language	Source		Target	
	# of Tokens	Longest Token	# of Tokens	Longest Token
Hindi	196	*augh*, *ough*	141	ɑjə (आय), ksə (क्स)
Kannada	197	*aine*	137	ɑjə, mjɑ
Tamil	179	*cque*	117	mij, ɑjə

Table 1: Overview of the substring alphabets generated in Step 2.

Feature Set	Description
U	Unigram: s_{-1}, s_0, and s_1
B	Bigram: $s_{-1}+s_0$
T	Trigram: $s_{-2}+s_{-1}+s_0$, $s_{-1}+s_0+s_1$ and $s_0+s_1+s_2$
P	Phoneme assigned to s_0 from dictionary lookup

Table 2: Feature sets used for CRF in Step 3. s_i is the substring relative to the current substring s_0.

the CMU Pronouncing Dictionary[2]. Just over a third of the English named entities have pronunciation information available for some or all the constituent words.

The CMU dictionary provides a sequence of phoneme symbols for an English word. We include these phonemes as CRF features if and only if a one-to-one correspondence exists between phonemes and substring tokens. For example, the English word *simon* has the segmentation ⟨*s i m o n*⟩ and pronunciation ⟨*S AY M AH N*⟩, both of length five. Additionally, a check is done to ensure that vowel phonemes do not align with consonant characters and vice-versa.

2.4 Step 4: Substring segmentation

In order to apply our trained model to unseen data, we must segment named entities into non-overlapping substrings that correspond to tokens in the source alphabet generated in Step 2. For instance, we need to convert the four character *desh* to the three token sequence ⟨*d e sh*⟩.

This is a non-trivial task. We must allow for the fact that substrings are not inserted *every* time the component character sequence appears. For instance, in our English/Hindi training set, the bigram *ti* always reduces to a single substring token when it occurs in the *-tion* suffix, but does not reduce in any other contexts (like *martini*). There are also cases where more than one non-trivial segmentation is possible. For example, two possible segmentations of *desh* are ⟨*d es h*⟩ and ⟨*d e sh*⟩, with the latter being the one that best corresponds to the three-character Hindi d̪eʃ (देश).

One solution is to greedily choose the most likely multi-character substring – in the example cited, we can choose ⟨*d e sh*⟩ because *sh* reduces more frequently than *es*. However, this creates the problem in cases where no reduction should occur, as with the *ti* in *martini*. Since contextual information is necessary to determine the correct substring segmentation, we model segmentation with a CRF, using a combination of character unigram, bigram, and trigram features.

We use an approach motivated by the Inside/Outside representation of NP-chunking which treats segmentation as a tagging process over words (Ramshaw and Marcus, 1995). As in NP-chunking, our goal is to identify non-overlapping, non-recursive segments in our input sequence. Our tagset is {**I**, **O**, **B**} where **I** indicates that a character is inside a substring, **O** indicates a character is outside a substring, and **B** marks a right boundary.

After the test data has been segmented into its substring representation, it can be passed as input to the CRF model trained in Step 3 to produce our final transliteration output.

3 Results

We first report our results on the development data provided by the NEWS task, for different feature sets and segmentation methods. We then present the performance of our system on the test data.[3]

3.1 Development Data

Table 3 shows the results across feature sets. Noting that the trigram feature **T** provides a sizable improvement, we compare results from **U+B+T+P** and **U+B+P** feature sets. Of the improved cases, 75-84% are a single vowel-to-vowel

[2]The CMU Pronouncing Dictionary (v0.7a). Available at http://www.speech.cs.cmu.edu/cgi-bin/cmudict

[3]For the development runs, we use the *training* set for training, and the *development* for testing. For the final test runs, we use both the *training* and *development* sets for training, and the *test* set for evaluation.

Language	Feature Set	ACC	F-Score
Hindi	U+P	24.6	86.2
	U+B+P	26.2	86.5
	U+B+T+P	**34.5**	**88.6**
	U+B+T	34.2	88.3
Tamil	U+P	26.7	87.8
	U+B+P	27.6	88.0
	U+B+T+P	**34.9**	**89.8**
	U+B+T	33.1	89.7
Kannada	U+P	22.5	86.0
	U+B+P	22.6	86.2
	U+B+T+P	**28.7**	**88.0**
	U+B+T	27.5	87.9

Table 3: Accuracy (ACC) and F-score results (in %) for CRF model on the ***development data***.

Language	Feature Set	ACC	F-Score
Hindi	**U+B+T+P**	**34.4**	**90.2**
	U+B+T	33.6	89.5
Tamil	**U+B+T+P**	**29.1**	**91.1**
	U+B+T	25.5	90.6
Kannada	**U+B+T+P**	**27.2**	**89.8**
	U+B+T	23.4	89.2

Table 4: Results on development data, restricted to NEs where **P** is included as a feature.

change, with the majority of the changes involving a schwa/central vowel.

We see small gains from using the phonetic feature in both accuracy and F-Score. We further examine only those named entities where dictionary information is applied, and as expected, this subset shows greater improvement (Table 4).

Table 5 compares our the Inside/Outside tagging approach with a greedy approach described earlier. The greedy approach only inserts a multi-character substring when that substring reduces more than 50% of the time in the overall training corpus. Since the Greedy method uses no local contextual information, results are significantly lower given the same feature set.

Language	Segmentation	ACC	F-Score
Hindi	I-O-B	**34.5**	**88.6**
	Greedy	30.3	86.7
Tamil	I-O-B	**34.9**	**89.8**
	Greedy	28.2	87.5
Kannada	I-O-B	**28.7**	**88.0**
	Greedy	25.0	86.7

Table 5: Comparison of segmentation methods on development data, using the **U+B+T+P** feature set.

3.2 Test Data

Our model produces 10 candidates for each named entity in the test data, ranked by the probability that the model assigns the candidate. We filter out candidates below the rank of 5 whose scores are less than 0.5 lower than that of the highest ranking candidate. Table 6 shows our results on the test data, using a CRF trained on the training and development data, with the feature set **U+B+T+P**.

	Hindi	Kannada	Tamil
Accuracy	41.8	36.3	43.5
F-Score	87.9	87.0	90.2
MRR	54.6	48.2	57.2
MAP_{ref}	41.2	35.5	43.0
MAP_{10}	18.3	16.4	19.5
MAP_{sys}	24.0	21.8	26.5

Table 6: Final results on the ***test data*** (in %).

References

Surya Ganesh, Sree Harsh, Prasad Pingali, and Vasudeva Varma. 2008. Statistical transliteration for cross language information retrieval using HMM alignment model and CRF. In *Proceedings of the 2nd Workshop on Cross Lingual Information Access*.

Taku Kudo. 2005. CRF++: Yet another CRF toolkit. Available at http://chasen.org/ taku/software/crf++/.

A. Kumaran and Tobias Kellner. 2007. A generic framework for machine transliteration. In *Proceedings of SIGIR-07*.

Haizhou Li, A Kumaran, Min Zhang, and Vladimir Pervouchine. 2009. Whitepaper of NEWS 2009 machine transliteration shared task. In *Proceedings of ACL-IJCNLP 2009 Named Entities Workshop (NEWS 2009)*.

Franz Josef Och and Hermann Ney. 2003. A systematic comparison of various statistical alignment models. *Computational Linguistics*, 29(1):19–51.

Franz Josef Och and Hermann Ney. 2004. The alignment template approach to statistical machine translation. *Computational Linguistics*, 30(4):417–449.

Lance Ramshaw and Mitch Marcus. 1995. Text chunking using transformation-based learning. In *Proceedings of WVLC-3*.

Tarek Sherif and Grzegorz Kondrak. 2007. Substring-based transliteration. In *Proceedings of ACL-07*.

Bing Zhao, Nguyen Bach, Ian Lane, and Stephan Vogel. 2007. A log-linear block transliteration model based on bi-stream HMMs. In *Proceedings of NAACL HLT 2007*.

A Syllable-based Name Transliteration System

Xue Jiang [1,2]
[1]Institute of Software, Chinese Academy of Science. Beijing China, 100190
jiangxue1024@yahoo.com.cn

Le Sun [1], Dakun Zhang [1]
[2]School of Software Engineering, Huazhong University of Science and Technology. Wuhan China, 430074
sunle@iscas.ac.cn
dakun04@iscas.ac.cn

Abstract

This paper describes the name entity transliteration system which we conducted for the "NEWS2009 Machine Transliteration Shared Task" (Li et al 2009). We get the transliteration in Chinese from an English name with three steps. We syllabify the English name into a sequence of syllables by some rules, and generate the most probable Pinyin sequence with the mapping model of English syllables to Pinyin (EP model), then we convert the Pinyin sequence into a Chinese character sequence with the mapping model of Pinyin to characters (PC model). And we get the final Chinese character sequence. Our system achieves an ACC of 0.498 and a Mean F-score of 0.786 in the official evaluation result.

1 Introduction

The main subject of shared task is to translate English names (source language) to Chinese names (target language). Firstly, we fix some rules and syllabify the English names into a sequence of syllables by these rules, in the meanwhile, we convert the Chinese names into Pinyin sequence. Secondly, we construct an EP model referring to the method of phrase-based machine translation. In the next, we construct a 2-gram language model on characters and a chart reflecting the using frequency of each character with the same pronunciation, both of which constitute the PC model converting Pinyin sequence into character sequence. When a Pinyin is mapped to several different characters, we can use them to make a choice. In our experiment, we adopt the corpus provided by NEWS2009 (Li et al 2004) and the LDC Name Entity Lists [1] respectively to conduct two EP models, while the NEWS2009 corpus for the PC model. The experiment indicates that the larger a training corpus is, the more precise the transliteration is.

2 Transliteration System Description

Knowing from the definition of transliteration, we must make the translating result maintain the original pronunciation in source language. We found that most English letters and letter compositions' pronunciation are relatively fixed, so we can take a syllabification on an English name, therefore the syllable sequence can represent its pronunciation. In Chinese, Pinyin is used to represent a character's pronunciation. Based on these analyses, we transliterate the English syllable sequence into a Pinyin sequence, and then translate the Pinyin sequence into characters.

We suppose that the probability of a transliteration from an English name to a Chinese name is denoted by P(Ch|En), the probability of a translation from an English syllable sequence to a Pinyin sequence is denoted by P(Py|En), and the probability of a translation from a Pinyin sequence to a characters is denoted by P(Ch|Py), then we can get the formula:

$$P(Ch|En) = P(Ch|Py) * P(Py|En) \qquad (1)$$

The character sequence in candidates having the max value of P(Ch|En) is the best transliteration(Wan and Verspoor, 1998).

2.1 Syllabification of English Names

English letters can be divided into vowel letters (VL) and consonant letters (CL). Usually, in a

[1]: Chinese <-> English Name Entity Lists v 1.0, LDC Catalog No.: LDC2005T34

Proceedings of the 2009 Named Entities Workshop, ACL-IJCNLP 2009, pages 96–99,
Suntec, Singapore, 7 August 2009. ©2009 ACL and AFNLP

word, a phonetic syllable can be constructed in a structure of CL+VL, CL+VL+CL, CL+VL+NL. To adapt for Chinese phonetic rule, we divide the continuous CLs into independent CLs(IC) and divide structure of CL+VL+CL into CL+VL and an IC. Take "Ronald" as an example, it can be syllabified into "Ro/na/l/d", "Ro" is CL+VL, "nal" is CL+VL+CL, and is divided into CL+VL and IC. 'd' is an independent CL(KUO et al. 2007). Of course there are some English names more complex to be syllabified, so we define seven rules for syllabification (JIANG et al. 2006):

(1) Define English letter set as O, vowel set as V={a, e, i, o, u}, consonant set as C=O-V.

(2) Replace all "x" in a name with "ks" before syllabification because it's always pronounced as "ks".

(3) The continuous VLs should be regarded as one VL.

(4) There are some special cases in rule (3), the continuous VLs like "oi", "io", "eo" are pronounced as two syllables, so they should be cut into two parts, so "Wilhoit" will be syllabifyd into "wi/l/ho/i/t".

(5) The continuous CLs should be cut into several independent CLs. If the last one is followed by some VLs, they will make up a syllable.

(6) Some continuous CLs are pronounced as a syllable, such as "ck", "th", these CLs will not be syllabifyd and be regarded as a single CL, "Jack" is syllabifyd into "Ja/ck".

(7) There are some other composition with the structure of VL+CL, such as "ing", "er", "an" and so on. If it's a consonant behind these compositions in the name, we can syllabify it at the end of the composition, while if it's a vowel behind them, we should double write the last letter and syllabify the word between the two same letters.

After syllabicating English names, we convert corresponding Chinese names into Pinyin. There are a few characters with multiple pronunciations in the training data, we find them out and ensure its pronunciation in a name manually.

We record all of these syllables got from the training data set, if we meet a syllable out of vocabulary when transliterating an English name, we will find a similar one with the shortest edit-distance in the vocabulary to replace that.

2.2 Mapping Model of English Syllables to Pinyins

The EP model consists of a phrase-based machine translation model with a trigram language model.

Given an English name **f**, we want to find its Chinese translation **e**, which maximize the conditional probability $\Pr(e \mid f)$, as shown below.

$$e^* = \arg\max_e \Pr(e \mid f) \quad (2)$$

Using Bayes rule, (1) can be decomposed into a Translation Model $\Pr(f \mid e)$ and a Language Model $\Pr(e)$ (Brown et al. 1993), which can both be trained separately. These models are usually regarded as features and combined with scaling factors to form a log-linear model (Och and Ney 2002). It can then be written as:

$$\Pr(e \mid f) = p_{\lambda_1^M}(e \mid f) = \frac{\exp[\sum_{m=1}^{M} \lambda_m h_m(e,f)]}{\sum_{e'} \exp[\sum_{m=1}^{M} \lambda_m h_m(e',f)]} \quad (3)$$

In our model, we use the following features:

- phrase translation probability $p(\bar{e} \mid \bar{f})$
- lexical weighting $lex(\bar{e} \mid \bar{f})$
- inverse phrase translation probability $p(\bar{f} \mid \bar{e})$
- inverse lexical weighting $lex(\bar{f} \mid \bar{e})$
- phrase penalty (always exp(1) = 2.718)
- word penalty (target name length)
- target language model, trigram

Thc first five features can be seen as a whole phrase translation cost and used as one during decoding.

In general, the translation process can be described as follows:

(1). Segmenting input English syllable sequence **f** into J syllables $\bar{f}_1^J$

(2). Translating each English syllable $\bar{f}_j$ into several Pinyins $\bar{e}_{jk}$

(3). Selecting the N-best words $e_1 \ldots e_n$, combined with reordering and Language Model and other features

(4). Rescoring the translation word set with additional features to find the best one.

We use SRI toolkit to train our trigram language model with modified Kneser-Ney smoothing (Chen and Goodman 1998). In the standard experiment, we use training data set provided by NEWS2009 (Li et al 2004) to train this language model, in the nonstandard one, we use that and the LDC Name Entity Lists to train this language model.

2.3 Mapping Model of Pinyins to Chinese Characters

Since the Chinese characters used in people names are limited, most of the conversions from Pinyin to character are fixed. But some Pinyins still have several corresponding characters, and we should make a choice among these characters. To solve this problem, we conduct a PC model consisting a frequency chart which reflects the using frequency of each character at different positions in the names and a 2-gram language model with absolute discounting smoothing.

A Chinese name is represented as $C_1C_2\cdots C_n$, C_i ($1 \leqslant i \leqslant n$) is a Chinese character. C_1 is at the first position, we call it FW; $C_2 \cdots C_{n-1}$ are in the middle, we call them MW; C_n is at the last position, we call it LW. Usually, each character has different frequencies at these three positions. In the training data set of NEWS2009, Pinyin "luo" can be mapped to three characters: "罗", "洛", and "萝", each of them has different frequencies at different positions.

	FW	MW	LW
罗	0.677	0.647	0.501
洛	0.323	0.352	0.499
萝	0	0.001	0

Table 1. Different frequencies at different positions

From this table, we can see that at FW and MW position, "罗" is more probable to be chosen than the others, but sometimes "洛" or "萝" is the correct one. In order to ensure characters with lower frequency like "洛" and "萝" can be chosen firstly in a certain context, we conduct a 2-gram language model.

If a Pinyin can be mapped to several characters, the condition probability ($P(Ch_i|py)$) indicating that how possible a character should be chosen is determined by the weighted average of its position frequency ($P(Ch_i|pos)$) and its probability in the 2-gram language model ($P(Ch_i|Ch_{i-1})$).

$$P(Ch_i|py) = a*P(Ch_i|pos)+(1-a)*P(Ch_i|Ch_{i-1}) \quad (4)$$

$0 < a < 1$. In our experiments, we set $a = 0.1$.

2.4 Experiments and Results

We carried out two experiments. The difference between them is the training data for EP model. The standard experiment adopts corpus provided by NEWS2009, while the nonstandard one adopts LDC Name Entity Lists.

Corpora	Name Num
LDC2005T34	572213
NEWS09_train_ench_31961	31961

Table 2. Corpora used for training the EP model

Considering that an English name may be translated to different Chinese names in different corpora, so we established a unique PC model with the training data set provided by NEWS2009 to avoid the model's deviation caused by different corpora.

The experimenting data is the development data set provided by NEWS2009 (Li et al 2004), testing script is also provided by NEWS2009.

First, we take a syllabification on testing names. Then we use the EP model to generate 5-best Pinyin sequences and their probabilities. For each Pinyin sequence, the PC model gives 3-best character sequences and their probabilities. In the end, we sort the results by probabilities of character sequences and corresponding Pinyin sequences.

The evaluation results are shown below.

Metrics	Standard	Nonstandard
ACC	0.490677	0.502417
Mean F-score	0.782039	0.784203
MRR	0.606424	0.611214
MAP_ref	0.490677	0.502417
MAP_10	0.189290	0.189782
MAP_sys	0.191476	0.192129

Table 3. Evaluation results of standard and nonstandard experiments

It's easy to see that nonstandard test is better than standard one on each metric. A larger corpus does make a contribution to a more accurate model.

For the official evaluation, we make two tests on the testing data set provided by NEWS2009 (Li et al 2004). The table 4 shows respectively the evaluation results of standard and nonstandard tests given by NEWS2009.

Metrics	Standard	Nonstandard
ACC	0.498	0.500
Mean F-score	0.786	0.786
MRR	0.603	0.607
MAP_ref	0.498	0.500
MAP_10	0.187	0.189
MAP_sys	0.189	0.191

Table 4. Official evaluation results of standard and nonstandard tests

3 Conclusion

We construct a name entity transliteration system based on syllable. This system syllabifies English names by rules, then translates the syllables to Pinyin and Chinese characters by statistics model. We found that a larger corpus may improve the transliteration. Besides, we can do something else to improve that. We need to fix more complex rules for syllabification. If we can get the name user's gender from some features of the name itself, then translate the male and female names on different Chinese character sets, the results may be more precise.

Acknowledgments

This work was supported by the National Science Foundation of China (60736044, 60773027), as well as 863 Hi-Tech Research and Development Program of China (2006AA010108 -5, 2008AA01Z145).

We also thank Haizhou Li, Min Zhang and Jian Su for providing the English-Chinese data.

Reference

Franz Josef Och and Hermann Ney. 2002. "Discriminative Training and Maximum Entropy Models for Statistical Machine Translation". In *Proceedings of the 40th Annual Meeting of the Association for Computational Linguistics (ACL).*

Haizhou Li, A Kumaran, Min Zhang, Vladimir Pervouchine, "Whitepaper of NEWS 2009 Machine Transliteration Shared Task". In *Proceedings of ACL-IJCNLP 2009 Named Entities Workshop (NEWS 2009)*, Singapore, 2009

Haizhou Li, Min Zhang, Jian Su. 2004. "A joint source channel model for machine transliteration", In *Proceedings of the 42nd ACL*, 2004

Jiang Long, Zhou Ming, and Chien Lee-feng. 2006. "Named Entity Translation with Web Mining and Transliteration". *Journal of Chinese Information Processing*, 21(1):1629--1634.

Jin-Shea Kuo, Haizhou Li, and Ying-Kuei Yang. 2007. "A Phonetic Similarity Model for Automatic Extraction of Transliteration Pairs". *ACM Trans. Asian Language Information Processing*, 6(2), September 2007.

Peter F. Brown, Stephen A. Della Pietra, et al. 1993. "The Mathematics of Statistical Machine Translation: Parameter Estimation". *Computational Linguistics* 19(2): 263-311.

Stanley F. Chen and Joshua Goodman. 1998. "An empirical study of smoothing techniques for language modeling". *Technical Report* TR-10-98, Harvard University.

Stephen Wan and Cornelia Maria Verspoor. 1998. "Automatic English-Chinese name transliteration for development of multilingual resources". In *Proceedings of the 17th international conference on Computational linguistics*, 2: 1352 – 1356.

Transliteration System using pair HMM with weighted FSTs

Peter Nabende
Alfa Informatica, CLCG,
University of Groningen, Netherlands
p.nabende@rug.nl

Abstract

This paper presents a transliteration system based on pair Hidden Markov Model (pair HMM) training and Weighted Finite State Transducer (WFST) techniques. Parameters used by WFSTs for transliteration generation are learned from a pair HMM. Parameters from pair-HMM training on English-Russian data sets are found to give better transliteration quality than parameters trained for WFSTs for corresponding structures. Training a pair HMM on English vowel bigrams and standard bigrams for Cyrillic Romanization, and using a few transformation rules on generated Russian transliterations to test for context improves the system's transliteration quality.

1 Introduction

Machine transliteration is the automatic transformation of a word in a source language to a phonetically equivalent word in a target language that uses a different writing system. Transliteration is important for various Natural Language Processing (NLP) applications including: Cross Lingual Information Retrieval (CLIR), and Machine Translation (MT). This paper introduces a system that utilizes parameters learned for a pair Hidden Markov Model (pair HMM) in a shared transliteration generation task[1]. The pair HMM has been used before (Mackay and Kondrak, 2005; Wieling *et al.*, 2007) for string similarity estimation, and is based on the notion of string Edit Distance (ED). String ED is defined here as the total edit cost incurred in transforming a source language string (S) to a target language string (T) through a sequence of edit operations. The edit operations include: (M)atching an element in S with an element in T; (I)nserting an element into T, and (D)eleting an element in S. Based on all representative symbols used for each of the two languages, emission costs for each of the edit operations and transition parameters can be estimated and used in measuring the similarity between two strings. To generate transliterations using pair HMM parameters, WFST (Graehl, 1997) techniques are adopted. Transliteration training is based mainly on the initial orthographic representation and no explicit phonetic scheme is used. Instead, transliteration quality is tested for different bigram combinations including all English vowel bigram combinations and n-gram combinations specified for Cyrillic Romanization by the US Board on Geographic Names and British Permanent Committee on Geographic Names (BGN/PCGN). However, transliteration parameters can still be estimated for a pair HMM when a particular phonetic representation scheme is used.

The quality of transliterations generated using pair HMM parameters is evaluated against transliterations generated from training WFSTs and transliterations generated using a Phrase-based Statistical Machine Translation (PBSMT) system. Section 2 describes the components of the transliteration system that uses pair HMM parameters; section 3 gives the experimental set up and results associated with the transliterations generated; and section 4 concludes the paper.

2 Machine Transliteration System

The transliteration system comprises of a training and generation components (Figure 1). In the training component, the Baum-Welch Expectation Maximization (EM) algorithm (Baum *et al.*, 1970) is used to learn the parameters of a pair HMM. In the generation component, WFST techniques (Graehl, 1997) model the learned pair HMM parameters for generating transliterations.

2.1 Parameter Estimation for a pair-HMM

A pair HMM has two output observations (Figure 2) that are aligned through the hidden states,

[1] The generation task is part of the NEWS 2009 machine transliteration shared task (Li et al., 2009)

Proceedings of the 2009 Named Entities Workshop, ACL-IJCNLP 2009, pages 100–103,
Suntec, Singapore, 7 August 2009.

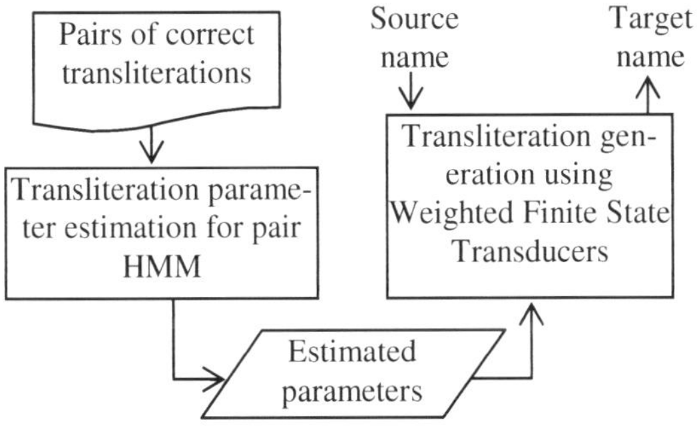

Figure 1: Machine Transliteration system

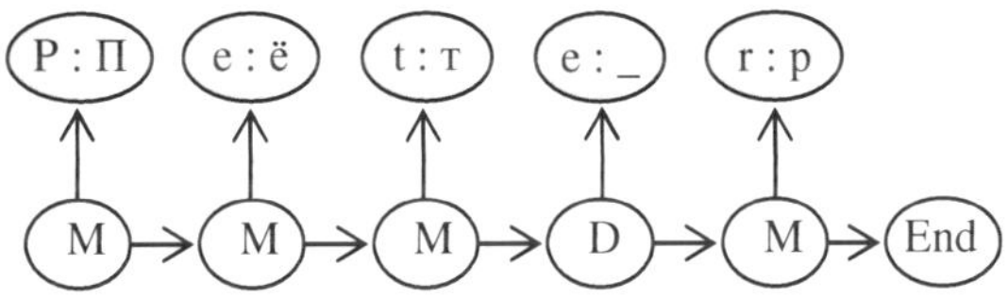

Figure 2: pair-HMM alignment for converting an English string "Peter" to a Russian string "Пётр"

unlike the classic HMMs that have only one observation sequence. The pair HMM structure differs from that of WFSTs in that in WFSTs the input and output symbols and associated weights occur on a transition arc while for the pair HMM, the input and output symbols and associated edit costs are encoded in a node. Two main sets of parameters are learned for the pair HMM: transition parameters (δ, ε, λ, τ_M, τ_{DI}) as shown in Figure 3 for different state transitions; and emission parameters in the (M)atch state and the other two gap states (D and I). s_i in Figure 3 is the ith symbol in the source language string S while t_j is the jth symbol in T.

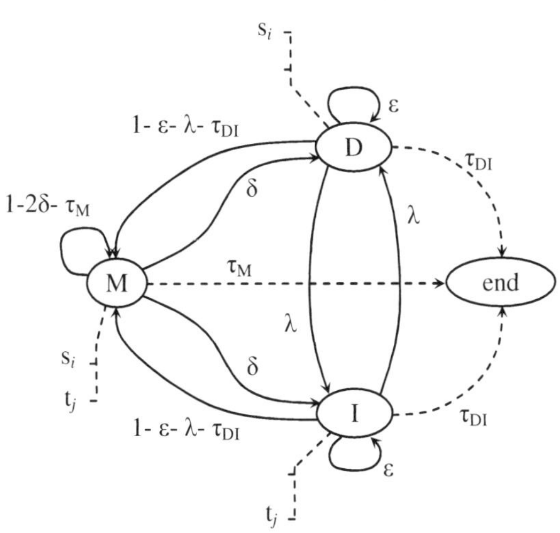

Figure 3: Pair Hidden Markov Model [Adapted from Mackay and Kondrak, 2005]

Pair HMM Emission parameters are stored in matrix form in three tables associated with the edit operations; transition parameters are also stored in matrix form in a table. The emission parameters are $(n \times m) + n + m$ in total; n and m are the numbers of symbols in the pair HMM source language alphabet (V_S) and target language alphabet (V_T) respectively. The parameters of starting in a given edit operation state are derived from the parameters of transiting from the match state (M) to either D or I or back to M.

Although pair HMM training is evaluated against WFST training, there is no major difference in the training approach used in both cases; a forward-backward EM algorithm is used in each case. The main difference is in the structure; for the pair-HMM, the state transition parameter is also incorporated into the weight that measures the level of relationship between the input and output symbol when transformed to a WFST arc.

2.2 Generating Transliterations in WFSTs

A Weighted Finite State Transducer is a finite automaton whose state transitions are labeled with input and output elements and weights that express the level of relationship between the input and output elements. Although the framework of WFSTs has mostly been applied in representing various models for speech recognition (Mohri *et al.*, 2008) including HMMs, WFSTs have as well been used for transliteration (Knight and Graehl, 1998), and are the most suitable for modeling pair HMM constraints for generating transliterations. In the WFST framework, it is possible to specify various configurations associated with constraints inherent in a particular model. Figure 4 shows a WFST that precisely corresponds to the structure of the pair

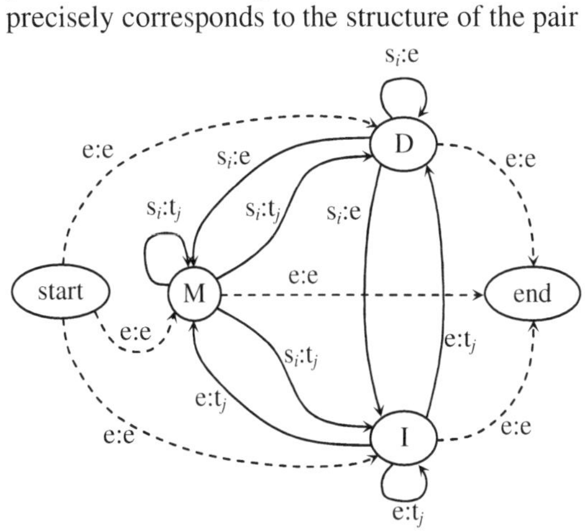

Figure 4: Finite State Transducer corresponding to the pair HMM.

HMM considering the constraints specified for the pair HMM. In Figure 4, e is an empty symbol while s_i and s_j are as defined for the pair HMM in Figure 3. Note that, in Figure 4, a start state is needed to model pair HMM parameter constraints for starting in any of the three edit states. However, it is possible to specify a WFST corresponding to the pair HMM with no start state. Various WFST configurations that do not conform to the bias corresponding to the pair HMM constraints had low transliteration quality and for space limitations, are not reported in this paper.

2.3 Transformation Rules

A look into the transliterations generated using pair HMM parameters on English-Russian development data showed consistent mistransliterations mainly due to lack of contextual modeling in the generated transliterations. For example in all cases where the Russian character л 'l' precedes the Russian soft sign ь ' ' ', the Russian soft sign was missing, resulting into a loss of transliteration accuracy. Two examples of mistransliterations that do not include the Russian soft sign ь are: крефелд instead of крефельд 'krefeld', and билбао instead of бильбао 'bilbao'. For such cases, simple transformation rules, such as "л→ль" were defined on the output transliterations in a post processing step. 25 transformation rules were specified for some of the mistransliterations to test the effect of modeling context.

2.4 Transliteration using PSMT system

Transliterations generated using pair HMM parameters and WFSTs are evaluated against those generated from a state of the art Phrase-based Statistical Machine Translation system called Moses. Moses has been used before for machine transliteration (Matthews, 2007) and performed way better than a baseline system that was associated with finding the most frequent mappings between source and target transliteration units in the training data. In the PBSMT system, bilingual phrase-tables are used and several components are combined in a log-linear model (translation models, reverse translation model, word and phrase penalties, language models, distortion parameters, etc.) with weights optimized using minimum error rate training. For machine transliteration: characters are aligned instead of words, phrases refer to character n-grams instead of word n-grams, and language models are defined over character sequences instead of word sequences. A major advantage of the PBSMT system over the pair HMM and a WFST models is that the phrase tables (character n-grams) cover a lot of contextual dependencies found in the data.

3 Experiments

3.1 Data Setup

The data used is divided according to the experimental runs that were specified for the NEWS 2009 shared transliteration task (Li *et al.*, 2009): a standard run and non-standard runs. The standard run involved using the transliteration system described above that uses pair HMM parameters combined with transformation rules. The English-Russian datasets used here were provided for the NEWS 2009 shared transliteration task (Kumaran and Kellner, 2009): 5977 pairs of names for training, 943 pairs for development, and 1000 for testing. For the non-standard runs, an additional English-Russian dataset extracted from the Geonames data dump was merged with the shared transliteration task data above to form 10481 pairs for training and development. For a second set of experiments (Table 2), a different set of test data (1000 pairs) extracted from the Geonames data dump was used. For the system used in the standard run, the training data was preprocessed to include representation of bigrams associated with Cyrillic Romanization and all English vowel bigram combinations.

3.2 Results

Six measures were used for evaluating system transliteration quality. These include (Li *et al.*, 2009): Accuracy (ACC), Fuzziness in Top-1 (Mean F Score), Mean Reciprocal Rank (MRR), Mean Average Precision for reference transliterations (MAP_R), Mean Average Precision in 10 best candidate transliterations (MAP_10), Mean Average Precision for the system (MAP_sys). Table 1 shows the results obtained using only the data sets provided for the shared transliteration task. The system used for the standard run is "phmm_rules" described in section 2 to sub section 2.3. "phmm_basic" is the system in which pair HMM parameters are used for transliteration generation but there is no representation for bigrams as described for the system used in the standard run. Table 2 shows the results obtained when additional data from Geonames data dump was used for training and development. In Table 2, "WFST_basic" and "WFST_rules" are systems associated with training WFSTs for the "phmm_basic" and "phmm_rules" systems

metrics / models	ACC	Mean F Score	MRR
phmm_basic	0.293	0.845	0.325
Moses_PSMT	0.509	0.908	0.619
phmm_rules	0.354	0.869	0.394
metrics / models	**MAP_R**	**MAP_10**	**MAP_sys**
phmm_basic	0.293	0.099	0.099
Moses_PSMT	0.509	0.282	0.282
phmm_rules	0.354	0.134	0.134

Table 1 Results from data sets for shared transliteration task.

metrics / models	ACC	Mean F Score	MRR
phmm_basic	0.341	0.776	0.368
phmm_rules	0.515	0.821	0.571
WFST_basic	0.321	0.768	0.403
WFST_rules	0.466	0.808	0.525
Moses_PSMT	0.612	0.845	0.660
metrics / models	**MAP_R**	**MAP_10**	**MAP_sys**
phmm_basic	0.341	0.111	0.111
phmm_rules	0.515	0.174	0.174
WFST_basic	0.321	0.128	0.128
WFST_rules	0.466	0.175	0.175
Moses_PSMT	0.612	0.364	0.364

Table 2 Results from additional Geonames data sets.

respectively. Moses_PSMT is the phrase-based statistical machine translation system. The results in both tables show that the systems using pair HMM parameters perform relatively better than the systems trained on WFSTs but not better than Moses. The low transliteration quality in the pair HMM and WFST systems as compared to Moses can be attributed to lack of modeling contextual dependencies unlike the case in PBSMT.

4 Conclusion

A Transliteration system using pair HMM parameters has been presented. Although its performance is better than that of systems based on only WFSTs, its transliteration quality is lower than the PBSMT system. On seeing that the pair HMM generated consistent mistransliterations, manual specification of a few contextual rules resulted in improved performance. As part of future work, we expect a technique that automatically identifies the mistransliterations would lead to improved transliteration quality. A more general framework, in which we intend to investigate contextual issues in addition to other factors such as position in source and target strings and edit operation memory in transliteration, is that of Dynamic Bayesian Networks (DBNs).

Acknowledgments

Funds associated with this work are from a second NPT Uganda project. I also thank Jörg Tiedemann for helping with experimental runs for the Moses PBSMT system.

References

A. Kumaran and Tobias Kellner. 2007. A Generic Framework for Machine Transliteration. *Proceedings of the 30th SIGIR.*

David Matthews. 2007. *Machine Transliteration of Proper Names.* Master's Thesis. School of Informatics. University of Edinburgh.

Jonathan Graehl. 1997. Carmel Finite-state Toolkit. http://www.isi.edu/licensed-sw/carmel/.

Haizhou Li, A. Kumaran, Min Zhang, Vladimir Pervouchine. 2009. Whitepaper of NEWS 2009 Machine Transliteration Shared Task. *Proceedings of ACL-IJCNLP 2009 Named Entities Workshop (NEWS* 2009), Singapore.

Kevin Knight and Jonathan Graehl. 1998. Machine Transliteration. *Computational Linguistics*, 24 (4): 599-612, MIT Press Cambridge, MA, USA.

Leonard E. Baum, Ted Petrie, George Soules, and Norman Weiss. 1970. A Maximization Technique Occurring in the Statistical Analysis of Probabilistic Functions of Markov Chains. *The Annals of Mathematical Statistics*, 41(1):164-171.

Martijn Wieling, Therese Leinonen and John Nerbonne. 2007. Inducing Sound Segment Differences using Pair Hidden Markov Models. In John Nerbonne, Mark Ellison and Grzegorz Kondrak (eds.) *Computing Historical Phonology: 9th Meeting of the ACL Special Interest Group for Computational Morphology and Phonology Workshop*, pp. 48-56, Prague.

Mehryar Mohri, Fernando C.N. Pereira, and Michael Riley. 2008. Speech Recognition with Weighte Finite State Transducers. In Larry Rabiner and Fred Juang, editors, *Handbook on Speech Processing and Speech Communication, Part E: Speech Recognition*. Springer-Verlag, Heidelberg, Germany.

Wesley Mackay and Grzegorz Kondrak. 2005. Computing Word Similarity and Identifying Cognates with Pair Hidden Markov Models. *Proceedings of the Ninth Conference on Computational Natural Language Learning* (CoNLL 2005), pp. 40-47, Ann-Arbor, Michigan.

English–Hindi Transliteration Using Context-Informed PB-SMT: the DCU System for NEWS 2009

Rejwanul Haque, Sandipan Dandapat, Ankit Kumar Srivastava, Sudip Kumar Naskar and Andy Way
CNGL, School of Computing
Dublin City University, Dublin 9, Ireland
{rhaque,sdandapat,snaskar,asrivastava,away}@computing.dcu.ie

Abstract

This paper presents English—Hindi transliteration in the NEWS 2009 Machine Transliteration Shared Task adding source context modeling into state-of-the-art log-linear phrase-based statistical machine translation (PB-SMT). Source context features enable us to exploit source similarity in addition to target similarity, as modelled by the language model. We use a memory-based classification framework that enables efficient estimation of these features while avoiding data sparseness problems.We carried out experiments both at character and transliteration unit (TU) level. Position-dependent source context features produce significant improvements in terms of all evaluation metrics.

1 Introduction

Machine Transliteration is of key importance in many cross-lingual natural language processing applications, such as information retrieval, question answering and machine translation (MT). There are numerous ways of performing automatic transliteration, such as noisy channel models (Knight and Graehl, 1998), joint source channel models (Li et al., 2004), decision-tree models (Kang and Choi, 2000) and statistical MT models (Matthews, 2007).

For the shared task, we built our machine transliteration system based on phrase-based statistical MT (PB-SMT) (Koehn et al., 2003) using Moses (Koehn et al., 2007). We adapt PB-SMT models for transliteration by translating characters rather than words as in character-level translation systems (Lepage & Denoual, 2006). However, we go a step further from the basic PB-SMT model by using source-language context features (Stroppa et al., 2007). We also create translation models by constraining the character-level segmentations, i.e. treating a consonant-vowel cluster as one transliteration unit.

The remainder of the paper is organized as follows. In section 2 we give a brief overview of PB-SMT. Section 3 describes how context-informed features are incorporated into state-of-art log-linear PB-SMT. Section 4 includes the results obtained, together with some analysis. Section 5 concludes the paper.

2 Log-Linear PB-SMT

Translation is modelled in PB-SMT as a decision process, in which the translation $e_1^I = e_1 \ldots e_I$ of a source sentence $f_1^J = f_1 \ldots f_J$ is chosen to maximize (1):

$$\arg\max_{I,e_1^I} P(e_1^I \mid f_1^J) = \arg\max_{I,e_1^I} P(f_1^J \mid e_1^I).P(e_1^I) \quad (1)$$

where $P(f_1^J \mid e_1^I)$ and $P(e_1^I)$ denote respectively the translation model and the target language model (Brown et al., 1993). In log-linear phrase-based SMT, the posterior probability $P(e_1^I \mid f_1^J)$ is directly modelled as a (log-linear) combination of features (Och and Ney, 2002), that usually comprise M translational features, and the language model, as in (2):

$$\log P(e_1^I \mid f_1^J) = \sum_{m=1}^{m} \lambda_m h_m (f_1^J, e_1^I, s_1^K) + \lambda_{LM} \log P(e_1^I) \quad (2)$$

where $s_1^K = s_1 \ldots s_k$ denotes a segmentation of the source and target sentences respectively into the sequences of phrases $(\hat{e}_1, \ldots, \hat{e}_k)$ and $(\hat{f}_1, \ldots, \hat{f}_k)$ such that (we set $i_0 = 0$) (3):

$$\forall 1 \le k \le K, \; s_k = (i_k; b_k, j_k), \quad \hat{e}_k = e_{i_{k-1}+1} \ldots e_{i_k}, \quad \hat{f}_k = f_{b_k} \ldots f_{j_k} \quad (3)$$

The translational features involved depend only on a pair of source/target phrases and do not take into account any context of these phrases. This means that each feature h_m in (2) can be rewritten as in (4):

Proceedings of the 2009 Named Entities Workshop, ACL-IJCNLP 2009, pages 104–107,
Suntec, Singapore, 7 August 2009.

$$h_m(f_1^J, e_1^I, s_1^K) = \sum_{k=1}^{K} \hat{h}_m(\hat{f}_k, \hat{e}_k, s_k) \quad (4)$$

where $\hat{h}_m$ is a feature that applies to a single phrase-pair. Thus (2) can be rewritten as:

$$\sum_{m=1}^{m} \lambda_m \sum_{k=1}^{K} \hat{h}_m(\hat{f}_k, \hat{e}_k, s_k) = \sum_{k=1}^{K} \hat{h}(\hat{f}_k, \hat{e}_k, s_k) \quad (5)$$

where, $\hat{h} = \sum_{m=1}^{m} \lambda_m \hat{h}_m$. In this context, the translation process amounts to: (i) choosing a segmentation of the source sentence, (ii) translating each source phrase.

3 Source Context Features in Log-Linear PB-SMT

The context of a source phrase $\hat{f}_k$ is defined as the sequence before and after a focus phrase $\hat{f}_k = f_{i_k} ... f_{j_k}$. Source context features (Stroppa et al., 2007) include the direct left and right context words (in our case, character/TU instead of word) of length l (resp. $f_{i_k - 1} ... f_{i_k - l}$ and $f_{j_k + 1} ... f_{j_k + l}$) of a given focus phrase $\hat{f}_k = f_{i_k} ... f_{j_k}$. A window of size $2l+1$ features including the focus phrase is formed. Thus lexical contextual information (CI) can be described as in (6):

$$\text{CI} = \{ f_{i_k - l} ... f_{i_k - 1}, f_{j_k + 1} ... f_{j_k + l} \} \quad (6)$$

As in (Haque et al., 2009), we considered a context window of ±1 and ±2 (i.e. l=1, 2) for our experiments.

One natural way of expressing a context-informed feature is as the conditional probability of the target phrase given the source phrase and its context information, as in (7):

$$\hat{h}_m(\hat{f}_k, CI(\hat{f}_k), \hat{e}_k, s_k) = \log P(\hat{e}_k \mid \hat{f}_k, CI(\hat{f}_k)) \quad (7)$$

3.1 Memory-Based Classification

As (Stroppa et al., 2007) point out, directly estimating $P(\hat{e}_k \mid \hat{f}_k, CI(\hat{f}_k))$ using relative frequencies is problematic. Indeed, Zens and Ney (2004) showed that the estimation of $P(\hat{e}_k \mid \hat{f}_k)$ using relative frequencies results in the overestimation of the probabilities of long phrases, so smoothing factors in the form of lexical-based features are often used to counteract this bias (Foster et al., 2006). In the case of context-informed features, since the context is also taken into account, this estimation problem can only become worse. To avoid such problems, in this work we use three memory-based classifiers: IGTree, IB1 and TRIBL [1] (Daelemans et al., 2005). When predicting a target phrase given a source phrase and its context, the source phrase is intuitively the feature with the highest prediction power; in all our experiments, it is the feature with the highest gain ratio (GR).

In order to build the set of examples required to train the classifier, we modify the standard phrase-extraction method of (Koehn et al., 2003) to extract the context of the source phrases at the same time as the phrases themselves. Importantly, therefore, the context extraction comes at no extra cost.

We refer interested readers to (Stroppa et al., 2007) and (Haque et al., 2009) as well as the references therein for more details of how Memory-Based Learning (MBL) is used for classification of source examples for use in the log-linear MT framework.

3.2 Implementation Issues

We split named entities (NE) into characters. We break NEs into transliteration units (TU), which bear close resemblance to syllables. We split English NEs into TUs having C*V* pattern and Hindi NEs are divided into TUs having Ch^+M pattern (M: Hindi *Matra* / vowel modifier, Ch: Characters other than *Matras*). We carry out experiments on both character-level (C-L) and TU-level (TU-L) data. We use a 5-gram language model for all our experiments. The Moses PB-SMT system serves as our baseline system.

The distribution of target phrases given a source phrase and its contextual information is normalised to estimate $P(\hat{e}_k \mid \hat{f}_k, CI(\hat{f}_k))$. Therefore our expected feature is derived as in (8):

$$\hat{h}_{mbl} = \log P(\hat{e}_k \mid \hat{f}_k, CI(\hat{f}_k)) \quad (8)$$

As for the standard phrase-based approach, their weights are optimized using Minimum Error Rate Training (MERT) of (Och, 2003) for each of the experiments.

As (Stroppa et al., 2007) point out, PB-SMT decoders such as Pharaoh (Koehn, 2004) or Moses (Koehn, 2007) rely on a static phrase-table represented as a list of aligned phrases accompanied with several features. Since these fea-

[1] An implementation of IGTree, IB1 and TRIBL is available in the TiMBL software package (http://ilk.uvt.nl/timbl).

tures do not express the context in which those phrases occur, no context information is kept in the phrase-table, and there is no way to recover this information from the phrase-table.

In order to take into account the context-informed features for use with such decoders, the devset and testset that need to be translated are pre-processed. Each token appearing in the testset and devset is assigned a unique id. First we prepare the phrase table using the training data. Then we generate all possible phrases from the devset and testset. These devset and testset phrases are then searched for in the phrase table, and if found, then the phrase along with its contextual information is given to MBL for classification. MBL produces class distributions according to the maximum-match of the features contained in the source phrase. We derive new scores from this class distribution and merge them with the initial information contained in the phrase table to take into account our feature functions ($\hat{h}_{mbl}$) in the log-linear model (2).

In this way we create a dynamic phrase table containing both the standard and the context-informed features. The new phrase table contains the source phrase (represented by the sequence of ids of the words composing the phrase), target phrase and the new score.

Similarly, replacing all the words by their ids in the development set, we perform MERT using our new phrase table to optimize the feature weights. We translate the test set (words represented by ids) using our new phrase table.

4 Results and Analysis

We used 10,000 NEs from the NEWS 2009 English—Hindi training data (Kumaran and Kellner, 2007) for the standard submission, and the additional English—Hindi parallel person names data (105,905 distinct name pairs) of the Election Commission of India[2] for the non-standard submissions. In addition to the baseline Moses system, we carried out three different set of experiments on IGTree, IB1 and TRIBL. Each of these experiments was carried out on both the standard data and the combined larger data, both at character level and the TU level, and considering ±1/±2 tokens as context. For each experiment, we produce the 10-best distinct hypotheses. The results are shown in Table 1.

We observed that many of the (unseen) TUs in the testset remain untranslated in TU-L systems due to the problems of data sparseness. Whenever a TU-L system fails to translate a TU, we fallback on the corresponding C-L system to translate the TU as a post-processing step.

The accuracy of the TU-L baseline system (0.391) is much higher compared to the C-L baseline system (0.290) on standard dataset. Furthermore, contextual modelling of the source language gives an accuracy of 0.416 and 0.399 for TU-L system and C-L system respectively. Similar trends are observed in case of larger dataset. However, the highest accuracy (0.445) has been achieved with the TU-L system using the larger dataset.

5 Conclusion

In this work, we employed source context modeling into the state-of-the-art log-linear PB-SMT for the English—Hindi transliteration task. We have shown that taking source context into account substantially improve the system performance (an improvement of 43.44% and 26.42% respectively for standard and larger datasets). IGTree performs best for TU-L systems while TRIBL seems to perform better for C-L systems on both standard and non-standard datasets.

Acknowledgements

We would like to thank Antal van den Bosch for his input on the use of memory based classifiers. We are grateful to SFI (http://www.sfi.ie) for generously sponsoring this research under grant 07/CE/I1142.

References

Adimugan Kumaran and Tobias Kellner. A generic framework for machine transliteration. *Proc. of the 30th SIGIR*, 2007.

Byung-Ju Kang and Key-Sun Choi. Automatic transliteration and back-transliteration by decision tree learning. 2000. *Proc. of LREC-2000*, Athens, Greece, pp. 1135-1141.

David Matthews. 2007. Machine Transliteration of Proper Names. Master's Thesis, University of Edinburgh, Edinburgh, United Kingdom.

Franz Och and Hermann Ney. 2002. Discriminative training and maximum entropy models for statistical machine translation. *Proc. of ACL 2002*, Philadelphia, PA, pp. 295–302.

George Foster, Roland Kuhn, and Howard Johnson. 2006. Phrasetable smoothing for statistical machine translation. *Proc. of EMNLP-2006*, Sydney, Australia, pp. 53-61.

[2] http://www.eci.gov.in/DevForum/Fullname.asp

	S/B	C/TU	Context	ACC	M-F-Sc	MRR	MAP_ref	MAP_10	MAP_sys
Baseline Moses	S	C	0	.290	.814	.393	.286	.131	.131
		TU	0	.391	.850	.483	.384	.160	.160
	B	C	0	.352	.830	.463	.346	.156	.156
		TU	0	.407	.853	.500	.402	.165	.165
IB1	S	C	±1	.391	.858	.501	.384	.166	.166
			±2	.386	.860	.479	.379	.155	.155
		TU	±1	**.406**	.858	.466	.398	.178	.178
			±2	.359	.838	.402	.349	.165	.165
	B	C	±1	**.431**	.865	.534	.423	.177	.177
			±2 (NSD1)	*.420*	*.867*	*.519*	*.413*	*.170*	*.170*
		TU	±1	**.437**	.863	.507	.429	.191	.191
			±2	**.427**	.862	.487	.418	.194	.194
IGTree	S	C	±1	.372	.849	.482	.366	.160	.160
			±2	.371	.847	.476	.364	.156	.156
		TU	±1	**.412**	.859	.486	.404	.164	.164
			±2	**.416**	.860	.493	.409	.166	.166
	B	C	±1	.413	.855	.518	.406	.173	.173
			±2 (NSD2)	*.407*	*.856*	*.507*	*.399*	*.168*	*.168*
		TU	±1	**.445**	.864	.527	.440	.176	.176
			±2	**.427**	.861	.516	.422	.173	.173
TRIBL	S	C	±1	.382	.854	.493	.375	.164	.164
			±2 (SD)	*.399*	*.863*	*.488*	*.392*	*.157*	*.157*
		TU	±1	**.408**	.858	.474	.400	.181	.181
			±2	.395	.857	.453	.385	.182	.182
	B	C	±1	**.439**	.866	.543	.430	.179	.179
			±2 (NSD3)	*.421*	*.864*	*.519*	*.415*	*.171*	*.171*
		TU	±1	**.444**	.863	.512	.436	.193	.193
			±2	**.439**	.865	.497	.430	.197	.197
	S*	C	±2 (NSD4)	*.419*	*.868*	*.464*	*.419*	*.338*	*.338*

Table1: Experimental Results (S/B → Standard / Big data, S*→ TM on Standard data, but LM on Big data, C/TU → Character / TU level, SD→ Standard submission, NSD→ Non-standard submission). Better results with bold faces have not been submitted in the NEWS 2009 Machine Transliteration Shared Task.

Haizhou Li, Zhang Min and Su Jian. 2004. A joint source-channel model for machine transliteration. *Proc. of ACL 2004*, Barcelona, Spain, pp.159-166.

Kevin Knight and Jonathan Graehl. 1998. Machine Transliteration. *Computational Linguistics*, 24(4):559-612.

Nicolas Stroppa, Antal van den Bosch and Andy Way. 2007. Exploiting Source Similarity for SMT using Context-Informed Features. *Proc. of TMI-2007*, Skövde, Sweden, pp. 231-240.

Peter F. Brown, S. A. D. Pietra, V. J. D. Pietra and R. L. Mercer. 1993. The mathematics of statistical machine translation: parameter estimation. *Computational Linguistics* 19 (2), pp. 263-311.

Philipp Koehn, F. J. Och, and D. Marcu. 2003. Statistical phrase-based translation. *Proc. of HLT-NAACL 2003*, Edmonton, Canada, pp. 48-54.

Philipp Koehn. 2004. Pharaoh: a beam search decoder for phrase-based statistical machine translation models. *Machine translation: from real users to research: Proc. of AMTA 2004,* Berlin: Springer Verlag, 2004, pp. 115-124.

Philipp Koehn, H. Hoang, A. Birch, C. Callison-Burch, M. Federico, N. Bertoldi, B. Cowan, W. Shen, C. Moran, R. Zens, C. Dyer, O. Bojar, A. Constantin and E. Herbst. 2007. Moses: open source toolkit for statistical machine translation. *Proc. of ACL*, Prague, Czech Republic, pp. 177-180.

Rejwanul Haque, Sudip Kumar Naskar, Yanjun Ma and Andy Way. 2009. Using Supertags as Source Language Context in SMT. *Proc. of EAMT-09*, Barcelona, Spain, pp. 234-241.

Richard Zens and Hermann Ney. 2004. Improvements in phrase-based statistical machine translation. Proc. of *HLT/NAACL 2004*, Boston, MA, pp. 257–264.

Walter Daelemans & Antal van den Bosch. 2005. *Memory-based language processing*. Cambridge, UK, Cambridge University Press.

Yves Lepage and Etienne Denoual. 2006. Objective evaluation of the analogy-based machine translation system ALEPH. *Proc. of the 12th Annual Meeting of the Association of NLP*, pp. 873-876.

A Hybrid Approach to English-Korean Name Transliteration

Gumwon Hong*, **Min-Jeong Kim***, **Do-Gil Lee**[+] **and Hae-Chang Rim***
*Department of Computer Science & Engineering, Korea University, Seoul 136-713, Korea
{gwhong,mjkim,rim}@nlp.korea.ac.kr
[+]Institute of Korean Culture, Korea University, Seoul 136-701, Korea
motdg@korea.ac.kr

Abstract

This paper presents a hybrid approach to English-Korean name transliteration. The base system is built on MOSES with enabled factored translation features. We expand the base system by combining with various transliteration methods including a Web-based n-best re-ranking, a dictionary-based method, and a rule-based method. Our standard run and best non-standard run achieve 45.1 and 78.5, respectively, in top-1 accuracy. Experimental results show that expanding training data size significantly contributes to the performance. Also we discover that the Web-based re-ranking method can be successfully applied to the English-Korean transliteration.

1 Introduction

Often, named entities such as person names or place names from foreign origin do not appear in the dictionary, and such out of vocabulary words are a common source of errors in processing natural languages. For example, in statistical machine translation (SMT), if a new word occurs in the input source sentence, the decoder will at best drop the unknown word or directly copy the source word to the target sentence. Transliteration, a method of mapping phonemes or graphemes of source language into those of target language, can be used in this case in order to identify a possible translation of the word.

The approaches to automatic transliteration between English and Korean can be performed through the following ways: First, in learning how to write the names of foreign origin, we can refer to a transliteration standard which is established by the government or some official linguistic organizations. No matter where the standard comes from, the basic principle of the standard is based on the correct pronunciation of foreign words. Second, since constructing such rules are very costly in terms of time and money, we can rely on a statistical method such as SMT. We believe that the rule-based method can guarantee to increase accuracy for known cases, and the statistical method can be robust to handle various exceptions.

In this paper, we present a variety of techniques for English-Korean name transliteration. First, we use a phrase-base SMT model with some factored translation features for the transliteration task. Second, we expand the base system by applying Web-based n-best re-ranking of the results. Third, we apply a pronouncing dictionary-based method to the base system which utilizes the pronunciation symbols which is motivated by linguistic knowledge. Finally, we introduce a phonics-based method which is originally designed for teaching speakers of English to read and write that language.

2 Proposed Approach

In order to build our base system, we use MOSES (Koehn et al., 2007), a well-known phrase-based system designed for SMT. MOSES offers a convenient framework which can be directly applied to machine transliteration experiments. In this framework, the transliteration can be performed in a very similar process of SMT task except the following changes. First, the unit of translation is changed from *words* to *characters*. Second, a *phrase* in transliteration refers to any contiguous block of character sequence which can be directly matched from a source word to a target word. Also, we do not have to worry about any distortion parameters because decoding can be performed in a totally monotonic way.

The process of the general transliteration approach begins by matching the unit of a source

Proceedings of the 2009 Named Entities Workshop, ACL-IJCNLP 2009, pages 108–111,
Suntec, Singapore, 7 August 2009. ©2009 ACL and AFNLP

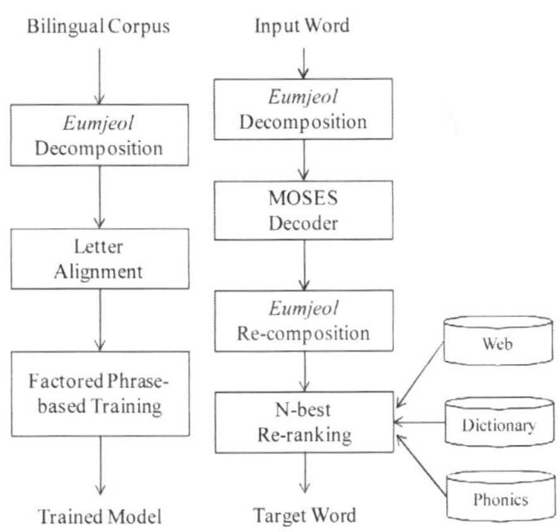

Figure 1: System Architecture

word to the unit of a target word. The unit can be based on graphemes or phonemes, depending on language pairs or approaches. In English-Korean transliteration, both grapheme-to-grapheme and grapheme-to-phoneme approaches are possible. In our method, we select grapheme-to-grapheme approach as a base system, and we apply grapheme-to-phoneme functions in pronouncing dictionary-based approach.

The transliteration between Korean and other languages requires some special preprocessing techniques. First of all, Korean alphabet is organized into syllabic blocks called *Eumjeol*. Korean transliteration standard allows each *Eumjeol* to consist of either two or three of the 24 Korean letters, with (1) leading 14 consonants, (2) intermediate 10 vowels, and (3) optionally, trailing 7 consonants (out of the possible 14). Therefore, Korean *Eumjeol* should be decomposed into letters before performing training or decoding any input. Consequently, after the letter-unit transliteration is finished, all the letters should be re-composed to form a correct sequence of *Eumjeols*.

Figure 1 shows the overall architecture of our system. The alignment between English letter and Korean letter is performed using GIZA++ (Och and Ney, 2003). We use MOSES decoder in order to search the best sequence of transliteration.

In this paper we focus on describing factored phrase-based training and n-best re-ranking techniques including a Web-based method, a pronouncing dictionary-based method, and a phonics-based method.

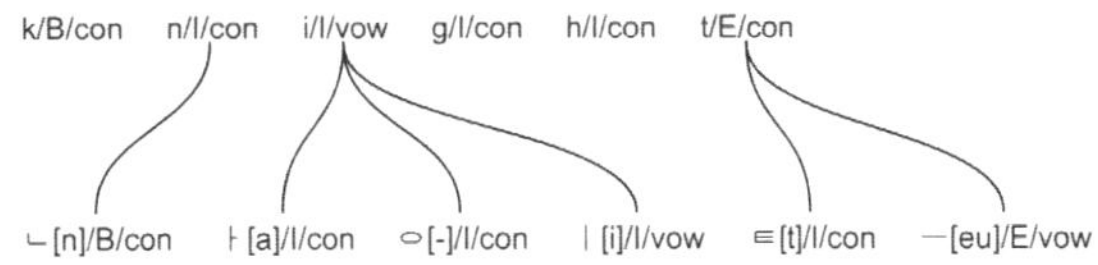

Figure 2: Alignment example between 'Knight' and '나이트 [*naiteu*]'

2.1 Factored Phrase-based Training

Koehn and Hoang (2007) introduces an integration of different information for phrase-based SMT model. We report on experiments with three factors: surface form, positional information, and the type of a letter. Surface form indicates a letter itself. For positional information, we add a BIO label to each input character in both the source words and the target words. The intuition is that certain character is differently pronounced depending on its position in a word. For example, 'k' in 'Knight' or 'h' in 'Sarah' are not pronounced. The type of a letter is used to classify whether a given letter is a vowel or a consonant. We assume that a consonant in source word would more likely be linked to a consonant in a target word. Figure 2 shows an example of alignment with factored features.

2.2 Web-based Re-ranking

We re-ranked the top n results of the decoder by referring to how many times both source word and target word co-occur on the Web. In news articles on the Web, a translation of a foreign name is often provided near the foreign name to describe its pronunciation or description. To reflect this observation, we use Google's proximity search by restricting two terms should occur within four-word distance. The frequency is adjusted as relative frequency form by dividing each frequency by total frequency of all n-best results.

Also, we linearly interpolate the n-best score with the relative frequency of candidate output. To make fair interpolation, we adjust both scores to be between 0 and 1. Also, in this method, we decide to remove all the candidates whose frequencies are zero.

2.3 Pronouncing Dictionary-based Method

According to "*Oeraeeo pyogibeop*[1]" (Korean orthography and writing method of borrowed for-

[1] http://www.korean.go.kr/08_new/data/rule03.jsp

Methods	Acc.$_1$	Mean F$_1$	Mean F$_{dec}$	MRR	MAP$_{ref}$	MAP$_{10}$	MAP$_{sys}$
BS	0.451	0.720	0.852	0.576	0.451	0.181	0.181
ER	0.740	0.868	0.930	0.806	0.740	0.243	0.243
WR	0.784	0.889	0.944	0.840	0.784	0.252	0.484
PD	0.781	0.885	0.941	0.839	0.781	0.252	0.460
PB	0.785	0.887	0.943	0.840	0.785	0.252	0.441

Table 1: Experimental Results (EnKo)

eign words), the primary principle of English-to-Korean transliteration is to spell according to the mapping table between the international phonetic alphabets and the Korean alphabets. Therefore, we can say that a pronouncing dictionary-based method is very suitable for this principle.

We use the following two resources for building a pronouncing dictionary: one is an English-Korean dictionary that contains 130,000 words. The other is the CMU pronouncing dictionary[2] created by Carnegie Mellon University that contains over 125,000 words and their transcriptions.

Phonetic symbols for English words in the dictionaries are transformed to their pronunciation information by using an internal code table. The internal code table represents mappings from each phonetic symbol to a single character within ASCII code table. Our pronouncing dictionary includes a list of words and their pronunciation information.

For a given English word, if the word exists in the pronouncing dictionary, then its pronunciations are translated to Korean graphemes by a mapping table and transformation rules, which are defined by "*Oeraeeo pyogibeop*".

2.4 Phonics-based Method

Phonics is a pronunciation-based linguistic teaching method, especially for children (Strickland, 1998). Originally, it was designed to connect the sounds of spoken English with group of English letters. In this research, we modify the phonics in order to connect English sounds to Korean letter because in Korean there is nearly a one-to-one correspondence between sounds and the letter patterns that represent them. For example, alphabet 'b' can be pronounced to 'ㅂ'(*bieup*) in Korean. Consequently, we construct about 150 rules which map English alphabet into one or more several Korean graphemes, by referring to the phonics. Though phonics cannot reveal all of the pronunciation of English words, the conversion from English alphabet into Korean letter is performed simply and efficiently. We apply the phonics in serial order from left to right of each input word. If multiple rules are applicable, the most specific rules are fist applied.

3 Experiments

3.1 Experimental Setup

We participate in both standard and non-standard tracks for English-Korean name transliteration in NEWS 2009 Machine Transliteration Shared Task (Li et al., 2009). Experimenting on the development data, we determine the best performing parameters for MOSES as follows.

- ***Maximum Phrase Length***: 3
- ***Language Model N-gram Order***: 3
- ***Language Model Smoothing***: Kneser-Ney
- ***Phrase Alignment Heuristic***: grow-diag-final
- ***Reordering***: Monotone
- ***Maximum Distortion Length***: 0

With above parameter setup, the results are produced from the following five different systems.

- ***Baseline System (BS)***: For the standard task, we use only given official training data [3] to construct translation model and language model for our base system.
- ***Expanded Resource (ER)***: For all four non-standard tasks, we use the examples of writing foreign names as additional training data. The examples are provided from the National Institute of the Korean Language[4]. The data originally consists of around 27,000 person names and around 7,000 place names including non-Ascii characters for English side words as well as duplicate entries. We preprocess the data in order to use 13,194 dis-

[2] http://www.speech.cs.cmu.edu/cgi-bin/cmudict

[3] Refer to Website http://www.cjk.org for more information

[4] The resource is open to public. See http://www.korean.go.kr/eng for more information.

tinct pairs of English names and Korean transliteration.

- ***Web-based Re-ranking (WR)***: We re-rank the result of *ER* by applying the method described in section 2.2.
- ***Pronouncing Dictionary-based Method (PD)***: The re-ranking of *WR* by combining with the method described in section 2.3.
- ***Phonics-based Method (PB)***: The re-ranking of *WR* by combining with the method described in section 2.4.

The last two methods re-rank the *WR* method by applying pronouncing dictionary-based method and Phonics-based method. We restrict that the pronouncing dictionary-based method and Phonics-based method can produce only one output, and use the outputs of the two methods to re-rank (again) the result of Web-based re-ranking. When re-ranking the results, we heuristically combined the outputs of *PD* or *PB* with the n-best result of *WR*. If the outputs of the two methods exist in the result of *WR*, we add some positive scores to the original scores of *WR*. Otherwise, we inserted the result into fixed position of the rank. The fixed position of rank is empirically decided using development set. We inserted the output of *PD* and *PB* at second rank and at sixth rank, respectively.

3.2 Experimental Results

Table 1 shows our experimental results of the five systems on the test data. We found that the use of additional training data (*ER*) and web-based re-ranking (*WR*) have a strong effect on transliteration performance. However, the integration of the *PD* or *PB* with *WB* proves not to significantly contribute the performance. To find more elaborate integration of those results will be one of our future work.

The MAP_{sys} value of the three re-ranking methods *WR*, *PD*, and *PB* are relatively higher than other methods because we filter out some candidates in n-best by their Web frequencies. In addition to the standard evaluation measures, we include the Mean F_{dec} to measure the Levenshtein distance between reference and the output of the decoder (decomposed result).

4 Conclusions

In this paper, we proposed a hybrid approach to English-Korean name transliteration. The system is built on MOSES with factored translation features. When evaluating the proposed methods, we found that the use of additional training data can significantly outperforms the baseline system. Also, the experimental result of using three n-best re-ranking techniques shows that the Web-based re-ranking is proved to be a useful method. However, our two integration methods with dictionary-based or rule-based method does not show the significant gain over the Web-based re-ranking.

For future work, we plan to devise more elaborate way to integrate statistical method and dictionary or rule-based method to further improve the transliteration performance. Also, we will apply the proposed techniques to possible applications such as SMT or Cross Lingual Information Retrieval.

References

Philipp Koehn and Hieu Hoang. 2007. Factored translation models. In *Proceedings of the 2007 Joint Conference on Empirical Methods in Natural Language Processing and Computational Natural Language Learning (EMNLP-CoNLL)*, pages 868–876, Prague, Czech Republic, June. Association for Computational Linguistics.

Philipp Koehn, Hieu Hoang, Alexandra Birch, Chris Callison-Burch, Marcello Federico, Nicola Bertoldi, Brooke Cowan, Wade Shen, Christine Moran, Richard Zens, Chris Dyer, Ondřej Bojar, Alexandra Constantin, and Evan Herbst. 2007. Moses: Open Source Toolkit for Statistical Machine Translation. In *ACL 2007, Demo and Poster Sessions*, June.

Haizhou Li, A Kumaran, Min Zhang, and Vladimir Pervouchine. 2009. Whitepaper of news 2009 machine transliteration shared task. In *Proceedings of ACL-IJCNLP 2009 Named Entities Workshop (NEWS 2009)*, Singapore.

Franz Josef Och and Hermann Ney. 2003. A systematic comparison of various statistical alignment models. *Computational Linguistics*, 29.

D.S. Strickland. 1998. *Teaching phonics today: A primer for educators*. International Reading Association.

Language Independent Transliteration system using phrase based SMT approach on substrings

Sara Noeman

IBM Cairo Technology & Development Center
Giza, Egypt
noemans@eg.ibm.com

Abstract

Everyday the newswire introduce events from all over the world, highlighting new names of persons, locations and organizations with different origins. These names appear as *Out of Vocabulary* (OOV) words for Machine translation, cross lingual information retrieval, and many other NLP applications. One way to deal with OOV words is to *transliterate* the unknown words, that is, to render them in the orthography of the second language.

We introduce a statistical approach for transliteration only using the bilingual resources released in the shared task and without any previous knowledge of the target languages. Mapping the Transliteration problem to the Machine Translation problem, we make use of the *phrase based SMT* approach and apply it on *substrings* of names. In the English to Russian task, we report ACC (*Accuracy in top-1*) of 0.545, Mean F-score of 0.917, and MRR (*Mean Reciprocal Rank*) of 0.596.

Due to time constraints, we made a single experiment in the English to Chinese task, reporting ACC, Mean F-score, and MRR of 0.411, 0.737, and 0.464 respectively.

Finally, it is worth mentioning that the system is language independent since the author is not aware of either languages used in the experiments.

1. Introduction

Named entities translation is strongly required in the field of Information retrieval (IR) as well as its usage in Machine translation. A significant proportion of OOV words are named entities and typical analyses find around 50% of OOV words to be named entities, yet these can be the most important words in the queries. Larkey et al (2003) showed that average precision of cross language retrieval reduced more than 50% when named entities in the queries were not translated.

Transliteration may be considered as a phonetic translation or mapping of a *sequence of characters* in the source language in the alphabet of the target language, thus we can use the analogy with the Machine translation problem, which translates a *sequence of words* in the source language into a semantically equivalent *sequence of words* in the target language.

In a statistical approach to machine translation, given a foreign word F, we try to find the English word Ê that maximizes P(E\F). Using Bayes' rule, we can formulate the task as follows:

$$\hat{E} = \underset{E}{\operatorname{argmax}} \frac{P(F\backslash E)*P(E)}{P(F)}$$

$$= \underset{E}{\operatorname{argmax}}\ P(F\backslash E)*P(E)$$

This is known as the noisy channel model, which splits the problem into two sub-tasks. The translation model provides an estimate for the P(F\E) for the foreign word ***F*** being a translation for the English word ***E***, while the language model provides an estimate of the probability P(E) is an English word.

In this paper we use the phrase based statistical Machine Translation (PBSMT) approach introduced by (Koehn et al.) to build English to Russian, and English to Chinese transliteration systems capable of learning the substring to substring mapping between source and target languages.

Section 2 includes a detailed description of our approach, section 3 describes our experimental set up and the results. The conclusions and future work are explained in section 4.

2. System architecture

Our approach is a formulation of the Transliteration problem using the PBSMT technique that proved improvement in Machine translation domain, making use of the analogy between the two problems.

The phrase-based approach developed for statistical machine translation (Koehn et al., 2003) is designed to overcome the restrictions of many-to-many mappings in word-based translation models. We applied the phrase based statistical approach used in Machine translation on our problem, mapping the "word", and

Proceedings of the 2009 Named Entities Workshop, ACL-IJCNLP 2009, pages 112–115,
Suntec, Singapore, 7 August 2009.

"phrase" in PBSMT terminology into "character", and "substring" in our system, where the substring in our notation represents a *sequence of adjacent characters*.

Figure (1) shows an overview of the whole system architecture.

Figure (1)

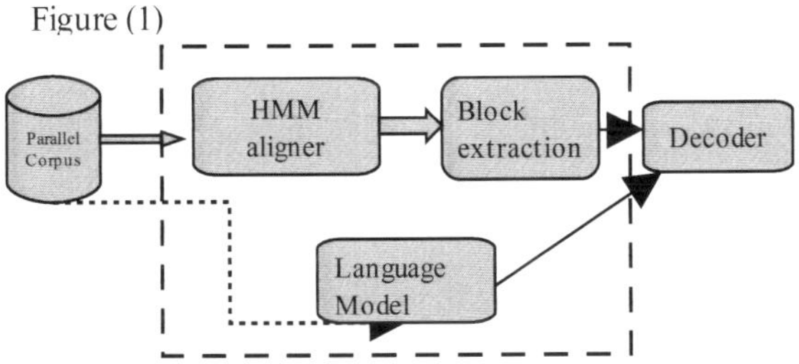

We used an HMM aligner similar to Giza++ (Och. et al., 1999) over the parallel character sequences using forward-backward alignment intersection. Heuristics were used to extend substring to substring mappings based on character-to-character alignment, with the constraint that no characters within the substring pair are linked to characters outside the substring pair. Thus we generated a substring to substring translation model with relative frequencies. We deploy heuristics to extract character sequence mapping similar to the heuristics used in PBSMT (Koehn et al., 2003). Figure (2) shows the heuristics used for block extraction over substrings in the English to Russian task using character to character alignments.

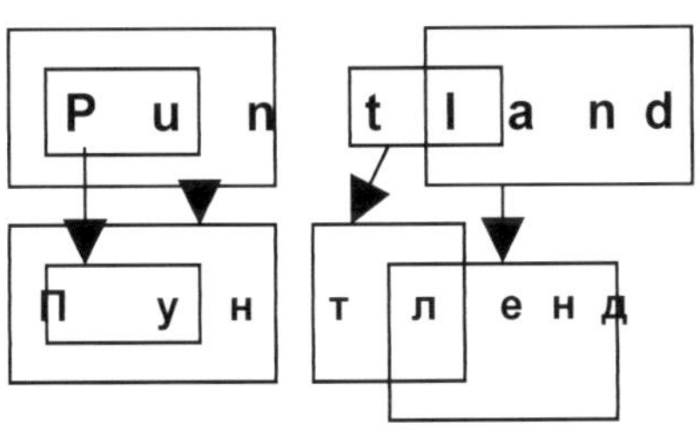

Figure (2)

Unlike the Machine Translation task, in transliteration we do not need any reordering during decoding which makes the decoding phase easier. We used monotone beam search decoder generating the *best k* transliteration candidates, where the translation model and the language model are used by the decoder to get best Viterbi paths of character sequences as a phonetic translation for the input English character sequence. (Tillmann, et al., 2003).

Finally, all transliteration candidates are weighted using their translation and language model probabilities as follows:

$P(w_r \backslash w_e) = P(w_e \backslash w_r) * P(w_r \in R)$

Here, we explain our system for the English to Russian task, while the English to Chinese system will follow the same criteria and their results are mentioned later.

a. Data and Resources

Standard Runs:

In the English to Russian task, we used the parallel corpus (EnRu) released by NEWS 2009 Shared Task on Transliteration to build the translation model. For the English to Chinese standard run, we used the parallel English-Chinese (EnCh) corpus released by NEW2009 availed by (Li et al., 2004). The target language side (Russian, Chinese) of the parallel data was used to build the language model. NEWS2009 released 5977 of EnRu names pairs as a training set, and 943 pairs as a development set. The EnCh corpus had 31,961 pairs as a training set, and 2896 pairs as a development set.

Non-Standard Runs:

For the English to Russian task we used the Russian data in UMC 0.1 Czech-English-Russian, from the Institute of Formal and Applied Linguistics (ÚFAL), to build a larger Russian LM, in addition to the data resources used in the standard run. No Named Entity tagging has been applied on this data because we lack the tools. However, we are just validating the character n-gram sequences in the target language with larger corpus of character sequences.
We didn't use any additional resources for the Chinese task.

b. Training

The training is held in two phases; first learning the list of Russian characters aligned to multiple English characters, and thus we obtain a table of English character n-grams to be added to unigram inventory of the source language. The second stage learns the transliteration model over this new inventory. (Larkey et al., 2003).

Table 1 shows the list of English n-gram characters added to unigram inventory.

Table (1)

s h c h	shch
s z c z	szcz
s c h	sch
z h	zh
c k	ck
p h	ph
k h	kh
c h	ch
s h	sh
s z	sz
c z	cz
š č	šč

A substring (phrase) table of Russian substrings mapped to English substrings is considered as the

translation model P(E\R). A language model P(R) is built using a monolingual Russian corpus.
Figure (3) shows a sample of the *substring feature table* generated during training using the block extraction heuristics over HMM alignments.

а к о н ‖ e a c o n 0 1
а ф ‖ e a f 0 1
а ф э ‖ e a f ă 0 1
е н е р и ф ‖ e n e r i f 0 1
е н е р и ф е ‖ e n e r i f e 0 1
н е р с ‖ e n e r s 0 1
н е р с р ‖ e n e r s r 0 1
н е р с р ю ‖ e n e r s r ü 0 1

Figure (3) a sample of the substring table

c. Decoding

The source English word is fragmented into all its possible substring sequences, and the decoder applies a monotone beam search, without reordering, to generate the *best k* phonetic translation character sequences in the target language alphabet.
Experiments 1, 2, and 3 use a substring based transliteration system The experiments set up will be as follows:

i. The effect of true casing versus lowercasing Russian characters is explained through the first experiment (*Exp-1*).

ii. The released English data contains some unusual English characters not belonging to the English alphabet, some of which are vowels like "ế, ê, ē, é, ä, ã, ą, ö, ó, ō, ú, û, ŭ", and others are consonants as "ľ, ł, ť, ż, ž, ń, ñ, ň, ř". The effect of normalizing these unusual English characters is explained in the second experiment (*Exp-2*).

iii. In the third experiment (*Exp-3*) we used the unigram inventory described in Table (1).

N.B.: Chinese language has a very large number of characters representing syllables rather than characters (a syllables = a consonant + vowel, or a consonant + vowel + final), thus the unigram inventory used in the English to Chinese task wasn't generated using the statistical trend used with English-Russian task. General linguistic heuristics were used to re-merge character n-grams like "sh, th, gh, ph, etc…" as well as character repetitions like "ll, mm, nn … ss, tt, etc..."

3. Results

Evaluation Metrics:

The quality of the transliteration task was measured using the 6 metrics defined in the shared task white paper. The first metric is the *Word Accuracy in Top-1 (ACC)* which is the precision of the exact match with the Top-1 reference. The second one is the *Fuzziness in Top-1 (**Mean F-score**)* which reflects an average F-score of the normalized lowest common subsequence between the system output and the Top-1 reference. The ***(MRR)*** represents the *Mean Reciprocal Rank* of the Top-1 reference in the ***k*** candidates generated by the system. The last three metrics ***MAP_{ref}***, ***MAP₁₀***, ***MAP_{sys}*** measure how the ***k*** candidates generated by the transliteration system are mapped to the ***n*** references available for each input in the testset.

English to Russian task

The results of experiments 1, 2, and 3 on the Development set, using the 6 evaluation metrics explained before, are written in Table (2). Exp-2 reflects the effect of normalizing all the unusual English characters that existed in the training data. Referring to the results of Exp-1, we conclude that this normalization decreases the ACC of the system around 2.5%. In the next experiments we only use the set up of Exp-3, which uses the statistical unigram inventory without true casing Russian characters or normalizing unusual English characters.

	Exp-1	Exp-2	Exp-3
ACC	0.705	0	0
Mean F-score	0.945	0.939	0
MRR	0.741	0.721	0
MAPref	0.705	0	0
MAP10	0.220	0.215	0
MAPsys	0.525	0	0

Table (2) explains Eng-Russian task results on the Development Set for experiments 1, 2, and 3.

- **Standard Run:**

Our Standard Run submission used the same setup used in Experiment-3, no lowercasing, no normalization, and using the list of English n-grams that were added to the unigram inventory after the first training phase. Table (3) contains the results of our Standard Submissions.

	Standard submission
ACC	0.545
Mean F-score	0.917
MRR	0.596
MAP_{ref}	0.545
MAP_{10}	0.286
MAP_{sys}	0.299

Table (3) explains Eng-Russian task results on the blind Test Set. This was the Standard submission.
N.B.: We submitted the previous output in true-cased Russian characters as our standard submission, and then we submitted the same system output after lower casing as a Non-Standard run because we were not sure that the evaluation tool used by the Shared Task

will be able to map true case and lower case variations.
The same will be done in the next run, where 2 submissions are submitted for the same output, one of which was true-cased and the other was lower cased.

- **Non-Standard Run:**

Using (*UMC 0.1*) additional LM on the blind Test set. The results are in table(5)

	Non-Standard submission
ACC	0.524
Mean F-score	0.913
MRR	0.579
MAP_{ref}	0.524
MAP_{10}	0.277
MAP_{sys}	0.291

Table (5) explains Eng-Russian task results on the blind Test Set. This was the Non-Standard submission.

English to Chinese task

Finally the previous setup with slight modifications was applied to the Eng-Chinese transliteration task. Tables (6), and (7) represent the results on the Chinese Development set and Test set respectively.

	Exp-3
ACC	0.447
Mean F-score	0.748
MRR	0.489
MAP_{ref}	0.447
MAP_{10}	0.147
MAP_{sys}	0.191

Table (6) explains Eng-Chinese task results on the Development Set.

- **Standard Run:**

	Standard submission
ACC	0.411
Mean F-score	0.737
MRR	0.464
MAP_{ref}	0.411
MAP_{10}	0.141
MAP_{sys}	0.173

Table (7) explains Eng-Chinese task results on the blind Test Set. This was the Standard submission

4. Conclusion and Future Work

In this paper we presented a substring based transliteration system, making use of the analogy between the Machine translation task and Transliteration. By applying the phrase based SMT approach in the transliteration domain, and without any previous knowledge of the target languages, we built an English to Russian system with ACC of 54.5% and an English to Chinese system with ACC of 41.2%.

In the future we are planning to hold some experiments to filter out the generated phrase table (substring table) and try other decoding techniques.

5. Acknowledgement

I would like to thank Dr. Hany Hassan in IBM Cairo TDC for his helpful comments and technical support.

6. References

N. AbdulJaleel and L. S. Larkey. 2003. Statistical transliteration for English-Arabic cross language information retrieval. In *CIKM*, pages 139–146.

Y. Al-Onaizan and K. Knight. 2002. Machine Transliteration of Names in Arabic Text. In Proceed-ings of the ACL Workshop on Computational Approaches to Semitic Languages.

P. F. Brown, V. J. Della Pietra, S. A. Della Pietra, and R. L. Mercer. 1993. The Mathematics of Statistical Machine Translation: Parameter Estimation. Computational Linguistics, 19(2):263–311.

P. Koehn, F.J. Och, and D. Marcu. 2003. Statistical Phrase-Based Translation. *Proc. Of the Human Language Technology Conference, HLT-NAACL'2003*, May.

H. Li, M. Zhang, J. Su: A Joint Source-Channel Model for Machine Transliteration. ACL 2004: 159-166

F. J. Och, C. Tillmann, and H. Ney. 1999. Improved Alignment Models for Statistical Machine Translation. In June 1999, EMNLP.

T. Sherif and G. Kondrak. 2007. Substring-Based Transliteration. In Proceedings of the ACL Workshop on Computational Approaches to Semitic Languages.

C. Tillmann and H. Ney. 2003.Word Re-ordering and DP-based Search in Statistical Machine Translation. In *COLING*, pages 850-856.

J. Zobel and P. Dart. 1996. Phonetic String Matching. Lessons from Information Retrieval. SIGIR Forum, special issue:166—172.

Combining MDL Transliteration Training with Discriminative Modeling

Dmitry Zelenko
4300 Fair Lakes Ct.
Fairfax, VA 22033, USA
dmitry_zelenko@sra.com

Abstract

We present a transliteration system that introduces minimum description length training for transliteration and combines it with discriminative modeling. We apply the proposed approach to transliteration from English to 8 non-Latin scripts, with promising results.

1 Introduction

Recent research in transliteration and translation showed utility of increasing the n-gram size in transliteration models and phrase tables (Koehn et al., 2003). Yet most learning algorithms for training n-gram transliteration models place restrictions on the size of n-gram due to tractability and overfitting issues, and, in the case of machine translation, construct the phrase table after training the model, in an ad-hoc manner. In this paper, we present a minimum description length (MDL) approach (Grunwald, 2007) for learning transliteration models comprising n-grams of unrestricted size. Given a bilingual dictionary of transliterated data we seek to derive a transliteration model so that the combined size of the data and the model is minimized.

Use of discriminative modeling for transliteration and translation is another promising direction allowing incorporation of arbitrary features in the transliteration process (Zelenko and Aone, 2006; Goldwasser and Roth, 2008). Here we propose to use the transliteration model derived via MDL training as a starting point and learn the model weights in the discriminative manner. The discriminative approach also provides a natural way to integrate the language modeling component into the transliteration decoding process.

We experimentally evaluate the proposed approach on the standard datasets for the task of transliterating from English to 8 non-Latin scripts

2 MDL Training for Transliteration

In our transliteration setting, we are given a string e written in an alphabet V_1 (e.g., Latin), which is to be transliterated into a string f written in an alphabet V_2 (e.g., Chinese). We consider a transliteration process that is conducted by a transliteration model T, which represents a function mapping a pair of strings (e_i, f_i) into a score $T(e_i, f_i) \in R$. For an alignment [1] $A = \{(e_i, f_i)\}$ of e and f, we define the alignment score $T(A) = \sum_i T(e_i, f_i)$. For a string e and a model T, the decoding process seeks the optimal transliteration $T(e)$ with respect to the model T:

$$T(e) = arg\max_f \{\ T(A) \mid \exists A = \{(e_i, f_i)\}\ \}$$

Different assumptions for transliteration models lead to different estimation algorithms. A popular approach is to assume a *joint* generative model for pairs (e, f), so that given an alignment $A = \{(e_i, f_i)\}$, a probability $P(e, f)$ is defined to be $\prod_i p(e_i, f_i)$. The probabilities $p(e_i, f_i)$ are estimated using the EM algorithm, and the corresponding transliteration model is $T(e_i, f_i) = \log(p(e_i, f_i))$. We can alternatively model the *conditional* probability directly: $P(f|e) = \prod_i p(f_i|e_i)$, where we again estimate the conditional probabilities $p(f_i|e_i)$ via the EM algorithm, and define the transliteration model accordingly: $T(e_i, f_i) = \log(p(f_i|e_i))$. We can also combine joint estimation with conditional decoding, observing that $p(f_i|e_i) = \frac{p(e_i, f_i)}{\sum_f p(e_i, f_i)}$ and using the conditional transliteration model after estimating a joint generative model.

Increasing the maximum n-gram size in probabilistic modeling approaches, at some point, degrades model accuracy due to overfitting. Therefore, probabilistic approaches typically use a small n-gram size, and perform additional modeling *post*

[1] Here we consider only monotone alignments.

Proceedings of the 2009 Named Entities Workshop, ACL-IJCNLP 2009, pages 116–119,
Suntec, Singapore, 7 August 2009.

factum: examples include joint n-gram modeling and phrase table construction in machine translation.

We propose to apply the MDL principle to transliteration modeling by seeking the model that compresses the transliteration data so that the combined size of the compressed data and the model is minimized. If T corresponds to a joint probabilistic model $P = \{p(e_i, f_i)\}$, then we can use the model to encode the data $D = \{(e, f)\}$ in

$$\begin{aligned} C_D(P) &= -\sum_{(e,f)} \log P(e, f) \\ &= -\sum_{(e,f)} max_A \sum_i \log p(e_i, f_i) \end{aligned}$$

bits, where $A = \{(e_i, f_i)\}$ is an alignment of e and f.

We can encode each symbol of an alphabet V using $\log |V|$ bits so encoding a string s of length $|s|$ from alphabet V takes $C_V(s) = \log |V|(|s| + 1)$ bits (we add an extra string termination symbol for separability). Therefore, we encode each transliteration model in

$$C_T(P) = \sum_{(e_i, f_i)} C_T(e_i, f_i)$$

bits, where $C_T(e_i, f_i) = C_{V_1}(e_i) + C_{V_2}(f_i) - \log p(e_i, f_i)$ is the number of bits used to encode both the pair (e_i, f_i) and its code according to P. Thus, we seek a probability distribution P that minimizes $C(P) = C_D(P) + C_T(P)$.

Let P be an initial joint probability distribution for a transliteration model T such that a string pair (e_i, f_i) appeared $n(e_i, f_i)$ times, and $p(e_i, f_i) = n(e_i, f_i)/N$, where $N = \sum_{(e_i, f_i)} n(e_i, f_i)$. Then, encoding a pair (e_i, f_i) takes on average $C(e_i, f_i) = \frac{C_T(e_i, f_i)}{n(e_i, f_i)} - \log p(e_i, f_i)$ bits - here we distribute the model size component to all occurrences of (e_i, f_i) in the data. Notice that the combined data and model size $C(P) = \sum_{(e_i, f_i)} n(e_i, f_i) C(e_i, f_i)$. It is this quantity $C(e_i, f_i)$ that we propose to use when conducting the MDL training algorithm below.

1. Pick an initial P. Compute $C(e_i, f_i) = \frac{C_T(e_i, f_i)}{n(e_i, f_i)} - \log p(e_i, f_i)$. Set combined size $C(P) = \sum_{(e_i, f_i)} n(e_i, f_i) C(e_i, f_i)$.

2. Iterate: during each iteration, for each $(e, f) \in D$, find the minimum codesize alignment $A = arg \min_A \sum_i C(e_i, f_i)$ of (e, f). Use the alignments to re-estimate P and re-compute C. Exit when there is no improvement in the combined model and data size.

Experimentally, we observed fast convergence of the above algorithm just after a few iterations, though we cannot present a convergence proof as yet. We picked the initial model by computing co-occurrence counts of n-gram pairs in D, that is, $n(e_i, f_i) = \sum_{(e,f)} \min(n_e(e_i), n_f(f_i))$, where $n_e(e_i)$ ($n_f(f_i)$) is the number of times the n-gram e_i (f_i) appeared in the string e (f).

Note that a Bayesian interpretation of the proposed approach is not straightforward due to the use of empirical component $-\log p(e_i, f_i)$ in model encoding. Changing the model encoding to use, for example, a code for $n(e_i, f_i)$ would allow for a direct Bayesian interpretation of the proposed code, and we plan to pursue this direction in the future.

The output of the MDL training algorithm is the joint probability model P that we use to define the transliteration model weights as the logarithm of corresponding conditional probabilities: $T(e_i, f_i) = \log \frac{p(e_i, f_i)}{\sum_f p(e_i, f)}$. During the decoding process of inferring f from e via an alignment A, we integrate the language model probability $p(f)$ via a linear combination: $T_{GEN}(e) = arg \max_f \{T(A) + \mu \log p(f)/|f|\}$, where μ is a combination parameter estimated via cross-validation.

3 Discriminative Training

We use the MDL-trained transliteration model T as a starting point for discriminative training: we consider all n-gram pairs (e_i, f_i) with nonzero probabilities $p(e_i, f_i)$ as features of a linear discriminative model T_{DISCR}. We also integrate the normalized language modeling probability $p_0(f) = p(f)^{\frac{1}{|f|}}$ in the discriminative model as one of the features: $T_{DISCR}(e) = arg \max_f \{T(A) + T_0 p_0(f)\}$. We learn the weights $T(e_i, f_i)$ and T_0 of the discriminative model using the average perceptron algorithm of (Collins, 2002). Since both the transliteration model and the language model are required to be learned from the same data, and the language modeling probability is integrated into our decoding process, we remove the string e from the language model before processing the example (f, e) during training; we re-incorporate the string e in the language model after the example (f, e) is processed by the averaged perceptron algorithm. We use the discriminatively trained model as the "standard" system in our experiments.

4 Experiments

We use the standard data for transliterating from English into 8 non-Latin scripts: Chinese (Haizhou et al., 2004); Korean, Japanese (Kanji), and Japanese (Katakana) (CJK Institute, 2009); Hindi, Tamil, Kannada, and Russian (Kumaran and Kellner, 2007). The data is provided as part of the Named Entities Workshop 2009 Machine Transliteration Shared Task (Li et al., 2009).

For all 8 datasets, we report scores on the standard tests sets provided as part of the evaluation. Details of the evaluation methodology are presented in (Li et al., 2009).

4.1 Preprocessing

We perform the same uniform processing of data: names are considered sequences of Unicode characters in their standard decomposed form (NFD). In particular, Korean Hangul characters are decomposed into Jamo syllabary. Since the evaluation data are provided in the re-composed form, we re-compose output of the transliteration system.

We split multi-word names (in Hindi, Tamil, and Kannada datasets) in single words and conducted training and evaluation on the single word level. We assume no word order change for multi-word names and ignore name pairs with different numbers of words.

4.2 System Parameters and Tuning

We apply pre-set system parameters with very little tuning. In particular, we utilize a 5-gram language model with Good-Turing discounting. The MDL training algorithm requires only the cardinalities of the corresponding alphabets as parameters, and we use the following approximate vocabulary sizes typically rounded to the closest power of 2 (except for Chinese and Japanese): for English, Russian, Tamil, and Kannada, we set $|V| = 32$; for Katakana and Hindi, $|V| = 64$; for Korean Jamo, $|V| = 128$; for Chinese and Japanese Kanji, $|V| = 1024$.

We perform 10 iterations of the average perceptron algorithm for discriminative training. For both alignment and decoding, we use a beam search decoder, with the beam size set to 100.

	Init	Comp	Ratio	Dict
Chinese	333 Kb	158 Kb	0.48	5780
Hindi	159 Kb	72 Kb	0.45	1956
Japanese (Kanji)	170 Kb	82 Kb	0.48	4394
Kannada	131 Kb	62 Kb	0.48	2010
Japanese (Katakana)	289 Kb	136 Kb	0.47	3383
Korean	69 Kb	31 Kb	0.45	1181
Russian	78 Kb	37 Kb	0.48	865
Tamil	134 Kb	62 Kb	0.46	1827

Table 1: MDL Data and Model Compression showing initial data size, final combined data and model size, the compression ratio, and the number of n-gram pairs in the final model.

	T1(Acc)	T2(Acc)	T2(F)	T2(MRR)
Chinese	0.522	0.619	0.847	0.711
Hindi	0.312	0.409	0.864	0.527
Japanese (Kanji)	0.484	0.509	0.675	0.6
Kannada	0.227	0.345	0.854	0.462
Japanese (Katakana)	0.318	0.420	0.807	0.541
Korean	0.339	0.413	0.702	0.524
Russian	0.488	0.566	0.919	0.662
Tamil	0.267	0.374	0.880	0.512

Table 2: Experimental results for transliteration from English to 8 non-Latin scripts comparing performance of generative (T1) and corresponding discriminative (T2) models.

4.3 Results

Our first set of experiments illustrates compression achieved by MDL training. Table 1 shows for each for the training datasets, the original size of the data, compressed size of the data including the model size, the compression ratio, and the number of n-gram pairs in the final model.

We see very similar compression for all languages. The number of n-gram pairs for the final model is also relatively small. In general, MDL training with discriminative modeling allows us to discover a flexible small set of features (n-gram pairs) without placing any restriction on n-gram size. We can interpret MDL training as searching implicitly for the best bound on the n-gram size together with searching for appropriate features. Our preliminary experiments also indicate that performance of models produced by the MDL approach roughly corresponds to performance of models trained with the optimal bound on the size of n-gram features.

Table 2 demonstrates that discriminative modeling significantly improves performance of the corresponding generative models. In this setting, the MDL training step is effectively used for feature construction: its goal is to automatically hone in on a small set of features whose weights are later learned by discriminative methods.

From a broader perspective, it is an open question whether seeking a compact representation of sequential data leads to robust and best-performing models, especially in noisy environments. For example, state-of-the-art phrase translation models eschew succinct representations, and instead employ broad redundant sets of features (Koehn et al., 2003). On the other hand, recent research show that small translation models lead to superior alignment (Bodrumlu et al., 2009). Therefore, investigation of the trade-off between robust redundant and succinct representation present an interesting area for future research.

5 Related Work

There is plethora of work on transliteration covering both generative and discriminative models: (Knight and Graehl, 1997; Al-onaizan and Knight, 2002; Huang et al., 2004; Haizhou et al., 2004; Zelenko and Aone, 2006; Sherif and Kondrak, 2007; Goldwasser and Roth, 2008). Application of the minimum description length principle (Grunwald, 2007) in natural language processing has been heretofore mostly limited to morphological analysis (Goldsmith, 2001; Argamon et al., 2004). (Bodrumlu et al., 2009) present a related approach on optimizing the alignment dictionary size in machine translation.

6 Conclusions

We introduced a minimum description length approach for training transliteration models that allows to avoid overfitting without putting apriori constraints of the size of n-grams in transliteration models. We plan to apply the same paradigm to other sequence modeling tasks such as sequence classification and segmentation, in both supervised and unsupervised settings.

References

Y. Al-onaizan and K. Knight. 2002. Machine transliteration of names in arabic text. In *ACL Workshop on Comp. Approaches to Semitic Languages*, pages 34–46.

S. Argamon, N. Akiva, A. Amir, and O. Kapah. 2004. Efficient unsupervised recursive word segmentation using minimum description length. In *Proceedings of COLING*.

T. Bodrumlu, K. Knight, and S. Ravi. 2009. A new objective function for word alignment. In *Proceedings NAACL Workshop on Integer Linear Programming for NLP*.

CJK Institute. 2009. http://www.cjk.org.

M. Collins. 2002. Discriminative training methods for hidden markov models: Theory and experiments with perceptron algorithms. In *Proceedings of EMNLP*.

J. Goldsmith. 2001. Unsupervised learning of the morphology of a natural language. *Computational Linguistics*, pages 153–198.

D. Goldwasser and D. Roth. 2008. Transliteration as constrained optimization. In *Proceedings of EMNLP*.

P. Grunwald. 2007. *The Minimum Description Length principle*. MIT Press.

L. Haizhou, Z. Min, and S. Jian. 2004. A joint source-channel model for machine transliteration. In *Proceedings of ACL*.

F. Huang, S. Vogel, , and A. Waibel. 2004. Improving named entity translation combining phonetic and semantic similarities. In *Proceedings of HLT/NAACL*.

K. Knight and J. Graehl. 1997. Machine transliteration. *Computational Linguistics*, pages 128–135.

P. Koehn, F. Och, and D. Marcu. 2003. Statistical phrase-based translation. In *Proceedings of NLT/NAACL*.

A. Kumaran and T. Kellner. 2007. A generic framework for machine transliteration. In *Proceedings of SIGIR*.

Haizhou Li, A. Kumaran, Min Zhang, and V. Pervouchine. 2009. Whitepaper of news 2009 machine transliteration shared task. In *Proceedings of ACL-IJCNLP 2009 Named Entities Workshop (NEWS 2009)*.

T. Sherif and G. Kondrak. 2007. Substring-based transliteration. In *Proceedings of ACL*.

D. Zelenko and C. Aone. 2006. Discriminative methods for transliteration. In *Proceedings of EMNLP*.

ϵ-extension Hidden Markov Models and Weighted Transducers for Machine Transliteration

Balakrishnan Vardarajan
Dept. of Electrical and Computer Engineering
Johns Hopkins University
bvarada2@jhu.edu

Delip Rao
Dept. of Computer Science
Johns Hopkins University
delip@cs.jhu.edu

Abstract

We describe in detail a method for transliterating an English string to a foreign language string evaluated on five different languages, including Tamil, Hindi, Russian, Chinese, and Kannada. Our method involves deriving substring alignments from the training data and learning a weighted finite state transducer from these alignments. We define an ϵ-extension Hidden Markov Model to derive alignments between training pairs and a heuristic to extract the substring alignments. Our method involves only two tunable parameters that can be optimized on held-out data.

1 Introduction

Transliteration is a letter by letter mapping of one writing system to another. Apart from the obvious use in writing systems, transliteration is also useful in conjunction with translation. For example, machine translation BLEU scores are known to improve when named entities are transliterated. This engendered several investigations into automatic transliteration of strings, named entities in particular, from one language to another. See Knight and Graehl(1997) and later papers on this topic for an overview.

Hidden Markov Model (HMM) (Rabiner, 1989) is a standard sequence modeling tool used in various problems in natural language processing like machine translation, speech recognition, part of speech tagging and information extraction. There have been earlier attempts in using HMMs for automatic transliteration. See (Abdul Jaleel and Larkey, 2003; Zhou et al., 2008) for example. In this paper, we define an ϵ-extension Hidden Markov Model that allows us to align source and target language strings such that the characters in the source string may be optionally aligned to the ϵ symbol. We also introduce a heuristic that allows us to extract high quality sub-alignments from the ϵ-aligned word pairs. This allows us to define a weighted finite state transducer that produces transliterations for an English string by minimal segmentation.

The overview of this paper is as follows: Section 2 introduces ϵ-extension Hidden Markov Model and describes our alignment procedure. Section 3 describes the substring alignment heuristic and our weighted finite state transducer to derive the final n-best transliterations. We conclude with a result section describing results from the NEWS 2009 shared task on five different languages.

2 Learning Alignments

The training data $\mathcal{D}$ is given as pairs of strings $(\mathbf{e}, \mathbf{f})$ where $\mathbf{e}$ is the English string with the corresponding foreign transliteration $\mathbf{f}$. The English string $\mathbf{e}$ consists of a sequence of English letters $(e_1, e_2, \ldots, e_N)$ while $\mathbf{f} = (f_1, f_2, \ldots, f_M)$.

We represent $\mathcal{E}$ as the set of all English symbols and $\mathcal{F}$ as the set of all foreign symbols.[1] We also assume both languages have a special null symbol ϵ, that is $\epsilon \in \mathcal{E}$ and $\epsilon \in \mathcal{F}$.

Our alignment model is a Hidden Markov Model $\mathcal{H}(X, Y, \mathcal{S}, \mathbf{T}, \mathbf{P}_s)$, where

- X is the start state and Y is the end state.
- $\mathcal{S}$ is the set of emitting states with $S = |\mathcal{S}|$. The emitting states are indexed from 1 to S. The start state X is indexed as state 0 and the end state Y is indexed as state $S+1$.
- $\mathbf{T}$ is an $(S+1) \times (S+1)$ stochastic matrix with $\mathbf{T} = [t_{ij}]$ for $i \in \{0, 1, \ldots, S\}$ and $j \in \{1, 2, \ldots, S+1\}$.

[1] Alphabets and diacritics are treated as separate symbols.

Proceedings of the 2009 Named Entities Workshop, ACL-IJCNLP 2009, pages 120–123,
Suntec, Singapore, 7 August 2009. ©2009 ACL and AFNLP

- $\mathbf{P}_s = [p_{ef}]$ is an $|\mathcal{E}| \times |\mathcal{F}|$ matrix of joint emission probabilities with $p_{ef} = P(e, f|s)$ $\forall s \in \mathcal{S}$.

We define $\tilde{\mathbf{s}}$ to be an ϵ-extension of a string of characters $\mathbf{s} = (c_1, c_2, \ldots, c_k)$ as the string obtained by pumping an arbitrary number of ϵ symbols between any two adjacent characters c_l and c_{l+1}. That is, $\tilde{\mathbf{s}} = (d_{i_1}, \ldots, d_{i_2}, \ldots, d_{i_k})$ where $d_{i_j} = c_j$ and $d_l = \epsilon$ for $i_m < l < i_{m+1}$ where $1 \leq l < k$. Observe that there are countably infinite ϵ-extensions for a given string $\mathbf{s}$ since an arbitrary number of ϵ symbols can be inserted between characters c_m and c_{m+1}. Let $\mathcal{T}(\mathbf{s})$ denote the set of all possible ϵ-extensions for a given string $\mathbf{s}$.

For a given pair of strings $(\mathbf{u}, \mathbf{v})$, we define a *joint* ϵ-extension of $(\mathbf{u}, \mathbf{v})$ as the pair $(\tilde{\mathbf{u}}, \tilde{\mathbf{v}})$ s.t. $\tilde{\mathbf{u}} \in \mathcal{T}(\mathbf{u})$ and $\tilde{\mathbf{v}} \in \mathcal{T}(\mathbf{v})$ with $|\tilde{\mathbf{u}}| = |\tilde{\mathbf{v}}|$ and $\nexists i$ s.t. $\tilde{u}_i = \tilde{v}_i = \epsilon$. Due to this restriction, there are finite ϵ-extensions for a pair $(\mathbf{u}, \mathbf{v})$ with the length of $\tilde{\mathbf{u}}$ and $\tilde{\mathbf{v}}$ bounded above by $|\mathbf{u}| + |\mathbf{v}|$. [2] Let $J(\mathbf{u}, \mathbf{v})$ denote the set of all joint ϵ-extensions of $(\mathbf{u}, \mathbf{v})$.

Given a pair of strings $(\mathbf{e}, \mathbf{f})$ with $\mathbf{e} = (e_1, e_2, \ldots, e_N)$ and $\mathbf{f} = (f_1, f_2, \ldots, f_M)$, we compute the probability $\alpha(\mathbf{e}, \mathbf{f}, s')$ that they are transliteration pairs ending in state s' as

$$\alpha(\mathbf{e}, \mathbf{f}, s') = \sum_{(\tilde{\mathbf{e}}, \tilde{\mathbf{f}}) \in J(\mathbf{e}, \mathbf{f})} \sum_{0 = s_0, \ldots, s_{|\tilde{\mathbf{e}}|} = s'} t_{0, s_1} \prod_{i=1}^{|\tilde{\mathbf{e}}|} t_{s_i, s_{i+1}} P(\tilde{e}_i, \tilde{f}_i | s_i)$$

In order to compute the probability $Q(\mathbf{e}, \mathbf{f})$ of a given transliteration pair, the final state has to be the end state $S+1$. Hence

$$Q(\mathbf{e}, \mathbf{f}) = \sum_{s=1}^{S} \alpha(\mathbf{e}, \mathbf{f}, s) t_{s, S+1} \qquad (1)$$

We also write the probability $\beta(\mathbf{e}, \mathbf{f}, s')$ that they are transliteration pairs starting in state s' as

$$\beta(\mathbf{e}, \mathbf{f}, s') = \sum_{(\tilde{\mathbf{e}}, \tilde{\mathbf{f}}) \in J(\mathbf{e}, \mathbf{f})} \sum_{s' = s_0, \ldots, s_{|\tilde{\mathbf{e}}|+1} = S+1} t_{s_0, s_1} \prod_{i=1}^{|\tilde{\mathbf{e}}|} t_{s_i, s_{i+1}} P(\tilde{e}_i, \tilde{f}_i | s_i)$$

Again noting that the start state of the HMM $\mathcal{H}$ is 0, we have $Q(\mathbf{e}, \mathbf{f}) = \sum_{s=1}^{S} \beta(\mathbf{e}, \mathbf{f}, s) t_{0,s}$. We denote a subsequence of a string $\mathbf{u}$ as $\mathbf{u}_n^m = (u_n, u_{n+1}, \ldots, u_m)$. Using these definitions, we can define $\alpha(\mathbf{e}_1^i, \mathbf{f}_1^j, s)$ as

$$\begin{cases} 1 & i = j = 0, s = 0 \\ 0 & i = j = 0, s \neq 0 \\ t_{0,s} P(e_1, f_1 | s) & i = j = 1 \\ \sum_{s'=1}^{S} t_{s',s} \alpha(\mathbf{e}_1^i, \mathbf{f}_1^{j-1}, s') P(\epsilon, f_j | s) & i = 1, j > 1 \\ \sum_{s'=1}^{S} t_{s',s} \alpha(\mathbf{e}_1^{i-1}, \mathbf{f}_1^j, s') P(e_i, \epsilon | s) & i > 1, j = 1 \end{cases}$$

Finally for $i > 1$ and $j > 1$,

$$\alpha(\mathbf{e}_1^i, \mathbf{f}_1^j, s) = \sum_{s' \in \mathcal{S}} t_{s',s} [\alpha(\mathbf{e}_1^i, \mathbf{f}_1^{j-1}, s') P(\epsilon, f_j | s) + \alpha(\mathbf{e}_1^{i-1}, \mathbf{f}_1^j, s') P(e_i, \epsilon | s) + \alpha(\mathbf{e}_1^{i-1}, \mathbf{f}_1^{j-1}, s') P(e_i, f_j | s)]$$

Similarly the recurrence for $\beta(\mathbf{e}_i^N, \mathbf{f}_j^M, s)$

$$\begin{cases} t_{s,S+1} & i = N+1, \\ & j = M+1 \\ \sum_{s'=1}^{S} t_{s,s'} \beta(\mathbf{e}_i^N, \mathbf{f}_{j+1}^M, s') P(\epsilon, f_j | s') & i = N, j < M \\ \sum_{s'=1}^{S} t_{s,s'} \beta(\mathbf{e}_{i+1}^N, \mathbf{f}_j^M, s') P(e_i, \epsilon | s') & i < N, j = M \end{cases}$$

For $i < N$ and $j < M$, $\beta(\mathbf{e}_i^N, \mathbf{f}_j^M, s) =$

$$\sum_{s' \in \mathcal{S}} t_{s,s'} [\beta(\mathbf{e}_i^N, \mathbf{f}_{j+1}^M, s') P(\epsilon, f_j | s') + \beta(\mathbf{e}_{i+1}^N, \mathbf{f}_j^M, s') P(e_i, \epsilon | s') + \beta(\mathbf{e}_{i+1}^N, \mathbf{f}_{j+1}^M, s') P(e_i, f_j | s')]$$

In order to proceed with the E.M. estimation of the parameters $\mathbf{T}$ and $\mathbf{P}_s$, we collect the *soft* counts $c(e, f|s)$ for emission probabilities by looping over the training data $\mathcal{D}$ as shown in Figure 1.

Similarly the soft counts $c_t(s', s)$ for the transition probabilities are estimated as shown in Figure 2.

Finally the probabilities $P(e, f|s)$ and t_{ij} are re-estimated as

$$\hat{P}(e, f|s) = \frac{c(e, f|s)}{\sum_{e \in \mathcal{E}, f \in \mathcal{F}} c(e, f|s)} \qquad (2)$$

$$\hat{t}_{s',s} = \frac{c_t(s', s)}{\sum_s c_t(s', s)} \qquad (3)$$

We can also compute the most probable alignment $(\tilde{\mathbf{e}}, \tilde{\mathbf{f}})$ between the two strings $\mathbf{e}$ and $\mathbf{f}$ as

[2] $|\tilde{\mathbf{u}}| = |\tilde{\mathbf{v}}| > |\mathbf{u}| + |\mathbf{v}|$ would imply $\exists i$ s.t. $\tilde{u}_i = \tilde{v}_i = \epsilon$ which contradicts the definition of joint ϵ-extension.

$$
\begin{aligned}
c(e, f|s) = & \sum_{(\mathbf{e},\mathbf{f})\in\mathcal{D}} \frac{1}{Q(\mathbf{e},\mathbf{f})} \sum_{i=1}^{N}\sum_{j=1}^{M}\sum_{s'} \alpha(\mathbf{e}_1^{i-1}, \mathbf{f}_1^{j-1}, s') t_{s',s} P(e_i, f_j|s) \beta(\mathbf{e}_i^N, \mathbf{f}_j^M, s) \mathbf{1}(e_i = e, f_j = f) \\
& + \sum_{(\mathbf{e},\mathbf{f})\in\mathcal{D}} \frac{1}{Q(\mathbf{e},\mathbf{f})} \sum_{i=1}^{N}\sum_{j=1}^{M}\sum_{s'} \alpha(\mathbf{e}_1^{i-1}, \mathbf{f}_1^{j}, s') t_{s',s} P(e_i, \epsilon|s) \beta(\mathbf{e}_i^N, \mathbf{f}_j^M, s) \mathbf{1}(e_i = e, f_j = f) \\
& + \sum_{(\mathbf{e},\mathbf{f})\in\mathcal{D}} \frac{1}{Q(\mathbf{e},\mathbf{f})} \sum_{i=1}^{N}\sum_{j=1}^{M}\sum_{s'} \alpha(\mathbf{e}_1^{i}, \mathbf{f}_1^{j-1}, s') t_{s',s} P(\epsilon, f_j|s) \beta(\mathbf{e}_i^N, \mathbf{f}_j^M, s) \mathbf{1}(e_i = e, f_j = f)
\end{aligned}
$$

Figure 1: EM soft count $c(e, f|s)$ estimation.

$$
\begin{aligned}
c_t(s', s) = & \sum_{(\mathbf{e},\mathbf{f})\in\mathcal{D}} \frac{1}{Q(\mathbf{e},\mathbf{f})} \sum_{i=1}^{N}\sum_{j=1}^{M} \alpha(\mathbf{e}_1^{i-1}, \mathbf{f}_1^{j-1}, s') t_{s',s} P(e_i, f_j|s) \beta(\mathbf{e}_i^N, \mathbf{f}_j^M, s) \\
& + \sum_{(\mathbf{e},\mathbf{f})\in\mathcal{D}} \frac{1}{Q(\mathbf{e},\mathbf{f})} \sum_{i=1}^{N}\sum_{j=1}^{M} \alpha(\mathbf{e}_1^{i-1}, \mathbf{f}_1^{j}, s') t_{s',s} P(e_i, \epsilon|s) \beta(\mathbf{e}_i^N, \mathbf{f}_j^M, s) \\
& + \sum_{(\mathbf{e},\mathbf{f})\in\mathcal{D}} \frac{1}{Q(\mathbf{e},\mathbf{f})} \sum_{i=1}^{N}\sum_{j=1}^{M} \alpha(\mathbf{e}_1^{i}, \mathbf{f}_1^{j-1}, s') t_{s',s} P(\epsilon, f_j|s) \beta(\mathbf{e}_i^N, \mathbf{f}_j^M, s) \\
& + \sum_{(\mathbf{e},\mathbf{f})\in\mathcal{D}} \frac{1}{Q(\mathbf{e},\mathbf{f})} \alpha(\mathbf{e}_1^{N}, \mathbf{f}_1^{M}, s') t_{s',S+1} \mathbf{1}(s = S+1)
\end{aligned}
$$

Figure 2: EM soft count $c_t(s', s)$ estimation.

$$\arg\max_{(\tilde{\mathbf{e}},\tilde{\mathbf{f}})\in J(\mathbf{e},\mathbf{f})} \sum_{0=s_0,\ldots,s_{|\tilde{\mathbf{e}}|+1}=S+1} t_{0,s_1} \prod_{i=1}^{|\tilde{\mathbf{e}}|} t_{s_i,s_{i+1}} P(\tilde{e}_i, \tilde{f}_i | s_i)$$

The pair $(\tilde{\mathbf{e}}, \tilde{\mathbf{f}})$ is considered as an alignment between the training pair $(\mathbf{e}, \mathbf{f})$.

3 Transduction of the Transliterated Output

Given an alignment $(\tilde{\mathbf{e}}, \tilde{\mathbf{f}})$, we consider all possible *sub-alignments* $(\tilde{\mathbf{e}}_i^j, \tilde{\mathbf{f}}_i^j)$ as pairs of substrings obtained from $(\tilde{\mathbf{e}}, \tilde{\mathbf{f}})$ such that $\tilde{e}_i \neq \epsilon$, $\tilde{f}_i \neq \epsilon$, $\tilde{e}_{j+1} \neq \epsilon$ and $\tilde{f}_{j+1} \neq \epsilon$. We extract all possible sub-alignments of all the alignments from the training data. Let $\mathcal{A}$ be the bag of all sub-alignments obtained from the training data. We build a weighted finite state transducer that transduces any string in $\mathcal{E}^+$ to $\mathcal{F}^+$ using these sub-alignments.

Let $(\mathbf{u}, \mathbf{v})$ be an element of $\mathcal{A}$. From the training data $\mathcal{D}$, observe that $\mathcal{A}$ can have multiple realizations of $(\mathbf{u}, \mathbf{v})$. Let $N(\mathbf{u}, \mathbf{v})$ be the number of times $(\mathbf{u}, \mathbf{v})$ is observed in $\mathcal{A}$. The empirical probability of transducing string $\mathbf{u}$ to $\mathbf{v}$ is simply

$$P(\mathbf{v}|\mathbf{u}) = \frac{N(\mathbf{u}, \mathbf{v})}{\sum_{\mathbf{v}:(\mathbf{u},\mathbf{v}')\in\mathcal{A}} N(\mathbf{u}, \mathbf{v}')}$$

For every pair $(\mathbf{u}, \mathbf{v}) \in \mathcal{A}$, we also compute the probability of transliteration from the HMM $\mathcal{H}$ as $Q(\mathbf{u}, \mathbf{v})$ from Equation 1.

We construct a finite state transducer $\mathbf{F}_{\mathbf{u},\mathbf{v}}$ that accepts *only* $\mathbf{u}$ and emits $\mathbf{v}$ with a weight $w_{\mathbf{u},\mathbf{v}}$ defined as

$$w_{\mathbf{u},\mathbf{v}} = -\log(P(\mathbf{v}|\mathbf{u})) - \lambda \log(Q(\mathbf{u}, \mathbf{v})) + \delta \quad (4)$$

Finally we construct a global weighted finite state transducer $\mathbf{F}$ by taking the union of all the $\mathbf{F}_{\mathbf{u},\mathbf{v}}$ and taking its closure.

$$\mathbf{F} = \left[\bigcup_{(\mathbf{u},\mathbf{v})\in\mathcal{A}} \mathbf{F}_{u,v} \right]^+ \quad (5)$$

The weight δ is typically sufficiently high so that a new english string is favored to be broken into fewest possible sub-strings whose transliterations are available in the training data.

We tune the weights λ and δ by evaluating the accuracy on the held-out data. The n-best paths in the weighted finite state transducer $\mathbf{F}$ represent our n-best transliterations.

4 Results

We evaluated our system on the standard track data provided by the NEWS 2009 shared task organizers on five different languages – Tamil, Hindi, Russian, and Kannada was derived from (Kumaran and Kellner, 2007) and Chinese from (Li et al., 2004). The results of this evaluation on the test data is shown in Table 1. For a detailed description

Language	Top-1 Accuracy	mean F_1 score	MRR
Tamil	0.327	0.870	0.458
Hindi	0.398	0.855	0.515
Russian	0.506	0.901	0.609
Chinese	0.450	0.755	0.514
Kannada	0.235	0.817	0.353

Table 1: Results on NEWS 2009 test data.

of the evaluation measures used we refer the readers to NEWS 2009 shared task whitepaper (Li et al., 2009).

5 Conclusion

We described a system for automatic transliteration of pairs of strings from one language to another using ϵ-extension hidden markov models and weighted finite state transducers. We evaluated our system on all the languages for the NEWS 2009 standard track. The system presented is language agnostic and can be trained for any language pair within a few minutes on a single core desktop computer.

References

Nasreen Abdul Jaleel and Leah Larkey. 2003. Statistical transliteration for english-arabic cross language information retrieval. In *Proceedings of the twelfth international conference on Information and knowledge management*, pages 139–146.

Kevin Knight and Jonathan Graehl. 1997. Machine transliteration. In *Computational Linguistics*, pages 128–135.

A. Kumaran and Tobias Kellner. 2007. A generic framework for machine transliteration. In *SIGIR '07: Proceedings of the 30th annual international ACM SIGIR conference on Research and development in information retrieval*, pages 721–722, New York, NY, USA. ACM.

Haizhou Li, Min Zhang, and Jian Su. 2004. A joint source-channel model for machine transliteration. In *ACL '04: Proceedings of the 42nd Annual Meeting on Association for Computational Linguistics*, page 159, Morristown, NJ, USA. Association for Computational Linguistics.

Haizhou Li, A Kumaran, Min Zhang, and Vladimir Pervouchine. 2009. Whitepaper of news 2009 machine transliteration shared task. In *Proceedings of ACL-IJCNLP 2009 Named Entities Workshop (NEWS 2009)*.

Lawrence Rabiner. 1989. A tutorial on hidden markov models and selected applications in speech recognition. In *Proceedings of the IEEE*, pages 257–286.

Yilu Zhou, Feng Huang, and Hsinchun Chen. 2008. Combining probability models and web mining models: a framework for jproper name transliteration. *Information Technology and Management*, 9(2):91–103.

Modeling Machine Transliteration as a Phrase Based Statistical Machine Translation Problem

Taraka Rama, Karthik Gali
Language Technologies Research Centre,
IIIT, Hyderabad, India.
{taraka,karthikg}@students.iiit.ac.in

Abstract

In this paper we use the popular phrase-based SMT techniques for the task of machine transliteration, for English-Hindi language pair. Minimum error rate training has been used to learn the model weights. We have achieved an accuracy of 46.3% on the test set. Our results show these techniques can be successfully used for the task of machine transliteration.

1 Introduction

Transliteration can be defined as the task of transcribing the words from a source script to a target script (Surana and Singh, 2008). Transliteration systems find wide applications in Cross Lingual Information Retrieval Systems (CLIR) and Machine Translation (MT) systems. The systems also find use in sentence aligners and word aligners (Aswani and Gaizauskas, 2005). Transcribing the words from one language to another language without the use of a bilingual lexicon is a challenging task as the output word produced in target language should be such that it is acceptable to the readers of the target language. The difficulty arises due to the huge number of Out Of Vocabulary (OOV) words which are continuously added into the language. These OOV words include named entities, technical words, borrowed words and loan words.

In this paper we present a technique for transliterating named entities from English to Hindi using a small set of training and development data. The paper is organised as follows. A survey of the previous work is presented in the next subsection. Section 2 describes the problem modeling which we have adopted from (Rama et al., 2009) which they use for L2P task. Section 3 describes how the parameters are tuned for optimal performance. A brief description of the data sets is provided in Section 4. Section 5 has the results which we have obtained for the test data. Finally we conclude with a summary of the methods and a analysis of the errors.

1.1 Previous Work

Surana and Singh (2008) propose a transliteration system in which they use two different ways of transliterating the named entities based on their origin. A word is classified into two classes either Indian or foreign using character based n-grams. They report their results on Telugu and Hindi data sets. Sherif and Kondrak (2007) propose a hybrid approach in which they use the Viterbi-based monotone search algorithm for searching the possible candidate transliterations. Using the approach given in (Ristad et al., 1998) the sub-string translations are learnt. They integrate the word-based unigram model based on (Knight and Graehl, 1998; Al-Onaizan and Knight, 2002) with the above model for improving the quality of transliterations.

Malik (2006) tries to solve a special case of transliteration for Punjabi in which they convert from Shahmukhi (Arabic script) to Gurumukhi using a set of transliteration rules. Abdul Jaleel (2003) show that, in the domain of information retrieval, the cross language retrieval performance was reduced by 50% when the name entities were not transliterated.

2 Problem Modeling

Assume that given a word, represented as a sequence of letters of the source language $\mathbf{s} = s_1^J = s_1...s_j...s_J$, needs to be transcribed as a sequence of letters in the target language, represented as $\mathbf{t} = t_1^I = t_1...t_i...t_I$. The problem of finding the best target language letter sequence among the transliterated candidates can be represented as:

Proceedings of the 2009 Named Entities Workshop, ACL-IJCNLP 2009, pages 124–127,
Suntec, Singapore, 7 August 2009.

$$\mathbf{t}_{best} = \arg\max_{\mathbf{t}} \{\Pr(\mathbf{t} \mid \mathbf{s})\} \quad (1)$$

We model the transliteration problem based on the noisy channel model. Reformulating the above equation using Bayes Rule:

$$\mathbf{t}_{best} = \arg\max_{\mathbf{t}} p(\mathbf{s} \mid \mathbf{t})\, p(\mathbf{s}) \quad (2)$$

This formulation allows for a target language letters' n-gram model $p(\mathbf{t})$ and a transcription model $p(\mathbf{s} \mid \mathbf{t})$. Given a sequence of letters **s**, the argmax function is a search function to output the best target letter sequence.

From the above equation, the best target sequence is obtained based on the product of the probabilities of transcription model and the probabilities of a language model and their respective weights. The method for obtaining the transcription probabilities is described briefly in the next section. Determining the best weights is necessary for obtaining the right target language sequence. The estimation of the models' weights can be done in the following manner.

The posterior probability $\Pr(\mathbf{t} \mid \mathbf{s})$ can also be directly modeled using a log-linear model. In this model, we have a set of M feature functions $h_m(\mathbf{t}, \mathbf{s}), m = 1...M$. For each feature function there exists a weight or model parameter $\lambda_m, m = 1...M$. Thus the posterior probability becomes:

$$\Pr(\mathbf{t} \mid \mathbf{s}) = p_{\lambda_1^M}(\mathbf{t} \mid \mathbf{s}) \quad (3)$$

$$= \frac{\exp\left[\Sigma_{m=1}^{M} \lambda_m h_m(\mathbf{t}, \mathbf{s})\right]}{\sum_{\acute{t}_1^I} \exp\left[\Sigma_{m=1}^{M} \lambda_m h_m(\acute{t}_1^I, \mathbf{s})\right]} \quad (4)$$

with the denominator, a normalization factor that can be ignored in the maximization process.

The above modeling entails finding the suitable model parameters or weights which reflect the properties of our task. We adopt the criterion followed in (Och, 2003) for optimising the parameters of the model. The details of the solution and proof for the convergence are given in Och (2003). The models' weights, used for the transliteration task, are obtained from this training.

All the above tools are available as a part of publicly available MOSES (Koehn et al., 2007) tool kit. Hence we used the tool kit for our experiments.

3 Tuning the parameters

The source language to target language letters are aligned using GIZA++ (Och and Ney, 2003). Every letter is treated as a single word for the GIZA++ input. The alignments are then used to learn the phrase transliteration probabilities which are estimated using the scoring function given in (Koehn et al., 2003).

The parameters which have a major influence on the performance of a phrase-based SMT model are the alignment heuristics, the maximum phrase length (MPR) and the order of the language model (Koehn et al., 2003). In the context of transliteration, *phrase* means a sequence of letters(of source and target language) mapped to each other with some probability (i.e., the *hypothesis*) and stored in a phrase table. The *maximum phrase length* corresponds to the maximum number of letters that a hypothesis can contain. Higher phrase length corresponds a larger phrase table during decoding.

We have conducted experiments to see which combination gives the best output. We initially trained the model with various parameters on the training data and tested for various values of the above parameters. We varied the maximum phrase length from 2 to 7. The language model was trained using SRILM toolkit (Stolcke, 2002). We varied the order of language model from 2 to 8. We also traversed the alignment heuristics spectrum, from the parsimonious *intersect* at one end of the spectrum through *grow, grow-diag, grow-diag-final, grow-diag-final-and* and *srctotrg* to the most lenient *union* at the other end.

We observed that the best results were obtained when the language model was trained on 7-gram and the alignment heuristic was *grow-diag-final*. No significant improvement was observed in the results when the value of MPR was greater than 7. We have done post-processing and taken care such that the alignments are always monotonic and no letter was left unlinked.

4 Data Sets

We have used the data sets provided by organisers of the NEWS 2009 Machine Transliteration Shared Task (Kumaran and Kellner, 2007). Prior to the release of the test data only the training data and development data was available. The training data and development data consisted of a parallel corpus having entries in both English and Hindi.

The training data and development data had 9975 entries and 974 entries respectively. We used the training data given as a part of the shared task for generating the phrase table and the language model. For tuning the parameters mentioned in the previous section, we used the development data.

From the training and development data we have observed that the words can be roughly divided into following categories, Persian, European (primarily English), Indian, Arabic words, based on their origin. The test data consisted of 1000 entries. We proceeded to experiment with the test set once the set was released.

5 Experiments and Results

The parameters described in Section 3 were the initial settings of the system. The system was tuned on the development set, as described in Section 2, for obtaining the appropriate model weights. The system tuned on the development data was used to test it against the test data set. We have obtained the following model weights. The other features available in the translation system such as *word penalty, phrase penalty* donot account in the transliteration task and hence were not included.

```
language model = 0.099
translation model = 0.122
```

Prior to the release of the test data, we tested the system without tuning on development data. The default model weights were used to test our system on the development data. In the next step the model weights were obtained by tuning the system. Although the system allows for a distortion model, allowing for phrase movements, we did not use the distortion model as distortion is meaningless in the domain of transliteration. The following measures such as Word Accuracy (ACC), Mean F-Score, Mean Reciprocal Rank (MRR), MAP_{ref}, MAP_{10}, MAP_{sys} were used to evaluate our system performance. A detailed description of each measure is available in (Li et al., 2009).

Measure	Result
ACC	0.463
Mean F-Score	0.876
MRR	0.573
MAP_{ref}	0.454
MAP_{10}	0.201
MAP_{sys}	0.201

Table 1: Evaluation of Various Measures on Test Data

6 Conclusion

In this paper we show that we can use the popular phrase based SMT systems successfully for the task of transliteration. The publicly available tool GIZA++ was used to align the letters. Then the phrases were extracted and counted and stored in phrase tables. The weights were estimated using minimum error rate training as described earlier using development data. Then beam-search based decoder was used to transliterate the English words into Hindi. After the release of the reference corpora we examined the error results and observed that majority of the errors resulted in the case of the foreign origin words. We provide some examples of the foreign origin words which were transliterated erroneously.

MONTAGUE	मॉन्टैग
AGAMEMNON	अगामेम्नों
HEINEKEN	हेनकेन
KLUANE	क्लुआने

Figure 1: Error Transliterations of Some Foreign Origin Words

References

N. AbdulJaleel and L.S. Larkey. 2003. Statistical transliteration for english-arabic cross language information retrieval.

Y. Al-Onaizan and K. Knight. 2002. Machine transliteration of names in Arabic text. In *Proceedings of the ACL-02 workshop on Computational approaches to semitic languages*, pages 1–13. Association for Computational Linguistics Morristown, NJ, USA.

N. Aswani and R. Gaizauskas. 2005. A hybrid approach to align sentences and words in English-Hindi parallel corpora. *Building and Using Parallel Texts: Data-Driven Machine Translation and Beyond*, page 57.

K. Knight and J. Graehl. 1998. Machine transliteration. *Computational Linguistics*, 24(4):599–612.

P. Koehn, F.J. Och, and D. Marcu. 2003. Statistical phrase-based translation. In *Proceedings of the 2003 Conference of the NAACL:HLT-Volume 1*, pages 48–54. ACL Morristown, NJ, USA.

P. Koehn, H. Hoang, A. Birch, C. Callison-Burch, M. Federico, N. Bertoldi, B. Cowan, W. Shen, C. Moran, R. Zens, et al. 2007. Moses: Open Source Toolkit for Statistical Machine Translation. In *ACL*, volume 45, page 2.

A. Kumaran and T. Kellner. 2007. A generic framework for machine transliteration. In *Proceedings of the 30th annual international ACM SIGIR conference on Research and development in information retrieval*, pages 721–722. ACM New York, NY, USA.

H. Li, A. Kumaran, M. Zhang, and V. Pervouchine. 2009. Whitepaper of NEWS 2009 Machine Transliteration Shared Task. In *Proceedings of ACL-IJCNLP 2009 Named Entities Workshop (NEWS 2009)*. ACL, Singapore, 2009.

M.G.A. Malik. 2006. Punjabi machine transliteration. In *Proceedings of the 21st International Conference on Computational Linguistics and the 44th annual meeting of the Association for Computational Linguistics*, pages 1137–1144. Association for Computational Linguistics Morristown, NJ, USA.

F.J. Och and H. Ney. 2003. A Systematic Comparison of Various Statistical Alignment Models. *Computational Linguistics*, 29(1):19–51.

F.J. Och. 2003. Minimum error rate training in statistical machine translation. In *Proceedings of the 41st Annual Meeting on ACL-Volume 1*, pages 160–167. ACL, Morristown, NJ, USA.

T. Rama, A.K. Singh, and S. Kolachina. 2009. Modeling letter to phoneme conversion as a phrase based statistical machine translation problem with minimum error rate training. In *The NAACL Student Research Workshop*, Boulder, Colorado.

ES Ristad, PN Yianilos, M.T. Inc, and NJ Princeton. 1998. Learning string-edit distance. *IEEE Transactions on Pattern Analysis and Machine Intelligence*, 20(5):522–532.

T. Sherif and G. Kondrak. 2007. Substring-based transliteration. In *ANNUAL MEETING-ASSOCIATION FOR COMPUTATIONAL LINGUISTICS*, volume 45, page 944.

A. Stolcke. 2002. Srilm – an extensible language modeling toolkit.

H. Surana and A.K. Singh. 2008. A more discerning and adaptable multilingual transliteration mechanism for indian languages. In *Proceedings of the Third International Joint Conference on Natural Language Processing*.

Maximum N-gram HMM-based Name Transliteration: Experiment in NEWS 2009 on English-Chinese Corpus

Yilu Zhou
George Washington University
yzhou@gwu.edu

Abstract

We propose an English-Chinese name transliteration system using a maximum N-gram Hidden Markov Model. To handle special challenges with alphabet-based and character-based language pair, we apply a two-phase transliteration model by building two HMM models, one between English and Chinese Pinyin and another between Chinese Pinyin and Chinese characters. Our model improves traditional HMM by assigning the longest prior translation sequence of syllables the largest weight. In our non-standard runs, we use a Web-mining module to boost the performance by adding online popularity information of candidate translations. The entire model does not rely on any dictionaries and the probability tables are derived merely from training corpus. In participation of NEWS 2009 experiment, our model achieved 0.462 Top-1 accuracy and 0.764 Mean F-score.

1 Introduction

It is in general difficult for human to translate unfamiliar personal names, place names and names of organizations (Lee et al., 2006). One reason is the variability in name translation. In many situations, there is more than one correct translation for the same name. In some languages, such as Arabic, it can go up to as many as forty (Arbabi et al., 1994). Even professional translators find it difficult to identify all variations. For example, when translating "Phelps" into Chinese, there are at least 5 different ways to translate this name: "费尔普斯," "菲尔普斯," "弗尔普斯," "菲尔普思," and "菲尔普丝," with some more popular than others.

The variability in translation implies the complexity in name translation that can hardly be addressed in typical machine translation systems. Machine translation systems are often black boxes where only one translation is provided, which do not offer a solution to variability issue. The accuracy of a machine translation system, whether statistical or example-based, largely depends on sentence context information. This context information is often not available with name translation. Furthermore, emerging names are difficult to capture in regular machine translation systems if they have not been included in training corpus or translation dictionary. Thus, being able to translate proper names not only has its own application area, it will also enhance the performance of current machine translation systems.

In our previous English-Arabic name transliteration work (Zhou et al., 2008), we proposed a framework for name transliteration using a 2-gram and a 3-gram Hidden Markov Model (HMM). In this research, we extend our 2-gram and 3-gram HMM to an N-gram HMM where N is the maximum number of prior translation mapping sequence that can be identified in the training corpus. In our non-standard runs, we also integrated a Web mining module. The rest of the paper is structured as follows. Section 2 reviews related work; Section 3 describes our algorithm; Section 4 discusses implementation and evaluation results are provided in Section 5. Section 6 concludes our work.

2 Related Work

Research in translating proper names has focused on two strategies: One is to mine translation pairs from bilingual online resources or corpora (Lee et. al, 2006). The second approach is a direct translation approach (Chen and Zong, 2008).

The first approach is based on the assumption that the two name equivalents should share similar relevant context words in their languages. Correct transliteration is then extracted from the closest matching proper nouns. The second approach, direct translation, is often done by transliteration. Transliteration is the representation of a word or phrase in the closest corresponding letters or characters of a language with different alphabet so that the pronunciation is as close as possible to the original word or phrase (AbdulJaleel and Larkey, 2003). Unlike mining-based approach, transliteration can deal with low-frequency proper names, but may generate ill-formed translations.

Proceedings of the 2009 Named Entities Workshop, ACL-IJCNLP 2009, pages 128–131,
Suntec, Singapore, 7 August 2009.

Transliteration models can be categorized into rule-based approach and statistical approach. A rule-based approach maps each letter or a set of letters in the source language to the closest sounding letter or letters in the target language according to pre-defined rules or mapping tables. It relies on manual identification of all transliteration rules and heuristics, which can be very complex and time consuming to build (Darwish et al., 2001). A statistical approach obtains translation probabilities from a training corpus: pairs of transliterated words. When new words come, the statistical approach picks the transliteration candidate with the highest transliteration probabilities generated as the correct transliteration. Most statistical-based research used phoneme-based transliteration, relying on a pronunciation dictionary. Al-Onaizan and Knight showed that a grapheme-based approach out-performed a phoneme-based approach in Arabic-English transliteration (Al-Onaizan and Knight, 2002).

3 Challenges with Chinese Language

There are several challenges in transliterating English names into Chinese. First, written Chinese is a logogram language. Thus, a phonetic representation of Chinese characters, Pinyin, is used as an intermediate Romanization. Our process of translating an English name into Chinese consists of two steps: translating English word into Pinyin and then mapping Pinyin into Chinese characters.

Second, Chinese is not only monosyllabic, but the pronunciation of each Chinese character is always composed of one (or none) Consonant unit and one Vowel unit with the Consonant always appears at the beginning. For example, /EKS/ is one syllable in English but is three syllables in Chinese (/E/ + /KE/ + /SI/). English syllables need to be processed in a way that can be mapped to Chinese Pinyin.

4 Proposed Maximum N-gram HMM

Figure 1 illustrates our name translation framework. The framework consists of three major components: 1) Training, 2) Hidden Markov Model-based Transliteration, and 3) Web Mining-enhanced ranking.

4.1 Training

The training process (Figure 1 Module 1) generates two transliteration probability tables based on a training corpus of English-Pinyin pair and Pinyin-Chinese name pairs. Pinyin is not provided in the training corpus, but is easy to obtain from a Chinese Pinyin table.

In order to perform mapping from English names to Chinese Pinyin, an English name is divided into sub-syllables and this process is called **Syllabification**. Although many English syllabification algorithms have been proposed, they need to be adjusted. During syllabification, light vowels are inserted between two continuous consonants and silent letters are deleted. We use a finite state machine to implement the syllabification process. For example, "Phelps" becomes {/ph/ /e/ /l/ /@/ /p/ /@/ /s/ /@/} with "@" being inserted light vowels.

Alignment process maps each sub-syllable in an English name to target Pinyin. The accuracy of **Alignment** process largely depends on the accuracy of Syllabification. Pinyin to Chinese character alignment is more straightforward where each Pinyin syllable (consonant + vowel) is mapped to the corresponding Chinese character. Once the alignment is done, occurrence of each translation pair can be calculated. Using this occurrence information, we can derive probabilities under various situations to support probability models.

We use the Hidden Markov Model which is one of the most popular probability models and has been used in speech recognition, the human genome project, consumer decision modeling, etc. (Rabiner, 1989). In transliteration, traditional HMM can be viewed as a 2-gram model where the current mapping selection depends on the previous mapping pair. We expand it to an N-gram model and use the combination of 1-gram, 2-gram, ... , (N-1)-gram and N-gram HMM where N is the maximum number of mapping sequence that can be found in training corpus.

The goal of our model is to find the candidate transliteration with the highest transliteration probabilities:

$$(1)\quad \operatorname{argmax} P(t \mid s) = \operatorname{argmax} P(t_1 t_2 . t_n \mid s_1 s_2 .. s_n)$$

Where s is the source name to be transliterated, which contains letter string $s_1 s_2 \ldots s_i$; t is the target name, which contains letter string $t_1 t_2 \ldots t_i$.

In a simple statistical model, or a **1-gram** model, transliteration probability is estimated as:

$$(2)\quad P(t_1, t_2, t_3, \ldots\ldots, t_n \mid s_1, s_2, s_3, \ldots\ldots, s_n) = P(t_1 \mid s_1) P(t_2 \mid s_2) \ldots\ldots P(t_n \mid s_n)$$

Where

$$P(t_i \mid s_i) = \frac{\#\, of\ times\ s_i\ translates\ to\ t_i\ in\ corpus}{\#\, of\ times\ s_i\ appears\ in\ corpus}$$

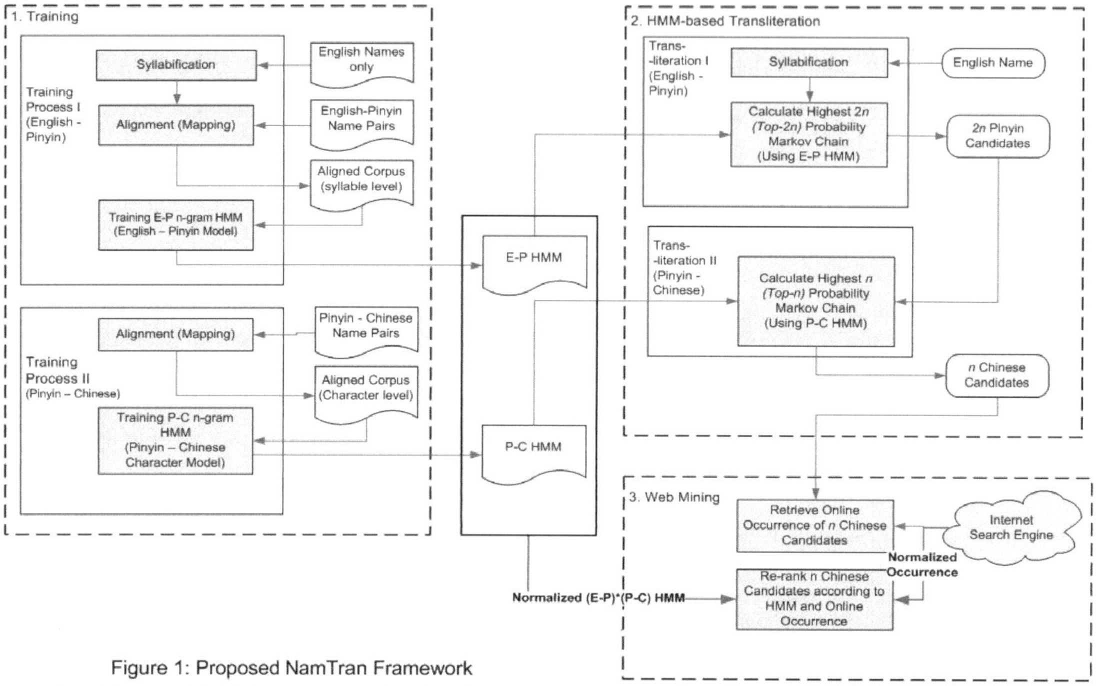

Figure 1: Proposed NamTran Framework

The **bigram** HMM improves the simple statistical model in that it incorporates context information into a probability calculation. The transliteration of the current letter is dependent on the transliteration of **ONE** previous letter (one previous state in HMM). Transliteration probability is estimated as:

(3)

$$P(t_1,t_2,t_3,......,t_n \mid s_1,s_2,s_3,......,s_n) = P(t_1 \mid s_1)P(t_2 \mid s_2,t_1)(t_3 \mid s_3,t_2)......p(t_n \mid s_n,t_{n-1})$$

Where $P(t_i \mid s_i) = \dfrac{\#\,of\ times\ s_i\ translates\ to\ t_i}{\#\,of\ times\ s_i\ occurs}$

and

$$P(t_i \mid s_i,t_{i-1}) = \frac{\#\,of\ times\ s_i\ translates\ to\ t_i\ given\ s_{i-1} -> t_{i-1}}{\#\,of\ times\ s_{i-1}\ translates\ to\ t_{i-1}}$$

The **trigram** HMM intends to capture even more context information by translating the current letter dependent on the **TWO** previous letters. Transliteration probability is estimated as:

(4)

$$P(t_1,t_2,t_3,......,t_n \mid s_1,s_2,s_3,......,s_n) = P(t_1 \mid s_1)p(t_2 \mid s_2,t_1)P(t_3 \mid s_3,t_2,t_1)......p(t_n \mid s_n,t_{n-1},t_{n-2})$$

Where

$$P(t_i \mid s_i) = \frac{\#\,of\ times\ s_i\ translates\ to\ t_i}{\#\,of\ times\ s_i\ occurs}$$

$$P(t_i \mid s_i,t_{i-1}) = \frac{\#of\,times s_i\,translates to t_i\,given s_{i-1} -> t_{i-1}}{\#of\,times s_{i-1}\,translates to t_{i-1}}$$

and

$$P(t_i \mid s_i,t_{i-1},t_{i-2}) = \frac{\#\,of\ times\ s_3\ translates\ to\ t_i\ given\ s_{i-1} -> t_{i-1}\ and\ s_{i-2} -> t_{i-2}}{\#\,of\ times\ s_{i-1}\ translates\ to\ t_{i-1} and\ s_{i-2}\ translates\ to\ t_{i-2}}$$

This process is continued until the maximum mapping sequence is found in the transliteration corpus. The final probability estimation is a weighted combination of all N-grams:

$$FinalTranslitenationScore = \alpha_1(1-gramHMM) + \alpha_2(2-gramHMM) + ... + \alpha_n(N-gramHMM)$$

In our submitted results, we applied $\alpha_1=1$, $\alpha_2=2$, …., $\alpha_n=N$ such that longer matched sequence has a larger contribution in the final probability. The rationale is that the longer the prior sequence identified in training data, the higher probability that the translation sequence is the correct tone. These α parameters can be tuned in the future. We call this approach **Maximum N-gram HMM**. The same process is conducted for Pinyin to Chinese character translation as shown in the lower part of Figure 1 Module 1.

4.2 Translation and Ranking

Once the two Maximum N-gram HMM Model are obtained, new incoming names are translated by obtaining a letter sequence that maximizes the overall probability through the HMM (Figure 1 Module 2). This step uses a modified Viterbi's search algorithm (Viterbi 1967). The original Viterbi's algorithm only keeps the most optimal path. To cope with name translation variations, we keep the top-20 optimal paths for further analysis.

4.3 Web Mining Component

To boost the transliteration performance we propose to use the Web mining approach, which analyzes candidates' occurrence on the Web

(Figure 1 Module 3). Each one of the top-20 transliterations obtained from the previous step is sent to a Web search engine using a meta-search program which records the number of documents retrieved, referred to as Web frequency. By examining the popularity of all possible transliterations on the Internet, bad transliterations can be filtered and their online popularity can serve as an indicator of transliteration correctness. The popularity is estimated by acquiring the number of documents returned from a search engine using the translation candidate as query. The final rank of transliterations is derived from a weighted score of the normalized Web frequency and the probability score.

5 Evaluation

Named Entity Workshop (NEWS) 2009 Machine Transliteration Shared Task provided a training corpus with 31,961 pairs of English and Chinese name translations and 2,896 testing cases. We submitted one standard run with Maximum N-gram HMM *(N-HMM)* setting, and two non-standard runs with 3-gram HMM *(3-HMM)*, and Maximum N-gram HMM + Web mining *(N-HMM+W)*. There are two other runs that we submitted which contains error in the results and they are not discussed here. We present our evaluation results in Table 1.

	Top-1 Acc	F-score	MRR	MAP (Ref)	MAP (10)
N-HMM	0.456	0.763	0.587	0.456	0.185
N-HMM+W	**0.462**	**0.764**	0.564	**0.462**	0.175
3-HMM	0.458	0.763	**0.602**	0.458	**0.191**

Table 1: Evaluation Results with Top-10 Candidates

It is confirmed that Web-mining module boosted the performance of N-gram HMM in all measure except for $MAP_{(10)}$. However, the boosting effect is small (1.3%). To our surprise, 3-gram HMM outperformed Maximum N-gram HMM slightly (3% in $MAP_{(10)}$). Our best Top-1 accuracy is 0.462, and best Mean F-score is 0.764 both achieved by N-gram HMM with Web mining module. We believe this slightly lower performance of Maximum N-gram HMM can be improved with some tuning of weight parameters.

6 Conclusions

We propose an English-Chinese name transliteration system using a maximum N-gram Hidden Markov Model. To handle special challenges with alphabet-based and character-based language pair, we apply a two-phase transliteration model by building two HMM models, one between English and Chinese Pinyin and another between Chinese Pinyin and Chinese characters. In participation of NEWS 2009 experiment, our model achieved 0.462 Top-1 accuracy and 0.764 Mean F-score. We plan to conduct further study the impact of Web mining component and find optimal set of parameters. Our model does not rely on any existing dictionary and the translation results are entirely based on learning the corpus data. In the future, this framework can be extended to other language pairs.

Acknowledgment

We thank the data source provider of this shared task from

English-Chinese (EnCh): Haizhou Li, Min Zhang, Jian Su, "A joint source channel model for machine transliteration", Proc. of the 42nd ACL, 2004

References

AbdulJaleel, N., and Larkey, L. S., Statistical transliteration for English-Arabic Cross Language Information Retrieval, in *Proceedings of (CIKM)* New Orleans, LA, pp. 139 (2003).

Al-Onaizan, Y., and Knight, K., Machine Transliteration of Names in Arabic Text, in *Proceedings of the ACL-02 Workshop on Computational Approaches to Semitic Languages* Philadelphia, Pennsylvania pp. 1 (2002).

Arbabi, M., Fischthal, S. M., Cheng, V. C., and Bart, E., Algorithms for Arabic Name Transliteration, *IBM Journal of Research and Development*, 38, 183 (1994).

Chen, Y., and Zong, C., A Structure-based Model for Chinese Organization Name Translation, *ACM Transactions on ACL*, 7, 1 (2008).

Darwish, K., Doermann, D., Jones, R., Oard, D., and Rautiainen, M., TREC-10 Experiments at University of Maryland CLIR and Video in *TREC*, Gaithersburg, Maryland (2001).

Lee, C.J., Chang, J. S., Jang, J.S.R, Extraction of transliteration pairs from parallel corpora using a statistical transliteration model, Information Sciences, 176(1), 67-90 (2006).

Rabiner, L. R., A Tutorial on Hidden Markov Models and Selected Applications in Speech Recognition, *Proceedings of the IEEE*, 77, 257–286 (1989).

Viterbi, A. J., Error Bounds for Convolutional Codes and an Asymptotically Optimum Decoding Algorithm, *IEEE Transactions on Information Theory*, 13, 260 (1967).

Zhou, Y., Huang, F., and Chen, H., Combining probability Models and Web Mining Models: A Framework for Proper Name transliteration, *Information Technology and Management*, 9, 91 (2008).

Name Transliteration with Bidirectional Perceptron Edit Models

Dayne Freitag
SRI International
freitag@ai.sri.com

Zhiqiang (John) Wang
SRI International
johnwang@ai.sri.com

Abstract

We report on our efforts as part of the shared task on the NEWS 2009 Machine Transliteration Shared Task. We applied an orthographic perceptron character edit model that we have used previously for name transliteration, enhancing it in two ways: by ranking possible transliterations according to the sum of their scores according to two models, one trained to generate left-to-right, and one right-to-left; and by constraining generated strings to be consistent with character bigrams observed in the respective language's training data. Our poor showing in the official evaluation was due to a bug in the script used to produce competition-compliant output. Subsequent evaluation shows that our approach yielded comparatively strong performance on all alphabetic language pairs we attempted.

1 Introduction

While transliteration is a much simpler problem than another linguistic transduction problem, language translation, it is rarely trivial. At least three phenomena complicate the automatic transliteration between two languages using different scripts—differing phoneme sets, lossy orthography, and non-alphabetic orthographies (e.g., syllabaries).

For most language pairs, these difficulties stand in the way of a rule-based treatment of the problem. For this reason, many machine learning approaches to the problem have been proposed. We can draw a rough distinction between learning approaches that attempt to model the phonetics of a transliteration problem explicitly, and those that treat the problem as simply one of orthographic transduction, leaving it to the learning algorithm to acquire phonetic distinctions directly from orthographic features of the training data. For example, Knight and Graehl (1998) address the problem through cascaded finite state transducers, with explicit representations of the phonetics. Subsequently, Al-Onaizan and Knight (2002) realize improvements by adding a "spelling" (i.e., orthographic) model. There has been an increasing emphasis on purely orthographic models, probably because they require less detailed domain knowledge (e.g., (Lee and Chang, 2003)).

2 Approach

The approach we explored as part of the NEWS 2009 Machine Transliteration Shared Task (Li et al., 2009) is strictly orthographic. We view the conversion of a name in one language to its representation in another as the product of a series of single-character edits, and seek to learn a character edit model that maximizes the score of correct name pairs. Our approach follows that described in Freitag and Khadivi (2007), a "structured perceptron" with cheaply computed character n-grams as features. Here, we give a brief description, and present the successful enhancements we tried specifically for the shared task.

2.1 Perceptron Edit Model

Suppose we are given two sequences, $\boldsymbol{s}_1^m \in \Sigma_s^*$ and $\boldsymbol{t}_1^n \in \Sigma_t^*$. We desire a function $A(\boldsymbol{s}, \boldsymbol{t}) \mapsto \mathcal{N}$ which assigns high scores to correct pairs $\boldsymbol{s}, \boldsymbol{t}$. If we stipulate that this score is the sum of the individual scores of a series of edits, we can find the highest-scoring such series through a generalization of the standard edit distance:

$$A(\boldsymbol{s}_1^i, \boldsymbol{t}_1^j) = \max \begin{cases} a_{\epsilon,t_j}(\boldsymbol{s}, i, \boldsymbol{t}, j) + A(\boldsymbol{s}_1^i, \boldsymbol{t}_1^{j-1}) \\ a_{s_i,\epsilon}(\boldsymbol{s}, i, \boldsymbol{t}, j) + A(\boldsymbol{s}_1^{i-1}, \boldsymbol{t}_1^j) \\ a_{s_i,t_j}(\boldsymbol{s}, i, \boldsymbol{t}, j) + A(\boldsymbol{s}_1^{i-1}, \boldsymbol{t}_1^{j-1}) \end{cases} \quad (1)$$

Proceedings of the 2009 Named Entities Workshop, ACL-IJCNLP 2009, pages 132–135,
Suntec, Singapore, 7 August 2009.

with $A(\emptyset, \emptyset) = 0$. The function $a_{s_i,t_j}(\boldsymbol{s}, i, \boldsymbol{t}, j)$ represents the score of substituting t_j for s_i; a_{ϵ,t_j} and $a_{s_i,\epsilon}$ represent insertion and deletion, respectively.

In the experiments reported in this paper, we assume that each local function a is defined in terms of $p + q$ features, $\{f_1, \cdots, f_p, f_{p+1}, \cdots, f_{p+q}\}$, defined over the source and target alphabets, respectively, and that these features have the functional form $\Sigma^* \times \mathcal{N} \mapsto \mathcal{R}$.

In this paper we exclusively use character n-gram indicator features. The "order" of a model is the size of the largest n-grams; for a model of order 2, features would be the bigrams and unigrams immediately adjacent to a given string position. Since the shared task is to *generate* target strings, only features for preceding n-grams are used in the target language.

The score of a particular edit is a linear combination of the corresponding feature values:

$$a(\boldsymbol{s}, i, \boldsymbol{t}, j) = \sum_{k=1}^{p} \alpha_k \cdot f_k(\boldsymbol{s}, i) + \sum_{k=p+1}^{p+q} \alpha_k \cdot f_k(\boldsymbol{t}, j) \tag{2}$$

The weights α_k are what we seek to optimize in order to tune the model for our particular application.

We optimize these weights through an extension of perceptron training for sequence labeling, due to Collins (2002). Take α to be a model parameterization, and let $A_\alpha(\boldsymbol{s}, \boldsymbol{t})$ return an optimal edit sequence $\boldsymbol{e}$, with its score v, given input sequences $\boldsymbol{s}$ and $\boldsymbol{t}$ under α. Elements of sequence $\boldsymbol{e}$ are character pairs $\langle c_s, c_t \rangle$, with $c_s \in \Sigma_s \cup \{\epsilon\}$ and $c_t \in \Sigma_t \cup \{\epsilon\}$, where ϵ represents the empty string. Let $\Phi(\boldsymbol{s}, \boldsymbol{t}, \boldsymbol{e})$ be a feature vector for a source string, target string, and corresponding edit sequence.

Table 1 shows the training algorithm. Starting with a zero parameter vector, we iterate through the collection of source sequences. For each sequence, we pick two target sequences, one the "true" transliteration t of the source string s, and one chosen by searching for a string t' that yields a maximal score according to the current model A_α (Line 6). If the model fails to assign t a higher score than t' (Line 9), we apply the perceptron training update (Line 10).

Note that because generation *constructs* the target sequence, the search in Line 6 for a target string t' that yields maximal $A_\alpha(\boldsymbol{s}, \boldsymbol{t'})$ is not trivial, and does not correspond to a simple recurrence relation like Equation 1. Both in training and testing, we use a beam search for target string generation. In training, this may mean that we find a t' with lower score than the correct target t. In such cases (Line 9 returns false), the model has correctly ordered the two alternative transliterations, and does not require updating.

1: Given training set $\boldsymbol{S} = \{\langle s, t \rangle\}$
2: $V \leftarrow []$, an empty list
3: $\alpha \leftarrow \mathbf{0}$, a weight vector
4: **for** some number of iterations **do**
5:     **for** $\langle s, t \rangle$ in $\boldsymbol{S}$ **do**
6:         $t' \leftarrow \text{maxarg}_{t'} A_\alpha(\boldsymbol{s}, \boldsymbol{t'})$
7:         $\langle \boldsymbol{e}, v \rangle \leftarrow A_\alpha(\boldsymbol{s}, \boldsymbol{t})$
8:         $\langle \boldsymbol{e'}, v' \rangle \leftarrow A_\alpha(\boldsymbol{s}, \boldsymbol{t'})$
9:         **if** $v' \geq v$ **then**
10:             $\alpha \leftarrow \alpha + \Phi(\boldsymbol{s}, \boldsymbol{t}, \boldsymbol{e}) - \Phi(\boldsymbol{s}, \boldsymbol{t'}, \boldsymbol{e'})$
11:         **end if**
12:         Append α to V
13:     **end for**
14: **end for**
15: Return the mean α from V

Table 1: The training algorithm. A_α is the affinity function under model parameters α, returning edit sequence $\boldsymbol{e}$ and score v.

2.2 Shared Task Extensions

This approach has been used effectively for practical transliteration of names from English to Arabic and Mandarin (and vice versa). As part of the NEWS shared task, we experimented with two simple extensions, both of which yielded improvements over the baseline described above. These extensions were used in our official submission for alphabetic language pairs. We treated English-to-Chinese somewhat differently, as described below.

Simple character n-gram constraints. The described approach sometimes violates target language spelling conventions by interpolating clearly inappropriate characters into a string that is otherwise a reasonable transliteration. We take this behavior as symptomatic of a kind of under-training in some portion of the problem space, a possible byproduct of 1-best perceptron training. One principled solution may be to optimize against n-best lists (Bellare et al., 2009).

Instead, we address this shortcoming in a straightforward way—by prohibiting the creation of n-grams, for some small n, that do not occur in the training data. Under a bigram restriction, if 'ab' is not seen in training, then an operation that inserts 'b' after 'a' is disallowed. In essence, we impose a very simple character language model of the target domain.

Our non-standard English-to-Chinese contributions, which involved transliterating from English to pinyin, employed a similar idea. In these experiments, rather than character bigrams, the model was constrained to produce only legal pinyin sequences.

Bidirectional generation. Character n-gram restrictions yielded modest but universal improvements on development data. Larger improvements were obtained through an equally simple idea: Instead of a single left-to-right model, we trained two models, one generating left-to-right, the other right-to-left, each model constrained by n-gram tables, as described above. At evaluation time, each of the constituent models was used to generate a large number of candidate strings (100, typically). All strings in the union of these two sets were then assigned a score, which was the unweighted sum of scores according to the constituent models, and reranked according to this score. The 10 highest-scoring were retained for evaluation.

A buggy implementation of this two-model idea accounts for our poor showing in the official evaluation. Because of a trivial error in the script we used to produce output, right-to-left models were treated as if they were left-to-right. The resulting strings and scores were consequently erroneous.

3 Evaluation

We experimented with models of order 2 and 3 (2-gram and 3-gram features) on shared task data for English to Hindi, Kannada, Russian, and Tamil (Kumaran and Kellner, 2007). Based on development accuracy scores, we found models of order 3 to be consistently better than order 2, and our submitted results use only order-3 models, with one exception. English-to-native-Chinese (Li et al., 2004) was treated as a special case. Using trigram features in the target language results in an explosion in the feature space, and a model that is slow to train and performs poorly. Thus, only for this language pair, we devised a mixed-order model, one using trigram features over English strings, and unigram features over Chinese. Because of the large target-language branching factor, the mixed-order native Chinese model remaining one of the slowest to train.

Languages	Accuracy	Delta
EnHi	0.465	-0.033
EnHi baseline	0.421	-0.077
EnKa	0.396	-0.002
EnKa baseline	0.370	-0.028
EnRu	0.609	-0.004
EnRu baseline	0.588	-0.025
EnTa	0.475	+0.001
EnTa baseline	0.422	-0.052
EnCh standard	0.672	-0.059
EnCh non-standard 1	0.673	-0.236
EnCh non-standard 2	0.5	-0.409

Table 2: Post-contest accuracy on evaluation set, including delta from highest-scoring contest participant.

We trained all models for 20 epochs, evaluating the 1-best accuracy of intervening models on the development data. In all cases, we observed that accuracy increased steadily for some number of iterations, after which it plateaued. Consequently, for all language pairs, we submitted the predictions of the latest model.

Table 2 lists accuracy reported by the official evaluation script on the contest evaluation data. All non-Chinese runs in the table are "standard," and are trained exclusively on shared task training data. Those labeled "baseline" are left-to-right models with no character n-gram constraints. These results were obtained after release of the evaluation data, but differ from our official submission in only two ways: First, and most importantly, the bug described previously was corrected. Second, in some cases training runs that had not completed at evaluation time were allowed to run to the full 20 epochs, and the resulting models were used. The exceptions are Hindi and native Chinese, each of which reflect performance at approximately 10 epochs. Without exception, a beam of size 100 was used to generate these results.

With the exception of "EnCh standard," all results in the table employed the bidirectional scheme described above. The Chinese non-standard runs differ from standard only in that models were trained to perform English-to-pinyin transliteration, followed by a conversion from pinyin to native Chinese using tables provided by the Unicode consortium. Non-standard Run 1 retains pinyin tonal diacritics, while Run 2 omits them. The mapping from pinyin to native Chinese characters introduces indeterminacy, which we accounted for in a simple fashion: First, in constructing a pinyin-to-Chinese conversion table, we discarded any Chinese characters that were used in the training data fewer than some small fraction of cases. Then, given a ranked list of pinyin transliterations, we generated all possible native Chinese sequences, ranked by the product of observed pinyin-to-Chinese probabilities, according to training frequencies.

It will be observed that our non-standard English-to-Chinese results lag considerably behind the best results. We suspect this is due in part to the fact that no additional training data was used in these experiments–only a change in representation.

4 Discussion and Conclusion

Treating the transliteration problem as one of orthographic transduction appears viable, particularly for conversion between alphabetic languages. An empirical character edit model based on a structured perceptron and character n-gram features, and using a simple training procedure that discovers appropriate weights for latent character alignment operations, yields performance that is generally as good as alternative approaches explored in the shared task. The key is model combination, particularly the combination of left-to-right and right-to-left models, respectively.

In contrast to the alphabetic language pairs, our performance on Chinese falls somewhat short. Nevertheless, it is possible that simple modifications of the basic procedure would render it competitive on English-Chinese, as well. In converting from English to native Chinese, we relied on a mixed-order model, with order-3 English features. It is possible that trigrams are too small in some cases to identify the appropriate Chinese character, and that 4-grams, if we can afford them, will make the difference. There is virtue in the idea of transliterating to pinyin as an intermediate step; converting to tonal pinyin yields accuracy at the same level as English-to-native-Chinese, even with the indeterminacy it introduces. Future work includes more principled approaches to resolving this indeterminacy, and combined pinyin/native models.

Acknowledgments

This material is based upon work supported by the Defense Advanced Research Projects Agency (DARPA) under Contract No. HR0011-06-C-0023 (approved for public release, distribution unlimited). Any opinions, findings and conclusions or recommendations expressed in this material are those of the authors and do not necessarily reflect the view of DARPA.

References

Y. Al-Onaizan and K. Knight. 2002. Machine transliteration of names in Arabic text. In *Proceedings of the ACL-02 workshop on computational approaches to semitic languages*.

K. Bellare, K. Crammer, and D. Freitag. 2009. Loss-sensitive discriminative training of machine transliteration models. In *Proceedings of the Student Research Workshop and Doctoral Consortium at NLT/NAACL 2009*.

M. Collins. 2002. Discriminative training methods for hidden Markov models: theory and experiments with perceptron algorithms. In *Proceedings of EMNLP-2002*.

D. Freitag and S. Khadivi. 2007. A sequence alignment model based on the averaged perceptron. In *Proceedings of EMNLP-CoNLL 2007*.

K. Knight and J. Graehl. 1998. Machine transliteration. *Computational Linguistics*, 24(4).

A. Kumaran and T. Kellner. 2007. A generic framework for machine transliteration. In *Proceedings of the 30th SIGIR*.

C.-J. Lee and J.S. Chang. 2003. Acquisition of English-Chinese transliterated word pairs from parallel-aligned texts using a statistical machine transliteration model. In *Proceedings of the HLT-NAACL 2003 Workshop on Building and Using Parallel Texts*.

H. Li, M. Zhang, and J. Su. 2004. A joint source channel model for machine transliteration. In *Proceedings of the 42nd ACL*.

H. Li, A. Kumaran, M. Zhang, and V. Pervouchine. 2009. Whitepaper of NEWS 2009 Machine Transliteration Shared Task. In *Proceedings of ACL-IJCNLP 2009 Named Entities Workshop (NEWS 2009)*.

Bridging Languages by SuperSense Entity Tagging

Davide Picca and **Alfio Massimiliano Gliozzo*** and **Simone Campora****
University of Lausanne, CH 1015-Lausanne-Switzerland
*Semantic Technology Lab (STLab - ISTC - CNR), Via Nomentana 56-0016, Rome, Italy
**Ecole Polytechnique Federale de Lausanne (EPFL)
davide.picca@unil.ch, alfio.gliozzo@istc.cnr.it, simone.campora@gmail.com

Abstract

This paper explores a very basic linguistic phenomenon in multilingualism: the lexicalizations of entities are very often identical within different languages while concepts are usually lexicalized differently. Since entities are commonly referred to by proper names in natural language, we measured their distribution in the lexical overlap of the terminologies extracted from comparable corpora. Results show that the lexical overlap is mostly composed by unambiguous words, which can be regarded as anchors to bridge languages: most of terms having the same spelling refer exactly to the same entities. Thanks to this important feature of Named Entities, we developed a multilingual super sense tagging system capable to distinguish between concepts and individuals. Individuals adopted for training have been extracted both by YAGO and by a heuristic procedure. The general F1 of the English tagger is over 76%, which is in line with the state of the art on super sense tagging while augmenting the number of classes. Performances for Italian are slightly lower, while ensuring a reasonable accuracy level which is capable to show effective results for knowledge acquisition.

1 Introduction

The Semantic Web paradigm is often required to provide a structured view of the unstructured information expressed in texts (Buitelaar et al., 2005; Cimiano, 2006). Semantic technology requires abundance of such kind of knowledge in order to cover the web scale in almost any language. Natural Language Processing (NLP) has been adopted with the purpose of knowledge acquisition, and in particular for ontology learning and information extraction. Structured information in ontologies is often expressed by taxonomies of concepts, and then populated by instances.

Nonetheless, automatically distinguish concepts from entities in taxonomies is not an easy task, especially as far as the problem of acquiring such knowledge from texts is concerned (Zirn et al., 2008; Picca and Popescu, 2007; Miller and Hristea, 2006). First of all because such a distinction is quite vague. From a description logics perspective, that is incidently widely adopted in ontology engineering, instances are the leaves of any taxonomy as they cannot be further subcategorized and populated by other instances. For example,"Bill Clinton" is clearly an individual, since it is instance of many concepts, such as *person* or *president*, but at the same time it is a non sense describing individuals belonging to the class *Bill Clinton*.

In order to tackle this issue, we aim to provide empirical evidence to a very basic linguistic phenomenon in multilingualism, which allows the exploitation of comparable corpora for bilingual lexical acquisition. It consists on the fact that the lexicalizations of entities is very often identical within different languages while concepts are usually lexicalized differently (de Pablo et al., 2006). The existence of this phenomenon is quite intuitive and can be easily justified by considering entities as often referred to by means of ostensive acts (i.e. the act of nominating objects by indicating them), performed *in presentia* during every day life. Since entities are usually referred to using proper names in natural language, we measured their distribution in the lexical overlap of the terminologies extracted from comparable corpora in two different sample languages (i.e. Italian and English).

Named Entities are instances of particular concepts (such as person or location) and are referred

Proceedings of the 2009 Named Entities Workshop, ACL-IJCNLP 2009, pages 136–142,
Suntec, Singapore, 7 August 2009. ©2009 ACL and AFNLP

to by proper names. Named Entity Recognition (NER) is a basic task in NLP that has the intent of automatically recognizing Named Entities. Incidentally, NER systems can be a useful step for broad-coverage ontology engineering but they have two main limitations:

- Traditional categories (e.g., person, location, and organization) are too few and generic. It is quite evident that taxonomies require more categories than the three mentioned above.

- Even though NER systems are supposed to recognize *individuals*, very often they also returns common names and no clear distinction with *concepts* is made.

A Super Sense Tagger (SST) (Ciaramita and Johnson, 2003) is an extended NER system that uses the wider set of categories composed by the 41 most general concepts defined by WordNet. WordNet has been organized according to psycholinguistic theories on the principles governing lexical memory (Beckwith et al., 1991). Thus the broadest WordNet's categories can serve as basis for a set of categories which exhaustively covers, at least as a first approximation, all possible concepts occurring in a sentence.

The aim of this paper is to develop and explore the property of instances being lexicalized identically in different languages in order to produce a SST having the following two features:

- Make explicit distinction between instances and concepts.

- Analyze the terminology of different languages adopting a common category set.

Nevertheless, the first point demands to face with the vague distinction between concepts and individuals belonging to those concepts. So one of the main issues explored in this paper is the automatic tagging of which categories clearly have this distinction.

The paper is organized as follows. In Section 2 we describe the multilingual SST, an Italian extension of the English SST that we exploited in Section 3 to show that the lexical overlap between languages is mostly composed by unambiguous words, which can be also regarded as anchors to bridge the two languages. Most of terms having the same spelling in the two languages exactly refer to the same entities. We measured those occurrencies with respect to all different ontological types identified by our tagging device, observing that most of the overlapped terms are proper names of persons, organization, locations and artifact, while the remaining ontological types are mostly lexicalized by common nouns and have a quite empty overlap. This confirms our claim that entities of tangible types are always lexicalized by the same terms.

In Section 4 we extended the SuperSense Tagger in order to distinguish instances from individuals, while Section 5 is about evaluation. Finally Section 6 concludes the paper proposing new directions for future investigation.

2 Multilingual Supersense Tagging

SuperSense Tagging is the problem to identify terms in texts, assigning a "supersense" category (e.g. `person`, `act`) to their senses within their context and apply it to recognize concepts and instances in large scale textual collections of texts. An example of tagging is provided here:

Guns$_{B-noun.group}$ and$_{I-noun.group}$ Roses$_{I-noun.group}$ plays$_{B-verb.communication}$ at$_O$ the$_O$ stadium$_{B-noun.location}$

These categories are extracted from WordNet. WordNet (Fellbaum, 1998) defines 45 lexicographer's categories, also called *supersenses* (Ciaramita and Johnson, 2003). They are used by lexicographers to provide an initial broad classification for the lexicon entries [1].

Although simplistic in many ways, the supersense ontology has several attractive features for NLP purposes. First of all, concepts are easily recognizable, however very general. Secondly, the small number of classes makes the implementation of state of the art methods possible (e.g. sequence taggers) to annotate text with supersenses. Finally, similar word senses tend to be merged together reducing ambiguity. This technology has been also adopted for Ontology Learning (Picca et al., 2007), as the top level WordNet supersenses cover almost any high level ontological type of interest in ontology design. Compared to other semantic tagsets, supersenses have the advantage of being designed to cover all possible open class words. Thus, in principle there is a supersense cat-

[1] We have used the WordNet version 2.0 for all the experiments in the paper.

egory for each word, known or novel. Additionally, no distinction is made between proper and common nouns, whereas standard NER systems tends to be biased towards the former.

Following the procedure described in (Picca et al., 2008), we developed a multilingual SST working on both Italian and English languages by training the same system on MultiSemcor (Bentivogli et al., 2004), a parallel English/Italian corpus composed of 116 texts which are the translation of their corresponding English texts in SemCor. This resource has been developed by manually translating the English texts to Italian. Then, the so generated parallel corpus has been automatically aligned at the Word Level. Finally, sense labels have been automatically transferred from the English words to their Italian translations.

The sense labels adopted in the Italian part of MultiSemCor (Bentivogli et al., 2004) have been extracted by Multi WordNet [2]. It is a multilingual computational lexicon, conceived to be strictly aligned with the Princeton WordNet. The available languages are Italian, Spanish, Hebrew and Romanian. In our experiment we used the English and the Italian components. The last version of the Italian WordNet contains around 58,000 Italian word senses and 41,500 lemmas organized into 32,700 synsets aligned with WordNet English synsets. The Italian synsets are created in correspondence with the Princeton WordNet synsets whenever possible, and the semantic relations are ported from the corresponding English synsets. This implies that the synset index structure is the same for the two languages.

The full alignment between the English and the Italian WordNet is guaranteed by the fact that both resources adopts the same synset IDs to refer to concepts. This nice feature has allowed us to infer the correct super-sense for each Italian sense by simply looking at the English structure. In this way, we assign exactly the same ontological types to both Italian and English terms, thus obtaining an Italian corpus tagged by its supersenses as shown below:

I_{O} $\mathrm{Guns}_{B-noun.group}$ $\mathrm{and}_{I-noun.group}$ $\mathrm{Roses}_{I-noun.group}$ $\mathrm{suonano}_{B-verb.communication}$ allo_{O} $\mathrm{stadio}_{B-noun.location}$

[2] Available at *http://multi WordNet.itc.it*.

3 Lexical Overlap in Comparable Corpora

Comparable corpora are collections of texts in different languages that regard similar topics (e.g. a collection of news published by press agencies in the same period). More restrictive requirements are expected for parallel corpora (i.e. corpora composed of texts which are mutual translations), while the class of the multilingual corpora (i.e. collection of texts expressed in different languages without any additional requirement) is the more general. Obviously parallel corpora are also comparable, while comparable corpora are also multilingual.

In comparable corpora, most of the individuals preserve the same spelling across different languages, while most concepts are translated differently. The analysis of the acquired terms for different ontological types shows a huge percentage of overlapped Named Entities. For our experiments, we assumed that the distinction between common names and proper names reflect as well the difference between concepts and entities in a formal ontology. Since proper names are recognized by the PoS tagger with relatively high precision, we interpreted occurrences of proper names in the acquired terminology as an evidence for detecting entities.

The Leipzig Corpora Collection (Quasthoff, 2006) presents corpora in different languages using the same format and comparable sources. The corpora are identical in format and similar in size and content. They contain randomly selected sentences in the language of the corpus. For the experiments reported in this paper, we used the Italian and the English part composed by 300,000 sentences. As shown in Figure 1 and in Figure 2, Named Entities are mostly concentrated into tangible types: Groups (organizations), Locations, Persons and Artifacts.

The results analysis is more impressive. Figure 3 shows that the lexical overlap (i.e. the subset of terms in common between English and Italian) is composed almost exclusively by entities (i.e. proper nouns). Instead if we take a look at Figure 4, we can observe that concepts are generally not shared, having an average percentage lower than 0.1%, independently of the ontological type. We can also observe the predictable result that ontological categories denoting material objects (i.e. persons, locations and groups, artifacts) still have

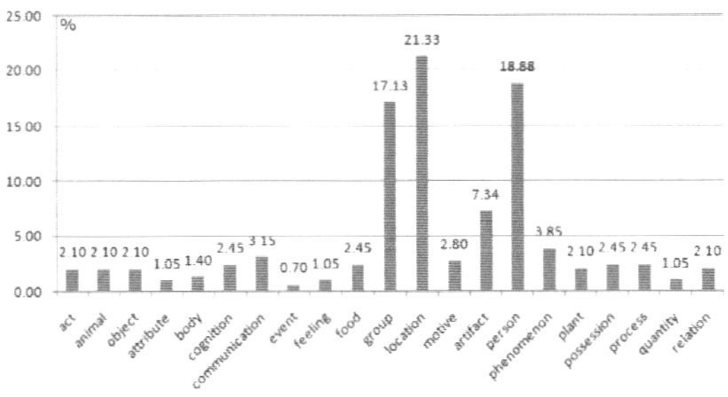

Figure 1: Distribution of discovered entity types in English

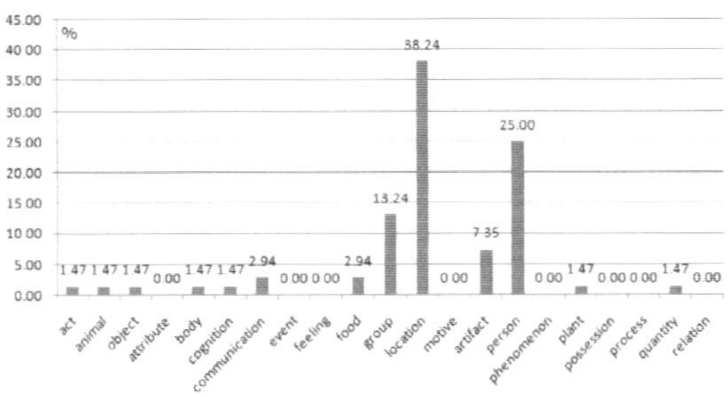

Figure 2: Distribution of discovered entity types in Italian

greater percentage of shared entities.

This is in line with the common practice of training NER on these categories. Examples of shared terms (entities) in concrete categories are:

- **noun.group**: e.g. NATO, Boeing, NASA;
- **noun.location**: e.g. Canada, Austria, Houston;
- **noun.person**: e.g. Romano_Prodi, Blair, Kofi_Annan.

Incidentally, exceptions can be found to our hypothesis (i.e. some concept is also shared).

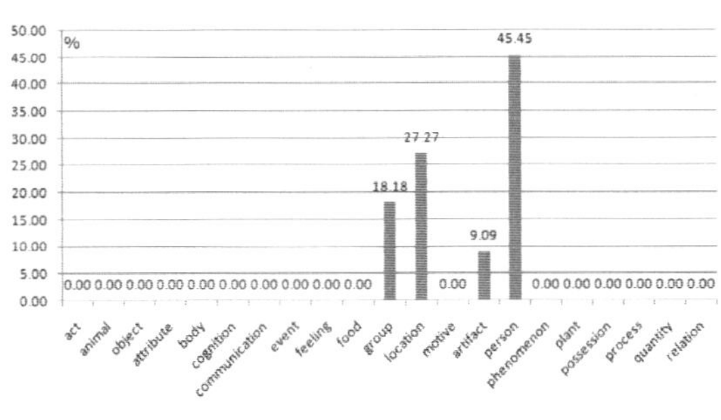

Figure 3: Shared Named Entities in both languages

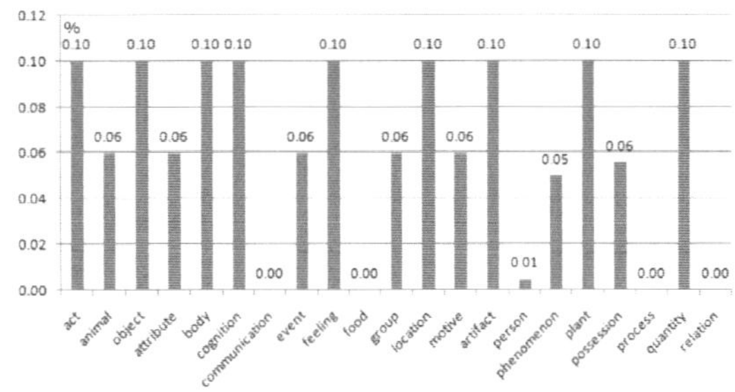

Figure 4: Shared Concepts in both languages

Examples are terms belonging to the supersense `noun.object` such as Radio and Computer. Anyhow, being them ported from one language to another, they generally do not cause problems, since they tend to share the same meaning. In our experiments (i.e. in the sample we manually analyzed), we did not find any false friend, suggesting that the impact of those words is relatively small, in spite of the fact that it is very often overemphasized.

Inversely, many abstract types (e.g. *noun.possession* and *noun.feeling*) do not share terminology at all.

4 Distinguishing entities from concepts

Successively, we subdivided each category into two sub-categories for both languages, *Instance* and *Concept* so that now the term "president" is tagged as *noun.person_Concept* and the term "Bill Clinton" as *noun.person_Instance*. In order to automate this task and create a reliable training set, we adopted the following strategy.

We used the concept/instances distinction provided by YAGO (Suchanek et al., 2007b). YAGO is a huge semantic knowledge base developed by the Max-Plack-Institute of Saarbrcken. YAGO knows over 1.7 million entities (like persons, organizations, cities, etc.). YAGO, exploits Wikipedia's info-boxes and category pages. Infoboxes are standardized tables that contain basic information about the entity described in the article (Suchanek et al., 2007a). For our purposes it is fundamental that YAGO's components are represented as entities. In our experiment we exploit entities as proper names and we use only YAGO entity database containing named entities.

For each term belonging to one of the concrete categories, we check if it appears in YAGO entity dataset, otherwise, if the term is not found in

YAGO, it has to satisfy all the following conditions to be tagged as *Instance*:

- The part of speech of the term belongs to one of the noun categories as "NN", "NNS", "NNP" or "NNPS".
- The first letter of the term is a capital letter.
- The term does not come after a full stop.

Upon a total of 12817 instances, almost $\frac{1}{4}$ have been found in YAGO, 3413 have been found using the heuristic strategy and the rest have been classified as concepts. If we take the previous example, the new output has now this form:

- Guns$_{B-noun.group_Instance}$ and$_{I-noun.group_Instance}$ Roses$_{I-noun.group_Instance}$ plays$_{B-verb.communication}$ at$_{O}$ the$_{O}$ stadium$_{B-noun.location_Concept}$

or

- Guns$_{B-noun.group_Instance}$ and$_{I-noun.group_Instance}$ Roses$_{I-noun.group_Instance}$ suonano$_{B-verb.communication}$ allo$_{O}$ stadio$_{B-noun.location_Concept}$

Afterwards, we trained the SST engine. It implements a Hidden Markov Model, trained with the perceptron algorithm introduced in (Collins, 2002) and it achieves a recall of 77.71% and a precision of 76.65% . Perception sequence learning provides an excellent trade-off accuracy/performance, sometimes outperforming more complex models such as Conditional Random Fields (Nguyen and Guo, 2007). We optimized the required parameters by adopting a cross validation technique. As for the settings developed by (Ciaramita and Johnson, 2003), the best results have been obtained by setting 50 trials and 10 epochs to train the perceptron algorithm. The basic feature set used for the training process, includes:

- *word* = lower-cased form of each token for the current position i and in addition for i-1 and i+1
- *sh* = shape of the token as a simple regular expression-like representation
- *pos* = POS of i, i-1 and i+1

Category	Recall	Prec.	F1
noun.artifact_Concept	0.72	0.73	0.73
noun.artifact_Instance	0.59	0.64	0.62
noun.group_Concept	0.72	0.73	0.73
noun.group_Instance	0.68	0.70	0.69
noun.location_Concept	0.68	0.65	0.66
noun.location_Instance	0.75	0.80	0.77
noun.person_Concept	0.83	0.80	0.82
noun.person_Instance	0.92	0.88	0.90

Table 1: Recall, precision and F1 for each category for English

- *sb*= bi- and tri-grams of characters of the suffix of word_i
- *pr*= bi- and tri-grams of characters of the prefix of word_i
- *rp* = coarse relative position of word_i, rp=begin if i = 0, rp=end if i = —sentence—-1, sb=mid otherwise
- *kf* = constant features on each token for regularization purposes

Finally, we trained the SST engine in the Italian corpus generated so far, and we evaluated the super sense tagging accuracy by adopting the same evaluation method as described in (Ciaramita and Johnson, 2003), obtaining F1 close to 0.70. However quite lower than the English F1, this result is in line with the claim, since the Italian corpus is smaller and lower in quality.

5 SST Performance and Evaluation

We evaluated the performances of the SST generated so far by adopting a n-fold cross validation strategy on the Semcor adopted for training. Results for the chosen categories are illustrated in Table 1 and Table 2, reporting precision, recall and F1 for any Supersense. If we cast a deeper glance at the tables, we can clearly notice that for some category the F1 is exceptionally high. Some of those best categorized categories are really essential for ontology learning. For example, important labels as *noun.person* or *noun.group* achieve results among the 70%. For some categories we have found a F1 over 0.80% as *noun.person_Instance* (F1 0.90%) or *noun.person_Concept* (F1 0.85%)

On the other hand, the Italian tagger achieved lower performances if compared with the English.

Category	Recall	Prec.	F1
noun.artifact_Concept	0.64	0.63	0.63
noun.artifact_Instance	0.66	0.67	0.66
noun.group_Concept	0.61	0.65	0.63
noun.group_Instance	0.66	0.66	0.66
noun.location_Concept	0.55	0.53	0.54
noun.location_Instance	0.56	0.76	0.64
noun.person_Concept	0.81	0.76	0.78
noun.person_Instance	0.88	0.81	0.85

Table 2: Recall, precision and F1 for each category for Italian

It can be explained by (i) the lower quality of the training resource, (ii) the lower quantity of training data and (iii) the unavailability of the first sense info.

Regarding the first point, it is worthwhile to remark that even if the quality of transfer developed by (Bentivogli et al., 2004) is high, many incorrect sense transfers (around 14%) can be found. Because of that our work suffers of the same inherited faults by the automatic alignment. For instance, we report here the most relevant errors we faced with during the preprocessing step. One of the main errors that has badly influenced the training set especially for multiword recognition is the case in which the translation equivalent is indeed a cross-language synonym of the source expression but not a lexical unit. It occurs when a language expresses a concept with a lexical unit whereas the other language expresses the same concept with a free combination of words (for instance *occhiali da sole* annotated with the sense of *sunglasses*).

Regarding the second problem, we noticed that the quantity of sense labeled words adopted for English is higher than 200,000, whereas the amount of Italian tokens adopted is around 92,000. Therefore, the amount of Italian training data is sensibly lower, explaining the lower performances.

Moreover, the italian SST lacks in one of the most important feature used for the English SST, first sense heuristics. In fact, for the Italian language, the first sense baseline cannot be estimated by simply looking at the first sense in WordNet, since the order of the Italian WordNet does not reflect the frequency of senses. Therefore, we did not estimate this baseline for the Italian SST, in contrast to what has been done for the English SST.

6 Conclusion and Future Work

In this work, we presented an empirical investigation about the role of Named Entities in comparable corpora, showing that they largely contribute in finding bridges between languages since they tend to refer to the same entities. This feature allows us to discover bridges among languages by simply looking for common Named Entities in corpora that are generally not parallels since such terms are usually associated to the same objects in the external world. We demonstrated that most terms in the lexical overlap between languages are entities, and we showed that they belong to few fundamentals categories (including persons, locations and groups).

A predominant amount of entities in the lexical overlap could be conceived as a support to our claim that Named Entities can be used to bridge the languages, since they preserve meaning and provide a set of highly accurate anchors to bridge languages in multilingual knowledge bases. Those anchors can be used as a set of seeds to boost further statistical or logical lexical acquisition processes. In addition, the impact of false friends revealed to be less problematic than expected.

We trained a multilingual super sense tagger on the Italian and English language and we introduced the distinction between concept and instance in a subset of its target classes, where our investigation suggested to look for concrete types. The resulting tagger largely extend the capabilities of the state of art supersense technology, by providing a multilingual tool which can be effectively used for multilingual knowledge induction.

For the future, we are going to further explore the direction of multilingual knowledge induction, exploiting the tagger developed so far for ontology engineering and knowledge retrieval. In addition, we plan to leverage more on the lexical overlap property analyzed in this paper, for example to develop unsupervised super sense taggers for all languages where annotated corpora are not available.

Acknowledgments

Alfio Massimiliano Gliozzo has been supported by the BONy project, financed by the Education and culture DG of the EU, grant agreement N 135263-2007-IT-KA3-KA3MP, under the Lifelong Learning Programme 2007 managed by EACEA.

References

R. Beckwith, C. Fellbaum, D. Gross, and G. Miller. 1991. 9. wordnet: A lexical database organized on psycholinguistic principles. *Lexicons: Using On-Line Resources to Build a Lexicon*, pages 211–232, Jan.

L. Bentivogli, P. Forner, and E. Pianta. 2004. Evaluating cross-language annotation transfer in the multisemcor corpus. In *COLING '04: Proceedings of the 20th international conference on Computational Linguistics*, page 364, Morristown, NJ, USA. Association for Computational Linguistics.

P. Buitelaar, P. Cimiano, and B. Magnini. 2005. *Ontology learning from texts: methods, evaluation and applications*. IOS Press.

M. Ciaramita and M. Johnson. 2003. Supersense tagging of unknown nouns in wordnet. In *Proceedings of EMNLP-03*, pages 168–175, Sapporo, Japan.

P. Cimiano. 2006. *Ontology Learning and Population from Text: Algorithms, Evaluation and Applications*. Springer-Verlag New York, Inc., Secaucus, NJ, USA.

M. Collins. 2002. Discriminative training methods for hidden markov models: Theory and experiments with perceptron algorithms. In *Proceedings of EMNLP-02*.

C. de Pablo, J.L. Martínez, and P. Martínez. 2006. Named entity processing for cross-lingual and multilingual ir applications. In *proceedings of the SIGIR2006 workshop on New Directions In Multilingual Information Access*.

C. Fellbaum. 1998. *WordNet. An Electronic Lexical Database*. MIT Press.

G. A. Miller and F. Hristea. 2006. Wordnet nouns: Classes and instances. *Computational Linguistics*, 32(1):1–3.

N. Nguyen and Y. Guo. 2007. Comparison of sequence labeling algorithms and extensions. In *Proceedings of ICML 2007*, pages 681–688.

D. Picca and A. Popescu. 2007. Using wikipedia and supersense tagging for semi-automatic complex taxonomy construction. *In proceedings RANLP*.

D. Picca, A. Gliozzo, and M. Ciaramita. 2007. Semantic domains and supersens tagging for domain-specific ontology learning. In *proceedings RIAO 2007*.

D. Picca, A. M. Gliozzo, and M. Ciaramita. 2008. Supersense tagger for italian. In *proceedings of the sixth international conference on Language Resources and Evaluation (LREC 2008)*.

C. B. Quasthoff, U. M. Richter. 2006. Corpus portal for search in monolingual corpora,. In *Proceedings of the fifth international conference on Language Resources and Evaluation, LREC*, pages pp. 1799–1802.

F. Suchanek, G. Kasneci, and G. Weikum. 2007a. Yago: A large ontology from wikipedia and wordnet. *Technical Report*.

F. M. Suchanek, G. Kasneci, and G. Weikum. 2007b. Yago: a core of semantic knowledge. In *WWW '07: Proceedings of the 16th international conference on World Wide Web*, pages 697–706, New York, NY, USA. ACM Press.

C. Zirn, V. Nastase, and M. Strube. 2008. Distinguishing between instances and classes in the wikipedia taxonomy. *Lecture notes in computer science*, Jan.

Chinese-English Organization Name Translation Based on Correlative Expansion

Feiliang Ren, Muhua Zhu, Huizhen Wang, Jingbo Zhu
Natural Language Processing Lab, Northeastern University, Shenyang, China
{renfeiliang,zhumuhua}@gmail.com
{wanghuizhen,zhujingbo}@mail.neu.edu.cn

Abstract

This paper presents an approach to translating Chinese organization names into English based on correlative expansion. Firstly, some candidate translations are generated by using statistical translation method. And several correlative named entities for the input are retrieved from a correlative named entity list. Secondly, three kinds of expansion methods are used to generate some expanded queries. Finally, these queries are submitted to a search engine, and the refined translation results are mined and re-ranked by using the returned web pages. Experimental results show that this approach outperforms the compared system in overall translation accuracy.

1 Introduction

There are three main types of named entity: location name, person name, and organization name. Organization name translation is a subtask of named entity translation. It is crucial for many NLP tasks, such as cross-language information retrieval, machine translation, question and answering system. For organization name translation, there are two problems among it which are very difficult to handle.

Problem I: There is no uniform rule that can be abided by to select proper translation methods for the inside words of an organization name. For example, a Chinese word "东北", when it is used as a modifier for a university, it is translated to ***Northeastern*** for "***东北***大学/***Northeastern*** University", and is translated to ***Northeast*** for "***东北***林业大学/***Northeast*** Forestry University", and is mapped to Chinese Pinyin ***Dongbei*** for "***东北***财经大学/***Dongbei*** University of Finance and Economics". It is difficult to decide which translation method should be chosen when we translate the inside words of an organization name.

Problem II: There is no uniform rule that can be abided by to select proper translation order and proper treatment of particles Here particles refer to prepositions and articles) for an input organization name. For example, the organization name "中国建设银行/China Construction Bank" and the organization name "中国农业银行/Agricultural Bank of China", they are very similar both in surface forms and in syntax structures, but their translation orders are different, and their treatments of particles are also different.

Generally, there are two strategies usually used for named entity translation in previous research. One is alignment based approach, and the other is generation based approach. Alignment based approach (Chen et al. 2003; Huang et al. 2003; Hassan and Sorensen, 2005; and so on) extracts named entities translation pairs from parallel or comparable corpus by some alignment technologies, and this approach is not suitable to solve the above two problems. Because new organization names are constantly being created, and alignment based method usually fails to cover these new organization names that don't occur in the bilingual corpus.

Traditional generation based approach (Al-Onaizan and Knight, 2002; Jiang et al .2007; Yang et al. 2008; and so on) usually consists of two parts. Firstly, it will generate some candidate translations for the input; then it will re-rank these candidate translations to assign the correct translations high ranks. Cheng and Zong [2008] proposed another generation based approach for organization name translation, which directly translates organization names according to their inherent structures. But their approach still can't solve the above two problems. This is because the amount of organization names is so huge and many of them have their own special translation rules to handle the above two problems. And the inherent structures don't reveal these translation rules. Traditional generation based approach is suitable for organization name translation. But in previous research, the final translation performance depends on the candidate translation gen-

Proceedings of the 2009 Named Entities Workshop, ACL-IJCNLP 2009, pages 143–151,
Suntec, Singapore, 7 August 2009.

eration process greatly. If this generation process failed, it is impossible to obtain correct result from the re-ranking process. In response to this, Huang et al. [2005] proposed a novel method that mined key phrase translation form web by using topic-relevant hint words. But in their approach, they removed the candidate translation generation process, which will improve extra difficult during mining phrase. Besides, in their approach, the features considered to obtain topic-relevant words are not so comprehensive, which will affect the quality of returned web pages where the correct translations are expected to be included. There is still much room for the improvement process of the topic-relevant words extraction.

Inspired by the traditional generation based named entity translation strategy and the approach proposed by Huang et al., we propose an organization name translation approach that mining the correct translations of input organization name from the web. Our aim is to solve the above two problems indirectly by retrieving the web pages that contain the correct translation of the input and mining the correct translation from them. Given an input organization name, firstly, some candidate translations are generated by using statistical translation method. And several correlative named entities for the input are retrieved from a correlative named entity list. Secondly, expanded queries are generated by using three kinds of query expansion methods. Thirdly, these queries are submitted to a search engine, and the final translation results are mined and re-ranked by using the returned web pages.

The rest of this paper is organized as follows, section 2 presents the extraction process of correlative named entities, section 3 presents a detail description of our translation method for Chinese organization name, and section 4 introduces our parameter evaluation method, and section 5 is the experiments and discussions part, finally conclusions and future work are given in section 6.

2 Extraction of Correlative Named Entities

The key of our approach is to find some web pages that contain the correct translation of the input. With the help of correlative named entities (here if two named entities are correlative, it means that they are usually used to describe the same topic), it is easier to find such web pages. This is because that in the web, one web page usually has one topic. Thus if two named entities are correlative, they are very likely to occur in pair in some web pages.

The correlative named entity list is constructed in advance. During translation, the correlative named entities for the input organization name are retrieved from this list directly. To set up this correlative named entity list, an about 180GB-sized collection of web pages are used. Totally there are about 100M web pages in this collection. Named entities are recognized from every web page by using a NER tool. This NER tool is trained by CRF model[1] with the corpus from SIGHAN-2008[2].

2.1 Features Used

During the extraction of correlative named entities, the following features are considered.

Co-occurrence in a Document The more often two named entities co-occur in a document, the more likely they are correlative. This feature is denoted as $CoD_i(n_1, n_2)$, which means the co-occurrence of named entities n_1 and n_2 in a document D_i. This feature is also the main feature used in Huang et al. [2005].

Co-occurrence in Documents The more often two named entities co-occur in different documents, the more likely they are correlative. This feature is denoted as $CoDs(n_1, n_2)$, which means the number of documents that both n_1 and n_2 occur in.

Distance The closer two named entities is in a document, the more likely they are correlative. This feature is denoted as $DistD_i(n_1, n_2)$, which means the number of words between n_1 and n_2 in a document D_i.

Mutual Information Mutual information is a metric to measure the correlation degree of two words. The higher two named entities' mutual information, the more likely they are correlative. And the mutual information of named entities n_1 and n_2 in a document D_i is computed as following formula.

$$MID_i(n_1, n_2) = p(n_1, n_2)\log\frac{p(n_1, n_2)}{p(n_1)\cdot p(n_2)} \quad (1)$$

Jaccard Similarity Jaccard similarity is also a metric to measure the correlative degree of two words. The higher two named entities' Jaccard

[1] http://www.chasen.org/~taku/software/CRF++/
[2] http://www.china-language.gov.cn/bakeoff08/

similarity, the more likely they are correlative. And Jaccard similarity is computed as following formula.

$$Jaccard(n_1,n_2)=\frac{CoDs(n_1,n_2)}{D(n_1)+D(n_2)-CoDs(n_1,n_2)} \quad (2)$$

where $D(n_i)$ is the number of documents that n_i occurs in, and $CoDs(n_i,n_j)$ is the number of documents that both n_i and n_j occur in.

TF-IDF TF-IDF is a weight computation method usually used in information retrieval. Here for a named entity n_i, TF-IDF is used to measure the importance of its correlative named entities. The TF-IDF value of n_j in a document D_i is computed as following formula.

$$TF-IDF_i(n_j)=tf_{ij}\times\log\frac{N}{D(n_j)} \quad (3)$$

where tf_{ij} is the frequency of n_j in document D_i, N is the number of total documents, and $D(n_j)$ is the number of documents that n_j occurs in.

2.2 Feature Combination

During the process of feature combination, every feature is normalized, and the final correlative degree of two named entities is the linear combination of these normalized features, and it is computed as following formula.

$$\begin{aligned}C(n_i,n_j)&=\lambda_1\frac{\sum_k CoD_k(n_i,n_j)}{\sum_j\sum_k CoD_k(n_i,n_j)}+\lambda_2\frac{CoDs(n_i,n_j)}{\sum_j CoDs(n_i,n_j)}\\&+\lambda_3\frac{\sum_k 1/DistD_k(n_i,n_j)}{\sum_j\sum_k 1/DistD_k(n_i,n_j)}+\lambda_4\frac{\sum_k MID_k(n_i,n_j)}{\sum_j\sum_k MID_k(n_i,n_j)}\\&+\lambda_5\frac{Jaccard(n_i,n_j)}{\sum_j Jaccard(n_i,n_j)}+\lambda_6\frac{\sum_k TF-IDF_k(n_j)}{\sum_k\sum_j TF-IDF_k(n_j)}\end{aligned} \quad (4)$$

Finally, for every organization name n_i, its top-K correlative named entities are selected to construct the correlative named entity list.

During translation, the correlative words for the input can be retrieved from this correlative list directly. If the input is not included in this list, the same method as in Huang et al. [2005] is used to obtain the needed correlative words.

3 Organization Name Translation Based on Correlative Expansion

3.1 Statistical Translation Module

The first step of our approach is to generate some candidate translations for every input organization name. As shown in table 1, these candidate translations are used as query stems during query expansion. We use Moses[3], a state of the art public machine translation tool, to generate such candidate translations. Here Moses is trained with the bilingual corpus that is from the 4th China Workshop on Machine Translation[4]. Total there are 868,947 bilingual Chinese-English sentence pairs on news domain in this bilingual corpus. Moses receives an organization name as input, and outputs the N-best results as the candidate translations of the input organization name. Total there are six features used in Moses: phrase translation probability, inverse phrase translation probability, lexical translation probability, inverse lexical translation probability, language model, and sentence length penalty. All the needed parameters are trained with MERT method (Och, 2003) by using a held-out development set.

3.2 Query Expansions

Because the amount of available web pages is so huge, the query submitted to search engine must be well designed. Otherwise, the search engine will return large amount of un-related web pages. This will enlarge the difficulty of mining phase. Here three kinds of expansion methods are proposed to generate some queries by combining the clues given by statistical translation method and the clues given by correlative named entities of the input. And these correlative named entities are retrieved from the correlative named entities list before the query expansions process. These three kinds of expansions are explained as follows.

3.2.1 Monolingual Expansion

Given an input organization name n_i, suppose s_i is one of its candidate translations, and n_j is one of its correlative named entities. If n_j can be reliably translated[5], we expand s_i with this reli-

---

[3] http://www.statmt.org/moses/

[4] http://www.nlpr.ia.ac.cn/cwmt-2008

[5] A word can be reliably translated means either it has a unique dictionary translation or it is a Chinese

able translation $t(n_j)$ to form a query "$s_i + t(n_j)$". This kind of expansion is called as monolingual expansion.

For two named entities, if they are correlative, their translations are likely correlative too. So their translations are also likely to occur in pair in some web pages. Suppose a query generated by this expansion is "$s_i + t(n_j)$", if the candidate translation s_i is the correct translation of the input, there must be some returned web pages that contain s_i completely. Otherwise, it is still possible to obtain some returned web pages that contain the correct translation. This is because that the search engine will return both the web pages that include the query completely and the web pages that include the query partly. And for a translation candidate s_i and the correct translation s_i', they are very likely to have some common words, so some of their returned web pages may overlap each other. Thus it can be expected that when we submit "$s_i + t(n_j)$" to search engine, it will return some web pages that include "$s_i' + t(n_j)$" or include s_i'. This is very helpful for the mining phase.

3.2.2 Bilingual Expansion

Given an input organization name n_i, suppose s_i is one of its candidate translations, we expand s_i with n_i to form a query "$s_i + n_i$". This kind of expansion is called as bilingual expansion.

Bilingual expansion is very useful to verify whether a candidate translation is the correct translation. To give readers more information or they are not sure about the translation of original named entity, the Chinese authors usually include both the original form of a named entity and its translation in the mix-language web pages [Fei Huang et al, 2005]. So the correct translation pair is likely to obtain more supports from the returned web pages than those incorrect translation pairs. Thus bilingual expansion is very useful for the re-ranking phase.

Besides, for an input organization name, if one of its incorrect candidate translations s_i is very similar to the correct translation s_i' in surface form, the correct translation is also likely to be contained in the returned web pages by using this kind of queries. The reason for this is the search mechanism of search engine, which has been explained above in monolingual expansion.

3.2.3 Mix-language Expansion

Given an input organization name n_i, suppose s_i is one of its candidate translations, and n_j is one of its correlative named entities. We expand s_i with n_j to form a query "$s_i + n_j$". This kind of expansion is called as mix-language expansion.

Mix-language expansion is a necessary complement to the other two expansions. Besides, this mix-language expansion is more prone to obtain some mix-language web pages that may contain both the original input organization name and its correct translation.

3.3 Mining

When the expanded queries are submitted to search engine, the correct translation of the input organization name may be contained in the returned web pages. Because the translation of an organization name must be also an organization name, we mine the correct translation of the input among the English organization names. Here we use the Stanford named entity recognition toolkits[6] to recognize all the English organization names in the returned web pages. Then align these recognized organization names to the input by considering the following features.

Mutual Translation Probability The translation probability measures the semantic equivalence between a source organization name and its target candidate translation. And mutual translation probability measures this semantic equivalence in two directions. For simplicity, here we use IBM model-1(Brown et al. 1993), which computes two organization names' translation probability using the following formula.

$$p(f \mid e) = \frac{1}{L^J} \prod_{j=1}^{J} \sum_{l=1}^{L} p(f_j \mid e_l) \tag{6}$$

where $p(f_j \mid e_l)$ is the lexical translation probability. Suppose the input organization name is n_i, s_i is one of the recognized English organi-

person name and can be translated by Pinyin mapping.

[6] http://nlp.stanford.edu/software/CRF-NER.shtml

zation names, the mutual translation probability of n_i and s_i is computed as:

$$mp(n_i, s_i) = \lambda p(n_i \mid s_i) + (1-\lambda) p(s_i \mid n_i) \quad (7)$$

Golden Translation Ratio For two organization names, their golden translation ratio is defined as the percentage of words in one organization name whose reliable transactions can be found in another organization name. This feature is used to measure the probability of one named entity is the translation of the other. It is computed as following formula.

$$GR(n_i, s_j) = \lambda \frac{G(n_i, s_j)}{|n_i|} + (1-\lambda) \frac{G(s_j, n_i)}{|s_j|} \quad (8)$$

where $G(n_i, s_j)$ is the number of golden translated words from n_i to s_j, and $G(s_j, n_i)$ is the number of golden translated words from s_j to n_i.

Co-occurrence In Web Pages For an input organization name n_i and a recognized candidate translation s_j, the more often they co-occur in different web pages, the more likely they are translations of each other. This feature is denoted as $CoS(n_i, s_j)$, which means the number of web pages that both n_1 and s_j occur in.

Input Matching Ratio This feature is defined as the percentage of the words in the input that can be found in a returned web page. For those mix-language web pages, this feature is used to measure the probability of the correct translation occurring in a returned web page. It is computed as the following formula.

$$IMR(n_i, s_k) = \frac{|n_i \cap s_k|}{|n_i|} \quad (9)$$

where s_k is the $k-th$ returned web page.

Correlative Named Entities Matching Ratio This feature is defined as the percentage of the words in a correlative named entity that can be found in a returned web page. This feature is also used to measure the probability of the correct translation occurring in a returned web page. It is computed as the following formula.

$$CW\_MR(c_i, s_k) = \frac{|c_i \cap s_k|}{|c_i|} \quad (10)$$

The final confidence score of n_i and t_j to be a translation pair is measured by following formula. As in formula 4, here every factor will be is normalized during computation.

$$\begin{aligned} C(n_i,t_j) &= \lambda_1 mp(n_i,t_j) + \lambda_2 GR(n_i,t_j) \\ &+ \lambda_3 \frac{CoSs(n_i,n_j)}{\sum_j CoS(n_i,n_j)} + \frac{\lambda_4}{K}\sum_k IMR(n_i,s_k) \\ &+ \frac{\lambda_5}{K \times I}\sum_i \sum_k CW\_MR(c_i,s_k) \end{aligned} \quad (11)$$

where K is the number of returned web pages, I is the number of correlative named entities for the input organization name.

For every input organization name, we remain a fixed number of mined candidate translations with the highest confidence scores. And add them to the original candidate translation set to form a revised candidate translation set.

3.4 Re-ranking

The aim of mining is to improve recall. And in the re-ranking phase, we hope to improve precision by assigning the correct translation a higher rank. The features considered here for the re-ranking phase are listed as follows.

Confidence Score The confidence score of n_i and t_j is not only useful for the mining phase, but also is useful for the re-ranking phase. The higher this score, the higher rank this candidate translation should be assigned.

Inclusion Ratio For Bilingual Query This feature is defined as the percentage of the returned web pages that the bilingual query is completely matched. It is computed as the following formula.

$$EHR\_BQ(q_i) = \frac{h(q_i)}{H(q_i)} \quad (12)$$

where $h(q_i)$ is the number of web pages that match the query q_i completely, and $H(q_i)$ is the total number of returned web pages for query q_i.

Candidate Inclusion Ratio for Monolingual Query and Mix-language Query This feature is defined as the percentage of the returned web pages that the candidate translation is completed matched. This feature for monolingual query is computed as formula 13, and this feature for mix-language query is computed as formula 14.

$$ECHR\_MlQ(s_i) = h(s_i) / H(q_i) \quad (13)$$

$$ECHR\_MixQ(s_i) = h(s_i) / H(q_i) \quad (14)$$

where $h(s_i)$ is the number of web pages that match the candidate translation s_i completely, and

$H(q_i)$ is the total number of returned web pages for query q_i.

Finally, the above features are combined with following formula.

$$R(n_i,t_j)=\lambda_1 C(n_i,t_j)+\frac{\lambda_2}{N}\sum_i EHR\_BQ(q_i)$$
$$+\frac{\lambda_3}{M}\sum_i ECHR\_MlQ(s_i)$$
$$+\frac{\lambda_4}{L}\sum_i ECHR\_MixQ(s_i) \quad (15)$$

where N is the number of candidate translations, M and L are the number of monolingual queries and mix-language queries respectively.

At last the revised candidate translation set is re-ranked according to this formula, and the top-K results are outputted as the input's translation results.

4 Parameters Evaluations

In above formula (4), formula (11) and formula (15), the parameters λ_i are interpolation feature weights, which reflect the importance of different features. We use some held-our organization name pairs as development set to train these parameters. For those parameters in formula (4), we used those considered features solely one by one, and evaluated their importance according to their corresponding inclusion ratio of correct translations when using mix-language expansion and the final weights are assigned according to the following formula.

$$\lambda_i=\frac{InclusionRate_i}{\sum_i InclusionRate_i} \quad (16)$$

Where $InclusionRate_i$ is the inclusion rate when considered feature f_i only. The inclusion rate is defined as the percentage of correct translations that are contained in the returned web pages as Huang et al.[2005] did.

To obtain the parameters in formula (11), we used those considered features solely one by one, and computed their corresponding precision on development set respectively, and final weights are assigned according to following formula.

$$\lambda_i=P_i \Big/ \sum_i P_i \quad (17)$$

Where P_i is the precision when considered feature f_i only. And for the parameters in formula (15), their assignment method is the same with the method used for formula (11).

5 Experiments and Discussions

We use a Chinese to English organization name translation task to evaluate our approach. The experiments consist of four parts. Firstly, we evaluate the contribution of the correlative named entities for obtaining the web pages that contain the correct translation of the input. Secondly, we evaluate the contribution of different query expansion methods. Thirdly, we investigate to which extents our approach can solve the two problems mentioned in section 1. Finally, we evaluate how much our approach can improve the overall recall and precision. Note that for simplicity, we use 10-best outputs from Moses as the original candidate translations for every input. And the search engine used here is Live[7].

5.1 Test Set

The test set consists of 247 Chinese organization names recognized from 2,000 web pages that are downloaded from Sina[8]. These test organization names are translated by a bilingual speaker given the text they appear in. And these translations are verified from their official government web pages respectively. During translation, we don't use any contextual information.

5.2 Contribution of Correlative Named Entities

The contribution of correlative named entities is evaluated by inclusion rate, and we compare the inclusion rate with different amount of correlative named entities and different amount of returned web pages. The experimental results are shown in Table 1 (here we use all these three kinds of expanding strategies).

		# of correlative named entities used		
		1	5	10
#of web pages used	1	0.17	0.39	0.47
	5	0.29	0.63	0.78
	10	0.32	0.76	0.82

Table 1. Comparisons of inclusion rate

From these results we can find that our approach obtains an inclusion rate of 82% when we use 10 correlative named entities and 10 returned web pages. We notice that there are some Chinese organization names whose correct English translations have multiple standards. For example, the organization name "国防部"is translated

[7] http://www.live.com/

[8] http://news.sina.com.cn/

into "Department of Defense" when it refers to a department in US, but is translated into "Ministry of Defence" when it refers to a department in UK or in Singapore. This problem affects the actual inclusion rate of our approach. Another factor that affects the inclusion rate is the search engine used. There is a small difference in the inclusion rate when different search engines are used. For example, the Chinese organization name "中信银行/China CITIC Bank", because the word "中信" is an out-of-vocabulary word, the best output from Moses is "of the bank". With such candidate translation, none of our three expansion methods works. But when we used Google as search engine instead, we mined the correct translation.

From these results we can conclude that by using correlative named entities, the returned web pages are more likely to contain the correct translations of the input organization names.

5.3 Contribution of Three Query Expansion Methods

In this section, we evaluate the contribution of these three query expansion methods respectively. To do this, we use them one by one during translation, and compare their inclusion rates respectively. Experimental results are shown in Table 2.

			#of web pages used		
			1	5	10
# of correlative named entities used	Monolingual Expansion Only	1	0.002	0.002	0.004
		5	0.017	0.019	0.019
		10	0.021	0.037	0.051
	Bilingual Expansion Only	1	0.112	0.159	0.174
		5	0.267	0.327	0.472
		10	0.285	0.414	0.669
	Mix-language Expansion Only	1	0.098	0.138	0.161
		5	0.231	0.307	0.386
		10	0.249	0.398	0.652

Table 2. Inclusion rate of different kinds of query expansion methods

From Table 2 we can see that bilingual expansion and mix-language expansion play greater roles than monolingual expansion in obtaining the web pages that contain the correct translations of the inputs. This is because the condition of generating monolingual queries is too strict, which requires a reliable translation for the correlative named entity. In most cases, this condition cannot be satisfied. So for many input organization names, we cannot generate any monolingual queries for them at all. This is the reason why monolingual expansion obtains so poorer an inclusion rate compared with the other two expansions. To evaluate the true contribution of monolingual expansion method, we carry out another experiment. We select 10 organization names randomly from the test set, and translate all of their correlative named entities into English by a bilingual speaker. Then we evaluate the inclusion rate again on this new test set. The experimental results are shown in Table 3.

		# of correlative named entities used		
		1	5	10
#of web pages used	1	0.2	0.3	0.6
	5	0.4	0.7	0.9
	10	0.4	0.8	0.9

Table 3. Inclusion rate for monolingual expansion on new test set

From Table 3 we can conclude that, if most of the correlative named entities can be reliably translated, the queries generated by this monolingual expansion will play greater role in obtaining the web pages that contain the correct translations of the inputs.

From those results in Table 2 we can conclude that, these three kinds of expansions complement each other. Using them together can obtain higher inclusion rate than using anyone of them only.

5.4 Efficiency on Solving Problem I and Problem II

In this section, we investigate to which extents our approach can solve the two problems mentioned in section 1.We compare the wrong translation numbers caused by these two problems (another main kind of translation error is caused by the translation of out-of-vocabulary words) between Moses and our approach. The experimental results are shown in Table 4.

	Moses Results	Our method
Problem I	44	3
Problem II	30	0

Table 4. Comparison of error numbers

From Table 4 we can see that our approach is very effective on solving these two problems. Almost all of the errors caused by these two problems are corrected by our approach. Only three wrong translations are not corrected. This is because that there are some Chinese organization names whose correct English translations have multiple standards, such as the correct translation of organization name "国防部"depends on its nationality, which has been explained in section 5.2.

5.5 Our Approach vs. Other Approaches

In this section, we compare our approach with other two methods: Moses and the approach proposed by Huang et al. [2005]. We compare their accuracy of Top-K results. For both our approach and Huang et al.'s approach, we use 10 correlative words for each input organization name and use 10 returned web pages for mining the correct translation result. The experimental results are shown in Table 5.

	Moses Results	Huang's Results	Our Results
Top 1	0.09	0.44	0.53
Top 5	0.18	0.61	0.73
Top 10	0.31	0.68	0.79

Table 5. Moses results vs. our results

Moses is a state-of-the-art translation method, but it can hardly handle the organization name translation well. In addition to the errors caused by the above two problems mentioned in section 1, the out-of-vocabulary problem is another obstacle for Moses. For example, when translating the organization name "国际海啸信息中心 /International Tsunami Information Centre", because the word "海啸" is an out-of-vocabulary word, Moses fails to give correct translation. But for those approaches that have a web mining process during translation, both the out-of-vocabulary problem and the two problems mentioned in section 1 are less serious. This is the reason that Moses obtains the lowest performance compared with the other two approaches. Our approach is also superior to Huang's method, as shown in the above table. We think this is because of the following three reasons. The first reason is that in our approach, we use a translation candidate generation process. Although these candidates are usually not so good, they can still provide some very useful clue information for the web retrieval process. The second reason is that the features considered for correlative words extraction in our approach are more comprehensive. Most of the time (except for the case that the input is not included in the correlative word list) our approach is more prone to obtain better correlative words for the input. The third reason is that our approach use more query expansion strategies than Huang's approach. These expansion strategies may complement each other and improve the probability of obtaining the web pages that contain the correct translations For example, both Moses and Huang's approach failed to translate the organization name "国际海啸信息中心". But in our approach, with the candidate translation "International Information Centre" that is generated by Moses, our approach still can obtain the web page that contains the correct translation when using bilingual expansion. Thus the correct translation "International Tsunami Information Centre" is mined out during the sequent mining process.

From table 5 we also notice that the final recall of our approach is a little lower than the inclusion rate as show in table 1. This means that our approach doesn't mine all the correct translations that are contained in the returned web pages. One of the reasons is that some of the input organization names are not clearly expressed. For example, an input organization name "伯克利分校", although its correct translation "University of California, Berkeley" is contained in the returned web pages, this correct translation cannot be mined out by our approach. But if it is expressed as "加利福尼亚大学伯克利分校", its correct translation can be mined from the returned web pages easily. Besides, the recognition errors of NER toolkits will also reduce the final recall of our approach.

6 Conclusions and Future Work

In this paper, we present a new organization name translation approach. It uses some correlative named entities of the input and some query expansion strategies to help the search engine to retrieve those web pages that contain the correct translation of the input. Experimental results show that for most of the inputs, their correct translations are contained in the returned web pages. By mining these correct translations and re-ranking them, the two problems mentioned in section 1 are solved effectively. And recall and precision are also improved correspondingly.

In the future, we will try to improve the extraction perform of correlative named entities. We will also try to apply this approach to the person name translation and location name translation.

Acknowledgments

This work was supported by the open fund of National Laboratory of Pattern Recognition, Institute of Automation Chinese Academy of Science, P.R.C, and was also supported in part by National Science Foundation of China (60873091), Natural Science Foundation of Liaoning Province (20072032) and Shenyang Science and Technology Plan (1081235-1-00).

References

Chen Hsin-Hsi, Changhua Yang, and Ying Lin. 2003. Learning formulation and transformation rules for multilingual named entities. Proceedings of the ACL 2003 Workshop on Multilingual and Mixed-language Named Entity Recognition. pp1-8.

Dekang Lin, Shaojun Zhao, Durme Benjamin Van Drume, Marius Pasca. Mining Parenthetical Translations from the Web by Word Alignment, ACL08. pp994-1002.

Fan Yang, Jun Zhao, Bo Zou, Kang Liu, Feifan Liu. 2008. Chinese-English Backward Transliteration Assisted with Mining Monolingual Web Pages. ACL2008. pp541-549.

Fei Huang, Stephan Vogel and Alex Waibel. 2003. Automatic Extraction of Named Entity Translingual Equivalence Based on Multi-feature Cost Minimization. Proceedings of the 2003 Annual Conference of the Association for Computational Linguistics, Workshop on Multilingual and Mixed-language Named Entity Recognition.

Fei Huang, Stephan vogel and Alex Waibel. 2004. Improving Named Entity Translation Combining Phonetic and Semantic Similarities. Proceedings of the HLT/NAACL. pp281-288.

Fei Huang, Ying Zhang, Stephan Vogel. 2005. Mining Key Phrase Translations from Web Corpora. HLT-EMNLP2005, pp483-490.

Feng, Donghui, Yajuan LV, and Ming Zhou. 2004. A new approach for English-Chinese named entity alignment. Proceedings of the Conference on Empirical Methods in Natural Language Processing (EMNLP 2004), pp372-379.

Franz Josef Och. 2003. Minimum Error Rate Training in Statistical Machine Translation. ACL2003. pp160-167.

Jin-Shea Kuo, Haizhou Li, Ying-Kuei Yang. Learning Transliteration Lexicon from the Web. COLING/ACL2006. pp1129-1136.

Hany Hassan and Jeffrey Sorensen. 2005. An Integrated Approach for Arabic-English Named Entity Translation. Proceedings of ACL Workshop on Computational Approaches to Semitic Languages. pp87-93.

Lee, Chun-Jen and Jason S.Chang and Jyh-Shing Roger Jang. 2004a. Bilingual named-entity pairs extraction from parallel corpora. Proceedings of IJCNLP-04 Workshop on Named Entity Recognition for Natural Language Processing Application. pp9-16.

Lee, Chun-Jen, Jason S.Chang and Thomas C. Chuang. 2004b. Alignment of bilingual named entities in parallel corpora using statistical model. Lecture Notes in Artificial Intelligence. 3265:144-153.

Lee, Chun-Jen, Jason S.Chang, and Jyh-Shing Roger Jang. 2005. Extraction of transliteration pairs from parallel corpora using a sta Acquisition of English-Chinese transliterated word pairs from parallel-aligned text using a statistical transliteration model. Information Sciences.

Long Jiang, Ming Zhou, Lee-Feng Chien, Cheng Niu. [2007]. Named Entity Translation with Web Mining and Transliteration. IJCAI-2007.

Moore, Robert C. 2003. Learning translations of named-entity phrases form parallel corpora. ACL-2003. pp259-266.

Peter F. Brown, Vincent J. Della Pietra, Stephen A. Della Pietra, and Robert L. Mercer. 1993. The Mathematics of Statistical Machine Translation: Parameter Estimation. Computational Linguistics, 19(2):263-311.

Y. Al-Onaizan and K. Knight. 2002. Translating named entities using monolingual and bilingual resources. In Proceedings of the 40th Annual Meeting of the Association for Computational Linguistics, pp400-408.

Ying Zhang and Phil Vines Using the Web for Automated Translation Extraction in Cross-Language Information Retrieval. SIGIR2004,pp162-169.

Yufeng Chen, Chengqing Zong. A Structure-based Model for Chinese Organization Name Translation. ACM Transactions on Asian Language Information Processing, 2008, 7(1), pp1-30.

Name Matching Between Chinese and Roman Scripts: Machine Complements Human

Ken Samuel, Alan Rubenstein, Sherri Condon, and Alex Yeh
The MITRE Corporation; M/S H305; 7515 Colshire Drive; McLean, Virginia 22102-7508
samuel@mitre.org, rubenstein@mitre.org, scondon@mitre.org, **and** asy@mitre.org

Abstract

There are generally many ways to transliterate a name from one language script into another. The resulting ambiguity can make it very difficult to "untransliterate" a name by reverse engineering the process. In this paper, we present a highly successful cross-script name matching system that we developed by combining the creativity of human intuition with the power of machine learning. Our system determines whether a name in Roman script and a name in Chinese script match each other with an F-score of 96%. In addition, for name pairs that satisfy a computational test, the F-score is 98%.

1 Introduction

There are generally many ways to transliterate a person's name from one language script into another. For example, writers have transliterated the Arabic name, الشكري, into Roman characters in at least 13 ways, such as Al Choukri, Ash-shukri, and al-Schoukri. This ambiguity can make it very difficult to "untransliterate" a name by reverse engineering the process.

We focused on a task that is related to transliteration. Cross-script name matching aims to determine whether a given name part in Roman script matches a given name part in Chinese (Mandarin) script,[1] where a name part is a single "word" in a person's name (such as a surname), and two names match if one is a transliteration of the other.[2] Cross-script name matching has many applications, such as identity matching, improving search engines, and aligning parallel corpora.

We combine a) the creative power of human intuition, which can come up with clever ideas and b) the computational power of machine learning, which can analyze large quantities of data. Wan and Verspoor (1998) provided the human intuition by designing an algorithm to divide names into pieces that are just the right size for Roman-Chinese name matching (Section 2.2.). Armed with Wan and Verspoor's algorithm, a machine learning approach analyzes hundreds of thousands of matched name pairs to build a Roman-Chinese name matching system (Section 3).

Our experimental results are in Section 4. The system correctly determines whether a Roman name and a Chinese name match each other with F = 96.5%.[3] And F = 97.6% for name pairs that satisfy the Perfect Alignment hypothesis condition, which is defined in Section 2.2.

2 Related Work

Wan and Verspoor's (1998) work had a great impact on our research, and we explain how we use it in Section 2.2. In Section 2.1, we identify other related work.

2.1 Chinese-English Name Matching

Condon et al. (2006) wrote a paper about the challenges of matching names across Roman and Chinese scripts. In Section 6 of their paper, they offered an overview of several papers related to Roman-Chinese name matching. (Cohen et al., 2003; Gao et al., 2004; Goto et al., 2003; Jung et al., 2000; Kang and Choi, 2000; Knight and Graehl, 1997; Kondrak, 2000; Kondrak and Dorr, 2004; Li et al., 2004; Meng et al., 2001; Oh

[1] In this paper, we often use the word "Roman" to refer to "Roman script", and similarly, "Chinese" usually stands for "Chinese script".

[2] Sometimes a third script comes between the Roman and Chinese versions of the name. For example, a Roman name might be transliterated into Arabic, which is then transliterated into Chinese, or an Arabic name could be transliterated into Roman and Chinese independently.

[3] F stands for F-score, which is a popular evaluation metric. (Andrade et al., 2009)

Proceedings of the 2009 Named Entities Workshop, ACL-IJCNLP 2009, pages 152–160,
Suntec, Singapore, 7 August 2009. ©2009 ACL and AFNLP

Roman Characters:	Albertson
Phonemes:	AE,L,B,ER,T,S,AH,N
Syllables:	AEL,BERT,SAHN
Subsyllable Units:	AE,L,BER,T,SAHN
Chinese:	阿尔贝特松
Chinese Phonemes:	/a/,/ər/,/pei/,/tʰə/,/suŋ/

Table 1. Subsyllable Units

and Choi, 2006; Virga and Khudanpur, 2003; Wellner et al., 2005; Winkler, 2002)

The Levenshtein algorithm is a popular way to compute string edit distance. (Levenshtein, 1966) It can quantify the similarity between two names. However, this algorithm does not work when the names are written in different scripts. So Freeman et al. (2006) developed a strategy for Roman-Arabic string matching that uses equivalence classes of characters to normalize the names so that Levenshtein's method can be applied. Later, Mani et al. (2006) transformed that system from Roman-Arabic to Roman-Chinese name matching and extended the Levenshtein approach, attaining F = 85.2%. Then when they trained a machine learning algorithm on the output, the performance improved to F = 93.1%

Mani et al. also tried applying a phonological alignment system (Kondrak, 2000) to the Roman-Chinese name matching task, and they reported an F-score of 91.2%. However, when they trained a machine learning approach on that system's output, the F-score was only 90.6%.

It is important to recognize that it would be inappropriate to present a side-by-side comparison between Mani's work and ours (F = 96.5%), because there are many differences, such as the data that was used for evaluation.

2.2 Subsyllable Units

Transliteration is usually based on the way names are pronounced.[4] However, each character in a Roman name generally corresponds to a single phoneme, while a Chinese character (CC) generally corresponds to a subsyllable unit (SSU). A phoneme is the smallest meaningful unit of sound, and a subsyllable unit is a sequence of one to three phonemes that conform to the following three constraints. (Wan and Verspoor, 1998)

(1) There is exactly one vowel phoneme.[5]
(2) At most, one consonant phoneme may precede the vowel phoneme.
(3) The vowel phoneme may be followed by, at most, one nasal phoneme.[6]

Consider the example in Table 1. The name "Albertson" consists of eight phonemes in three syllables.[7] The last syllable, SAHN, satisfies the definition of SSU, and the other two are split into smaller pieces, resulting in a total of five SSUs. There are also five CCs in the Chinese version, 阿尔贝特松. We note that the fourth and sixth rows in the table show similarities in their pronunciations. For example, the first SSU, AE, sounds like the first CC, /a/. And, although the sounds are not always identical, such as BER and /pei/, Wan and Verspoor claimed that these SSU-CC correspondences can be generalized in the following way:

Perfect Alignment (PA) hypothesis

If a Roman name corresponds to a sequence of n SSUs, $S_1, S_2, \ldots, S_n$, and the Chinese form of that name is a sequence of n CCs, $C_1, C_2, \ldots, C_n$, then C_i matches S_i for all $1 \le i \le n$.

In Section 4, we show that the PA hypothesis works very well. However, it is not uncommon to have more SSUs than CCs in a matching name pair, in which case, the PA hypothesis does not apply. Often this happens because an SSU is left out of the Chinese transliteration, perhaps because it is a sound that is not common in Chinese. For example, suppose "Carlberg" (KAA, R,L,BER,G) is transliterated as 卡尔贝里. In this example, the SSU, R, does not correspond to any of the CCs. We generalize this phenomenon with another hypothesis:

SSUs Deletion (SSUD) hypothesis

If a Roman name corresponds to a sequence of n+k SSUs (k>0), $S_1, S_2, \ldots, S_{n+k}$, and the Chinese form of that name is a sequence of n CCs, $C_1, C_2, \ldots, C_n$, then, for some set of k S_i's, if those SSUs are removed from the sequence of SSUs, then the PA hypothesis holds.

And in the case where the number of CCs is greater than the number of SSUs, we make the

[4] Of course, there are exceptions. For example, when a name happens to be a word, sometimes that name is *translated* (rather than transliterated) into the other language. But our experimental results suggest that the exceptions are quite rare.

[5] Wan and Verspoor treat the phoneme, /ər/, as in Albertson, as a vowel phoneme.

[6] The nasal phonemes are /n/ and /ŋ/, as in "nothing".

[7] To represent phonemes, we use two different standards in this paper. The symbols between slashes (like /ər/) are in the IPA format (International Phonetic Association, 1999). And the phonemes written in capital letters (like ER) are in the ARPABET format (Klatt, 1990).

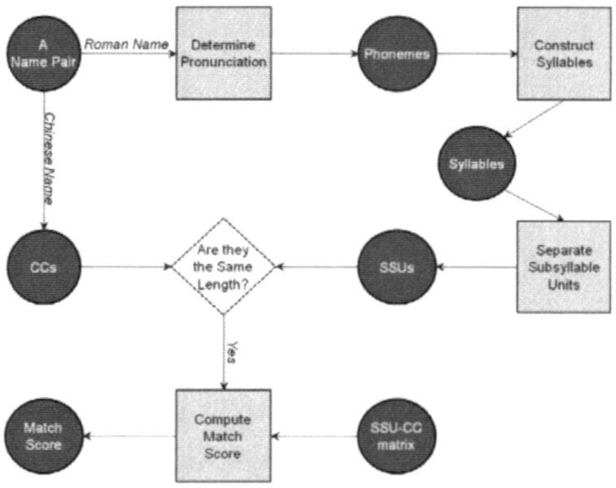

Figure 1. Application Mode

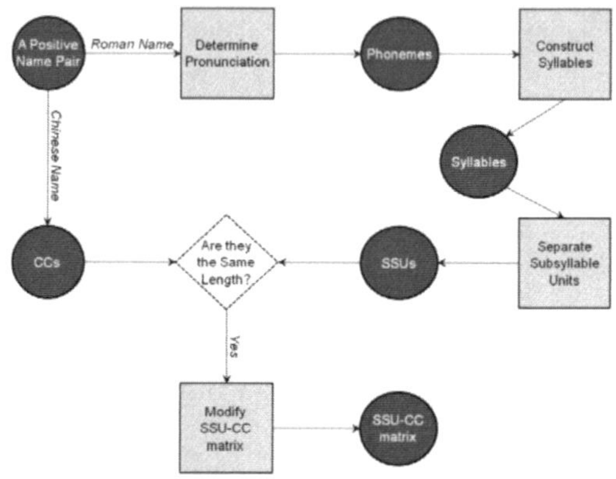

Figure 2. Training Mode

corresponding CCs Deletion (CCD) hypothesis. In the next section, we show how we utilize these hypotheses.

3 Machine Learning

We designed a machine learning algorithm to establish a mapping between SSUs and CCs. In Section 3.1, we show how our system can do Roman-Chinese name matching, and then we present the training procedure in Section 3.2.

3.1 Application Mode

Given a Roman-Chinese name pair, our system computes a match score, which is a number between 0 and 1 that is meant to represent the likelihood that two names match. This is accomplished via the process presented in Figure 1.

Starting in the upper-left node of the diagram with a Roman name and a Chinese name, the system determines how the Roman name should be pronounced by running it through the Festival system. (Black et al., 1999) Next, two algorithms designed by Wan and Verspoor (1998) join the phonemes to form syllables and divide the syllables into SSUs.[8] If the number of SSUs is equal to the number of characters in the Chinese name,[9] we apply the PA hypothesis to align each SSU with a CC.

The system computes a match score using a data structure called the SSU-CC matrix (subsyllable unit – Chinese character matrix), which has a nonnegative number for each SSU-CC pair, and this value should represent the strength of the correspondence between the SSU and the CC. Table 2 shows an example of an SSU-CC matrix. With this matrix, the name pair <Albert, 阿尔贝特> receives a relatively high match score, because the SSUs in Albert are AE, L, BER, and T, and the numbers in the SSU-CC matrix for <AE,阿>, <L,尔>, <BER,贝> and <T,特> are 2, 2, 3, and 2, respectively.[10] Alternatively, the system assigns a very low match score to <Albert, 尔贝特阿>, because the values of <AE,尔>, <L,贝>, <BER,格>, and <T,阿> are all 0.

	AE	BER	EH	G	KAA	L	LAHN	LIY	NAH	R	SAHN	T
伦	0	0	0	0	0	0	1	0	0	0	0	0
利	0	0	0	0	0	0	0	1	0	0	0	0
卡	0	0	0	0	1	0	0	0	0	0	0	0
叶	0	0	1	0	0	0	0	0	0	0	0	0
埃	0	0	1	0	0	0	0	0	0	0	0	0
娜	0	0	0	0	0	0	0	0	1	0	0	0
尔	0	0	0	0	0	2	0	0	0	1	0	0
松	0	0	0	0	0	0	0	0	0	0	1	0
特	0	0	0	0	0	0	0	0	0	0	0	2
贝	0	3	0	0	0	0	0	0	0	0	0	0
连	0	0	0	0	0	0	1	0	0	0	0	0
里	0	0	0	1	0	0	0	0	0	0	0	0
阿	2	0	0	0	0	0	0	0	0	0	0	0

Table 2. SSU-CC Matrix #1

3.2 Training Mode

To generate an SSU-CC matrix, we train our system on a corpus of Roman-Chinese name pairs

[8] This procedure passes through three separate modules, each of which introduces errors, so we would expect the system to suffer from compounding errors. However, the excellent evaluation results in Section 4 suggest otherwise. This may be because the system encounters the same kinds of errors during training that it sees in the application mode, so perhaps it can learn to compensate for them.

[9] Section 3.3 discusses the procedure used when these numbers are not equal.

[10] The equation used to derive the match score from these values can be found in Section 5.

Example #	1	2	3	4	5
Roman Characters	**Albert**	**Albertson**	**Carly**	**Elena**	**Ellenberg**
Subsyllable Units	AE,L,BER,T	AE,L,BER,T,SAHN	KAA,R,LIY	EH,LAHN,NAH	EH,LAHN,BER,G
Chinese Characters	阿尔贝特	阿尔贝特松	卡尔利	叶连娜	埃伦贝里

Table 3. Training Data

that match. Figure 2 shows a diagram of the training system. The procedure for transforming the Roman name into a sequence of SSUs is identical to that presented in Section 3.1. Then, if the number of SSUs is the same as the number of CCs,[9] we apply the PA hypothesis to pair the SSUs with the CCs. For example, the third name pair in Table 3 has three SSU-CC pairs: <KAA, 卡>, <R,尔>, and <LIY,利>. So the system modifies the SSU-CC matrix by adding 1 to each cell that corresponds to one of these SSU-CC pairs. Training on the five name pairs in Table 3 produces the SSU-CC matrix in Table 2.

3.3 Imperfect Alignment

The system makes two passes through the training data. In the first pass, whenever the PA hypothesis does not apply to a name pair (because the number of SSUs differs from the number of CCs), that name pair is skipped.

Then, in the second pass, the system builds another SSU-CC matrix. The procedure for processing each name pair that satisfies the PA hypothesis's condition is exactly the same as in the first pass (Section 3.2). But the other name pairs require the SSUD hypothesis or the CCD hypothesis to delete SSUs or CCs. For a given Roman-Chinese name pair:

CCs	Score	Scaled Score
Ø 卡尔贝里	0.00	0.00
卡 Ø 尔贝里	0.90	0.54
卡尔 Ø 贝里	0.76	0.46
卡尔贝 Ø 里	0.00	0.00
卡尔贝里 Ø	0.00	0.00

Table 4. Subsyllable Unit Deletion

```
For every d in D:
  Temporarily make the deletions in d.
  Evaluate the resulting name pair with Matrix #1.
Scale the evaluation scores of the d's to sum to 1.
For every d in D:
  Temporarily make the deletions in d.
  For every SSU-CC pair, ssu-cc, in the result:
    Add d's scaled score to cell [ssu,cc] in Matrix #2.
```

where D is the set of all deletion sets that make the PA hypothesis applicable. Note that the size of D grows exponentially as the difference between the number of SSUs and CCs grows.

As an example, consider adding the name pair <Carlberg, 卡尔贝里> to the data in Table 3. Carlberg has five SSUs: KAA,R,L,BER,G, but 卡尔贝里 has only four CCs. So the PA hypothesis is not applicable, and the system ignores this name pair in the first pass. Table 2 shows the values in Matrix #1 when it is completed.

In the second pass, we must apply the SSUD hypothesis to <Carlberg, 卡尔贝里> by deleting one of the SSUs. There are five ways to do this, as shown in the five rows of Table 4. (For instance, the last row represents the case where G is deleted — the SSU-CC pairs are <KAA,卡>, <R,尔>, <L,贝>, <BER,里>, and <G,Ø>.[11])

	Ø	BER	G	KAA	L	R	...
Ø		0.00	0.00	0.00	0.46	0.54	
卡	0.00	0.00	0.00	2.00	0.00	0.00	
尔	0.00	0.00	0.00	0.00	2.54	1.46	
贝	0.00	4.00	0.00	0.00	0.00	0.00	
里	0.00	0.00	2.00	0.00	0.00	0.00	
...							

Table 5. SSU-CC Matrix #2

Each of the five options are evaluated using the values in Matrix #1 (Table 2) to produce the scores in the second column of Table 4. Then the

[11] The Ø represents a deleted SSU. We include a row and column named Ø in Matrix #2 to record values for the cases in which the SSUs and CCs are deleted.

	LAHN (BER)	LAHN (NAH)	BER (G)	BER (T)
伦	1	0	0	0
贝	0	0	1	2
连	0	1	0	0

Table 6. Considering Context

system scales the scores to sum to 1, as shown in the third column, and it uses those values as weights to determine how much impact each of the five options has on the second matrix. Table 5 shows part of Matrix #2.

In application mode, when the system encounters a name pair that does not satisfy the PA hypothesis's condition it tries all possible deletion sets and selects the one that produces the highest match score.

3.4 Considering Context

It might be easier to estimate the likelihood that an SSU-CC pair is a match by using information found in surrounding SSU-CC pairs, such as the SSU that follows a given SSU-CC pair. We do this by increasing the number of columns in the SSU-CC matrix to separate the examples based on the surrounding context.

For example, in Table 2, we cannot determine whether LAHN should map to 伦 or 连. But the SSU that follows LAHN clears up the ambiguity, because when LAHN immediately precedes BER, it maps to 伦, but when it is followed by NAH, it corresponds to 连. Table 6 displays a portion of the SSU-CC matrix that accounts for the contextual information provided by the SSU that follows an SSU-CC pair.

3.5 The Threshold

Given an SSU-CC name pair, the system produces a number between 0 and 1. But in order to evaluate the system in terms of precision, recall, and F-score, we need the system to return a yes (a match) or no (not a match) response. So we use a threshold value to separate those two cases.

The threshold value can be manually selected by a human, but this is often difficult to do effectively. So we developed the following automated approach to choose the threshold. After the training phase finishes developing Matrix #2, the system processes the training data[12] one more time.

[12] We tried selecting the threshold with data that was not used in training, and we found no statistically significant improvement.

Alignment	% of Data
#SSUs - #CCs ≥ 3	1.62%
#SSUs - #CCs = 2	6.66%
#SSUs - #CCs = 1	20.00%
#SSUs - #CCs = 0	60.60%
#SSUs - #CCs = -1	10.48%
#SSUs - #CCs = -2	0.61%
#SSUs - #CCs ≤ -3	0.02%

Table 7. Statistics of the Data

But this time it runs in application mode (Section 3.1), computing a match score for each training example. Then the system considers all possible ways to separate the yes and no responses with a threshold, selecting the threshold value that is the most effective on the training data.

Building the SSU-CC matrices does not require any negative examples (name pairs that do not match). However, we do require negative examples in order to determine the threshold and to evaluate the system. Our technique for generating negative examples involves randomly rearranging the names in the data.[13]

4 Evaluation of the System

We ran several experiments to test our system under a variety of different conditions. After describing our data and experimental method, we present some of our most interesting experimental results.

We used a set of nearly 500,000 Roman-Chinese person name pairs collected from Xinhua News Agency newswire texts. (Huang, 2005) Table 7 shows the distribution of the data based on alignment. Note that the PA hypothesis applies to more than 60% of the data.

We used the popular 10-fold cross validation approach [14] to obtain ten different evaluation scores. For each experiment we present the average of these scores.

Our system's precision (P), recall (R), and F-score (F) are: P = 98.19%, R = 94.83%, and F = 96.48%. These scores are much better than we originally expected to see for the challenging task of Roman-Chinese name matching.

Table 8 shows P, R, and F for subsets of the test data, organized by the number of SSUs mi-

[13] Unfortunately, there is no standard way to generate negative examples.

[14] The data is divided into ten subsets of approximately the same size, testing the system on each subset when trained on the other nine.

Alignment	P	R	F
#SSUs - #CCs ≥ 3	72.38%	94.02%	81.79%
#SSUs - #CCs = 2	95.26%	92.67%	93.95%
#SSUs - #CCs = 1	99.07%	93.27%	96.08%
#SSUs - #CCs = 0	99.87%	95.33%	97.55%
#SSUs - #CCs = -1	98.33%	96.42%	97.37%
#SSUs - #CCs = -2	73.80%	94.98%	83.04%
#SSUs - #CCs ≤ -3	7.54%	78.04%	13.71%

Table 8. Varying Alignment of Name Pairs

nus the number of CCs in the name pairs. The differences between scores in adjacent rows of each column are statistically significant.[15] Perfectly aligned name pairs proved to be the easiest, with F = 97.55%, but the system was also very successful on the examples with the number of SSUs and the number of CCs differing by one (F = 96.08% and F = 97.37%). These three cases account for more than 91% of the positive examples in our data set. (See Table 7.)

4.1 Deletion Hypotheses

We ran tests to determine whether the second pass through the training data (in which the SSUD and CCD hypotheses are applied) is effective. Table 9 shows the results on the complete set of test data, and all of the differences between the scores are statistically significant.

The first row of Table 9 presents F when the system made only one pass through the training data. The second row's experiments utilized the CCD hypothesis but ignored examples with more SSUs than CCs during training. For the third row, we used the SSUD hypothesis, but not the CCD hypothesis, and the last row corresponds to system runs that used all of the training examples. From these results, it is clear that both of the deletion hypotheses are useful, particularly the SSUD hypothesis.

4.2 Context

In Section 3.4, we suggested that contextual information might be useful. So we ran some tests, obtaining the results shown in Table 10. For the second row, we used no contextual information. Row 5 corresponds to the case where we gave the system access to the SSU immediately following the SSU-CC pair being analyzed. In row 6's experiment, we used the SSU immediately preceding the SSU-CC pair under consideration, and row 7 corresponds to system runs that accounted for both surrounding SSUs.

Hypotheses	F
PA	75.25%
PA & CCD	83.74%
PA & SSUD	92.86%
PA & CCD & SSUD	96.48%

Table 9. Varying the Training Data

We also tried simplifying the contextual information to boolean values that specify whether an SSU-CC pair is at a boundary of its name or not, and rows 1, 3, and 4 of Table 10 show those results. "Left Border" is true if and only if the SSU-CC pair is at the beginning of its name, "Right Border" is true if and only if the SSU-CC pair is at the end of its name, and "Both Borders" is true if and only if the SSU-CC pair is at the beginning or end of its name. All differences in the table are statistically significant, except for those between rows 2, 3, and 4. These results suggest that the right border provides no useful information, even if the left border is also included in the SSU-CC matrix. But when the SSU-CC matrix only accounted for the left border, the F-score was significantly higher than the baseline. Providing more specific information in the form of SSUs actually made the scores go down significantly.

4.3 Sparse Data

We were initially surprised to discover that using the rich information in the surrounding SSUs made the results worse. The explanation for this is that adding contextual information increases the size of the SSU-CC matrix, and so several of the numbers in the matrix become smaller. (For example, compare the values in the "BER" columns in Table 2 and Table 6.) This means that the system might have been suffering from a sparse data problem, which is a situation where there are not enough training examples to distinguish correct answers from incorrect answers, and so incorrect answers can appear to be correct by random chance.

There are two factors that can contribute to a sparse data problem. One is the amount of training data available — as the quantity of training data increases, the sparse data problem becomes less severe. The other factor is the complexity of

#	Contextual Information	F
1	Left Border	96.48%
2	No Context	96.25%
3	Both Borders	96.24%
4	Right Border	96.19%
5	Next SSU	87.53%
6	Previous SSU	85.89%
7	Previous SSU and Next SSU	47.89%

Table 10. Evaluation with Context

Contextual Info.	All Cells	Cells > 10^{-7}
No Context	0.128	4.35
Right Border	0.071	3.45
Left Border	0.069	3.45
Both Borders	0.040	3.13
Next SSU	0.002	1.12
Previous SSU	0.001	0.78
Both SSUs	*far less*	*far less*

Table 11. Num. SSU-CC Pairs per Matrix Cell

the learned model — as the model becomes more complex, the sparse data problem worsens.

Our system's model is the SSU-CC matrix, and a reasonable measure of the its complexity is the number of entries in the matrix. The second column of Table 11 shows the number of SSU-CC pairs in training divided by the number of cells in the SSU-CC matrix. These ratios are quite low, suggesting that there is a sparse data problem. Even without using any context, there are nearly 8 cells for each SSU-CC pair, on average.[16]

It might be more reasonable to ignore cells with extremely low values, since we can assume that these values are effectively zero. The third column of Table 11 only counts cells that have values above 10^{-7}. The numbers in that column look better, as the ratio of cells to training pairs is better than 1:4 when no context is used. However, when using the previous SSU, there are still more cells than training pairs.

Another standard way to test for sparse data is to compare the system's results as a function of the quantity of training data. As the amount of training data increases, we expect the F-score to rise, until there is so much training data that the F-score is at its optimal value.[17] Figure 3 shows the results of all of the context experiments that we ran, varying the amount of training data. (90% of the training data was used to get the F-scores in Table 10.) The t test tells us that "No Context" is the only curve that does not increase significantly on the right end. This suggests that all of the other curves might continue increasing if we used more training data. So even the "Both SSUs" case could potentially achieve a competitive score, given enough training examples. Also,

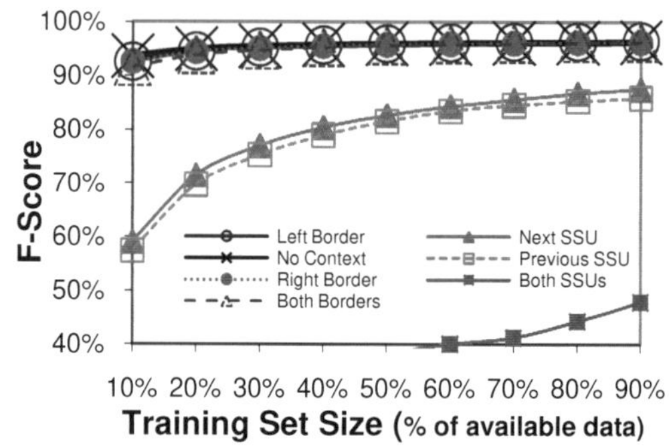

Figure 3. Testing for Sparse Data

more training data could produce higher scores than 96.48%.

5 Summary

We designed a system that achieved an F-score of 96.48%, and F = 97.55% on the 60.61% of the data that satisfies the PA hypothesis's condition.

Due to the paper length restriction, we can only provide short summaries of the other experiments that that we ran.

1) We experimentally compared six different equations for computing match scores and found that the best of them is an arithmetic or geometric average of Prob(SSU|CC) and Prob(CC|SSU).
2) We attempted to make use of two simple handcrafted rules, but they caused the system's performance to drop significantly.
3) We compared two approaches for automatically computing the pronunciation of a Roman name and found that using the Festival system (Black et al., 1999) alone is just as effective as using the CMU Pronunciation Dictionary (CMUdict, 1997) supplemented by Festival.
4) We tried computing the threshold value with data that was not used in training the system. However, this failed to improve the system's performance significantly.

6 Future Work

There are so many things that we still want to do, including:

1. modifying our system for the task of transliteration (Section 6.1),
2. running fair comparisons between our work and related research,
3. using Levenshtein's algorithm (Levenshtein, 1966) to implement the SSUD and

[16] It is true that a name pair can have multiple SSU-CC pairs, but even if the average number of SSU-CC pairs per name pair is as high as 8 (and it is not), one training name pair per SSU-CC matrix cell is still insufficient.

[17] Note that this value may not be 100%, because there are factors that can make perfection difficult to achieve, such as errors in the data.

CCD hypotheses, instead of exhaustively evaluating all possible deletion sets (Section 3.3),[18]
4. developing a standard methodology for creating negative examples,
5. when using contextual information, splitting rows or columns of the SSU-CC matrix only when they are ambiguous according to a metric such as Information Gain (Section 3.4),[19]
6. combining our system with other Roman-Chinese name matching systems in a voting structure (Van Halteren, Zavrel, and Daelemans, 1998),
7. independently evaluating the modules that determine pronunciation, construct syllables, and separate subsyllable units (Section 3),
8. converting phonemes into feature vectors (Aberdeen, 2006),
9. modifying our methodology to apply it to other similar languages, such as Japanese, Korean, Vietnamese, and Hawaiian.
10. manually creating rules based on information in the SSU-CC matrix, and
11. utilizing graphemic information.

6.1 Transliteration

We would like to modify our system to enable it to transliterate a given Roman name into Chinese in the following way. First, the system computes the SSUs as in Section 3.1. Then it produces a match score for every possible sequence of CCs that has the same length as the sequence of SSUs, returning all of the CC sequences with match scores that satisfy a predetermined threshold restriction.

For example, in a preliminary experiment, given the Roman name *Ellen*, the matcher produced the transliterations below, with the match scores in parentheses.[20]

埃 伦 (0.32)

埃 兰 (0.14)

埃 隆 (0.11)

埃 朗 (0.05)

[18] We thank a reviewer for suggesting this method of improving efficiency.

[19] We thank a reviewer for this clever way to control the size of the SSU-CC matrix when context is considered.

[20] A manually-set threshold of 0.05 was used in this experiment.

Based on our data, the first and fourth results are true transliterations of *Ellen*, and the only true transliteration that failed to make the list is 埃连.

7 Conclusion

There was a time when computational linguistics research rarely used machine learning. Researchers developed programs and then showed how they could successfully handle a few examples, knowing that their programs were unable to generalize much further. Then the language community became aware of the advantages of machine learning, and statistical systems almost completely took over the field. Researchers solved all kinds of problems by tapping into the computer's power to process huge corpora of data. But eventually, the machine learning systems reached their limits.

We believe that, in the future, the most successful systems will be those developed by people cooperating with machines. Such systems can solve problems by combining the computer's ability to process massive quantities of data with the human's ability to intuitively come up with new ideas.

Our system is a success story of human-computer cooperation. The computer tirelessly processes hundreds of thousands of training examples to generate the SSU-CC matrix. But it cannot work at all without the insights of Wan and Verspoor. And together, they made a system that is successful more than 96% of the time.

References

Aberdeen, J. (2006) "geometric-featurechart-jsa-20060616.xls". *Unpublished.*

Andrade, Miguel. Smith, S. Paul. Cowlisha, Mike F. Gantner, Zeno. O'Brien, Philip. Farmbrough, Rich. et al. "F1 Score." (2009) *Wikipedia: The Free Encyclopedia*. http://en.wikipedia.org/wiki/F-score.

Black, Alan W. Taylor, Paul. Caley, Richard. (1999) *The Festival Speech Synthesis System: System Documentation*. Centre for Speech Technology Research (CSTR). The University of Edinburgh. http://www.cstr.ed.ac.uk/projects/festival/manual

CMUdict. (1997) *The CMU Pronouncing Dictionary*. v0.6. The Carnegie Mellon Speech Group. http://www.speech.cs.cmu.edu/cgi-bin/cmudict.

Cohen, W. Ravikumar, P. Fienberg, S. (2003) "A Comparison of String Distance Metrics for Name-

Matching Tasks." *Proceedings of the IJCAI-03 Workshop on Information Integration on the Web*. Eds. Kambhampati, S. Knoblock, C. 73-78.

Condon, Sherri. Aberdeen, John. Albin, Matthew. Freeman, Andy. Mani, Inderjeet. Rubenstein, Alan. Sarver, Keri. Sexton, Mike. Yeh, Alex. (2006) "Multilingual Name Matching Mid-Year Status Report."

Condon, S. Freeman, A. Rubenstein, A. Yeh, A. (2006) "Strategies for Chinese Name Matching."

Freeman, A. Condon, S. Ackermann, C. (2006) "Cross Linguistic Name Matching in English and Arabic: A 'One to Many Mapping' Extension of the Levenshtein Edit Distance Algorithm." *Proceedings of NAACL/HLT*.

Gao, W. Wong, K. Lam, W. (2004) "Phoneme-Based Transliteration of Foreign Names for OOV Problem." *Proceedings of the First International Joint Conference on Natural Language Processing*.

Goto, I. Kato, N. Uratani, N. Ehara, T. (2003) "Transliteration Considering Context Information Based on the Maximum Entropy Method." *Proceedings of MT-Summit IX*.

Huang, Shudong. (2005) "LDC2005T34: Chinese <-> English Named Entity Lists v 1.0." *Linguistics Data Consortium*. Philadelphia, Pennsylvania. ISBN #1-58563-368-2. http://www.ldc.upenn.edu/Catalog/CatalogEntry.jsp?catalogId=LDC2005T34.

International Phonetic Association. (1999) *Handbook of the International Phonetic Association : A Guide to the Use of the International Phonetic Alphabet*. Cambridge University Press, UK. ISBN 0521652367. http://www.cambridge.org/uk/catalogue/catalogue.asp?isbn=0521652367.

Jung, S. Hong, S. Paek, E. (2000) "An English to Korean Transliteration Model of Extended Markov Window." *Proceedings of COLING*.

Kang, B.J. Choi, K.S. (2000) "Automatic Transliteration and Back-Transliteration by Decision Tree Learning." *Proceedings of the 2nd International Conference on Language Resources and Evaluation*.

Klatt, D.H. (1990) "Review of the ARPA Speech Understanding Project." *Readings in Speech Recognition*. Morgan Kaufmann Publishers Inc. San Francisco, CA. ISBN 1-55860-124-4. 554-575.

Knight, K. Graehl, J. (1997) "Machine Transliteration." *Proceedings of the Conference of the Association for Computational Linguistics (ACL)*.

Kondrak, G. (2000) "A New Algorithm for the Alignment of Phonetic Sequences." *Proceedings of the First Meeting of the North American Chapter of the Association for Computational Linguistics (NAACL)*. Seattle, Washington. 288-295.

Kondrak, G. Dorr, B. (2004) "Identification of Confusable Drug Names: A New Approach and Evaluation Methodology." *Proceedings of the Twentieth International Conference on Computational Linguistics (COLING)*. 952-958.

Levenshtein, V.I. (1966) "Binary Codes Capable of Correcting Deletions, Insertions and Reversals." *Sov. Phys. Dokl.* 6. 707-710.

Li, H. Zhang, M. Su, J. (2004) "A Joint Source-Channel Model for Machine Transliteration." *Proceedings of ACL 2004*.

Mani, Inderjeet. Yeh, Alexander. Condon, Sherri. (2006) "Machine Learning from String Edit Distance and Phonological Similarity."

Meng, H. Lo, W. Chen, B. Tang, T. (2001) "Generating Phonetic Cognates to Handle Named Entities in English-Chinese Cross-Language Spoken Document Retrieval." *Proceedings of ASRU*.

Oh, Jong-Hoon. Choi, Key-Sun. (2006) "An Ensemble of Transliteration Models for Information Retrieval." *Information Processing & Management*. 42(4). 980-1002.

"Student's t Test." (2009) *Wikipedia: The Free Encyclopedia*. http://en.wikipedia.org/wiki/T_test#Equal_sample_sizes.2C_equal_variance.

Van Halteren, H., Zavrel, J. Daelemans, W. (1998) "Improving Data Driven Word-Class Tagging by System Combination." *Proceedings of the 36th Annual Meeting of the Association for Computational Linguistics and the 17th International Conference on Computational Linguistics*. Montréal, Québec, Canada. 491-497.

Virga, P. Khudanpur, S. (2003) "Transliteration of Proper Names in Cross-Lingual Information Retrieval." *Proceedings of the ACL Workshop on Multi-lingual Named Entity Recognition*.

Wan, Stephen. Verspoor, Cornelia Maria. (1998). "Automatic English-Chinese Name Transliteration for Development of Multilingual Resources." *Proceedings of the 36th Annual Meeting of the Association for Computational Linguistics*. Montréal, Québec, Canada.

Wellner, B. Castano, J. Pustejovsky, J. (2005) "Adaptive String Similarity Metrics for Biomedical Reference Resolution." *Proceedings of the ACL-ISMB Workshop on Linking Biological Literature, Ontologies, and Databases: Mining Biological Semantics*. 9-16. http://www.cs.brandeis.edu/~wellner/pubs/Wellner-StringSim-BioLINK.pdf.

Winkler, W. "Methods for Record Linkage and Bayesian Networks." (2002) *Proceedings of the Section on Survey Research Methods, American Statistical Association*. http://www.census.gov/srd/www/byyear.html.

Analysis and Robust Extraction of Changing Named Entities

Masatoshi Tsuchiya[†] **Shoko Endo**[‡] **Seiichi Nakagawa**[‡]
[†]Information and Media Center / [‡]Department of Information and Computer Sciences,
Toyohashi University of Technology
tsuchiya@imc.tut.ac.jp, {shoko,nakagawa}@slp.ics.tut.ac.jp

Abstract

This paper focuses on the change of named entities over time and its influence on the performance of the named entity tagger. First, we analyze Japanese named entities which appear in Mainichi Newspaper articles published in 1995, 1996, 1997, 1998 and 2005. This analysis reveals that the number of named entity types and the number of named entity tokens are almost steady over time and that 70 $\sim$ 80% of named entity types in a certain year occur in the articles published either in its succeeding year or in its preceding year. These facts lead that 20 $\sim$ 30% of named entity types are replaced with new ones every year. The experiment against these texts shows that our proposing semi-supervised method which combines a small annotated corpus and a large unannotated corpus for training works robustly although the traditional supervised method is fragile against the change of name entity distribution.

1 Introduction

It is widely agreed that extraction of named entity (henceforth, denoted as *NE*) is an important subtask for various NLP applications, such as information retrieval, machine translation, information extraction and natural language understanding. Several conferences like Message Understanding Conference(Grishman and Sundheim, 1996) and the IREX workshop (Sekine and Eriguchi, 2000) were conducted to encourage researchers of NE extraction and to provide its common evaluation basis.

In Japanese NE extraction, it is quite common to apply morphological analysis as preprocessing stage which segments a sentence into a sequence of morphemes. After that, either a pattern matcher based on hand-crafted rules or a statistical chunker is employed to extract NEs from a sequence of morphemes. Various machine learning approaches such as maximum entropy(Uchimoto et al., 2000), decision list(Sassano and Utsuro, 2000; Isozaki, 2001), and Support Vector Machine(Yamada et al., 2002; Isozaki and Kazawa, 2002) were investigated for extracting NEs. These researches show that machine learning approaches are more promising than approaches based on hand-crafted rules if a large corpus whose NEs are properly annotated is available as training data.

However, it is difficult to obtain an enough corpus in the real world because of the increasing number of NE types and the increasing time gap between the training corpus and the test corpus. There is the increasing number of NE types like personal names and company names in the real world. For example, a large database of organization names(Nichigai Associates, 2007) already contains 171,708 types and is still increasing. Because annotation work is quite expensive, the annotated corpus may become obsolete in a short period of time. Both of two factors expands the difference of NE distribution between the training corpus and the test corpus, and it may decrease the performance of the NE tagger as shown in (Mota and Grishman, 2008). Therefore, a robust method to extract NEs which do not occur or occur few times in a training corpus is necessary.

This paper focuses on the change of NEs over time and its influence on the performance of the NE tagger. First, we annotate NEs in Mainichi Newspaper articles published in 1996, 1997, 1998 and 2005, and analyze NEs which appear in these texts and an existing corpus. It consists of Mainichi Newspaper articles published in 1995, thus, we get an annotated corpus that spans 10 years. This analysis reveals that the number of NE types and the number of NE tokens are almost

Proceedings of the 2009 Named Entities Workshop, ACL-IJCNLP 2009, pages 161–167,
Suntec, Singapore, 7 August 2009.

Table 1: Statistics of NE categories of IREX corpus

NE Categories	Frequency (%)
ARTIFACT	747 (4.0)
DATE	3567 (19.1)
LOCATION	5463 (29.2)
MONEY	390 (2.1)
ORGANIZATION	3676 (19.7)
PERCENT	492 (2.6)
PERSON	3840 (20.6)
TIME	502 (2.7)
Total	18677

steady over time and that that 70 $\sim$ 80% of NE types in a certain year occur in the articles published either in its succeeding year or in its preceding year. These facts lead that 20 $\sim$ 30% of named entity types are replaced with new ones every year. The experiment against these corpora shows that the traditional supervised method is fragile against the change of NE types and that our proposing semi-supervised method which combines a small annotated corpus and a large unannotated corpus for training is robust against the change of NE types.

2 Analysis of Changing Named Entities

2.1 Task of the IREX Workshop

The task of NE extraction of the IREX workshop (Sekine and Eriguchi, 2000) is to recognize eight NE categories in Table 1. The organizer of the IREX workshop provided a training corpus (henceforth, denoted as *IREX corpus*), which consists of 1,174 Mainichi Newspaper articles published from January 1st 1995 to 10th which include 18,677 NEs. In the Japanese language, no other corpora whose NEs are annotated are publicly available as far as we know.[1] Thus, IREX corpus is referred as a golden sample of NE distribution in this paper.

2.2 Data Description

The most homogeneous texts which are written in different days are desirable, to explore the influence of the text time frame on NE distribution. Because IREX corpus is referred as a golden sample

[1]The organizer of the IREX workshop also provides the testing data to its participants, however, we cannot see it because we did not join it.

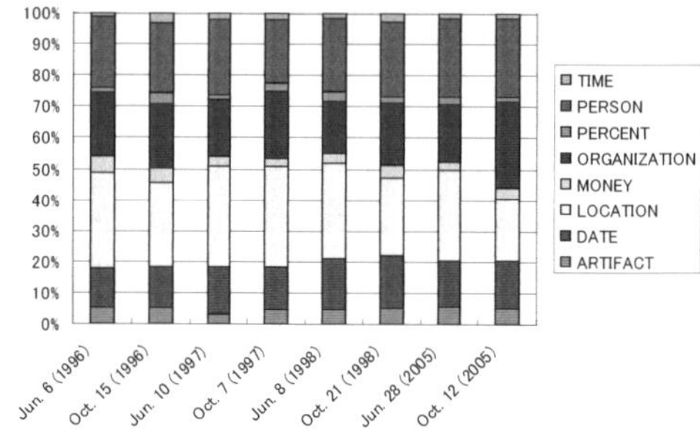

Figure 1: Distribution of NE categories

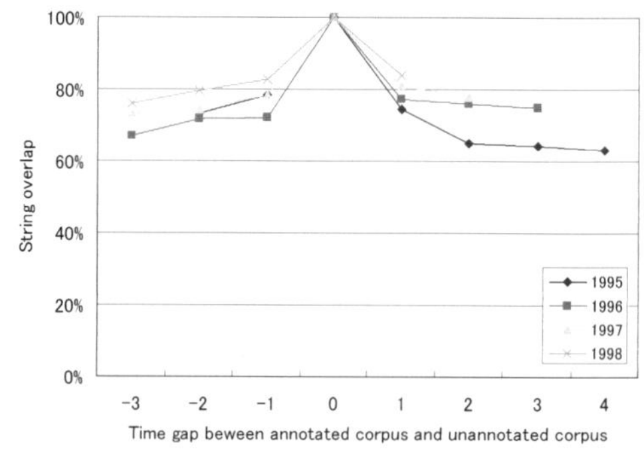

Figure 2: Overlap ratio of NEs over years

in this paper, Mainichi Newspaper articles written in different years than IREX corpus is suitable. Thus, ordinal days of June and October in 1996, 1997, 1998 and 2005 are randomly selected as sampling days.

Because annotating work is too expensive for us to annotate all articles published in sampling days, thirty percent of them are only annotated. Each article of Mainichi Newspaper belongs into 16 categories like front page articles, international stories, economical stories, political stories, editorial columns, and human interest stories. Because these categories may influence to NE distribution, it is important to keep the proportion of categories in the sampled texts to the proportion in the whole newspaper, in order to investigate NE distribution over the whole newspaper. Therefore, thirty percent articles of each category published at sampling days are randomly selected and annotated in accordance with the IREX regulation.

2.3 Analysis of Annotated Samples

Table 2 shows the statistics of our annotated corpus. The leftmost column of Table 2 (whose pub-

Table 2: Statistics of sampling texts

Published date	1995	1996		1997		1998		2005	
	Jan. 1∼10	Jun. 5	Oct. 15	Jun. 10	Oct. 7	Jun. 8	Oct. 21	Jun. 23	Oct. 12
# of articles	1174	120	133	106	117	96	126	90	99
# of characters	407881	60790	53625	46653	50362	51006	67744	49038	44344
# of NE types	6979	1446	1656	1276	1350	1190	1226	1230	1113
# of NE tokens	18677	2519	2652	2145	2403	2126	2052	1902	2007
# of NE types / # of characters	0.0171	0.0238	0.0309	0.0274	0.0268	0.0233	0.0181	0.0251	0.0251
# of NE tokens / # of characters	0.0458	0.0414	0.0495	0.0460	0.0477	0.0417	0.0303	0.0388	0.0453

Table 3: Overlap of NE types between texts published in different years

Published date of annotated corpus A	Published year of unannotated corpus U						
	1993	1994	1995	1996	1997	1998	1999
Jan. 1∼10 (1995)	73.2%	78.6%	—	74.4%	65.0%	64.4%	63.3%
Jun. 6, Oct. 15 (1996)	67.2%	71.7%	72.2%	—	77.3%	76.0%	75.1%
Jun. 6, Oct. 7 (1997)	71.2%	73.4%	74.4%	78.6%	—	80.8%	78.6%
Jun. 8, Oct. 21 (1998)	72.5%	74.6%	76.2%	79.7%	82.7%	—	84.0%
Jun. 23, Oct. 12 (2005)	62.3%	64.1%	66.8%	68.7%	71.2%	72.9%	73.8%

lish date is January 1st to 10th in 1995) is corresponding to IREX corpus, and other columns are corresponding to articles annotated by ourselves. Table 2 illustrates that the normalized number of NE types and the normalized number of NE tokens are almost steady over time. Figure 1 shows the distributions of NE categories for sampling texts and that there is no significant difference between them.

We also investigate the relation of the time gap between texts and NE types which appear in these texts. The overlap ratio of NE types between the annotated corpus A published in the year Y_A and the annotated corpus B published in the year Y_B was defined in (Mota and Grishman, 2008) as follows

$$type\_overlap(A, B) = \frac{|T_A \cap T_B|}{|T_A| + |T_B| - |T_A \cap T_B|},$$

where T_A and T_B are lists of NE types which appear in A and B respectively. However, it is impossible to compute reliable $type\_overlap$ in our research because enough annotated texts are unavailable. As an alternative of $type\_overlap$, the overlap ratio of NE types between the annotated corpus A and the unannotated corpus U published in the year Y_U is defined as follows

$$string\_overlap(A, U) = \frac{\sum_{s \in T_A} \delta(s, U)}{|T_A|},$$

where $\delta(s, U)$ is the binary function to indicate whether the string s occurs in the string U or not. Table 3 shows $string\_ratio$ values of annotated texts. It shows that $70 \sim 80\%$ of T_A appear in the preceding year of Y_A, and that $70 \sim 80\%$ of T_A appear in the succeeding year of Y_A.

Figure 2 shows the relation between the time gap $Y_U - Y_A$ and $string\_ratio(A, U)$. Suppose that all NEs are independent and equivalent on their occurrence probability and that $string\_ratio(A, U)$ is equal to 0.8 when the time gap $Y_U - Y_A$ is equal to one. When the time gap $Y_{U'} - Y_A$ is equal to two years, although this assumption leads that $string\_ratio(A, U')$ will be equal to 0.64, $string\_ratio(A, U')$ in Figure 2 is greater than 0.7. This suggests that NEs are not equivalent on their occurrence probability. And more, Table 4 shows that the longer time span of the annotated text increases the number of NE types. These facts lead that some NEs are short-lived and superseded by other new NEs.

3 Robust Extraction of Changing Named Entities

It is infeasible to prepare a large annotated corpus which covers all increasing NEs. A semi-supervised learning approach which combines a small annotated corpus and a large unannotated corpus for training is promising to cope this problem. (Miller et al., 2004) proposed the method using classes which are assigned to words based on the class language model built from a large unannotated corpus. (Ando and Zhang, 2005) pro-

Table 4: Number of NE types and Time Span of Annotated Text

	1995	1995∼1996	1995∼1997	1995∼1998	1995∼2005
ARTIFACT	541 (1.00)	743 (1.37)	862 (1.59)	1025 (1.89)	1169 (2.16)
DATE	950 (1.00)	1147 (1.21)	1326 (1.40)	1461 (1.54)	1583 (1.67)
LOCATION	1403 (1.00)	1914 (1.36)	2214 (1.58)	2495 (1.78)	2692 (1.92)
MONEY	301 (1.00)	492 (1.63)	570 (1.89)	656 (2.18)	749 (2.49)
ORGANIZATION	1487 (1.00)	1890 (1.27)	2280 (1.53)	2566 (1.73)	2893 (1.95)
PERCENT	249 (1.00)	319 (1.28)	353 (1.42)	401 (1.61)	443 (1.78)
PERSON	1842 (1.00)	2540 (1.38)	3175 (1.72)	3683 (2.00)	4243 (2.30)
TIME	206 (1.00)	257 (1.25)	291 (1.41)	314 (1.52)	332 (1.61)
Total	6979 (1.00)	9302 (1.33)	11071 (1.59)	12601 (1.81)	14104 (2.02)

(Values in brackets are rates of increase comparing to 1995.)

Morpheme Feature			Similar Morpheme Feature			Character Type Feature	Chunk Label
	(English translation)	POS		*(English translation)*	POS		
今日 (kyou)	*(today)*	Noun–Adverbial	今日 (kyou)	*(today)*	Noun–Adverbial	⟨1, 0, 0, 0, 0, 0⟩	O
の (no)	gen	Particle	の (no)	gen	Particle	⟨0, 1, 0, 0, 0, 0⟩	O
石狩 **(Ishikari)**	*(Ishikari)*	Noun–Proper	関東 **(Kantou)**	*(Kantou)*	Noun–Proper	⟨1, 0, 0, 0, 0, 0⟩	B-LOCATION
平野 (heiya)	*(plain)*	Noun–Generic	平野 (heiya)	*(plain)*	Noun–Generic	⟨1, 0, 0, 0, 0, 0⟩	I-LOCATION
の (no)	gen	Particle	の (no)	gen	Particle	⟨0, 1, 0, 0, 0, 0⟩	O
天気 (tenki)	*(weather)*	Noun–Generic	天気 (tenki)	*(weather)*	Noun–Generic	⟨1, 0, 0, 0, 0, 0⟩	O
は (ha)	top	Particle	は (ha)	top	Particle	⟨0, 1, 0, 0, 0, 0⟩	O
晴れ (hare)	*(fine)*	Noun–Generic	晴れ (hare)	*(fine)*	Noun–Generic	⟨1, 1, 0, 0, 0, 0⟩	O

Figure 3: Example of Training Instance for Proposed Method

posed the method using thousands of automatically generated auxiliary classification problems on an unannotated corpus. (**?**) proposed the semi-supervised discriminative model whose potential function can treat both an annotated corpus and an unannotated corpus.

In this paper, the method proposed by (Tsuchiya et al., 2008) is employed, because its implementation is quite easy. It consists of two steps. The first step is to assign the most similar and familiar morpheme to each unfamiliar morpheme based on their context vectors calculated from a large unannotated corpus. The second step is to employ Conditional Random Fields(CRF)[2](Lafferty et al., 2001) using both features of original morphemes and features of similar morphemes.

This section gives the detail of this method.

3.1 Chunking of Named Entities

It is quite common that the task of extracting Japanese NEs from a sentence is formalized as a chunking problem against a sequence of morphemes. For representing proper chunks, we employ IOB2 representation, one of representations which have been studied well in various chunking tasks of NLP (Tjong Kim Sang, 1999). This representation uses the following three labels.

- **B** Current token is the beginning of a chunk.
- **I** Current token is a middle or the end of a chunk consisting of more than one token.
- **O** Current token is outside of any chunk.

Actually, we prepare the 16 derived labels from the label **B** and the label **I** for eight NE categories, in order to distinguish them.

When the task of extracting Japanese NEs from a sentence is formalized as a chunking problem of a sequence of morphemes, the segmentation boundary problem arises as widely known. For example, the NE definition of IREX tells that a Chinese character "米 (bei)" must be extracted as an NE means *America* from a morpheme "訪米 (hou-bei)" which means *visiting America*. A naive chunker using a morpheme as a chunking unit cannot extract such a kind of NEs. In order to cope this problem, (Uchimoto et al., 2000) proposed employing translation rules to modify problematic morphemes, and (Asahara and Matsumoto, 2003; Nakano and Hirai, 2004) formalized the task of extracting NEs as a chunking problem of a sequence of characters instead of a sequence of morphemes. In this paper, we keep the naive formalization, because it is still enough to analyze the influence of

[2]http://chasen.org/~taku/software/CRF++/

the text time frame.

3.2 Assignment of Similar Morpheme

A context vector V_m of a morpheme m is a vector consisting of frequencies of all possible unigrams and bigrams,

$$V_m = \begin{pmatrix} f(m, m_0), & \cdots & f(m, m_N), \\ f(m, m_0, m_0), & \cdots & f(m, m_N, m_N), \\ f(m_0, m), & \cdots & f(m_N, m), \\ f(m_0, m_0, m), & \cdots & f(m_N, m_N, m) \end{pmatrix},$$

where $M \equiv \{m_0, m_1, \ldots, m_N\}$ is a set of all morphemes of the unannotated corpus, $f(m_i, m_j)$ is a frequency that a sequence of a morpheme m_i and a morpheme m_j occurs in the unannotated corpus, and $f(m_i, m_j, m_k)$ is a frequency that a sequence of morphemes m_i, m_j and m_k occurs in the unannotated corpus.

Suppose an unfamiliar morpheme $m_u \in M \cap \overline{M_F}$, where M_F is a set of familiar morphemes that occur frequently in the annotated corpus. The most similar morpheme $\hat{m_u}$ to the morpheme m_u measured with their context vectors is given by the following equation,

$$\hat{m_u} = \underset{m \in M_F}{\operatorname{argmax}}\, sim(V_{m_u}, V_m), \qquad (1)$$

where $sim(V_i, V_j)$ is a similarity function between context vectors. In this paper, the *cosine* function is employed as it.

3.3 Features

The feature set F_i at i-th position is defined as a tuple of the *morpheme feature* $MF(m_i)$ of the i-th morpheme m_i, the *similar morpheme feature* $SF(m_i)$, and the *character type feature* $CF(m_i)$.

$$F_i = \langle\, MF(m_i),\ SF(m_i),\ CF(m_i)\, \rangle$$

The morpheme feature $MF(m_i)$ is a pair of the surface string and the part-of-speech of m_i. The similar morpheme feature $SF(m_i)$ is defined as

$$SF(m_i) = \begin{cases} MF(\hat{m_i}) & \text{if } m_i \in M \cap \overline{M_F} \\ MF(m_i) & \text{otherwise} \end{cases},$$

where $\hat{m_i}$ is the most similar and familiar morpheme to m_i given by Eqn. 1. The character type feature $CF(m_i)$ is a set of six binary flags to indicate that the surface string of m_i contains a Chinese character, a *hiragana* character, a *katakana* character, an English alphabet, a number and an other character respectively.

	$\longrightarrow$ Chunking Direction $\longrightarrow$				
Feature set	F_{i-2}	F_{i-1}	F_i	F_{i+1}	F_{i+2}
Chunk label	c_{i-2}	c_{i-1}	$\boxed{c_i}$		

Figure 4: Chunking Direction

When we identify the chunk label c_i for the i-th morpheme m_i, the surrounding five feature sets $F_{i-2}, F_{i-1}, F_i, F_{i+1}, F_{i+2}$ and the preceding two chunk labels c_{i-2}, c_{i-1} are referred as shown in Figure 4.

Figure 3 shows an example of training instance of the proposed method for the sentence "今日 (kyou) の (no) 石狩 (Ishikari) 平野 (heiya) の (no) 天気 (tenki) は (ha) 晴れ (hare)" which means "*It is fine at Ishikari-plain, today*". "関東 (Kantou)" is assigned as the most similar and familiar morpheme to "石狩 (Ishikari)" which is unfamiliar in the training corpus.

3.4 Experimental Result

Figure 5 compares performances of the proposed method and the baseline method over the test texts which were published in 1996, 1997, 1998 and 2005. The proposed method combines a small annotated corpus and a large unannotated corpus as already described. This experiment refers IREX corpus as a small annotated corpus, and refers Mainichi Newspaper articles published from 1993 to the preceding year of the test text published year as a large unannotated corpus. For example, when the test text was published in 1998, Mainichi Newspaper articles published from 1993 to 1997 are used. The baseline method is trained from IREX corpus with CRF. But, it uses only MF and CF as features, and does not use SF. Figure 5 illustrates two points: (1) the proposed method outperforms the baseline method consistently, (2) the baseline method is fragile to changing of test texts.

Figure 6 shows the relation between the performance of the proposed method and the size of unannotated corpus against the test corpus published in 2005. It reveals that that increasing unannotated corpus size improves the performance of the proposed method.

4 Conclusion

In this paper, we explored the change of NE distribution over time and its influence on the per-

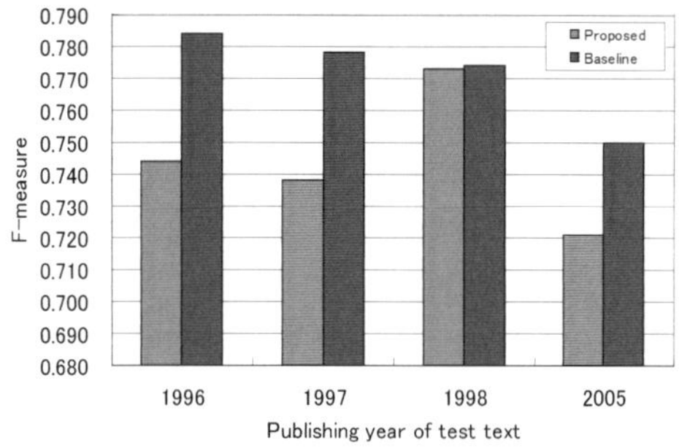

Figure 5: Comparison between proposed method and baseline method

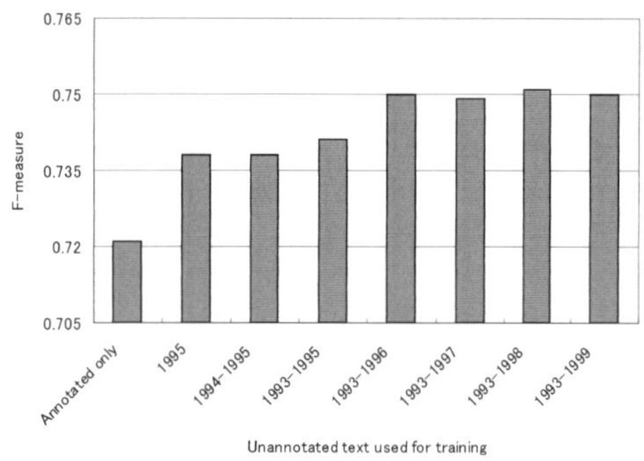

Figure 6: Relation of performance and unannotated corpus size

formance of the NE tagger. First, we annotated Mainichi Newspaper articles published in 1996, 1997, 1998 and 2005, and analyzed NEs which appear in these texts and IREX corpus which consists of Mainichi Newspaper articles published in 1995. This analysis illustrated that the number of NE types and the number of NE tokens are almost steady over time, and that 70 $\sim$ 80% of NE types seen in a certain year occur in the texts published either in its succeeding year or in its preceding year. The experiment against these texts showed that our proposing semi-supervised NE tagger works robustly although the traditional supervised NE tagger is fragile against the change of NE types. Based on the results described in this paper, we will investigate the relation between the performance of NE tagger and the similarity of its training corpus and its test corpus.

References

Rie Kubota Ando and Tong Zhang. 2005. A high-performance semi-supervised learning method for text chunking. In *Proc. of ACL '05*, pages 1–9, June.

Masayuki Asahara and Yuji Matsumoto. 2003. Japanese named entity extraction with redundant morphological analysis. In *Proc. of HLT–NAACL '03*, pages 8–15.

Ralph Grishman and Beth Sundheim. 1996. Message understanding conference-6: a brief history. In *Proc. of the 16th COLING*, pages 466–471.

Hideki Isozaki and Hideto Kazawa. 2002. Efficient support vector classifiers for named entity recognition. In *Proc. of the 19th COLING*, pages 1–7.

Hideki Isozaki. 2001. Japanese named entity recognition based on a simple rule generator and decision tree learning. In *Proc. of ACL '01*, pages 314–321.

John Lafferty, Andrew McCallum, and Fernando Pereira. 2001. Conditional Random Fields: Probabilistic Models for Segmenting and Labeling Sequence Data. In *Proceedings of ICML*, pages 282–289.

Scott Miller, Jethran Guinness, and Alex Zamanian. 2004. Name tagging with word clusters and discriminative training. In *Proc. of HLT-NAACL 2004*, pages 337–342, May.

Cristina Mota and Ralph Grishman. 2008. Is this NE tagger getting old? In *Proceedings of the Sixth International Language Resources and Evaluation (LREC'08)*, May.

Keigo Nakano and Yuzo Hirai. 2004. Japanese named entity extraction with bunsetsu features. *Transactions of Information Processing Society of Japan*, 45(3):934–941, Mar. (in Japanese).

Nichigai Associates, editor. 2007. *DCS Kikan-mei Jisho*. Nichigai Associates. (in Japanese).

Manabu Sassano and Takehito Utsuro. 2000. Named entity chunking techniques in supervised learning for japanese named entity recognition. In *Proc. of the 18th COLING*, pages 705–711.

Satoshi Sekine and Yoshio Eriguchi. 2000. Japanese named entity extraction evaluation: analysis of results. In *Proc. of the 18th COLING*, pages 1106–1110.

E. Tjong Kim Sang. 1999. Representing text chunks. In *Proc. of the 9th EACL*, pages 173–179.

Masatoshi Tsuchiya, Shinya Hida, and Seiichi Nakagawa. 2008. Robust extraction of named entity including unfamiliar word. In *Proceedings of ACL-08: HLT, Short Papers*, pages 125–128, Columbus, Ohio, June. Association for Computational Linguistics.

Kiyotaka Uchimoto, Ma Qing, Masaki Murata, Hiromi Ozaku, Masao Utiyama, and Hitoshi Isahara. 2000. Named entity extraction based on a maximum entropy model and transformation rules. *Journal of Natural Language Processing*, 7(2):63–90, Apr. (in Japanese).

Hiroyasu Yamada, Taku Kudo, and Yuji Matsumoto. 2002. Japanese named entity extraction using support vector machine. *Transactions of Information Processing Society of Japan*, 43(1):44–53, Jan. (in Japanese).

Tag Confidence Measure for Semi-Automatically Updating Named Entity Recognition

Kuniko Saito and **Kenji Imamura**
NTT Cyber Space Laboratories, NTT Corporation
1-1 Hikarinooka, Yokosuka-shi, Kanagawa, 239-0847, Japan
{saito.kuniko, imamura.kenji}@lab.ntt.co.jp

Abstract

We present two techniques to reduce machine learning cost, *i.e.*, cost of manually annotating unlabeled data, for adapting existing CRF-based named entity recognition (NER) systems to new texts or domains. We introduce the *tag* posterior probability as the tag confidence measure of an individual NE tag determined by the base model. Dubious tags are automatically detected as recognition errors, and regarded as targets of manual correction. Compared to entire *sentence* posterior probability, tag posterior probability has the advantage of minimizing system cost by focusing on those parts of the sentence that require manual correction. Using the tag confidence measure, the first technique, known as active learning, asks the editor to assign correct NE tags only to those parts that the base model could not assign tags confidently. Active learning reduces the learning cost by 66%, compared to the conventional method. As the second technique, we propose bootstrapping NER, which semi-automatically corrects dubious tags and updates its model.

1 Introduction

Machine learning, especially supervised learning, has achieved great success in many natural language tasks, such as part-of-speech (POS) tagging, named entity recognition (NER), and parsing. This approach automatically encodes linguistic knowledge as statistical parameters (models) from large annotated corpora. In the NER task, which is the focus of this paper, sequential tagging[1] based on statistical models is similarly used; studies include Conditional Random Fields (CRFs; Lafferty et al., 2001, Suzuki et al., 2006). However, the manual costs incurred in creating annotated corpora are extremely high.

On the other hand, Consumer Generated Media (CGM) such as blog texts has attracted a lot of attention recently as an informative resource for information retrieval and information extraction tasks. CGM has two distinctive features; enormous quantities of new texts are generated day after day, and new vocabularies and topics come and go rapidly. The most effective approach to keep up with new linguistic phenomena is creating new annotated corpora for model re-training at short intervals. However, it is difficult to build new corpora expeditiously because of the high manual costs imposed by traditional schemes.

To reduce the manual labor and costs, various learning methods, such as active learning (Shen et al., 2004, Laws and Schütze, 2008), semi-supervised learning (Suzuki and Isozaki, 2008) and bootstrapping (Etzioni, 2005) have been proposed. Active learning automatically selects effective texts to be annotated from huge raw-text corpora. The correct answers are then manually annotated, and the model is re-trained. In active learning, one major issue is data selection, namely, determining which sample data is most effective. The data units used in conventional methods are sentences.

Automatically creating annotated corpora would dramatically decrease the manual costs. In fact, there always are some recognition errors in any automatically annotated corpus and the editor has to correct errors one by one. Since sentences are used as data units, the editor has to pay attention to all tags in the selected sentence because it is not obvious where the recognition error is. However, it is a waste of manual effort to

[1]Tags are assigned to each input unit (e.g., word) one by one.

Proceedings of the 2009 Named Entities Workshop, ACL-IJCNLP 2009, pages 168–176,
Suntec, Singapore, 7 August 2009. ©2009 ACL and AFNLP

annotate all tags because most tags must be labeled correctly by the base model[2].

In this paper, we propose a confidence measure based on tag posterior probability for the NER task. Our method does not use the confidence of a sentence, but instead computes the confidence of the tag assigned to each word. The tag confidence measure allows the sentence to which the base model might assign an incorrect tag to be selected automatically. Active learning becomes more efficient because we correct only those tags that have low confidence (cf. Sec. 4).

We can realize the same effect as active learning if we can automatically correct the selected data based upon our tag confidence measure. Our proposal "Semi-Automatically Updating NER" automatically corrects erroneous data by using a seed NE list generated from other information sources. Semi-Automatically Updating NER easily keeps up with new words because it enables us to update the model simply by providing a new NE list (cf. Sec. 5).

2 Named Entity Recognition Task

The NER task is to recognize entity names such as organizations and people. In this paper, we use 17 NE tags based on the IOB2 scheme (Sang and De Meulder, 1999) combined with eight Japanese NE types defined in the IREX workshop (IREX 1999) as shown in Table 1.

For example, "東京(Tokyo)/都(City)/に(in)" is labeled like this:

"東京/B-<LOC> 都/I-<LOC> に/O".

This task is regarded as the sequential tagging problem, *i.e.,* assigning NE tag sequences $T = t_1 \cdots t_n$ to word sequences $W = w_1 \cdots w_n$. Recently, discriminative models such as Conditional Random Fields (CRFs) have been successfully applied to this task (Lafferty et al., 2001). In this paper, we use linear-chain CRFs based on the Minimum Classification Error framework (Suzuki et al., 2006). The posterior probability of a tag sequence is calculated as follows:

$$P(T \mid W) = \frac{1}{Z(W)} \exp\{\sum_{i=1}^{n} (\sum_a \lambda_a \cdot f_a(t_i, w_i) + \sum_b \lambda_b \cdot f_b(t_{i-1}, t_i))\}, \quad (1)$$

where w_i and t_i are the i-th word and its corresponding NE tag, respectively. $f_a(t_i, w_i)$ and $f_b(t_{i-1}, t_i)$ is a feature function[3]. λ_a and λ_b is a parameter to be estimated from the training data. $Z(W)$ is a normalization factor over all candidate paths expressed as follows:

$$Z(W) = \sum_T \exp\{\sum_{i=1}^{n} (\sum_a \lambda_a \cdot f_a(t_i, w_i) + \sum_b \lambda_b \cdot f_b(t_{i-1}, t_i))\}. \quad (2)$$

The best tag sequence that maximizes Formula (1) is located using the Viterbi algorithm.

Table 1. NE Types and Tags.

NE Types	NE Tags	
PERSON	B-<PSN>	I-<PSN>
LOCATION	B-<LOC>	I-<LOC>
ORGANIZATION	B-<ORG>	I-<ORG>
ARTIFACT	B-<ART>	I-<ART>
DATE	B-<DAT>	I-<DAT>
TIME	B-<TIM>	I-<TIM>
MONEY	B-<MNY>	I-<MNY>
PERCENT	B-<PCT>	I-<PCT>
outside an NE	O	

3 Error Detection with Tag Confidence Measure

3.1 Tag Posterior Probability

It is quite natural to consider *sentence* posterior probability as a confidence measure of the estimated tag sequences. We focus on *tag* posterior probability, and regard it as the confidence measure of the decoded tag itself. Our method tries to detect the recognition error of each tag by referring to the tag confidence measure.

Figure 1 overviews the calculation of tag confidence measure. The confidence score of tag $t_{i,j}$, which is a candidate tag for word w_i, is calculated as follows:

$$P(t_{i,j} \mid W) = \sum_T P(t_{i,j}, T \mid W), \quad (3)$$

where $\sum_T P(t_{i,j}, T \mid W)$ is the summation of all NE tag sequences that pass through $t_{i,j}$. This probability is generally called the marginal probability. $j = 1, \cdots, k$ represents the number of NE tags shown in Table 1(*i.e.*, k=17 in this paper).

The tag confidence score of $t_{i,j}$ can be calculated efficiently using forward and backward

[2] A base model is the initial model trained with the initial annotated corpora.

[3] We used n-grams (n=1, 2, 3) of surface forms and parts-of-speech within a five word window and 2-gram combinations of NE tags as the feature set.

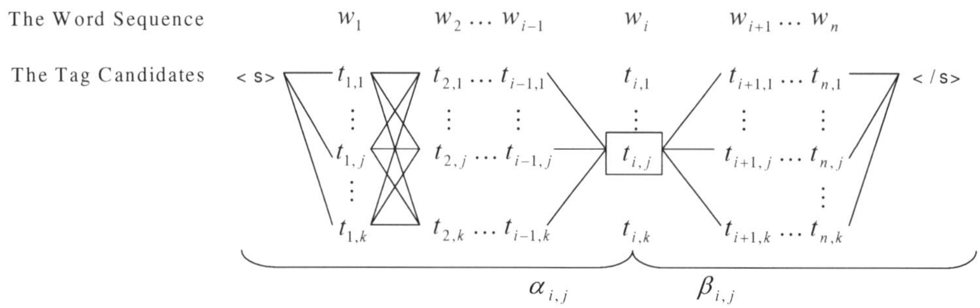

Figure 1. Overview of the tag confidence measure calculation.

algorithms as follows (Manning and Schütze, 1999):

$$P(t_{i,j} \mid W) = \frac{1}{Z(W)} \alpha_{i,j} \cdot \beta_{i,j}, \tag{4}$$

where

$$\alpha_{i,j} = \sum_k \{\alpha_{i-1,k} \cdot \exp\{\textstyle\sum_a \lambda_a \cdot f_a(t_i, w_i) + \sum_b \lambda_b \cdot f_b(t_{i-1}, t_i)\}\}, \tag{5}$$

$$\beta_{i,j} = \sum_k \{\beta_{i+1,k} \cdot \exp\{\textstyle\sum_a \lambda_a \cdot f_a(t_{i+1}, w_{i+1}) + \sum_b \lambda_b \cdot f_b(t_i, t_{i+1})\}\}, \tag{6}$$

$$\alpha_{0,j} = 1, \tag{7}$$

$$\beta_{n+1,j} = 1. \tag{8}$$

In this manner, the confidence scores of all tags of each word in a given sentence are calculated. The rejecter then refers to the highest tag confidence score in judging whether the decoded NE tag is correct or incorrect.

3.2 Rejecter

The rejecter tries to detect dubious tags in the NER result derived by the method described in Section 2. For each word, the rejecter refers to the decoded tag t_d, which maximizes Formula (1), and the most confident tag t_1, in terms of the posterior probability as defined in Formula (4). The judgment procedure is as follows:

[1] If t_d is NOT identical to t_1, then t_d is determined to be dubious, and so is rejected as an incorrect tag.[4]

[2] Else, if the confidence score of t_1, called cs_1, is below the predefined threshold, t_d is determined to be dubious, and so is rejected as an incorrect tag.

[3] Otherwise, t_d is accepted as a correct tag.

Increasing the threshold also increases the number of rejected tags and manual annotation cost. In practice, the threshold should be empirically set to achieve the lowest judgment error rate using development data. There are two types of judgment errors: false acceptance and false rejection. False rejection is to reject a correct tag, and false acceptance is to accept an incorrect tag in error. The judgment error rate is taken as the ratio of these two types of errors in all instances.

4 Active Learning

Tag-wise recognition error detection is also helpful for data selection in active learning. If a sentence contains several rejected tags, it contains some new information which the base model does not have. In other words, this sentence is worth learning. Our approach, then, is to base data selection (sentence selection) on the presence of rejected tags. However, it is not necessary to check and correct all tags in each selected sentence. We only have to check and correct the rejected tags to acquire the annotated sentences.

Figure 2 shows our active learning scheme.

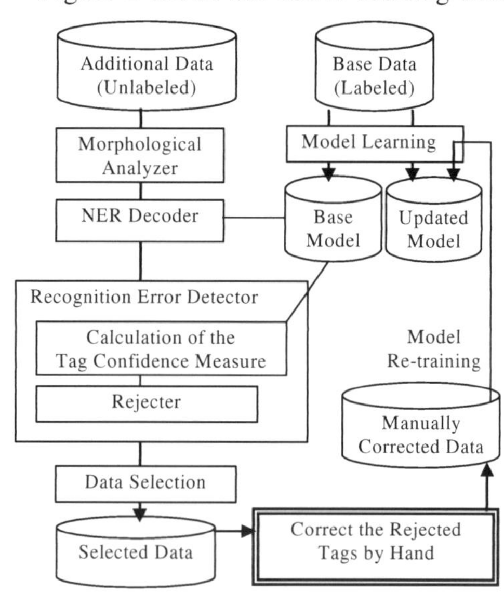

Figure 2. Active Learning Scheme

[4] The decoded tag t_d rarely disagrees with the most confident tag t_1 due to a characteristic of the CRFs.

First, the NER decoder assigns an NE tag to each word[5] of the additional data using the base model trained with the base data. The recognition error detector then determines whether each tag can be confidently accepted as described in Section 3. In this step, the confidence score is calculated using the same base model used for NER decoding. Next, the sentences with at least one rejected tag are selected. Only the rejected tags are manually checked and corrected. Finally, the model is retrained and updated with the merged data consisting of the manually corrected data and the base data.

4.1 Experiments

We evaluated the efficiency of our active learning method from the perspective of learning cost. A blog corpus consisting of 45,694 sentences in blog articles on the WWW was prepared for the experiments. This corpus was divided into four segments as shown in Table 2. All sentences were manually annotated including additional data. For additional data, these tags were initially hidden and used only for simulating manual correction as shown below. Development data was used for optimizing the threshold by measuring the rejecter's judgment error rate as described in Subsection 3.2.

Table 2. Data Used for Active Learning.

Base Data	11,553 sentences, 162,227 words
Development Data	1,000 sentences, 19,710 words
Additional Data	32,163 sentences, 584,077 words
Test Data	978 sentences, 17,762 words

We estimated the learning cost from the rate of hand-labeled tags. The Word Check Rate (WCR) represents the ratio of the number of the words in the additional data that need to be manually checked and annotated, to the total number of words in the additional data, and is expressed as follows:

WCR= Checked Tags / Total Words.

The system obtained various sizes of selected data as the rejecter changed its threshold from 0.1 to 1.0 for data selection. Only the rejected tags in the selected data were replaced with the tags originally assigned by hand (*i.e.*, correct tags). This procedure simulates manual correction. The manually corrected data was merged with the base data to update the base model.

[5] The morphological analyzer segments an input sentence into a word sequence and assigns parts-of-speech to each word.

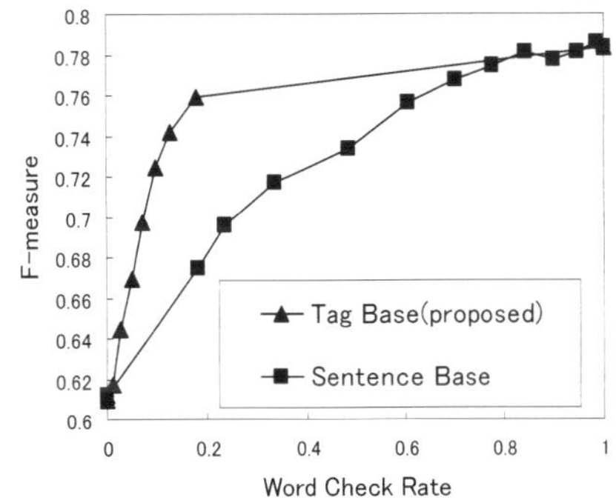

Figure 3. Learning Curves.

We compared our method with data selection based on the sentence confidence measure. Posterior probabilities of sentences were used as the confidence measure, and low-confidence scoring sentences were selected. In contrast to our active learning method, all tags in the selected sentences were replaced with the correct tags in this case.

We evaluated the effectiveness of the updated models against the test data by F-measure as follows:

$$F = \frac{2 \times recall \times precision}{recall + precision}. \quad (9)$$

4.2 Results and Discussions

4.2.1 Learning Curves and Accuracies

Figure 3 shows learning curves of two active learning methods; one is based on our tag confidence measure (Tag Based selection), and the other is based on the sentence confidence measure (Sentence Based selection). In order to reach the F-measure of approximately 0.76, Sentence Based selection requires approximately 60% of the entire data set to be checked by hand. In contrast, Tag Based selection requires only 20% or thereabouts. In other words, our Tag Based selection technique basically matches the performance of Sentence Based selection with only 1/3 of the learning cost.

4.2.2 Types of Tag Replacement

We further investigated the effects of tag-based judgment from the results of an experiment on our Tag Based selection. We categorized tag replacements of the rejected tags into the following four types:

- **No Change**: the rejected tag is replaced with the same tag.
- **O-to-BI**: the rejected tag is an O-tag. It is replaced with a B-tag or an I-tag.

- **BI-to-O**: the rejected tag is a B-tag or an I-tag. It is replaced with an O-tag.
- **BI-to-BI**: the rejected tag is a B-tag or an I-tag. It is replaced with another B-tag or I-tag.

Table 3 shows the distribution of these four categories in the selected data for the threshold of 0.5. This threshold achieves the lowest judgment error rate given the development set.

The rate of No Change replacement type is the highest. This means that the rejecter rejected too many tags, which actually did not need to be checked by hand. Although this result does not have a negative influence on the accuracy of the updated model, it is not preferable from the learning cost perspective. Further consideration should be given in order to improve the rejecter's judgment.

O-to-BI type accounts for the 2nd highest percentage of all replacements: it is almost one third of all changes. Excluding No Change type (*i.e.*, among O-to-BI, BI-to-O and BI-to-BI types), O-to-BI type makes up nearly 60% of these three replacement types. This result shows that there were many new NEs not recognized by the base model in the selected data.

Table 3. The Distribution of Replacement Types.

Replacement Type	Frequency	%
No Change	13,253	43.6
O-to-BI	10,042	33.0
BI-to-O	2,419	8.0
BI-to-BI	4,688	15.4
Total	30,402	100.0

5 Bootstrapping for NER

As mentioned in Section 4, we have to correct an O-tag to a B-tag or an I-tag in many cases, almost 60% of all actual corrections. This situation arises from a characteristic of the NER task. In the NER task, most NE tags in the entire corpus are O-tags. In fact, we found that 91 % of all tags were O-tags in the additional data discussed in Section 4. Thus, when a new NE appears in a sentence, this new NE is often mistakenly given an O-tag by the base model.

The fact that only O-tags are dominant implies that we have a chance to find a correct B-tag or I-tag when we look up the 2nd candidate. This is because one of these top two candidates is inevitably a B-tag or an I-tag. Thus, it is valuable to consider what the NEXT preferable tag is when the most preferable tag is rejected.

We examined in detail the accuracy of the tag candidates when the threshold is 0.5 as summarized in Table 4. When the top tag (*i.e.*, the tag with the highest tag confidence score) is accepted, its accuracy is 94 %, obviously high. On the other hand, the top tag's accuracy is only 43 % when it is rejected. However, focusing both on the top tag and on the 2nd tag provides an opportunity to correct the rejected tag in this case. If we consider these top two tags together when the 1st tag is rejected, the possibility of finding the correct tag is 72 %, relatively high. This suggests that the system is capable of correcting the rejected tag automatically by using the top two tag candidates. On this background, automatic correction is attempted for re-training the model through the use of a bootstrapping scheme.

Table 4. Accuracy of the Tags.

Rejecter's Judgment of the Top Tag		
ACCEPT	REJECT	
Top Tag	Top Tag	2nd Tag
94 %	43 %	29 %

Figure 4 shows an example of the top two tag candidates and their tag confidence scores when the top tag's confidence score is lower than the threshold (=0.5). We call this lattice the "tag graph" in this paper. The system failed to recognize the movie title "3丁目の夕日" ("*Sanchome no Yuuhi*", which means "Sunset on Third Street") as ARTIFACT only with the top tag candidates. However, it may find a correct tag sequence using the top two tag candidates (shaded cells in Figure 4). Once the system identifies the correct tag sequence automatically in the tag graph, the sequence is used as a manually annotated sequence. We introduce this new technique, Semi-Automatically Updating NER.

Figure 4. The Top Two Tag Candidates with Tag Confidence Measures.

	Top Tag		2nd Tag	
	Tag	score	Tag	score
今日(Today)	B-<DAT>	0.95		
「(“)	O	0.98		
3(Third)	O	**0.47**	**B-<ART>**	0.36
丁目(Street)	O	**0.38**	**I-<ART>**	0.36
の(on)	O	**0.49**	**I-<ART>**	0.38
夕日(Sunset)	**I-<ART>**	**0.39**	O	0.34
」(”)	O	0.99		
が(is)	O	0.99		
放映(broadcast)	O	0.99		

5.1 Semi-Automatically Updating NER

By extracting the correct tag sequence in each tag graph as shown in Figure 4, it is possible to obtain automatically corrected data, which also serve as new training data. Based on this idea, we propose Semi-Automatically Updating NER, which is hereafter simply referred to as Updating NER.

Figure 5 overviews Updating NER. The rejecter produces the sentences with tag graphs based on the tag confidence measure. In this new procedure, however, the rejecter's role differs from that described in Section 4 as follows:

[1] When the highest confidence score cs_1 equals or exceeds the threshold, the rejecter accepts only the top candidate tag t_1, otherwise it goes to Step 2.
[2] When cs_1 is less than the threshold, the rejecter accepts not only the top tag t_1 but also the 2nd tag t_2.

Sentences that contain the 2nd candidates are selected in data selection for subsequent processing. The correct tag sequence in each tag graph is identified in automatic correction as follows:

[1] Select the tag sequence that has the longest[6] and consistent NE from the tag graph.
[2] If the longest NE also exists in a seed NE list, which will be described below, the system extracts the entire sentence with its tag sequence as corrected data.

In Step 1, the system selects one preferable tag sequence based on the longest NE match. In the tag graph shown in Figure 4, there are 16 possible sequences because four words "3", "丁目(Street)", "の(on)" and "夕日(Sunset)" each have two tag candidates; O or B for "3", O or I for "丁目(Street)" and "の(on)", and I or O for "夕日(Sunset)". For example, "B I I I", "B I I O", "B I O O", "O O O I", "O O O O" and the rest. Because the sequence "B I I I" constructs the longest NE, the system selects the tag sequence that contains the ARTIFACT "3丁目の夕日." Other sequences that contain partial NEs such as "3", "3丁目", "3丁目の", which are all ARTIFACTs, are ignored.

In Step 2, the system judges whether the tag sequence selected in Step 1 is indeed correct.

[6] By longest, we mean the longest tag sequence that does *not* include any O-tags.

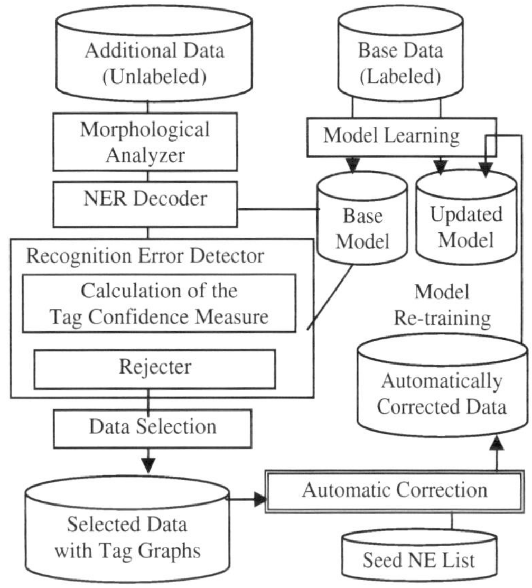

Figure 5. Semi-Automatically Updating NER Scheme.

However, the system requires some hints to judge the correctness, so we need to prepare a seed NE list, which contains surface forms and NE types. This list can be created by manually annotation of possible NEs or automatic generation from other sources such as dictionaries. When the same NE exists both in the selected tag sequence and the seed NE list, the system regards the selected tag sequence as reliable and extracts it as automatically corrected data. Finally, the model is updated by merging the automatically corrected data with the base data.

Bootstrapping means that data selection and correction of the selected data are completely automatic; we still have to prepare the seed NE list somehow. Thus the learning cost is quite low because we only need to provide an NE list as a seed. Updating NER is capable of modifying the model to keep up with the emergence of new named entities. Therefore, it is effective to analyze the large amount of texts that emerge everyday, such as blogs on the WWW.

5.2 Experiments

We tested our Updating NER with a large amount of blog texts from the WWW. One week's worth of blog texts was crawled on the WWW to generate the additional data. Table 5 shows the statistics of the data used in our experiments. The test data contained only the blog texts generated in December 2006, and the base data is about a half year older than the test data. Therefore, it is difficult for the base model to recognize new NEs in the test data. One week's worth of December 2006 blog texts were prepared for bootstrapping. The overlap between the test data and the additional data was removed in advance. We set the rejecter's threshold at 0.5 and selected the data with tag graphs from the additional data.

Japanese Wikipedia entries were used as the seed NE list. The titles of Wikipedia articles were regarded as surface forms. NE types were estimated from the category sections of each article, based on heuristic rules prepared in advance. We collected 104,296 entries as a seed NE list.

Using this seed list, Updating NER extracted the seed NE and its context from the selected data automatically. If the system found a match, it extracted the sentence with its tag sequence from the selected data. The automatically corrected data was then merged with the base data in order to re-train the base model.

For comparison, we evaluated the effect of the seed NE list itself. If there is a sequence of words that can be found in the seed list, then that sequence is always recognized as a NE. Note that the other words are simply decoded using the base model. We call this method 'user dictionary'. Here, we use recall and precision to evaluate the accuracy of the model.

Table 5. Data Description for Updating NER.

Base Data (blog in Sep. 04-Jun. 06)	43,716 sentences 746,304 words
Additional Data (one week's blog in Dec. 06)	240,474 sentences 3,677,077 words
Selected Data from the Additional Data	113,761 sentences 2,466,464 words
Test Data (blog in Dec.06)	1,609 sentences 21,813 words

5.3 Results

Table 6 shows the details of accuracy results regarding the following four NE types: PERSON, LOCATION, ORGANIZATION, and ARTIFACT, which are referred to hereafter as PSN, LOC, ORG and ART, respectively. Although we added Wikipedia as a user dictionary to the base model, it only slightly improved the recall. In fact, it has no positive and sometimes a negative effect on precision (e.g., ART decreased from 0.666 to 0.619). This indicates that adding an NE list as a dictionary is not enough to improve the accuracy of a NER system. This is because the NER system cannot discriminate an NE from surrounding unrelated words. It simply extracts matched sequences of words, so it overestimates the number of NEs.

On the contrary, our Updating NER improved both recall and precision (e.g., the recall and the precision in ART improved from 0.320 to 0.364 and from 0.666 to 0.694, respectively.). This means that not only the NE list but also the contexts are actually needed to retrain the model. Our Updating NER scheme has the advantage of finding the reliable context of a seed NE list automatically. Although some manual effort is needed to provide a seed NE list, its associated cost is lower than the cost of annotating the entire training data. Thus, we regard Updating NER as a promising solution for reducing learning cost in practical NER systems.

As shown in Table 6, neither user dictionary method nor Updating NER improves the accuracy in ORG. We assume that this is caused by the distribution of NE types in the seed NE list. In the seed list selected from the Wikipedia entries, PSN-type is dominant (74%). ORG-type is scant at only 11%, so the system did not have enough chances to retrain the ORG-type. Rather, it might be the case that the system had a tendency to recognize ORG-type as PSN-type because peoples' names are often used as organization names. Further investigation is needed to clarify the impact of the distribution and the quality of the seed NE list.

Table 6. Details of Accuracy.

		PSN	LOC	ORG	**ART**
Base Model	rec.	0.640	0.737	0.688	0.320
	prec.	0.699	0.811	0.652	0.666
+Wikipedia (user dic.)	rec.	0.686	0.729	0.688	0.354
	prec.	0.716	0.815	0.654	0.619
+Wikipedia (UpdatingNER)	rec.	0.649	0.747	0.678	0.364
	prec.	0.728	0.822	0.632	0.694

5.4 Discussions

Compared to conventional machine learning techniques, the most distinctive feature of Updating NER is that the system can focus on the top two candidates when the confidence score of the top candidate is low. This feature actually has a great advantage in the NER task, because the system is capable of determining what the next preferable tag is when a new NE appears which is assigned an O-tag by the base model.

Updating NER, however, has one weak point. That is, the following two strict conditions are required to correct the selected data automatically. First, the correct tag sequence must appear in tag graphs (*i.e.,* as one of the top two tag candidates). Second, the NE must also appear in the seed NE list. These conditions decrease the chance of extracting sentences with correct tag sequences from the selected data.

To overcome this weakness, one practical approach is to use Updating NER in combination with active learning. In the case of active learning, we do not need the correct tags in the top two candidates. The editor can assign correct tags without considering the order of candidates. In short, active learning has broad coverage in terms of learning, while Updating NER does not. Therefore, active learning is suitable for improving the performance level of the entire base model. Updating NER has the advantage of staying current with new named entities which emerge every day on the WWW. In practical use, for example, it will be better to update the model every week with Updating NER to keep up with new named entities, and occasionally perform active learning (every six months or so) to enhance the entire model. In the future, we plan to evaluate the efficiency of our two learning methods in practical applications, such as domain adaptation and acquisition of hot trend NE words from blog texts on the WWW.

6 Related Works

To date, there have been many related works on active learning not only for the NER task (Shen et al., 2004, Laws and Schütze, 2008) but also for other tasks, such as POS tagging (Engelson and Dagan, 1996), text classification (Lewis and Catlett, 1994), parsing (Hwa, 2000), and confusion set disambiguation (Banko and Brill, 2001). Active learning aims at effective data selection based on criterion measures, such as the confidence measure. Most previous works focus on the *Sentence*-Based criterion evaluation and data selection. Our proposal differs from those previous works in that we focus on the *Tag*-Based strategy, which judges whether each tag should be accepted or rejected. This approach maximizes the effectiveness of manual annotation by leaving the accepted tags in without any manual correction. As a result, our Tag-based approach reduces the manual annotation cost by 66 %, compared to the Sentence-Base method.

Semi-supervised learning has become an active area in machine learning; it utilizes not only annotated corpora but also huge amounts of plain text for model training. Several studies adapted semi-supervised learning to suit NLP tasks, such as word sense disambiguation (Yarowsky, 1995), text classification (Fujino et al., 2008), and chunking and NER (Suzuki and Isozaki, 2008). Suzuki and Isozaki (2008) suggest that a GIGA-word size plain text corpus may further improve the performance of the state-of-the-art NLP system. In this paper, however, we aim at model adaptation to the CGM domain to keep up with the new linguistic phenomena that are emerging every day. Because it is difficult to obtain GIGA-word size plain text sets that reflect such new linguistic phenomena, it is not practical to directly apply this approach to our task.

Bootstrapping is similar to semi-supervised learning in that it also allows the use of plain text (Etzioni 2005, Pantel and Pennacchioti 2006). In this learning method, it is possible to extract new instances automatically from plain text with small seed data prepared manually. Our Updating NER is similar to bootstrapping in that it extracts new annotated corpora automatically from plain text data starting with a seed NE list. However, the goal of conventional bootstrapping is to develop a new dictionary or thesaurus by extracting new instances. On the contrary, our goal is to acquire a new NE and its surrounding context in a sentence, not to build a NE dictionary (*i.e.*, correct tag sequence). It is the tag sequence and not a single NE that is needed for model training. Updating NER is a novel approach in the point of applying bootstrapping to the framework of supervised learning. This approach is quite effective in that it has the advantage of reducing learning cost compared with active learning because only a seed NE list is needed.

7 Conclusions

To reduce machine learning cost, we introduced two techniques that are based on a tag confidence measure determined from tag posterior probability. Dubious tags are automatically detected as recognition errors using the tag confidence measure. This approach maximizes the effectiveness of manual annotation by leaving the confident tags in without any manual correction.

We first applied this technique to active learning by correcting error tags manually. We found that it matches the performance of the learning method based on the sentence confidence measure with only 1/3 of the learning cost.

Next, we proposed Semi-Automatic Updating NER which has a bootstrap learning scheme, by expanding the scope from the top tag candidate to include the 2nd candidate. With this new scheme, it is possible to collect auto-labeled data from a large data source, such as blog texts on the WWW, by simply providing a seed NE list.

References

M. Banko and E. Brill. 2001. Scaling to Very Very Large Corpora for Natural Language Disambiguation. In *Proc. of ACL-2001*, pages 26-33.

S. A. Engelson and I. Dagan. 1999. Committee-Based Sample Selection for Probabilistic Classifiers. *Journal of Artificial Intelligence Research*, vol.11(1999), pages 335-360.

O. Etzioni, M. Cafarella, D. Downey, A. Popescu, T. Shaked, S. Soderland, D. S. Weld, and A. Yates. 2005. Unsupervised Named-Entity Extraction from the Web: An Experimental Study. *Artificial Intelligence*, 165(1), pages 91-134.

A. Fujino, N. Ueda, and K. Saito. 2008. Semisupervised Learning for a Hybrid Generative /Discriminative Classifier Based on the Maximum Entropy Principle. *IEEE Transactions on Pattern Analysis and Machine Intelligence (TPAMI)*, 30(3), pages 424-437.

R. Hwa. 2000. Sample Selection for Statistical Grammer Induction. In *Proc. of EMNLP/VLC-2000*, pages 45-52.

IREX Committee (ed.), 1999. In *Proc. of the IREX workshop*. http://nlp.cs.nyu.edu/irex/

J. Lafferty, A. McCallum, and F. Pereira. 2001. Conditional Random Fields: Probabilistic Models for Segmenting and Labeling Sequence Data. In *Proc. of ICML-2001*. pages 282-289.

F. Laws and H. Schütze. 2008. Stopping Criteria for Active Learning of Named Entity Recognition. In *Proc. of COLING-2008*, pages 465-472.

D. Lewis and J. Gatlett. 1994. Heterogeneous uncertainty sampling for supervised learning. In *Proc. of ICML-1994*, pages 148-156.

C. D. Manning and H. Schütze. 1999. Foundations of Statistical Natural Language Processing. The MIT Press.

P. Pantel and M. Pennacchiotti. 2006. Espresso: Leveraging Generic Patterns for Automatically Harvesting Semantic Relations. In *Proc. of COLING-ACL-2006*, pages 113-120.

E. F. T. K. Sang and F. De Meulder. 1999. Representing text chunks. In *Proc. of EACL-1999*, pages 173-179.

D. Shen, J. Zhang, J. Su, G. Zhou, and C. L. Tan. 2004. Multi-Criteria-based Active Learning for Named Entity Recognition. In *Proc. of ACL-2004*, pages 589-596.

J. Suzuki and H. Izozaki. 2008. Semi-Supervised Sequential Labeling and Segmentation using Giga-word Scale Unlabeled Data. In *Proc. of ACL-2008*, pages 665-673.

J. Suzuki, E. McDermott, and H. Isozaki. 2006. Training Conditional Random Fields with Multivariate Evaluation Measures. In *Proc. of COLING-ACL-2006*. pages 617-624.

D. Yarowsky. 1995. Unsupervised Word Sense Disambiguation Rivaling Supervised Methods. In *Proc. of ACL-1995*, pages 189-196.

X. Zhu. 2007. Semi-Supervised Learning, ICML-2007 Tutorial.

A Hybrid Model for Urdu Hindi Transliteration

Abbas Malik Laurent Besacier Christian Boitet
GETALP, Laboratoire d'Informatique Grenoble (LIG)
Université Joseph Fourier
Abbas.Malik, Laurent.Besacier,
Christian.Boitet@imag.fr

Pushpak Bhattacharyya
IIT Bombay
pb@cse.iitb.ac.in

Abstract

We report in this paper a novel hybrid approach for Urdu to Hindi transliteration that combines *finite-state machine (FSM)* based techniques with *statistical word language model* based approach. The output from the FSM is filtered with the word language model to produce the correct Hindi output. The main problem handled is the case of omission of diacritical marks from the input Urdu text. Our system produces the correct Hindi output even when the crucial information in the form of diacritic marks is absent. The approach improves the accuracy of the transducer-only approach from 50.7% to 79.1%. The results reported show that performance can be improved using a word language model to disambiguate the output produced by the transducer-only approach, especially when diacritic marks are not present in the Urdu input.

1 Introduction

Transliteration is a process to transcribe a word written in one language, in another language by preserving its articulation. It is crucial for handling out-of-vocabulary (OOV) words in different domains of Natural Language Processing (NLP), especially in Machine Translation (Knight and Graehl, 1998; Knight and Stall, 1998; Paola and Sanjeev, 2003), Cross-Lingual Information Retrieval (Pirkola *et al.*, 2003), the development of multi-lingual resources (Yan *et al.*, 2003) and multi-lingual text and speech processing. It is also useful for Inter-dialectal translation without lexical changes and sometimes it is mandatory when the dialects in question use mutually incomprehensible writing systems. Such cases exists in Malay (written in 2 different scripts), Turkish (2 scripts), Kurdish (3 scripts), Hindi/Urdu (2 scripts), Punjabi (2 scripts), *etc.*, where words are transliterated from one script to the other, irrespective of their type (noun, verb, *etc.*, and not only proper nouns and unknown words). In this study, we will focus on Hindi/Urdu example.

Hindi and Urdu are written in two mutually incomprehensible scripts, Devanagari and Urdu script – a derivative of Persio-Arabic script respectively. Hindi and Urdu are the official languages of India and the later is also the National language of Pakistan (Rahman, 2004). Table 1 gives an idea about the number of speakers of Hindi and Urdu.

	Native Speaker	2nd Lang. Speaker	Total
Hindi	366	487	853
Urdu	60.29	104	164.29
Total	426.29	591	1,017.29
Source: (Grimes, 2000) all numbers are in millions			

Table 1: Hindi and Urdu Speakers

Notwithstanding the transcriptional differences, Hindi and Urdu share phonology, grammar, morphology, literature, cultural heritage, *etc.* People from Hindi and Urdu communities can understand the verbal expressions of each other but the written expression of one community is alien to the other community.

A finite-state transliteration model for Hindi and Urdu transliteration using the Universal Intermediate Transcription (UIT – a pivot between the two scripts) was proposed by Malik *et al.* (2008). The non-probabilistic finite-state model is not powerful enough to solve all problems of Hindi ↔ Urdu transliteration. We visit and analyze Hindi ↔ Urdu transliteration problems in the next section and show that the solution of these problems is beyond the scope of a non-probabilistic finite-state transliteration model.

Proceedings of the 2009 Named Entities Workshop, ACL-IJCNLP 2009, pages 177–185,
Suntec, Singapore, 7 August 2009. ©2009 ACL and AFNLP

Following this, we show how a statistical model can be used to solve some of these problems, thereby enhancing the capabilities of the finite-state model.

Thus, we propose a hybrid transliteration model by combining the finite-state model and the *statistical word language model* for solving Hindi ↔ Urdu transliteration problems, discussed in section 2. Section 3 will throw light on the proposed model, its different components and various steps involved in its construction. In section 4, we will report and various aspects of different experiments and their results. Finally, we will conclude this study in section 5.

2 Hindi Urdu Transliteration

In this section, we will analyze Hindi ↔ Urdu transliteration problems and will concentrate on Urdu to Hindi transliteration only due to shortage of space and will discuss the reverse transliteration later. Thus, the remainder of the section analyzes the problems from Urdu to Hindi transliteration.

2.1 Vowel, Yeh (ی) and Waw (و)

Urdu is written in a derivation of Persio-Arabic script. Urdu vowels are represented with the help of four long vowels Alef-madda (آ), Alef (ا), Waw (و), Yeh (ی) and diacritical marks. One vowel can be represented in many ways depending upon its context or on the origin of the word, e.g. the vowel [ɑ] is represented by Alef-madda (آ) at the beginning of a word, by Alef (ا) in the middle of a word and in some Persio-Arabic loan word, it is represented by the diacritical mark Khari Zabar (◌ٰ). Thus Urdu has very complex vowel system, for more details see Malik *et al.* (2008). Urdu contains 10 vowels, and 7 of them also have their nasalization forms (Hussain, 2004; Khan, 1997) and 15 diacritical marks. Thou diacritical marks form the cornerstone of the Urdu vowel system, but are sparingly used (Zia, 1999). They are vital for the correct Urdu to Hindi transliteration using the finite-state transliteration model. The accuracy of the finite-state transliteration model decreases from above 80% to 50% in the absence of diacritical marks. Figure 1 shows two example Urdu phrases (i) with and (ii) without the diacritical marks and their Hindi transliteration using the finite-state transliteration model. Due to the absence of Zabar (◌َ) in the first and the last words in (1)(ii) and in the 5th word in (2)(ii), vowels ◌ै [æ] and औ [ɔ] are transliterated into vowels ◌े [e] and ओ [o] respectively. Similarly, due to the absence of Pesh (◌ُ) and Zer (◌ِ) in 3rd and 4th words respectively in (1)(ii), both vowels ◌ु [ʊ] and ि◌ [ɪ] are converted into the vowel [ə]. All wrongly converted words are underlined.

(1) (i) مَیں نے بہُت ادھِک کام نہیں کِیا ہَے
(ii) میں نے بہت ادھک کام نہیں کیا ہے
(i) मैं ने बहुत अधिक काम नहीं किया है
(ii) में ने बहत अधक काम नहें कया हे
I have not done a lot of work

(2) (i) کینْدْرِیّہ سْطر پر بھی اَور راجْیہ سْطر پر بھی
(ii) کیندریہ سطر پر بھی اور راجیہ سطر پر بھی
(i) केन्द्रीय स्तर पर भी और राज्य स्तर पर भी
(ii) केंदरय सतर पर भी ओर राजय सतर पर भी
Both at the central level and at the state level

Figure 1: Example Urdu Phrases

In Hindi, each vowel is represented by a character and a vowel sign except the vowel [ə], which is only represented by the character अ and do not have a vowel sign (Malik *et al.*, 2008). Table 2 gives all vowel conversion problems.

Sr.	IPA	Vowel Conversion Problems	Hindi
1	ɪ	ɪ → ə	इ or ि◌ → अ or 0*
2	ʊ	ʊ → ə	उ or ◌ु → अ or 0*
3	i	i → e	ई or ◌ी → ए or ◌े
4	æ	æ → e	ऐ or ◌ै → ए or ◌े
5	u	u → o	ऊ or ◌ू → ओ or ◌ो
6	ɔ	ɔ → o	औ or ◌ौ → ओ or ◌ो
7	j	j → e	य → ◌े
8	v	v → o	व → ◌ो

* Zero (0) means deleted.

Table 2: Vowel Problems from Urdu to Hindi

Long vowels Yeh (ی) [j] and Waw (و) [v] are also used as consonants and certain contextual rules help us to decide whether they are used as a consonant or as a vowel, *e.g.*, Yeh (ی) and Waw (و) are used as consonants at the start of a word and after the long vowel Alef-madda (آ), *etc.* Finite-state transliteration model can exploit such contextual rules but it is not possible to decide Yeh (ی) and Waw (و) as consonants in the absence of diacritics. Thus a finite-state transliteration model wrongly converts consonant Yeh (ی) and Waw (و) into vowels े [e] and ो [o], also given in Table 2, instead of consonants Ya (य) and Wa (व) respectively, *e.g.*, in the word کنور (prince) [kʊɲvr], Waw is wrongly converted into the vowel [o] due to the absence of Zabar (َ) after it and the word becomes [kʊnor], which is not a valid word of Hindi/Urdu.

2.2 Native Sounds

The Hindi writing system contains some native sounds/characters, *e.g.*, vocalic R (ऋ) [r̥], retroflex form of Na (ण) [ɳ], *etc.* On the other hand Urdu does not have their equivalents. Thus words containing such sounds are transcribed in Urdu with their approximate phonetic equivalents. All such cases are problematic for Urdu to Hindi transliteration and are given in Table 3.

Sr.	IPA	Hindi	Urdu
1	r̥	ऋ or ृ	ر [r]
2	ɳ	ण	ن [n]
3	ʃ	ष	ش [ʃ]
4	Half h	ः	ہ [h]

Table 3: Sounds of Sanskrit Origin

2.3 Conjunct Form

The Hindi alphabet is partly syllabic because each consonant inherits the vowel [ə]. Two or more consonants may be combined together to form a cluster called Conjunct that marks the absence of the inherited vowel [ə] between consonants (Kellogg, 1872; Montaut, 2004). Conjunction is also used to represent the gemination of a consonant, *e.g.*, क[k]+्+क[k]=क्क[kk] where ् is the conjunct marker and aspiration of some consonants like न [n], म [m], र [r] and ल [l] when used as conjunction with ह [h], *e.g.*, न[n] + ् + ह[h] = न्ह[n^h]. Conjunction has a special meaning but native speakers use conjunct forms without any explicit rule (Montaut, 2004).

On the other hand, Urdu uses Jazam (ْ – a diacritic) and Shadda (ّ) to mark the absence of a vowel between two consonants and gemination of a consonant respectively. In the absence of these diacritics in the input Urdu text, it is not possible to decide on the conjunct form of consonants except in the case of aspiration. In Urdu, aspiration of a consonant is marked with the special character Heh-Doachashmee (ھ) (Malik *et al.*, 2008), thus a finite-state transducer can easily decide about the conjunction for aspiration with a simple contextual rule, e.g. the word دُلھن (bride) [d̪ʊlʰn] is correctly transliterated by our finite-state transliteration model into दुल्हन.

2.4 Native Hindi Spellings and Sanskritized Vocabulary

Sanskrit highly influences Hindi and especially its vocabulary. In some words of Sanskrit origin, the vowel ी [i] and ू [u] are transcribed as ि [ɪ] and ु [ʊ] respectively at the end of a word. Javaid and Ahmed (2009) have pointed to this issue in these words "Hindi language can have words that end on short vowel…". Table 4 gives some examples of such native words. On the other hand in Urdu, short vowels can never come at the end of a word (Javaid and Ahmed, 2009; Malik *et al.*, 2008).

Vowel	Examples
ी [i]	व्यक्ति – ویکتی (person) [vjəkti]
	संस्कृति – سنسکرتی (culture) [səɲskrət̪i]
	उच्चकोटि – اُچکوٹی (high) [ʊʧʧkoʈi]
ू [u]	हेतु – ہیتو (for) [het̪u]
	किन्तु – کنتو (but) [kɪnt̪u]
	धातु – دھاتو (metal) [d̪at̪u]

Table 4: Hindi Word with Short vowel at End

It is clear from above examples that short vowels at the end of a Hindi word can easily be transliterated in Urdu using a contextual rule of a finite-state transducer, but it is not possible to do so for Urdu to Hindi transliteration using a non-probabilistic finite-state transliteration model. Thus Urdu to Hindi transliteration can also be considered as a special case of Back Transliteration.

In some words, the vowel ُ [u] is written as the vowel ُ [ʊ], *e.g.*, हुए – ہُوئے or हुआ – ہُوا (to be) [hue], राजनपुर (name of a city) [radʒənpur]. Some of these cases are regular and can be implemented as contextual rules in a finite-state transducer but it is not possible in every case.

2.5 Ain (ع)

Ain (ع – glottal stop) exists in the Arabic alphabet and native Arabic speakers pronounce it properly. Urdu also has adopted Ain (ع) in its alphabet as well as Arabic loan words but native speakers of the sub-continent cannot produce its sound properly, rather they produce a vowel sound by replacing Ain (ع) with Alef (ا). The Hindi alphabet follows one character for one sound rule and it does not have any equivalent of Ain (ع). Then, Ain (ع) in Urdu words is transcribed in Hindi by some vowel representing the pronunciation of the word by native sub-continent speakers. Thus it is always transliterated in some vowel in Hindi. For example, Ain (ع) gives the sound of the vowel [ə] in عجیب – अजीब (strange) [ədʒib] and the vowel [ɑ] with and without Alef (ا) in words عام – आम (common) [ɑm] and بعد – बाद (after) [bɑd̪] respectively. In some words, Ain (ع) is not pronounced at all and should be deleted while transliterating from Urdu to Hindi, *e.g.*, شرُوع – शुरू (to start) [ʃʊru], *etc.* Conversion of Ain (ع) is a big problem for transliteration.

2.6 Nasalization

Noonghunna (ں) [ɲ] is the nasalization marker of vowels in Urdu. Interestingly, it is only used to nasalize a vowel at the end of a word. In the middle of a word, Noon (ن) [n] is used to mark the nasalization of a vowel and it is also used as a consonant. It is difficult to differentiate between nasalized and consonant Noon (ن). There are certain contextual rules that help to decide that Noon (ن) is used as a consonant or a nasalization marker, but it not possible in all cases.

2.7 Persio-Arabic Vocabulary

Urdu borrows a considerable portion of it vocabulary from Persian and Arabic and transliteration of these words in Hindi is not regular. Table 5 explains it with few examples.

Urdu	Hindi	
	FST Conversion	Correct
بالکل	बालकुल (surely)	बिलकुल [bɪlkʊl]
بالواسطہ	बालवासता (with reference of)	बिलवासता [bɪlvas̪ta]
فی الحقیقت	फ़ीअलहक़ीक़त (in fact)	फ़िलहक़ीक़त [fɪlhəqiqət]

Table 5: Persio-Arabic Vocabulary in Urdu

3 Hybrid Transliteration Model

The analysis of the previous section clearly shows that solution of these problems is beyond the scope of the non-probabilistic Hindi Urdu Finite-state transliteration model (Malik *et al.*, 2008). We propose a hybrid transliteration model that takes the input Urdu text and converts it in Hindi using the Finite-state Transliteration Model (Malik et al, 2008). After that, it tries to correct the orthographic errors in the transducer-only Hindi output string using a *statistical word language model* for Hindi with the help of a *Hindi Word Map* described later. The approach used is rather similar to what is done in text recapitalization (Stolcke *et al.* 1998) for instance.

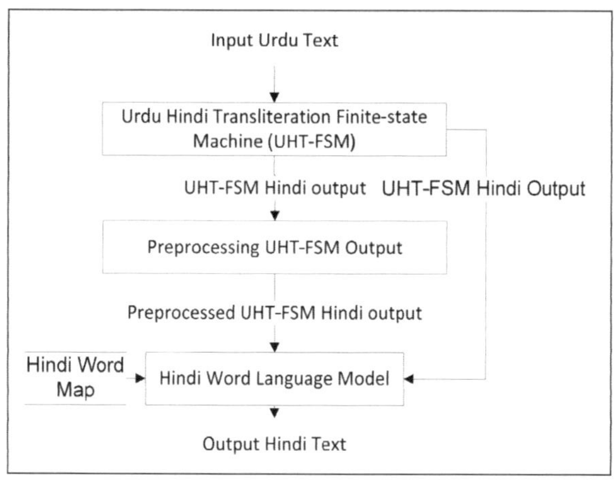

Figure 2: Hybrid Transliteration Model for Urdu Hindi

Normally, the Urdu text does not contain necessary diacritical marks that are mandatory for the correct transliteration by the finite-state component `Urdu Hindi Transliteration`

Finite-state Machine (UHT-FSM), described by Malik *et al.* (2008). The proposed hybrid model focuses on the correct transliteration of Urdu texts without diacritical marks. Figure 2 gives the proposed Model architecture.

3.1 Preprocessing UHT-FSM Output

The goal of this pre-processing is to generate a more "normalized" (and consequently more ambiguous) form of Hindi, e.g. pre-processing transforms both corpus words इस (this) [ɪs] and उस (that) [ʊs] (if encountered in the UHT-FSM Hindi output) into the default input Hindi word अस* [əs] (not a valid Hindi word but is a finite-state transliteration of the input Urdu word اس, a word without diacritical marks). Thus pre-processing is vital for establishing connections between the UHT-FSM Hindi output words (from the Urdu input without diacritical marks) and the Hindi corpus words. In the example above, the word अस* [əs] is aligned to two Hindi corpus words. All such alignments are recorded in the *Hindi Word Map*. This ambiguity will be solved by the `Hindi word language model`, trained on a large amount of Hindi data. Thus pre-processing is a process that establishes connections between the most likely expected input Hindi word forms (UHT-FSM Hindi output from the Urdu input without diacritical marks) and the correct Hindi word forms (words that are present in the Hindi corpus).

The `Preprocessing` component is a finite-state transducer that normalizes the Hindi output of `UHT-FSM` component for the `Hindi word language model`. The transducer converts all cases of gemination of consonants into a simple consonant. For example, the `UHT-FSM` converts the Urdu word رب (God) [rəbb] into रब्ब and the `Preprocessing` converts it into रब [rb]. The transducer also removes the conjunct marker (◌्) from the output of the `UHT-FSM` except when it is preceded by one of the consonant from the set {र [r], ल [l], म [m], न [n]} and also followed by the consonant ह [h] (first 3 lines of Figure 3), *e.g.*, `UHT-FSM` converts the Urdu words ہندی (Hindi) [hɪndi] and دُلھن (bride) [d̪ʊlʰn] into हिन्दी and दुल्हन respectively and the `Preprocessing` component converts them into हिनदी (removes ◌्) and दुल्हन (no change). Actually, Preprocessing deteriorates the accuracy of the output of the `UHT-FSM` component. We will come back to this point with exact figures in the next section.

The code of the finite-state transducer is given in XFST (Beesley and Karttunen, 2003) style in Figure 3. In XFST, the rules are applied in reverse order due to XFST's transducer stack, i.e. a rule written at the end of the XFST script file will apply first and so on.

```
read regex [◌् -> 0 || [? - [र | ल | म | न]] _ [? - ह]];
read regex [◌् -> 0 || [र | ल | म | न] _ [? - ह]];
read regex [◌् -> 0 || [? - [र | ल | म | न]] _ [ह]];
read regex [[क ◌् क] -> क, [क ◌् ख] -> ख, [ग ◌् ग] -> ग, [ग ◌् घ] -> घ, [च ◌् च] -> च, [च ◌् छ] -> छ, [ज ◌् ज] -> ज, [ज ◌् झ] -> झ, [ट ◌् ट] -> ट, [ट ◌् ठ] -> ठ, [ड ◌् ड] -> ड, [ड ◌् ढ] -> ढ, [त ◌् त] -> त, [त ◌् थ] -> थ, [द ◌् द] -> द, [द ◌् ध] -> ध, [प ◌् प] -> प, [प ◌् फ] -> फ, [ब ◌् ब] -> ब, [ब ◌् भ] -> भ, [म ◌् म] -> म, [य ◌् य] -> य, [र ◌् र] -> र, [ल ◌् ल] -> ल, [व ◌् व] -> व, [श ◌् श] -> श, [ष ◌् ष] -> ष, [स ◌् स] -> स, [ह ◌् ह] -> ह, [क़ ◌् क़] -> क़, [ख़ ◌् ख़] -> ख़, [ग़ ◌् ग़] -> ग़, [ज़ ◌् ज़] -> ज़, [ड़ ◌् ड़] -> ड़, [ढ़ ◌् ढ़] -> ढ़, [फ़ ◌् फ़] -> फ़];
```

Figure 3: Preprocessing Transducer

3.2 Hindi Word Language Model

The `Hindi Word Language Model` is an important component of the hybrid transliteration model. For the development of our *statistical word language model*, we have used the Hindi Corpus freely available from the Center for Indian Language Technology[1], Indian Institute of Technology Bombay (IITB), India.

First, we extracted all Hindi sentences from the Hindi corpus. Then we removed all punctuation marks from each sentence. Finally, we added '<s>' and '</s>' tags at the start and at the end of each sentence. We trained a tri-gram `Hindi Word Language Model` with the SRILM (Stolcke, 2002) tool. The processed Hindi corpus data contains total 173,087 unique sen-

[1] http://www.cfilt.iitb.ac.in/

tences and more than 3.5 million words. The SRILM toolkit command '*disambig*' is used to generate the final Hindi output using the *statistical word language model* for Hindi and the *Hindi Word Map* described in the next section.

3.3 Hindi Word Map

The *Hindi Word Map* is another very important component of the proposed hybrid transliteration model. It describes how each "normalized" Hindi word that can be seen after the `Preprocessing` step and can be converted to one or several correct Hindi words, the final decision being made by the *statistical word language model* for Hindi. We have developed it from the same processed Hindi corpus data that was used to build the `Hindi Word Language Model`. We extracted all unique Hindi words (120,538 unique words in total).

The hybrid transliteration model is an effort to correctly transliterate the input Urdu text without diacritical marks in Hindi. Thus we take each unique Hindi word and try to generate all possible Hindi word options that can be given as input to the `Hindi Word Language Model` component for the said word. Consider the Urdu word ربّ (God) [rəbb]; its correct Hindi spellings are रब्ब. If we remove the diacritical mark Shadda (◌ّ) after the last character of the word, then the word becomes رب and `UHT-FSM` transliterates it in रब*. Thus the `Hindi Word Language Model` will encounter either रब्ब or रब* for the Hindi word रब्ब (two possible word options). In other words, the *Hindi Word Map* is a computational model that records all possible alignments between the "normalized" or pre-processed words (most likely input word forms) and the correct Hindi words from the corpus.

We have applied a finite-state transducer that generates all possible word options for each unique Hindi word. We cannot give the full XFST code of the 'Default Input Creator' due to space shortage, but a sample XFST code is given in Figure 4. If the Urdu input contains all necessary diacritical marks, then pre-processing of the output of the `UHT-FSM` tries to remove the effect of some of these diacritical marks from the Hindi output. In the next section, we will show that actually it increases the accuracy at the end.

```
define CONSONANTS [क | ख | ग | घ | ङ | च |
छ | ज | झ | ञ | ट | ठ | ड | ढ | ण | त | थ | द | ध |
न | प | फ | ब | भ | म | य | र | ल | व | श | ष | स |
ह | क़ | ख़ | ग़ | ज़ | ड़ | ढ़ | फ़];
...
read regex [◌ै (->) ◌े, ◌ी (->) ◌े, ◌ृ (->) ◌ो, ◌ौ
(->) ◌ो, ◌ि (->) 0, ◌ु (->) 0 || [CONSONANTS]
_ ];
read regex [◌ी (->) ◌े || [CONSONANTS] _ [? -
.#.]];
read regex [◌ि -> ◌ी, ◌ु -> ◌ो, ◌ु -> ◌ृ ||
[CONSONANTS] _ .#.];
...
```

Figure 4: Default Input Creator Transducer

Practically, the *Hindi Word Map* is a file in which each line contains a possible input word to `Hindi Word Language Model`, followed by a list of one (see line 3 of Figure 5) or more (see line 1 of Figure 5) words from the corpus that are associated with this possible input word.

The 'Default Input Creator' transducer has generated in total 961,802 possible input words for 120,538 unique Hindi words. For implementation reasons, we also added non-ambiguous pair entries in the word map (see line 2 of Figure 5), thus the initial word map contains in total 1,082,340 entries. We extract unique option words and finally, *Hindi Word Map* contains in total 962,893 entries. Some examples from Hindi Word Map file are given in Table 5.

(1) कीजे कीजि कीजै
(2) कीजो कीजो
(3) रब रब्ब
(4) कीमयागरी कीमियागरी कीमियागिरी
(5) अस इस उस

Figure 5: Sample Hindi Word Map

4 Test and Results

For testing purposes, we extracted 200 Hindi sentences from the Hindi corpus before removing punctuation marks. These sentences were of course removed from the training corpus used to build the *statistical word language model* for Hindi. First we converted these 200 Hindi sentences in Urdu using Hindi Urdu Finite-state transliteration model (Malik *et al.*, 2008). Transliterated Urdu sentences were post edited manually for any error and we also made sure that the Urdu text contained all diacritical marks. 200 original Hindi sentences served as Hindi reference for evaluation purposes.

From the post-edited Urdu sentences, we developed two test corpora. The first test corpus was the Urdu test with all diacritical marks. In the second test corpus, all diacritical marks were removed. We calculated both word level and character level accuracy and error rates using the SCLITE[2] tool. Our 200 sentence test contains 4,250 words and 16,677 characters in total.

4.1 Test: UHT-FSM

First we converted both Urdu test data using `UHT-FSM` only and compared the transliterated Hindi texts with the Hindi reference. `UHT-FSM` shows a word error rate of 21.5% and 51.5% for the Urdu test data with and without diacritics respectively. Results are given in Table 6, row 1.

Urdu Test Data	With diacritics	Without diacritics
UHT-FSM Accuracy/Error	80.7% / 21.5%	50.7% / 51.5%
UHT-FSM + HLM	82.6% / 19.6%	79.1% / 23.1%
UHT-FSM + PrePro	67.5% / 32.4%	50.7% / 51.5%
UHT-FSM + PrePro + HLM	85.8% / 16.4%	79.1% / 23.1%

Table 6: Word Level Results

These results support our claims that the absence of diacritical marks considerably increases the error rate.

4.2 Test: UHT-FSM + Hindi Language Model

Both outputs of `UHT-FSM` are first passed directly to `Hindi Word Language Model` without preprocessing. The `Hindi Word Language Model` converts UHT-FSM Hindi output in the final Hindi output with the help of *Hindi Word Map*.

Two final outputs were again compared with the Hindi reference and results are given in Table 6, row 2. For Urdu test data without diacritics, error rate decreased by 28.4% due to the `Hindi Word Language Model` and *Hindi Word Map* as compared to the `UHT-FSM` error rate. The Hindi Word Language Model also decreases the error rate by 1.9% for the Urdu test data with diacritics.

4.3 Test: UHT-FSM + Preprocessing

In this test, both outputs of `UHT-FSM` were preprocessed and the intermediate Hindi outputs were compared with the Hindi reference. Results are given in Table 6, row 3. After the comparison of results of row 1 and row 3, it is clear that preprocessing deteriorates the accuracy of Urdu test data with diacritics and does not have any effect on Urdu test data without diacritics.

4.4 Test: UHT-FSM + Preprocessing + Hindi Language Model

Preprocessed UHT-FSM Hindi outputs of the test of Section 4.3 were passed to the `Hindi Word Language Model` that produced final Hindi outputs with the help of the *Hindi Word Map*. Results are given in Table 6, row 4. They show that the `Hindi Word Language Model` increases the accuracy by 5.1% and 18.3% when compared with the accuracy of `UHT-FSM` and `UHT-FSM` + Preprocessing tests respectively, for the Urdu test data with diacritical marks.

For the Urdu test data without diacritical marks, the `Hindi Word Language Model` increases the accuracy rate by 28.3% in comparison to the accuracy of the `UHT-FSM` output (whether pre-processed or not).

4.5 Character Level Results

All outputs of tests of Sections 4.1, 4.2, 4.3 and 4.4 and the Hindi reference are processed to calculate the character level accuracy and error rates. Results are given in Table 7.

Urdu Test Data	With diacritics	Without diacritics
UHT-FSM	94.1% / 6.5%	77.5% / 22.6%
UHT-FSM + HLM	94.6% / 6.1%	89.8% / 10.7
UHT-FSM + PreP	87.5% / 13.0%	77.5% / 22.6
UHT-FSM + PreP + HLM	94.5% / 6.1%	89.8% / 10.7

Table 7: Character Level Results

[2] http://www.itl.nist.gov/iad/mig//tools/

4.6 Results and Examples

The `Hindi Word Language Model` increases the accuracy of Urdu Hindi transliteration, especially for the Urdu input without diacritical marks.

Consider the examples of Figure 7. Figure 1 is reproduced here by adding the Hindi transliteration of example sentences using the proposed hybrid transliteration model and Hindi reference.

(1)
(i) مَیں نے بہُت ادھِک کام نہیں کِیا ہَے
(ii) میں نے بہت ادھک کام نہیں کیا ہے
(i) मैं ने बहुत अधिक काम नहीं किया है
(ii) में ने बहत अधक काम नहें कया हे
I have not done a lot of work

Output of Hybrid Transliteration Model
(i) मैं ने बहुत अधिक काम नहीं किया है
(ii) मैं ने बहुत अधिक काम नहीं किया है

Hindi Reference
मैंने बहुत अधिक काम नहीं किया है

(2)
(i) کینْدْرِیّہ سْطر پر بھی اور راجْیہ سْطر پر بھی
(ii) کیندریہ سطر پر بھی اور راجیہ سطر پر بھی
(i) केन्द्रीय स्तर पर भी और राज्य स्तर पर भी
(ii) केंदरय सतर पर भी ओर राजय सतर पर भी
Both at the central level and at the state level

Output of Hybrid Transliteration Model
(i) केन्द्रीय स्तर पर भी और राज्य स्तर पर भी
(ii) केंद्रिय स्तर पर भी और राज्य स्तर पर भी

Hindi Reference
केन्द्रीय स्तर पर भी और राज्य स्तर पर भी

Figure 7: Examples

By comparing Hindi outputs of `Hindi Word Language Model` with the Hindi reference, only the first word of (2)(ii) is wrong and other errors due to the absence of diacritical marks in the source Urdu sentences are corrected properly.

5 Conclusion

From the test results of the previous section we can conclude that the *statistical word language model* increases the accuracy of Urdu to Hindi transliteration, especially for Urdu input text without diacritical marks. The proposed Hybrid Transliteration Model improves the accuracy and produces the correct Hindi output even when the crucial information in the form of diacritical marks is absent. It increases the accuracy by 28.3% in comparison to our previous Finite-state Transliteration Model. This study also shows that diacritical marks are crucial and necessary for Hindi Urdu transliteration.

References

Beesley, Kenneth R. and Karttunen, Lauri. 2003. *Finite State Morphology*, CSLI Publication, USA.

Grimes, Barbara F. (ed). 2000. *Pakistan*, in Ethnologue: Languages of the World, 14th Edition Dallas, Texas; Summer Institute of Linguistics, pp: 588-598.

Hussain, Sarmad. 2004. *Letter to Sound Rules for Urdu Text to Speech System*, proceedings of Workshop on Computational Aproaches to Arabic Script-based Languages, COLING 2004, Geneva, Switzerland.

Jawaid, Bushra and Tafseer Ahmed. 2009. *Hindi to Urdu Conversion: Beyond Simple Transliteration*, in proceedings of Conference on Language & Technology, Lahore, Pakistan.

Kellogg, Rev. S. H. 1872. *A Grammar of Hindi Language*, Delhi, Oriental Book reprints.

Khan, Mehboob Alam. 1997. اُردو کا صوتی نظام (Sound System in Urdu), National Language Authority, Pakistan

Knight, K. and Graehl, J. 1998. *Machine Transliteration*, Computational Linguistics, 24(4).

Knight, K. and Stall, B. G. 1998. *Transliterating Names and Technical Terms in Arabic Text*, proceedings of COLING/ACL Workshop on Computational Approaches to Semitic Languages.

Malik, M. G. Abbas. Boitet, Christian. Bhattcharyya, Pushpak. 2008. *Hindi Urdu Machine Transliteration using Finite-state Transducers*, proceedings of COLING 2008, Manchester, UK.

Montaut, A. 2004. *A Linguistic Grammar of Hindi*, Studies in Indo-European Linguistics Series, Munchen, Lincom Europe.

Paola, V. and Sanjeev, K. 2003. *Transliteration of Proper Names in Cross-language Application*, proceedings of 26th Annual International ACM SIGIR Conference on Research and Development in Information Retrieval, Toronto, Canada.

Pirkola, A. Toivonen, J. Keshustalo, H. Visala, K. and Jarvelin, K. 2003. *Fuzzy Translation of Cross-lingual Spelling Variants*, proceedings of 26th Annual International ACM SIGIR Conference on Research and Development in Information Retrieval, Toronto, Canada.

Rahman, Tariq. 2004. *Language Policy and Localization in Pakistan: Proposal for a Paradigmatic*

Shift, Crossing the Digital Divide, SCALLA Conference on Computational Linguistics.

Stolcke, A. 2002. *SRILM – An Extensible Language Modeling Toolkit*, in proceedings of International Conference on Spoken Language Processing.

Stolcke, A. Shriberg, E. Bates, R. Ostendorf, M. Hakkani, D. Plauche, M. Tur, G. and Lu, Y. 1998. *Automatic Detection of Sentence Boundaries and Disfluencies based on Recognized Words.* Proceedings of International Conference on Spoken Language Processing (ICSLP), Sydney, Australia.

Yan, Qu. Gregory, Grefenstette. and David A. Evans. 2003. *Automatic Transliteration for Japanese-to-English Text Retrieval.* In proceedings of the 26th annual international ACM SIGIR conference on Research and Development in Information Retrieval, pp: 353 – 360.

Zia, Khaver. 1999. *Standard Code Table for Urdu.* Proceedings of 4th Symposium on Multilingual Information Processing (MILIT-4), Yangon, Myanmar, CICC, Japan.

Graphemic Approximation of Phonological Context for English-Chinese Transliteration

Oi Yee Kwong
Department of Chinese, Translation and Linguistics
City University of Hong Kong
Tat Chee Avenue, Kowloon, Hong Kong
Olivia.Kwong@cityu.edu.hk

Abstract

Although direct orthographic mapping has been shown to outperform phoneme-based methods in English-to-Chinese (*E2C*) transliteration, it is observed that phonological context plays an important role in resolving graphemic ambiguity. In this paper, we investigate the use of surface graphemic features to approximate local phonological context for *E2C*. In the absence of an explicit phonemic representation of the English source names, experiments show that the previous and next character of a given English segment could effectively capture the local context affecting its expected pronunciation, and thus its rendition in Chinese.

1 Introduction

Proper names including personal names, place names, and organization names, make up a considerable part of naturally occurring texts. Personal names, in particular, do not only play an important role in identifying an individual, but also carry the family history, parental expectation, as well as other information about a person. In natural language processing, the proper rendition of personal names, especially between dissimilar languages such as Chinese and English, often contributes significantly to machine translation accuracy and intelligibility, and cross-lingual information retrieval. This paper addresses the problem of automatic English-Chinese forward transliteration (referred to as *E2C* hereafter) of personal names.

Unlike many other languages, Chinese names are characteristic in their relatively free choice and combination of characters, particularly for given names. Such apparent flexibility does not only account for the virtually infinite number of authentic Chinese names, but also leads to a considerable sample space when foreign names are transliterated into Chinese. Underlying the large sample space, however, is not entirely a random distribution. On the one hand, there are no more than a few hundred Chinese characters which are used in names (e.g. Sproat *et al.*, 1996). On the other hand, beyond linguistic and phonetic properties, many other social and cognitive factors such as dialect, gender, domain, meaning, and perception, are simultaneously influencing the naming process and superimposing on the surface graphemic correspondence.

As the state-of-the-art approach, direct orthographic mapping (e.g. Li *et al.*, 2004), making use of graphemic correspondence between English and Chinese directly, has been shown to outperform phoneme-based methods (e.g. Virga and Khudanpur, 2003). In fact, transliteration of foreign names into Chinese is often based on the surface orthographic forms, as exemplified in the transliteration of Beckham, where the supposedly silent h in "ham" is taken as pronounced, resulting in 汉姆 *han4-mu3* in Mandarin Chinese and 咸 *haam4* in Cantonese[1].

However, as we have observed, there is considerable graphemic ambiguity in *E2C*, where an English segment might correspond to different Chinese segments. Such multiple mappings, to a large extent, is associated with the phonological context embedding the English segment, thus affecting its expected pronunciation. Hence, if such phonological context could be considered in

[1] Mandarin names are shown in simplified Chinese characters and transcribed in Hanyu Pinyin, while Cantonese names are shown in traditional Chinese characters and transcribed in Jyutping published by the Linguistic Society of Hong Kong.

Proceedings of the 2009 Named Entities Workshop, ACL-IJCNLP 2009, pages 186–193,
Suntec, Singapore, 7 August 2009.

the transliteration model, some of the graphemic ambiguity could be resolved. However, instead of going for an explicit phonemic representation, which might introduce an extra step for error propagation, in the current study we investigate the usefulness of surface graphemic features for approximating the local phonological context in *E2C*. Experiments show that the previous and next character of a given segment could effectively capture the local phonological context and improve transliteration accuracy.

A short note on terminology before we move on: We use "segment" to refer to a minimal graphemic transliteration unit in the names. For instance, in the data, the name Amyx is transliterated as 阿米克斯 *a1-mi3-ke4-si1*, the grapheme pairs are <a, 阿>, <my, 米>, and <x, 克斯>. There are three English segments: "a", "my" and "x"; and three Chinese segments: 阿, 米 and 克斯. A segment may or may not correspond to exactly a syllable, although it often does.

In Section 2, we will briefly review some related work. In Section 3, we will discuss some observations on graphemic ambiguity in *E2C*. The proposed method will be presented in Section 4. Experiments will be reported in Section 5, with results discussed in Section 6, followed by a conclusion in Section 7.

2 Related Work

There are basically two categories of work on machine transliteration. On the one hand, various alignment models are used for acquiring transliteration lexicons from parallel corpora and other resources (e.g. Lee *et al.*, 2006; Jin *et al.*, 2008; Kuo and Li, 2008). On the other hand, statistical transliteration models are built for transliterating personal names and other proper names, such as by means of noisy channel models or direct models amongst others, phoneme-based (e.g. Knight and Graehl, 1998; Virga and Khudanpur, 2003), or grapheme-based (e.g. Li *et al.*, 2004), or a combination of them (Oh and Choi, 2005), or based on phonetic (e.g. Tao *et al.*, 2006; Yoon *et al.*, 2007) and semantic (e.g. Li *et al.*, 2007) features.

Li *et al.* (2004), for instance, used a Joint Source-Channel Model under the direct orthographic mapping (DOM) framework, skipping the middle phonemic representation in conventional phoneme-based methods, and modelling the segmentation and alignment preferences by means of contextual n-grams of the transliteration units. Their method was shown to outperform phoneme-based methods and those based on the noisy channel model.

The n-gram model used in Li *et al.* (2004) was based on previous local context of grapheme pairs. However, as we are going to show in Section 3, contexts on both sides of a segment are important in determining the actual rendition of it in Chinese. In addition, graphemic ambiguity could in part be resolved by means of the phonological context embedding the segment. Hence in the current study, we propose a method modified from the Joint Source-Channel Model to take into account contexts on both sides of a segment, and to approximate local phonological context by means of surface graphemic features.

3 Some Observations

In this section, we will quantitatively analyse some properties of *E2C* based on our data, and show the importance of considering neighbouring context on both sides of a certain segment, as well as the possibility of approximating phonological properties graphemically.

3.1 Dataset

The data used in the current study are based on the English-Chinese (EnCh) training and development data provided by the organisers of the NEWS 2009 Machine Transliteration Shared Task. There are 31,961 English-Chinese name pairs in the training set, and 2,896 English-Chinese name pairs in the development set. The data were manually cleaned up and aligned with respect to the correspondence between English and Chinese segments, e.g. Aa/l/to 阿/尔/托. The analysis in this section is based on the training set.

The Chinese transliterations in the data basically correspond to Mandarin Chinese pronunciations of the English names, as used by media in Mainland China (Xinhua News Agency, 1992). Note that transliterations for English names could differ considerably in Chinese, depending on the dialect in question. Names transliterated according to Mandarin Chinese pronunciations are very different from those according to Cantonese pronunciations, for instance. Transliterations used in Mainland China are also different from those used in Taiwan region, despite both are based on Mandarin Chinese. A well cited example is a syllable initial /d/ may surface as in Baghdad 巴格达 *ba1-ge2-da2*, but the syllable final /d/ is not represented. This is true for transliteration based on Mandarin Chinese pronunciations. For Cantonese, however, it is different since ending stops like –p, –t and –k are allowed in Cantonese syllables. Hence the syllable final /d/ in Baghdad is already captured in the last syllable of 巴格達 *baa1-gaak3-daat6* in Cantonese.

Such phonological properties of Mandarin Chinese might also account for the observation that extra syllables are often introduced for certain consonant segments in the middle of an English name, as in Hamilton, transliterated as 汉密尔顿 *han4-mi4-er3-dun4* in Mandarin Chinese (c.f. 咸美頓 *haam4-mei5-deon6* in Cantonese); and Beckham, transliterated as 贝克汉姆 *bei4-ke4-han4-mu3* in Mandarin Chinese (c.f. 碧咸 *bik1-haam4* in Cantonese).

3.2 Graphemic Ambiguity

Table 1 quantitatively describes the training data. On average each English name has around 3.14 segments, or transliteration units. On average each English segment has around 1.7 different renditions in Chinese. On the other hand, although the number of unique Chinese segments is just a few hundred, on average one Chinese segment could correspond to about 10 different English segments. This suggests that English-Chinese graphemic segment correspondence could be quite ambiguous. Further analysis is therefore needed to see if any systematic patterns could be found among such ambiguity.

Unique English names	31,822
Total English segments	99,930
Unique English segments	2,822
Unique Chinese segments	458
Unique grapheme pairs	4,750

Table 1. Quantitative Aspects of the Data

Assume transliteration pair mappings are in the form <e_k, $\{c_{k1},c_{k2},\ldots,c_{kn}\}$>, where e_k stands for the *k*th unique English segment, and $\{c_{k1},c_{k2},\ldots,c_{kn}\}$ for the set of *n* unique Chinese segments observed for it in the data. It was found in the training data that *n* varies from 1 to 15, while 32.2% of the distinct English segments have multiple grapheme correspondence. Table 2 shows the degree of graphemic ambiguity with illustrative examples. Some of the ambiguity, however, is the result of homophones. The effect of homophones (whether or not tones are taken into account) in *E2C* transliteration is worth more in-depth investigation, but it is beyond the scope of the current study.

n	Proportion	Examples			
		English Segment	Chinese Segments	Source Name	Transliteration
≥5	4.8%	na	内 *nei4*	Aber**na**thy	阿伯**内**西
			娜 *na4*	Adami**na**	阿达米**娜**
			尼 *ni2*	Cra**na**ge	克拉**尼**奇
			拿 *na2*	Buo**na**parte	波**拿**巴
			瑙 *nao3*	Ke**na**ll	克**瑙**尔
			纳 *na4*	Stra**na**han	斯特拉**纳**汉
			诺 *nuo4*	Wid**na**ll	威德**诺**尔
4	2.9%	tain	丹 *dan1*	Lafon**tain**	拉方**丹**
			坦 *tan3*	S**tain**ton	斯**坦**顿
			廷 *ting2*	Sar**tain**	沙**廷**
			顿 *dun4*	Chas**tain**	查斯**顿**
3	7.3%	ran	兰 *lan2*	G**ran**berg	格**兰**伯格
			朗 *lang3*	F**ran**cine	佛**朗**辛
			伦 *lun2*	Kar**ran**	卡**伦**
2	17.2%	ty	蒂 *di4*	Chris**ty**	克里斯**蒂**
			太 *tai4*	S**ty**le	斯**太**尔
1	67.8%	gie	吉 *ji2*	An**gie**	安**吉**
				Cow**gie**l	考**吉**尔

Table 2. Graphemic Ambiguity of the Data

The other multiple correspondences are nevertheless genuine ambiguity. The same English graphemic segment, depending on its pronunciation within the name, could be rendered in various Chinese segments of very different pronunciations. To determine the expected pronunciation of the ambiguous English segment, however, the phonological context embedding the segment has an important role to play. For instance, the graphemic segment "na", when appearing at the end of a name, is often pronounced as /na/ and rendered as 娜 *na4*, especially for female names. But when it is in the middle of a name, and especially before "th", it is often pronounced as /nei/ and rendered as 内 *nei4*. Similarly, the segment "ty" is often pronounced as /ti/ at the end of a name and transliterated as 蒂 *di4*. On the other hand, if it is in the middle of a name, after an "s" or in front of "le" or "re", it is often pronounced as /tai/ and therefore transliterated as 太 *tai4*.

Take another segment "le" as an example. It is found to correspond to as many as 15 different Chinese segments, including 利 *li4*, 勒 *le4*, 历 *li4*, 尔 *er3*, 莱 *lai2*, 里 *li3*, etc. When "le" appears at the end of a name, all but a few cases are pronounced as /l/ and rendered as 尔 *er3*, particularly when it follows "a", e.g. Dale 戴尔 *dai4-er3* and Dipasquale 迪帕斯奎尔 *di2-pa4-si1-kui2-er3*. Exceptions are when "le" at the end of a name follows "r", where it is often rendered as 利 *li4* instead. On the other hand, when "le" appears at the beginning of a name where the vowel is often prominently pronounced, it is usually rendered as 勒 *le4* or 莱 *lai2*, e.g. Lepke 莱普克 *lai2-pu3-ke4*, except when it is followed by the vowel "o", where it is then often transliterated as 利 *li4*, e.g. Leonor 利奥诺 *li4-ao4-nuo4*. When "le" appears in the middle of a name, the transliteration is nevertheless more variable. Still it is remarkable that "le" is transliterated as 历 *li4* when it is followed by "c" or "x", e.g. Alex 阿历克斯 *a4-li4-ke4-si1*.

Such observations thus suggest two important points for *E2C*. First, contexts on both sides of a given segment do play a role in determining its likely rendition in Chinese. Second, the phonological context is important for determining the expected pronunciation of an English segment given its position in a name. Hence we propose a method, making use of contexts on both sides of a segment, to approximate the local phonological context of a segment via surface graphemic features.

4 Proposed Method

The Joint Source-Channel Model in Li *et al.* (2004) making use of direct orthographic mapping and a bigram language model for the segment pairs (or token pairs in their terms) is as follows:

$$\begin{aligned} P(E,C) &= P(e_1,e_2,\ldots,e_k,c_1,c_2,\ldots,c_k) \\ &= P(<e_1,c_1>,<e_2,c_2>,\ldots,<e_k,c_k>) \\ &\approx \prod_{k=1}^{K} P(<e_k,c_k>|<e_{k-1},c_{k-1}>) \end{aligned}$$

where E refers to the English source name and C refers to the transliterated Chinese name. With K segments aligned between E and C, e_k and c_k refer to the kth English segment and its corresponding Chinese segment respectively.

While we have grounds for orthographic mapping as mentioned in the introduction, there is some modification we hope to make to the above model. As pointed out in the last section, local contexts on both sides of a given segment should be important and useful for modelling the context embedding the segment, which in turn could help determine its expected pronunciation. In addition, the phonological environment might be sufficiently represented by a neighbouring phoneme instead of even a syllable. Thus we take the last character from the previous segment and the first character of the next segment (instead of the whole neighbouring segment) into account, irrespective of their corresponding Chinese segments. This could be considered an attempt to approximate the local phonological context of a given segment by means of surface graphemic features, even if we do not go for an explicit phonemic representation of the source name.

Hence we propose to make use of bigrams in both directions with equal weighting, and assign a score, *Score(E,C)*, to a transliteration candidate as below:

$$\prod_{k=1}^{K} P(<e_k,c_k>|\, lc(e_{k-1}))\, P(<e_k,c_k>|\, fc(e_{k+1}))$$

where $lc(e_{k-1})$ refers to the last character of the previous English segment, and $fc(e_{k+1})$ refers to the first character of the next English segment.

In the rest of this paper, we will refer to this method as GAP, which stands for Graphemic Approximation of Phonological context.

5 Experiments

The 31,961 English-Chinese name pairs from the NEWS shared task training set were used for training, and the 2,896 names in the development set were used for testing. The data were first manually cleaned up and aligned with respect to the correspondence between English segments and Chinese segments.

5.1 Segmentation of Test Names

Each test name was first segmented. All possible segmentations were obtained based on the unique English segments obtained from the manual alignment above.

The graphemic units are made case-insensitive. When finding all possible graphemic segmentations of the English source names, segments with length 1 are only allowed if no longer segment with that initial letter followed by a vowel is possible. For example, while "a", "k", "l", "o", "v", "s" and "y" are all observed segments in the training data, when computing the transliteration for the test name Akalovsky, only two of the possible segmentations, A/ka/lo/v/s/ky and A/kal/o/v/s/ky, were considered while the rest involving more single-letter segments were ignored. This is justified by three reasons. First, the more alternative segmentations, the more alternative transliteration candidates are to be evaluated. This is computationally expensive, and many alternatives are in fact quite unlikely. Second, single-letter segments are redundant if a longer segment is possible. On the one hand, transliterations are usually based on a consonant-vowel combination as a unit. A consonant will only be on its own as a segment if it occurs among a consonant cluster, which has no direct syllable correspondence in Chinese. For example, it is useless to single out the second "k" in Akalovsky as the longer segment "ka" is pronounceable anyway, unlike in names with consonant clusters like Akst. On the other hand, in the cases of doubling consonants like Ross, both "s" and "ss" will correspond to similar sounds. Third, the n-gram models favour transliterations with fewer segments anyway, so the segmentations with more single-letter segments will be less probable in any case.

The possible segmentations obtained were then ranked by a method similar to GAP. The score for each segmentation candidate *S*, *Score(S)*, is computed by:

$$\prod_{k=1}^{K} P(s_k \mid lc(s_{k-1}))\, P(s_k \mid fc(s_{k+1}))$$

where s_k is the *k*th segment in a name, $lc(s_{k-1})$ is the last character of the previous segment and $fc(s_{k+1})$ is the first character of the next segment.

In the experiments, we selected the top *N* segmentation candidates for use in subsequent steps, where *N* was varied from 1 to 3.

5.2 Transliteration Candidates

With the top *N* segmentation candidates, the transliteration candidates were generated by looking up the grapheme pairs obtained from manual alignment with frequency over a certain threshold *f*. We tested with $f \geq 3$ and $f \geq 5$. If there is no grapheme pair for a certain segment above the threshold, all pairs below the threshold would be considered. All combinations obtained were then subject to ranking by the GAP transliteration method.

5.3 Testing

The transliteration candidates were evaluated and ranked by the GAP method. For comparison, we also run the Joint Source-Channel Model (JSCM) described in Li *et al.* (2004) on the test data. In addition, we also tested a variation of GAP, called GAP-s, where the neighbouring characters are replaced by the neighbouring segments in the computation of the scores, that is, $lc(e_{k-1})$ is replace by $<e_{k-1},c_{k-1}>$ and $fc(e_{k+1})$ is replaced by $<e_{k+1},c_{k+1}>$. Note that similar changes were applied to the ranking of the source name segmentations for both methods accordingly.

System performance was measured by the Mean Reciprocal Rank (MRR) (Kantor and Voorhees, 2000), as well as the Word Accuracy in Top-1 (ACC) and Fuzziness in Top-1 (Mean F-score) used in the NEWS shared task. Only the top 10 transliteration candidates produced by the systems were considered.

6 Results and Discussion

6.1 Candidates Filtering

As mentioned in the last section, candidates were filtered in two stages. First, when the source English name was segmented, only the top *N* segmentation candidates were retained for subsequent processes. Second, when transliteration candidates were generated, only those grapheme pairs with frequency $\geq f$, where applicable, were considered for the candidates. Table 3 shows the results of GAP with various combinations of *N* and *f*.

	f \ *N*	1	2	3
ACC	3	0.6357	0.6443	**0.6450**
Mean F		0.8558	0.8600	**0.8598**
MRR		0.6961	0.7279	**0.7319**
ACC	5	0.6336	0.6423	0.6430
Mean F		0.8547	0.8597	0.8595
MRR		0.6910	0.7233	0.7280

Table 3. Performance of GAP

As seen in Table 3, although the top 1 segmentation candidate could already achieve a certain performance level, taking the top 3 segmentation candidates could nevertheless considerably improve the MRR. This apparently suggests that the source name segmentation step could have significantly affected the overall performance of transliteration. Taking more segmentation candidates into account could help raise some correct transliterations to a higher rank, but there was not much improvement in terms of the accuracy at the top 1 position.

In terms of the grapheme pair frequency, setting the threshold at 3 gave only slightly better results than setting it at 5. A possible reason is that about 70% of all unique grapheme pairs have frequency below 5, and out of these over 47% only have single correspondence. In other words, there are a lot of grapheme pairs of low frequency, and for those ambiguous English segments, the distribution of their corresponding Chinese segments could be relatively uneven.

Hence the following comparison between various transliteration methods was based on the combination of N=3 and $f \geq 3$.

6.2 System Performance

To show the effectiveness of our proposed method, GAP was compared with JSCM and GAP-s. Table 4 shows the results of the three methods.

	JSCM	**GAP-s**	**GAP**
ACC	0.5760	0.6174	**0.6450**
Mean F	0.8309	0.8507	**0.8598**
MRR	0.6881	0.7175	**0.7319**

Table 4. System Performance Comparison

As evident from Table 4, system GAP-s outperformed JSCM. The accuracy at top 1 position is much improved, thus boosting the MRR too. This improvement therefore supports our hypothesis that contexts on both sides of a given segment are important for determining its rendition in Chinese, where part of the graphemic ambiguity could be successfully resolved. Meanwhile, system GAP further improves the results from GAP-s, bringing ACC up to 0.6450 and MRR to 0.7319. This shows that the phonological context could be better captured, though only approximately, by means of the last character of the previous segment and the first character of the next segment, instead of the whole neighbouring segments. This is because the phonological context is often most closely related to the neighbouring phonemes instead of a whole syllable.

6.3 Examples

In this section we show two examples from the experimental outcomes to illustrate the usefulness of the GAP method.

The name Abercromby, according to the gold standard, should be transliterated as 阿伯克龙比 *a4-bo2-ke4-long2-bi3*. This transliteration came third in the JSCM system, whose top first and second candidates were 阿伯克罗姆比 *a4-bo2-ke4-luo2-mu3-bi3* and 阿贝尔克罗姆比 *a4-bei4-er3-ke4-luo2-mu3-bi3* respectively. On the contrary, the expected transliteration came first in the GAP system.

The top 3 source name segmentation candidates for both methods are shown in Table 5. The expected segmentation has already been identified as the best candidate in GAP, while it came third in JSCM.

Top	**JSCM**	**GAP**
1	a/ber/c/ro/m/by	a/ber/c/rom/by
2	a/be/r/c/ro/m/by	a/ber/c/ro/m/by
3	a/ber/c/rom/by	a/be/r/c/rom/by

Table 5. Segmentations for Abercromby

When it comes to the evaluation of the transliteration candidates, the longer candidates could even score higher than the expected outcome in JSCM. The statistical data show that the bigram c/克+ro/罗 is far more likely than c/克+rom/龙, but $P(<e_k,c_k>=<\text{rom},\text{龙}> \mid fc(e_{k+1})=\text{b})$ is much stronger than $P(<e_k,c_k>=<\text{m},\text{姆}> \mid fc(e_{k+1})=\text{b})$. Hence, taking the character on both sides of a segment, GAP managed to rank 阿伯克龙比 highest.

Another example is the name Regelson, which is transliterated as 里格尔森 *li3-ge2-er3-sen1* in the gold standard. The expected transliteration is ranked 8th in JSCM and 2nd in GAP. Although *P*(<e_k,c_k>=<ge,杰> | <e_{k-1},c_{k-1}>=<re,里>) is much higher than *P*(<e_k,c_k>=<ge,格> | <e_{k-1},c_{k-1}>=<re,里>), when taking the next segment <l,尔> into account, the likelihood of <ge,杰> is lowered. Hence the expected transliteration is ranked higher in GAP.

6.4 Error Analysis

As the proposed method stands, errors could have been propagated from two steps. The first is the source name segmentation step. If it happens that the top segmentation candidates are already wrong to start with, there is no way to reach the expected transliteration at all. Hence it is even more important to maintain a high accuracy for the segmentation step. The other error-propagation step is certainly when transliteration candidates are evaluated. The results for this step often heavily rely on the training data. If it happens that the grapheme pair distributions are somewhat skewed, particular Chinese segments would be preferred irrespective of relevant linguistic or other factors. On the other hand, if many homophones are used for a particular English segment, the chance of reaching the expected transliteration with one of the homophones is again loosened. More on this will be discussed in the next section.

For the latter error-propagation step, our attempt to make use of contexts on both sides of a segment has been shown to be able to improve the results. To see how much of the errors is attributable to the segmentation step, we roughly made an estimation by comparing the length of the top 1 candidates given in JSCM and GAP with the gold standard. It was found that 17.8% and 14.2% of the first candidates in JSCM and GAP respectively do not match the length of the gold standard. More detailed analysis of the segmentation results is in progress.

6.5 Current Limitations and Future Work

Our current treatment of neighbouring context and graphemic approximation of phonological context is shown to outperform pure DOM based on previous context only. Nevertheless, there are several directions of work which would require more investigation to further improve *E2C* performance.

First, the source name segmentation step needs further improvement to minimise error propagation from an early step. Phonological knowledge is obviously important in this regard as how a given English name should be segmented and pronounced is determined by its phonological context. Even without an explicit phonemic representation of the source names, more could be done in terms of modelling the phonological context via the surface graphemes.

Second, relating to the above, foreign names of different origins often have very different phonological properties leading to different pronunciations for the same orthographic forms. The silent h in Beckham mentioned earlier is one example, even though Chinese transliterations are often based on surface orthographic properties. Other problematic cases could be from languages like Russian and German where there are relatively more consonant clusters. For instance, the segment "scho" is often transliterated as one syllable (e.g. 绍 *shao4*, 肖 *xiao4*, or 舍 *she4*) but the segment "stro" often leads to three syllables (e.g. 斯特罗 *si1-te4-luo2*). It is therefore important to incorporate more phonological knowledge into the transliteration model, not only to generate more reliable and acceptable transliteration candidates, but also to reduce effort in evaluating phonologically invalid segmentation candidates and syllable structures, thus making the task computationally less expensive.

Third, as one of our separate ongoing studies shows, homophones are not only abundant in Chinese language per se, but also in *E2C* transliteration. The situation is particularly salient in Chinese transliterations based on Cantonese pronunciations. For example, while some names might have two transliterations with different pronunciations, like Jackson as 積遜 *zik1-seon3* or 積臣 *zik1-san4*, the same name might also be rendered in two forms with a different character having the same pronunciation, such as Adam as 亞當 or 阿當 (both pronounced as *aa3-dong1* in Cantonese). Two transliterations for the same name might have the same sound but different tones, e.g. Ashley as 艾殊利 *aai6-syu4-lei6* or 艾舒利 *aai6-syu1-lei6*. We therefore attempt to model the English-Chinese segment correspondence via an intermediate representation of the phonetic transcription of the Chinese characters. Preliminary results are reported in Kwong (2009). Although it happens that only one transliteration is given for each name in the gold standard data used in this study, the variability of *E2C* in reality is evident. It is therefore important for systems to be able to accommodate acceptable transliteration alternatives, particularly for transliteration extraction and information retrieval.

Fourth, given that tonal patterns could help distinguish some homophone ambiguity, the effect of the tonal factor and its potential association with the pitch and accent in the English names is worth further investigation.

7 Conclusion

Hence in this paper, we have reported our work on approximating phonological context for *E2C* with surface graphemic features. This is based on the observation that certain graphemic ambiguity is closely associated with the local contexts on both sides of a given segment, the phonological properties of which often determine its expected pronunciation. Experiments have shown that in the absence of an explicit phonemic representation of the English source names, the previous and next character of a given segment could be effectively employed to approximate the local phonological context affecting the rendition of a given segment in Chinese. Our proposed method GAP gives better results than the conventional JSCM which only makes use of previous context, and GAP-s which considers the whole neighbouring segments. Future work includes improving the source name segmentation step to minimise error propagation from an early stage, incorporating other factors like name origin and special phonological properties of different source languages into the transliteration model, as well as effectively handling homophones and tonal patterns in *E2C* transliteration.

Acknowledgements

The work described in this paper was substantially supported by a grant from City University of Hong Kong (Project No. 7002203).

References

Jin, C., Na, S-H., Kim, D-I. and Lee, J-H. (2008) Automatic Extraction of English-Chinese Transliteration Pairs using Dynamic Window and Tokenizer. In *Proceedings of the Sixth SIGHAN Workshop on Chinese Language Processing (SIGHAN-6)*, Hyderabad, India, pp.9-15.

Kantor, P.B. and Voorhees, E.M. (2000) The TREC-5 Confusion Track: Comparing Retrieval Methods for Scanned Text. *Information Retrieval, 2(2-3)*: 165-176.

Knight, K. and Graehl, J. (1998) Machine Transliteration. *Computational Linguistics, 24(4)*:599-612.

Kuo, J-S. and Li, H. (2008) Mining Transliterations from Web Query Results: An Incremental Approach. In *Proceedings of the Sixth SIGHAN Workshop on Chinese Language Processing (SIGHAN-6)*, Hyderabad, India, pp.16-23.

Kwong, O.Y. (2009) Homophones and Tonal Patterns in English-Chinese Transliteration. To appear in *Proceedings of ACL-IJCNLP 2009*, Singapore.

Lee, C-J., Chang, J.S. and Jang, J-S. R. (2006) Extraction of transliteration pairs from parallel corpora using a statistical transliteration model. *Information Sciences, 176*:67-90.

Li, H., Zhang, M. and Su, J. (2004) A Joint Source-Channel Model for Machine Transliteration. In *Proceedings of the 42nd Annual Meeting of the Association for Computational Linguistics (ACL 2004)*, Barcelona, Spain, pp.159-166.

Li, H., Sim, K.C., Kuo, J-S. and Dong, M. (2007) Semantic Transliteration of Personal Names. In *Proceedings of the 45th Annual Meeting of the Association for Computational Linguistics (ACL 2007)*, Prague, Czech Republic, pp.120-127.

Oh, J-H. and Choi, K-S. (2005) An Ensemble of Grapheme and Phoneme for Machine Transliteration. In R. Dale, K-F. Wong, J. Su and O.Y. Kwong (Eds.), *Natural Language Processing – IJCNLP 2005*. Springer, LNAI Vol. 3651, pp.451-461.

Sproat, R., Shih, C., Gale, W. and Chang, N. (1996) A stochastic finite-state word-segmentation algorithm for Chinese. *Computational Linguistics, 22(3)*: 377-404.

Tao, T., Yoon, S-Y., Fister, A., Sproat, R. and Zhai, C. (2006) Unsupervised Named Entity Transliteration Using Temporal and Phonetic Correlation. In *Proceedings of the 2006 Conference on Empirical Methods in Natural Language Processing (EMNLP 2006)*, Sydney, Australia, pp.250-257.

Virga, P. and Khudanpur, S. (2003) Transliteration of Proper Names in Cross-lingual Information Retrieval. In *Proceedings of the ACL2003 Workshop on Multilingual and Mixed-language Named Entity Recognition*.

Xinhua News Agency. (1992) *Chinese Transliteration of Foreign Personal Names*. The Commercial Press.

Yoon, S-Y., Kim, K-Y. and Sproat, R. (2007) Multilingual Transliteration Using Feature based Phonetic Method. In *Proceedings of the 45th Annual Meeting of the Association for Computational Linguistics (ACL 2007)*, Prague, Czech Republic, pp.112-119.

Czech Named Entity Corpus and SVM-based Recognizer

Jana Kravalová
Charles University in Prague
Institute of Formal and Applied Linguistics
kravalova@ufal.mff.cuni.cz

Zdeněk Žabokrtský
Charles University in Prague
Institute of Formal and Applied Linguistics
zabokrtsky@ufal.mff.cuni.cz

Abstract

This paper deals with recognition of named entities in Czech texts. We present a recently released corpus of Czech sentences with manually annotated named entities, in which a rich two-level classification scheme was used. There are around 6000 sentences in the corpus with roughly 33000 marked named entity instances. We use the data for training and evaluating a named entity recognizer based on Support Vector Machine classification technique. The presented recognizer outperforms the results previously reported for NE recognition in Czech.

1 Introduction

After the series of Message Understanding Conferences (MUC; (Grishman and Sundheim, 1996)), processing of named entities (NEs) became a well established discipline within the NLP domain, usually motivated by the needs of Information Extraction, Question Answering, or Machine Translation. For English, one can find literature about attempts at rule-based solutions for the NE task as well as machine-learning approaches, be they dependent on the existence of labeled data (such as CoNLL-2003 shared task data), unsupervised (using redundancy in NE expressions and their contexts, see e.g. (Collins and Singer, 1999)) or a combination of both (such as (Talukdar et al., 2006), in which labeled data are used as a source of seed for an unsupervised procedure exploiting huge unlabeled data). A survey of research on named entity recognition is available in (Ekbal and Bandyopadhyay, 2008).

There has been considerably less research done in the NE field in Czech, as discussed in (Ševčíková et al., 2007b). Therefore we focus on it in this paper, which is structured as follows. In Section 2 we present a recently released corpus of Czech sentences with manually annotated instances of named entities, in which a rich classification scheme is used. In Section 3 we describe a new NE recognizer developed for Czech, based on the Support Vector Machine (SVM) classification technique. Evaluation of such approach is presented in Section 4. The summary is given in Section 5.

2 Manually Annotated Corpus

2.1 Data Selection

We have randomly selected 6000 sentences from the Czech National Corpus[1] from the result of the query `([word=".*[a-z0-9]"] [word="[A-Z].*"])`. This query makes the relative frequency of NEs in the selection higher than the corpus average, which makes the subsequent manual annotation much more effective, even if it may slightly bias the distribution of NE types and their observed density.[2]

2.2 Annotation NE Instances with Two-level NE Classification

There is no generally accepted typology of Named Entities. One can see two trends: from the viewpoint of unsupervised learning, it is advantageous to have just a few coarse-grained categories (cf. the NE classification developed for MUC conferences or the classification proposed in (Collins and Singer, 1999), where only persons, locations, and organizations were distinguished), whereas those interested in semantically oriented applications prefer more informative (finer-grained) categories (e.g. (Fleischman and Hovy, 2002) with

[1] http://ucnk.ff.cuni.cz

[2] The query is trivially motivated by the fact that NEs in Czech (as well as in many other languages) are often marked by capitalization of the first letter. Annotation of NEs in a corpus without such selection would lower the bias, but would be more expensive due to the lower density of NE instances in the annotated material.

Proceedings of the 2009 Named Entities Workshop, ACL-IJCNLP 2009, pages 194–201,
Suntec, Singapore, 7 August 2009.

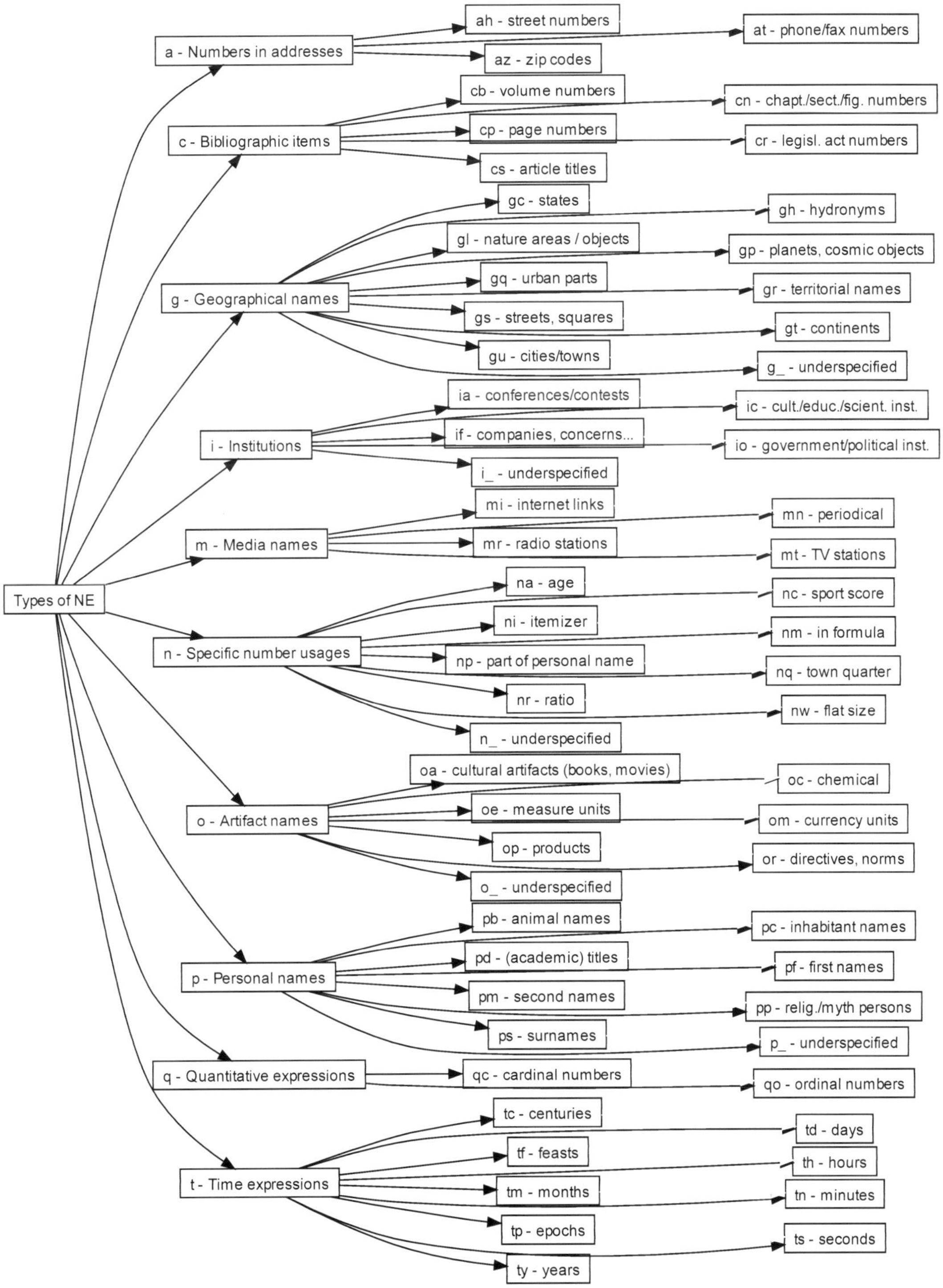

Figure 1: Two-level hierarchical classification of NEs used in the corpus. Note that the (detailed) NE types are divided into two columns just because of the space reasons here.

eight types of person labels, or Sekine's Extended NE Hierarchy, cf. (Sekine, 2003)).

In our corpus, we use a two-level NE classification depicted in Figure 1. The first level corresponds to rough categories (called *NE supertypes*) such as person names, geographical names etc. The second level provides a more detailed classification: e.g. within the supertype of geographical names, the *NE types* of names of cities/towns, names of states, names of rivers/seas/lakes etc. are distinguished.[3] If more robust processing is necessary, only the first level (NE supertypes) can be used, while the second level (NE types) comes into play when more subtle information is needed. Each NE type is encoded by a unique two-character tag (e.g., `gu` for names of cities/towns, `gc` for names of states; a special tag, such as `g_`, makes it possible to leave the NE type underspecified).

Besides the terms of NE type and supertype, we use also the term *NE instance*, which stands for a continuous subsequence of tokens expressing the entity in a given text. In the simple plain-text format, which we use for manual annotations, the NE instances are marked as follows: the word or the span of words belonging to the NE is delimited by symbols < and >, with the former one immediately followed by the NE type tag (e.g. `<pf` *John*> *loves* `<pf` *Mary*>).

The annotation scheme allows for the embedding of NE instances. There are two types of embedding. In the first case, the NE of a certain type can be embedded in another NE (e.g., the river name can be part of a name of a city as in `<gu` *Ústí nad* `<gh` *Labem*>>). In the second case, two or more NEs are parts of a (so-called) *container NE* (e.g., two NEs, a first name and a surname, form together a person name container NE such as in `<P<pf` *Paul*> `<ps` *Newman*>>). The container NEs are marked with a capital one-letter tag: `P` for (complex) person names, `T` for temporal expressions, `A` for addresses, and `C` for bibliographic items. A more detailed description of the NE classification can be found in (Ševčíková et al., 2007b).

[3]Given the size of the annotated data, further subdivision into even finer classes (such as persons divided into categories such as lawyer, politician, scientist used in (Fleischman and Hovy, 2002)) would result in too sparse annotations.

2.3 Annotated Data Cleaning

After collecting all the sentences annotated by the annotators, it was necessary to clean the data in order to improve the data quality. For this purpose, a set of tests was implemented. The tests revealed wrong or "suspicious" spots in the data (based e.g. on the assumption that the same lemma should manifest an entity of the same type in most its occurrences), which were manually checked and corrected if necessary. Some noisy sentences caused e.g. by wrong sentence segmentation in the original resource were deleted; the final size of the corpus is 5870 sentences.

2.4 Morphological Analysis of Annotated Data

The sentences have been enriched with morphological tags and lemmas using Jan Hajič's tagger shipped with Prague Dependency Treebank 2.0 (Hajič et al., 2006) integrated into the TectoMT environment (Žabokrtský et al., 2008). Motivation for this step was twofold

- Czech is a morphologically rich language, and named entities might be subject to paradigms with rich inflection too. For example, male first name *Tomáš* (Thomas) migh appear also in one of the following forms: *Tomáše, Tomášovi, Tomáši, Tomášem, Tomášové, Tomášům* ...(according to grammatical case and number), which would make the training data without lemmatization much sparser.
- Additional features (useful for SVM as well as for any other Machine Learning approach) can be mined from the lemma and tag sequences, as shown in Section 3.2.

2.5 Public Data Release

Manually annotated and cleaned 6000 sentences with roughly 33000 named entities were released as Czech Named Entity Corpus 1.0. The corpus consists of manually annotated sentences and morphological analysis in several formats: a simple plain text format, a simple xml format, a more complex xml format based on the Prague Markup Language (Pajas and Štěpánek, 2006) and containing also the above mentioned morphological analysis, and the html format with visually highlighted NE instances.

For the purposes of supervised machine learning, division of data into training, development and evaluation subset is provided in the corpus. The division into training, development and evaluation subsets was made by random division of sentences into three sets, in proportion 80% (training), 10% (development) and 10% (evaluation), see Table 1. Other basic quantitative properties are summarized in Table 2 and Table 3.

The resulting data collection, called Czech Named Entity Corpus 1.0, is now publicly available on the Internet at *http://ufal.mff.cuni.cz/tectomt*.

Set	#Sentences	#Words	#NE instances
train	4696	119921	26491
dtest	587	14982	3476
etest	587	15119	3615
total	5870	150022	33582

Table 1: Division of the annotated corpus into training, development test, and evaluation test sets.

Lenght	#Occurrences	Proportion
one-word	23057	68.66%
two-word	6885	20.50%
three-word	1961	5.84%
longer	1679	5.00%
total	33582	100.00%

Table 2: Occurrences of NE instances of different length in the annotated corpus.

3 SVM-based Recognizer

3.1 NER as a classification task

In this section, we formulate named entity recognition as a classification problem. The task of named entity recognition as a whole includes several problems to be solved:

- detecting "basic" one-word, two-word and multiword named entities,
- detecting complex entities containing other entities (e.g. an institution name containing a personal name).

Furthermore, one can have different requirements on what a correctly recognized named entity is (and train a separate recognizer for each case):

- an entity whose span and type are correctly recognized,

NE type	#Occurrences	Proportion
ps	4040	12.03%
pf	3072	9.15%
P	2722	8.11%
gu	2685	8.00%
qc	2040	6.07%
oa	1695	5.05%
ic	1410	4.20%
ty	1325	3.95%
th	1325	3.95%
s	1285	3.83%
gc	1107	3.30%
if	834	2.48%
io	830	2.47%
tm	559	1.66%
n_	512	1.52%
f	506	1.51%

Table 3: Distribution of several most frequent NE types in the annotated corpus.

- an entity whose span and supertype are correctly recognized,
- an entity whose span is correctly recognized (without regard to its type).

Therefore, we subdivide the classification problem into a few subproblems. Firstly, we independently evaluate the recognition system for one-word named entities, for two-word named entities and for multiword named entities. For each of these three problems, we define three tasks, ordered from the easiest to the most difficult:

- Named entity *span recognition* – all words of named entity must be found but the type is not relevant. For one-word entities, this reduces to 0/1 classification problem, that is, each word is either marked as named entity (1) or as regular word (0). For two-word entities, this 0/1 decision is made for each couple of subsequent words (bigram) in the sentence.
- Named entity *supertype recognition* – all words of named entity must be found and the supertype must be correct. This is a multiclass classification problem, where classes are named entity classes of the first level in hierarchy (`p, g, i, ...`) plus one class for regular words.

- Named entity *type recognition* – all words of named entity must be found and the type must be correct.

In our solution, a separate SVM classifier is built for one-word named entities, two-word named entities and three-word named entities. Then, as we proceed through the text, we apply the classifier on each "window" or "n-gram" of words – one-word, two-word and three-word, classifying the n-gram with the corresponding SVM classifier. We deliberately omit named entities containing four and more words, as they represent only a small portion of the instances (5%).

3.2 Features

Classification features which were used by the SVM classifier(s), are as follows:

- *morphological features* – part of speech, gender, case and number,
- *orthographic features* – boolean features such as capital letter at the beginning of the word or regular expression for time and year ,
- *lists* of known named entities – boolean features describing whether the word is listed in lists of Czech most used names and surnames, Czech cities, countries or famous institutions,
- *lemma* – some lemmas contain shortcuts describing the property of lemma, for example "Prahou" (Prague, 7th case) would lemmatize to "Praha_;G" with mark "_;G" hinting that "Praha" is a geographical name,
- *context features* – similar features for preceding and following words, that is, part of speech, gender, case and number for the preceding and following word, orthographic features, membership in a list of known entities and lemma hints for the preceding and following word.

All classification features were transformed into binary (boolean) features, resulting in roughly 200-dimensional binary feature space.

3.3 Classifier implementation

For the classification task, we decided to use Support Vector Machine classification method. First, this solution has been repeatedly shown to give better scores in NE recognition in comparison to other Machine Learning methods, see e.g. (Isozaki and Kazawa, 2002) and (Ekbal and Bandyopadhyay, 2008). Second, in our preliminary experiments on our data it outperformed all other solutions too (based on naive Bayes, k nearest neighbors, and decision trees).

As an SVM classifier, we used its CPAN Perl implementation `Algorithm-SVM`.[4]

Technically, the NE recognizer is implemented as a Perl module included into TectoMT, which is a modular open source software framework for implementing NLP applications, (Žabokrtský et al., 2008).[5]

4 Evaluation

4.1 Evaluation metrics

We use the following standard quantities for evaluating performance of the presented classifier:

- precision – the number of correctly predicted NEs divided by the number of all predicted NEs,
- recall – the number of correctly predicted NEs divided by the number of all NEs in the data,
- f-score – harmonic mean of precision and recall.

In our opinion, simpler quantities such as accuracy (the percentage of correctly marked words) are not suitable for this task, since the number of NE instances to be found is not known in advance.[6]

4.2 Results

The results for SVM classifier when applied on the evaluation test set of the corpus are summarized in Table 4. The table evaluates all subtasks as defined in Section 3.1, that is, for combination

[4] *http://www.cpan.org/authors/id/L/LA/LAIRDM/*

[5] One of the reasons for integrating the classifier into TectoMT is the fact that it requires the input texts to be sentence-segmented, tokenized, tagged and lemmatized; all the necessary tools for such preprocessing are already available in TectoMT.

[6] Counting also all non-NE words predicted as non-entities as a success would lead to very high accuracy value without much information content (obviously most words are not NE instances).

	All NEs			One-word NEs			Two-word NEs		
	P	R	F	P	R	F	P	R	F
span+type	0.75	0.62	0.68	0.80	0.71	0.75	0.68	0.62	0.65
span+supertype	0.75	0.67	0.71	0.87	0.78	0.82	0.71	0.64	0.67
span	0.84	0.70	0.76	0.89	0.80	0.84	0.76	0.69	0.72

Table 4: Summary of the SVM classifier performance (P=precision, R=recall, F=f-measure). Recognition of NEs of different length is evaluated separately. The other dimension corresponds to the gradually released correctness requirements.

true type	predicted type	true type description	predicted type description	errors
oa	x	cultural artifacts (books, movies)	no entity	184
ic	x	cult./educ./scient. inst.	no entity	74
x	gu	no entity	cities/towns	71
x	P	no entity	personal name container	66
if	x	companies, concerns ...	no entity	60
x	ic	no entity	cult./educ./scient. inst.	59
io	x	government/political inst.	no entity	57
x	ps	no entity	surnames	47
P	x	personal name container	no entity	43
ps	x	surnames	no entity	41
gu	x	cities/towns	no entity	37
x	td	no entity	days	35
op	x	products	no entity	33
x	pf	no entity	first names	31
T	x	time container	no entity	30

Table 5: The most frequent types of errors in NE recognition made by the SVM classifier.

of subtask defined for all entities, one-word entities and two-word entities and with gradually released requirements for correctness: correct span and correct (detailed) type, correct span and correct supertype, correct span only.

The most common SVM classification errors are shown in Table 5.

4.3 Discussion

As we can see in Table 4, the classifier recognizes span and type of all named entities in text with f-measure = 0.68. This improves the results reported on this data in (Ševčíková et al., 2007a), which was 0.62. For one-word named entities, the improvement is also noticeable, from 0.70 to 0.75.

In our opinion, the improvement is caused by better feature selection on one hand. We do not use as many classification features as the authors of (Ševčíková et al., 2007a), instead we made a preliminary manual selection of features we considered to be helpful. For example, we do not use the whole variety of 15 Czech morphological categories for every word in context, but we use only part of speech, gender, case and number. Also, we avoided using features based on storing words which occurred in training data, such as boolean feature, which is true for words, which appeared in training data as named entity. We tried employing such features, but in our opinion, they result in sparsity in space searched by SVM.

It would be highly difficult to correctly compare the achieved results with results reported on other languages (such as f-score 88.76% achieved for English in (Zhang and Johnson, 2003)), especially because of different task granularity (and obviously highly different baselines). Furthermore, in Czech the task is more complicated due to inflection: many named entities can appear in several many different forms. For example, the Czech capital city "Praha" appeared in these forms in training data: *Praha, Prahy, Prahou, Prahu*.

Table 5 describes the most common errors made by classifier. Clearly, the most problematic classes are objects (`oa`) and institutions (`ic, if, io`), which mostly remain unrecognized. The problem is that, cultural artifacts like books or movies, or institutions, tend to have quite new and unusual names, as opposed to personal names, for which fairly limited amount of choice exists, and cities, which do not change and can be listed easily.

Institutions also tend to have long and complicated names, for which it is especially difficult to find the ending frontier. We believe that dependency syntax analysis (such as dependency trees resulting from the maximum spanning tree parser, (McDonald et al., 2005)) might provide some clues here. By determining the head of the clause, e.g. *theatre, university, gallery* and it's dependants, we might get some hints about which words are part of the name and which are not.

Yet another improvement in overall performance could be achieved by incorporating hypernym discovery (making use e.g. of Wikipedia) as proposed in (Kliegr et al., 2008).

5 Conclusions

We have presented a new recently published corpus of Czech sentences with manually annotated named entities with fine-grained two-level annotation. We used the data for training and evaluating a named entity recognizer based on Support Vector Machines classification technique. Our classifier reached f-measure 0.68 in recognizing and classifying Czech named entities into 62 categories and thus outperformed the results previously reported for NE recognition in Czech in (Ševčíková et al., 2007a).

We intend to further improve our classifier, especially recognition of institution and object names, by employing dependency syntax features. Another improvement is hoped to be achieved using WWW-based ontologies.

Acknowledgments

This research was supported by MSM 0021620838, GAAV ČR 1ET101120503, and MŠMT ČR LC536.

References

Michael Collins and Yoram Singer. 1999. Unsupervised Models for Named Entity Classification. In *Proceedings of the Conference on Empirical Methods in Natural Language Processing and Very Large Corpora (EMNLP/VLC)*, pages 189–196.

Asif Ekbal and Sivaji Bandyopadhyay. 2008. Named Entity Recognition using Support Vector Machine: A Language Independent Approach . *International Journal of Computer Systems Science and Engineering*, 4(2):155–170.

Michael Fleischman and Eduard Hovy. 2002. Fine Grained Classification of Named Entities . In *Proceedings of the 19th International Conference on Computational Linguistics (COLING)*, volume I, pages 267–273.

Ralph Grishman and Beth Sundheim. 1996. Message Understanding Conference - 6: A Brief History. In *Proceedings of the 16th International Conference on Computational Linguistics (COLING)*, volume I, pages 466–471.

Jan Hajič, Jarmila Panevová, Eva Hajičová, Petr Sgall, Petr Pajas, Jan Štěpánek, Jiří Havelka, Marie Mikulová, Zdeněk Žabokrtský, and Magda Ševčíková. 2006. Prague Dependency Treebank 2.0.

Hideki Isozaki and Hideto Kazawa. 2002. Efficient Support Vector Classifiers For Named Entity Recognition. In *Proceedings of the 19th International Conference on Computational Linguistics (COLING'02)*.

Tomas Kliegr, Krishna Chandramouli, Jan Nemrava, Vojtech Svatek, and Ebroul Izquierdo. 2008. Wikipedia as the premiere source for targeted hypernym discovery. *WBBT ECML08*.

Ryan McDonald, Fernando Pereira, Kiril Ribarov, and Jan Hajič. 2005. Non-Projective Dependency Parsing using Spanning Tree Algorithms. In *Proceedings of Human Langauge Technology Conference and Conference on Empirical Methods in Natural Language Processing (HTL/EMNLP)*, pages 523–530, Vancouver, BC, Canada.

Petr Pajas and Jan Štěpánek. 2006. XML-based representation of multi-layered annotation in the PDT 2.0. In Richard Erhard Hinrichs, Nancy Ide, Martha Palmer, and James Pustejovsky, editors, *Proceedings of the LREC Workshop on Merging and Layering Linguistic Information (LREC 2006)*, pages 40–47, Paris, France.

Satoshi Sekine. 2003. Sekine's Extended Named Entity Hierarchy. http://nlp.cs.nyu.edu/ene/.

Magda Ševčíková, Zdeněk Žabokrtský, and Oldřich Krůza. 2007. Named Entities in Czech: Annotating Data and Developing NE Tagger. In Václav Matoušek and Pavel Mautner, editors, *Lecture Notes in Artificial Intelligence, Proceedings of the 10th International Conference on Text, Speech and Dialogue*, volume 4629 of *Lecture Notes in Computer Science*, pages 188–195, Pilsen, Czech Republic. Springer Science+Business Media Deutschland GmbH.

Partha Pratim Talukdar, Thorsten Brants, Mark Liberman, and Fernando Pereira. 2006. A Context Pattern Induction Method for Named Entity Extraction. In *Proceedings of the 10th Conference on Computational Natural Language Learning (CoNLL-X)*, pages 141–148.

Magda Ševčíková, Zdeněk Žabokrtský, and Oldřich Krůza. 2007. Zpracování pojmenovaných entit v českých textech. Technical report, ÚFAL MFF UK, Praha.

Zdeněk Žabokrtský, Jan Ptáček, and Petr Pajas. 2008. TectoMT: Highly Modular MT System with Tectogrammatics Used as Transfer Layer. In *Proceedings of the 3rd Workshop on Statistical Machine Translation, ACL.*

Tong Zhang and David Johnson. 2003. A robust risk minimization based named entity recognition system. In Walter Daelemans and Miles Osborne, editors, *Proceedings of CoNLL-2003*, pages 204–207. Edmonton, Canada.

Voted NER System using Appropriate Unlabeled Data

Asif Ekbal
Dept. of Computer Science &Engg.,
Jadavpur University, Kolkata-700032,
India
asif.ekbal@gmail.com

Sivaji Bandyopadhyay
Dept. of Computer Science &Engg.,
Jadavpur University, Kolkata-700032,
India
sivaji_cse_ju@yahoo.com

Abstract

This paper reports a voted Named Entity Recognition (NER) system with the use of appropriate unlabeled data. The proposed method is based on the classifiers such as Maximum Entropy (ME), Conditional Random Field (CRF) and Support Vector Machine (SVM) and has been tested for Bengali. The system makes use of the language independent features in the form of different contextual and orthographic word level features along with the language dependent features extracted from the Part of Speech (POS) tagger and gazetteers. Context patterns generated from the unlabeled data using an active learning method have been used as the features in each of the classifiers. A semi-supervised method has been used to describe the measures to automatically select effective documents and sentences from unlabeled data. Finally, the models have been combined together into a final system by weighted voting technique. Experimental results show the effectiveness of the proposed approach with the overall *Recall*, *Precision*, and *F-Score* values of 93.81%, 92.18% and 92.98%, respectively. We have shown how the language dependent features can improve the system performance.

1 Introduction

Named Entity Recognition (NER) is an important tool in almost all Natural Language Processing (NLP) application areas. Machine learning (ML) approaches are more popularly used in NER because these are easily trainable, adoptable to different domains and languages as well as their maintenance are also less expensive. Some of the very effective ML approaches used in NER are ME (Borthwick, 1999), CRF (Lafferty et al., 2001) and SVM (Yamada et al., 2002). In the earlier work (Florian et al., 2003), it has been shown that combination of several ML models yields better performance than any single ML model. One drawback of the ML techniques to NLP tasks is the requirement of a large amount of annotated data to achieve a reasonable performance.

Indian languages are resource-constrained and the manual preparation of NE annotated data is both time consuming and cost intensive. It is important to decide how the system should effectively select unlabeled data and how the size and relevance of data impact the performance. India is a multilingual country with great cultural diversities. Named Entity (NE) identification in Indian languages in general and Bengali in particular is difficult and challenging as:

1. Unlike English and most of the European languages, Bengali lacks capitalization information, which plays a very important role in identifying NEs.
2. Indian person names are generally found in the dictionary as common nouns with some specific meanings. For example, *kabitA* [Kabita] is a person name and can also be found in the dictionary as a common noun with the meaning 'poem'.
3. Bengali is an inflectional language providing one of the richest and most challenging sets of linguistic and statistical features resulting in long and complex wordforms. For example, the person name *sachin* [root] can appear as *sachi**ner*** [inflection:-*er*], *sachIn**ke*** [inflection:-*ke*], *sachIn**bAbu*** [inflection: -*bAbu*], *sachIn**dA*** [inflection:-*dA*] etc. The location name *kolkAtA* [root] can appear in different wordforms like *kolkAtA**r*** [inflection:-*r*], *kolkAtA**te*** [inflection:-*te*], *kolkAtA**i*** [inflection:-*i*] etc.
4. Bengali is a relatively free phrase order language. Thus, NEs can appear in any position of the sentence making the NER task more difficult.
5. Bengali, like other Indian languages, is a resource-constrained language. The annotated corpus, name dictionaries, good morphological

Proceedings of the 2009 Named Entities Workshop, ACL-IJCNLP 2009, pages 202–210,
Suntec, Singapore, 7 August 2009. ©2009 ACL and AFNLP

analyzers, POS taggers etc. are not yet available in the required measure.

6. Although Indian languages have a very old and rich literary history, technological developments are of recent origin.

7. Web sources for name lists are available in English, but such lists are not available in Bengali. This necessitates the use of transliteration for creating such lists.

A HMM based NER system for Bengali has been reported in Ekbal et al. (2007b), where additional contextual information has been considered during emission probabilities and NE suffixes are used for handling the unknown words. More recently, the works in the area of Bengali NER can be found in Ekbal et al. (2008a), and Ekbal and Bandyopadhyay (2008b) with the CRF, and SVM approach, respectively. Other than Bengali, the works on Hindi can be found in Li and McCallum (2004) with CRF and Saha et al. (2008) with a hybrid feature set based ME approach. Various works of NER involving Indian languages are reported in IJCNLP-08 NER Shared Task on South and South East Asian Languages (NERSSEAL) [1] using various techniques.

2 Named Entity Recognition in Bengali

We have used a Bengali news corpus (Ekbal and Bandyopadhyay, 2008c), developed from the web-archive of a widely read Bengali newspaper for NER. A portion of this corpus containing 200K wordforms has been manually annotated with the four NE tags namely, *Person, Location, Organization* and *Miscellaneous*. We have also used the NE annotated data of 122K wordforms, collected from the NERSSEAL shared task. The shared task data was originally annotated with a fine-grained NE tagset of twelve tags. We consider only those tags that represent person, location, organization, and miscellaneous names (NEN [number], NEM [Measurement] and NETI [Time]). Other tags have been mapped to the NNE tags that represent the "other-than-NE" category. In order to properly denote the boundaries of NEs, four NE tags are further divided into the following forms:

B-XXX: Beginning of a multiword NE, I-XXX: Internal of a multiword NE consisting of more than two words, E-XXX: End of a multiword NE, XXX→PER/LOC/ORG/MISC. For example, the name *sachin ramesh tendulkar* is tagged as *sachin*/B-PER *ramesh*/I-PER *tendulkar*/E-PER. The single word NE is tagged as, PER: Person name, LOC: Location name, ORG: Organization name and MISC: Miscellaneous name. In the output, sixteen NE tags are replaced with the four NE tags.

2.1 Our Approaches

Initially, we started with the development of a NER system using an active learning method. This is used as the *baseline* model. Four supervised NER systems based on ME, CRF and SVM have been developed. Two different systems with the SVM model, one using **forward parsing** (SVM-F) that parses from left to right and other using **backward parsing** (SVM-B) that parses from right to left, have been developed. The SVM system has been developed based on (Valdimir, 1995), which perform classification by constructing an N-dimensional hyperplane that optimally separates data into two categories. We have used *YamCha* toolkit (http://chasen-org/~taku/software/yamcha), an SVM based tool for detecting classes in documents and formulating the NER task as a sequential labeling problem. Here, the *pairwise* multi-class decision method and *polynomial kernel function* have been used. The TinySVM-0.0[2] classifier has been used for classification. The C^{++} based CRF++ package (http://crfpp.sourceforge.net) and the C^{++} based ME package [3] have been used for NER.

Performance of the supervised NER models is limited in part by the amount of labeled training data available. A part of the available unlabeled corpus (Ekbal and Bandyopadhyay, 2008c) has been used to address this problem. Based on the original training on the labeled corpus, there will be some tags in the unlabeled corpus that the taggers will be very sure about. We have proposed a semi-supervised learning technique that selects appropriate data from the available large unlabeled corpora and adds to the initial training set in order to improve the performance of the taggers. The models are retrained with this new training set and this process is repeated in a bootstrapped manner.

2.2 Named Entity Features

The main features for the NER task have been identified based on the different possible combinations of available word and tag contexts. In

[1] http://ltrc.iiit.ac.in/ner-ssea-08/proc/index.html

[2] http://cl.aist-nara.ac.jp/~taku ku/software/TinySVM

[3] http://homepages.inf.ed.ac.uk/s0450736/software/maxent/maxent-20061005.tar.bz2

addition to these, various gazetteer lists have been developed for use in the NER tasks.

The set of features 'F' contains language independent as well as language dependent features. The set of language independent features includes the context words, fixed length prefixes and suffixes of all the words, dynamic NE information of the previous word(s), first word, length of the word, digit and infrequent word information. Language dependent features include the set of known suffixes that may appear with the various NEs, clue words that help in predicting the location and organization names, words that help to recognize measurement expressions, designation words that help to identify person names, various gazetteer lists that include the first names, middle names, last names, location names, organization names, function words, weekdays and month names. We have also used the part of speech (POS) information of the current and/or the surrounding word(s) as the features.

Language independent NE features can be applied for NER in any language without any prior knowledge of that language. The lists or gazetteers are basically language dependent at the lexical level and not at the morphology or syntax level. Also, we include the POS information in the set of language dependent features as the POS information depends on some language specific phenomenon such as person, number, tense, gender etc. Also, the particular POS tagger, used in this work, makes use of the several language specific resources such as lexicon, inflection lists and a NER system to improve its performance. Evaluation results have demonstrated that the use of language specific features is helpful to improve the performance of the NER system. In the resource-constrained Indian language environment, the non-availability of language specific resources acts as a stimulant for the development of such resources for use in NER systems. This leads to the necessity of apriori knowledge of the language. The features are described below very briefly.

•Context words: Such words include the preceding and succeeding words of the current word. This is based on the observation that the surrounding words carry effective information for the identification of NEs.

•Word suffix and prefix: Fixed length word suffixes and prefixes are helpful to identify NEs. In addition, variable length word suffixes are also used. Word suffixes and prefixes are the effective features and work well for the inflective Indian languages like Bengali.

•Named Entity Information: This is the only dynamic feature in the experiment. The previous word NE tag is very informative in deciding the current word NE tag.

•First word (binary valued): This feature checks whether the current token is the first word of the sentence or not. Though Bengali is a relatively free phrase order language, the first word of the sentence is most likely a NE as it appears most of the time in the subject position.

•Length of the word (binary valued): This feature checks whether the length of the token is less than three or not. We have observed that very short words are most probably not the NEs.

•Infrequent word (binary valued): A cut off frequency has been chosen in order to consider the infrequent words in the training corpus. This is based on the observation that the infrequent words are rarely NEs.

•Digit features: Several digit features have been considered depending upon the presence and/or the number of digit(s) in a token. These binary valued features are helpful in recognizing miscellaneous NEs such as time, monetary and date expressions, percentages, numerical numbers etc.

•Position of the word (binary valued): Position of the word (whether last word or not) in a sentence is a good indicator of NEs.

•Part of Speech (POS) Information: We have used an SVM-based POS tagger (Ekbal and Bandyopadhyay, 2008d) that was originally developed with 26 POS tags, defined for the Indian languages. For SVM models, we have used this POS tagger. However, for the ME and CRF models, we have considered a coarse-grained POS tagger that has the following tags: Nominal, PREP (Postpositions) and Other.

•Gazetteer Lists: Gazetteer lists, developed manually as well as semi-automatically from the news corpus (Ekbal and Bandyopadhyay, 2008c), have been used as the features in each of the classifiers. The set of gazetteers along with the number of entries are as follows:

(1). Organization clue word (e.g., *ko.m* [Co.], *limited* [Limited] etc): 94, Person prefix words (e.g., *shrimAn* [Mr.], *shrImati* [Mrs.] etc.): 145, Middle names: 2,491, Surnames: 5,288, NE suffixes (e.g., *-bAbu* [-babu], *-dA* [-da], *-di* [-di] for person and *-lyAnd* [-land] *-pur*[-pur], *-liyA* [-lia] etc for location):115, Common location (e.g., *sarani* [Sarani], *roDa* [Road] etc.): 147, Action verb (e.g., *balen* [says], *ballen* [told] etc.):141, Function words:743, Designation words (e.g., *netA*[leader], *sA.msad* [MP] etc.): 139, First names:72,206, Location names:7,870, Organization names:2,225, Month name (English and Bengali calendars):24, Weekdays (English and Bengali calendars):14

(2). Common word (521 entries): Most of the Indian language NEs appears in the dictionary with some meanings. For example, the word *kamol* may be the name of a person but also appears in the dictionary with another meaning *lotus*, the name of a flower; the word *dhar* may be a verb and also can be the part of a person name. We have manually created a list, containing the words that can be NEs as well as valid dictionary words.

3 Active Learning Method for Baseline NER System

We have used a portion, containing 35,143 news documents and approximately 10 million wordforms, of the Bengali news corpus (Ekbal and Bandyopadhyay, 2008c) for developing the *baseline* NER system.

The frequently occurring words have been collected from the *reporter*, *location* and *agency* tags of the Bengali news corpus. The unlabeled corpus is tagged with the elements from the seed lists. In addition, various gazetteers have been used that include surname, middle name, person prefix words, NE suffixes, common location and designations for further tagging of the NEs in the training corpus. The following linguistic rules have been used to tag the training corpus:

(i). If there are two or more words in a sequence that represent the characters of Bengali or English alphabet, then such words are part of NEs. For example, *bi e* (B A), *ci em di e* (C M D A), *bi je pi* (B J P) are all NEs.

(ii). If at the end of a word, there are strings like *- era*(-er), *-eraa* (-eraa), *-ra* (*-ra*), *-rA* (-raa), *-ke* (-ke), *-dera* (-der) then the word is likely to be a person name.

(iii). If a clue word like *saranI* (sarani), *ro.Da* (road), *lena* (lane) etc. is found after an unknown word then the unknown word along with the clue word may be a location name.

(iv). A few names or words in Bengali consist of the characters *chandrabindu* or *khanda ta*. So, if a particular word W is not identified as NE by any of the above rules but includes any of these two characters, then W may be a NE. For example *o.NrI* (*onry*) is a person name.

(v). The set of action verbs like *balen* (says), *ballen* (told), *ballo* (told), *shunla* (heared), *ha.Nslo* (*haslo*) etc. often determines the presence of person names. If an unknown word W appears in the sentence followed by the action verbs, then W is most likely a person name. Otherwise, W is not likely to be a NE.

(vi). If there is reduplication of a word W in a sentence then W is not likely to be a NE. This is so because rarely name words are reduplicated. In fact, reduplicated name words may signify something else. For example, *rAm rAm* (ram ram) is used to greet a person.

(vii). If at the end of any word W there are suffixes like *-gulo* (-gulo), *-guli* (guli), *-khAnA* (-*khana*) etc., then W is not a NE.

For each tag T inserted in the training corpus, the algorithm generates a *lexical* pattern *p* using a context window of maximum width 6 (excluding the tagged NE) around the left and the right tags, e.g.,

p = [$l_{-3} l_{-2}\ l_{-1}$ <T> ...</T> $l_{+1}\ l_{+2}\ l_{+3}$],

where, $l_{\pm i}$ are the *context* of p. All these patterns, derived from the different tags of the labeled and unlabeled training corpora, are stored in a Pattern Table (or, set P), which has four different fields namely, pattern *id* (identifies any particular pattern), pattern *example* (pattern), pattern *type* (*Person/Location/Organization*) and *relative frequency* (indicates the number of times any pattern of a particular *type* appears in the entire training corpus relative to the total number of patterns generated of that *type*). This table has 20,967 distinct entries.

Every pattern p in the set P is matched against the same unlabeled corpus. In a place, where the context of p matches, p predicts the occurrence of the left or right boundary of name. POS information of the words as well as some linguistic rules and/or length of the entity have been used in detecting the other boundary. The extracted entity may fall in one of the following categories:

- *positive example*: The extracted entity is of the same NE *type* as that of the pattern.
- *negative example:* The extracted entity is of the different NE *type* as that of the pattern.
- *error example*: The extracted entity is not at all a NE.

The *type* of the extracted entity is determined by checking whether it appears in any of the seed lists; otherwise, its *type* is determined manually. The *positive* and *negative* examples are then added to the appropriate seed lists. The *accuracy* of the pattern is calculated as follows:

accuracy(p)= |*positive* (p)|/[| *positive* (p)| + |*negative* (p)| + |*error*(p)|]

A threshold value of *accuracy* has been chosen in order to discard the patterns below this threshold. A pattern is also discarded if its total *positive count* is less than a predetermined threshold value. The remaining patterns are ranked by their *relative frequency* values. The *n* top high frequent patterns are retained in the pattern set P and this set is denoted as *Accept Pattern*.

All the *positive* and *negative* examples extracted by a pattern p can be used to generate further patterns from the same training corpus. Each new *positive* or *negative* instance (not appearing in the seed lists) is used to further tag the training corpus. We repeat the previous steps for each new NE until no new patterns can be generated. A newly generated pattern may be identical to a pattern that is already in the set P. In such a case, the *type* and *relative frequency* fields in the set P are updated accordingly. Otherwise, the newly generated pattern is added to the set with the *type* and *relative frequency* fields set properly. The algorithm terminates after 13 iterations and there are 20,176 distinct entries in the set P.

4 Semi-supervised Approach for Unlabeled Document and Sentence Selection

A method for automatically selecting the appropriate unlabeled data from a large collection of unlabeled documents for NER has been described in Ekbal and Bandyopadhyay (2008e). This work reported the selection of unlabeled documents based on the overall *F-Score* value of the individual system. In this work, the unlabeled documents have been selected based on the *Recall*, *Precision* as well as the *F-Score* values of the participating systems. Also, we have considered only the SVM-F model trained with the language independent, language dependent and context features for selecting the appropriate sentences to be included into the initial training data. The use of single model makes the training faster compared to Ekbal and Bandyopadhyay (2008e). The SVM-F model has been considered as it produced the best results for the development set as well as during the 10-fold cross validation test. The unlabeled 35,143 news documents have been divided based on news sources/types in order to create segments of manageable size, separately evaluate the contribution of each segment using a gold standard development test set and reject those that are not helpful and to apply the latest updated best model to each subsequent segment. It has been observed that incorporation of unlabeled data can only be effective if it is related to the target problem, i.e., the test set. Once the appropriate documents are selected, it is necessary to select the tagged sentences that are useful to improve both the *Recall* and *Precision* values of the system. Appropriate sentences are selected using the SVM-F model depending upon the structure and/or contents of the sentences.

4.1 Unlabeled Document Selection

The unlabeled data supports the acquisition of new names and contexts to provide new evidences to be incorporated in the models. Unlabeled data can degrade rather than improve the classifier's performance on the test set if it is irrelevant to the test document. So, it is necessary to measure the relevance of the unlabeled data to our target test set. We construct a set of key words from the test set T to check whether an unlabeled document d is useful or not.

- We do not use all words in the test set T as the key words since we are only concerned about the distribution of name candidates. So, each document is tested with the CRF model using the language independent features, language dependent features and the context features.
- We take all the name candidates in the top N best hypotheses (N=10) for each sentence of the test set T to construct a query set Q. Using this query set, we find all the relevant documents that include three (heuristically set) names belonging to the set Q. In addition, the documents are not considered if they contain fewer than seven (heuristic) names.

4.2 Sentence Selection

All the tagged sentences of a relevant document are not added to training corpus as incorrectly tagged or irrelevant sentences can lead to the degradation in model performance. Our main concern is on how much new information is extracted from each sentence of the unlabeled data compared to the training corpus that already we have in our hand.

The SVM-F model has been used to select the relevant sentences. All the relevant documents are tagged with the SVM-F model developed with the language independent, language dependent and context features along with the class decomposition technique. If both *Recall* and *Precision* values of the SVM-F model increase then that sentence is selected to be added to the initial training corpus. A close investigation reveals the fact that this criterion often selects a number of sentences which are too short or do not include any name. These words may make the model worse if added to the training data. For example, the distribution of non-names may increase significantly that may lead to degradation of model performance. In this experiment, we have not included the sentences that include fewer than *five* words or do not include any names. The bootstrapping procedure is given as follows:

1. Select a relevant document *RelatedD* from a large corpus of unlabeled data with respect to the test set T using the document selection method described in Section 4.1.
2. Split *RelatedD* into n subsets and mark them C_1, C_2, …., C_n.
3. Call the development set *DevT*.
4. For I=1 to n

4.1. Run SVM-F model, developed with the language independent features, language dependent feature and context features along with the class decomposition technique, on C_i.

4.2. If the length of each tagged sentence S is less than five or it does not contain any name then discard S.

4.3. Add C_i to the training data and retrain SVM-F model. This produces the updated model.

4.4. Run the updated model on *DevT*; if the *Recall* and *Precision* values reduce then don't use C_i and use the old model.

5. Repeat steps 1-4 until *Recall* and *Precision* values of the SVM-F model either become equal or differ by some threshold values (set to 0.01) in consecutive two iterations.

5 Evaluation Results and Discussions

Out of 200K wordforms, 150K wordforms along with the IJCNLP-08 shared task data has been used for training the models. Out of 200K wordforms, 50K wordforms have been used as the development data. The system has been tested with a gold standard test set of 35K wordforms. Each of the models has been evaluated in two different ways, being guided by language independent features (language independent system denoted as LI) and being guided by language independent as well as language dependent features (language dependent system denoted as LD).

5.1 Language Independent Evaluation

A number of experiments have been carried out in order to identify the best-suited set of language independent features for NER in each of models. Evaluation results of the development set for the NER models are presented in Table 1 in terms of percentages of Recall (R), Precision (P) and F-Score (FS). The ME based system has demonstrated the F-Score value of 74.67% for the context word window of size three, i.e., previous one word, current word and the next word, prefixes and suffixes of length up to three characters of only the current word, dynamic NE tag of the previous word, first word, infrequent word, length and the various digit features. The CRF based system yielded the highest F-Score value of 76.97% for context window of size five, i.e., two preceding, current and two succeeding words along with the other set of features as in the ME model. Both the SVM based systems have demonstrated the best performance for the context window of size seven, i.e., three preceding, current and two succeeding words, dynamic NE information of the previous two words along with the other set of features as in the ME and CRF based systems. In SVM models, we have conducted experiments with the different polynomial kernel functions and observed the highest F-Score value with degree 2. It has been also observed that *pairwise* multiclass decision method performs better than the one vs rest method. For all the models, context words and prefixes and/or suffixes have been found to be the most effective features.

Model	R	P	FS
ME	76.82	72.64	74.67
CRF	78.17	75.81	76.97
SVM-F	79.14	77.26	**78.19**
SVM-B	79.09	77.15	78.11

Table 1. Results on the development set for the language independent supervised models

5.2 Language Dependent Evaluation

Evaluation results of the systems that include the POS information and other language dependent features are presented in the Table 2. During the experiments, it has been observed that all the language dependent features are not equally important. POS information is the most effective followed by NE suffixes, person prefix words, designations, organization clue words and location clue words. Table 1 and Table 2 show that the language dependent features can improve the overall performance of the systems significantly.

Model	R	P	FS
ME	87.02	80.77	83.78
CRF	87.63	84.03	85.79
SVM-F	87.74	85.89	**86.81**
SVM-B	87.69	85.17	86.72

Table 2. Results on the development set for the language dependent supervised models

5.3 Use of Context Features as Features

Now, the high ranked patterns of the *Accept Pattern* set (Section 3) can be used as the features of the individual classifier. A feature 'ContextInf' is defined by observing the three preceding and succeeding words of the current word. Evaluation results are presented in Table 3. Clearly, it is evident from the results of Table 2 and Table 3 that context features are very effective to improve the *Precision* values in each of the models.

Model	R	P	FS
ME	88.22	83.71	85.91
CRF	89.51	85.94	87.69
SVM-F	89.67	86.49	**88.05**
SVM-B	89.61	86.47	88.01

Table 3. Results on the development set by including context features

5.4 Results on the Test Set

A gold standard test set of 35K wordforms has been used to report the evaluation results. The models have been trained with the language independent, language dependent and the context features. Results have been presented in Table 4 for the test set. In the *baseline* model, each pattern of the *Accept Pattern* set is matched against the test set. Results show that SVM-F model performs best for the test set.

Error analyses have been conducted with the help of confusion matrix. In order to improve the performance of the classifiers, we have used some post-processing techniques.

Output of the ME based system has been post-processed with a set of heuristics (Ekbal and Bandyopadhyay, 2009) to improve the performance further. The post-processing as described in Ekbal and Bandyopadhyay (2008e) tries to assign the correct tag according to the n-best results for every sentence of the test set in the CRF framework. In order to remove the unbalanced class distribution between names and non-names in the training set, we have considered the class decomposition technique (Ekbal and Bandyopadhyay, 2008e) for SVM. Evaluation results of the post-processed systems are presented in Table 5.

Model	R	P	FS
Baseline	68.11	71.37	69.32
ME	86.04	84.98	85.51
CRF	87.94	87.12	87.53
SVM-F	89.91	85.97	**87.89**
SVM-B	89.82	85.93	87.83

Table 4. Results on the test set

Model	R	P	FS
ME	87.29	86.81	87.05
CRF	89.19	88.85	89.02
SVM-F	90.23	88.62	**89.41**
SVM-B	90.05	88.61	89.09

Table 5. Results of the post-processed models on the test set

Each of the models has been also evaluated for the 10-fold cross validation tests. Initially all the models have been developed with the language independent features along with the context features. Then, language dependent features have been included into the models. In each run of the 10 tests, the outputs have been post-processed with the several post-processing techniques as described earlier. Results are shown in Table 6.

	Model	R	P	FS
LI	ME	81.34	79.01	80.16
	CRF	82.66	80.75	81.69
	SVM-F	83.87	81.83	82.83
	SVM-B	83.87	81.77	82.62
LD	ME	87.54	87.97	87.11
	CRF	89.5	88.73	89.19
	SVM-F	89.97	88.61	89.29
	SVM-B	89.76	88.51	89.13

Table 6. Results of the 10-fold cross validation tests

Statistical ANOVA tests (Anderson and Scolve, 1978) demonstrated that the performance improvement in each of the language dependent model is statistically significant over the language independent model. We have also carried out the statistical tests to show that performance improvement in CRF over ME and SVM-F over CRF are statistically significant.

5.5 Impact of Unlabeled Data Selection

In order to investigate the contribution of document selection in bootstrapping, the post-processed models are run on 35,143 news documents. This yields the gradually improving performance for the SVM-F model as shown in Table 7. After selection of the appropriate unlabeled data, all the models have been retrained by including the unlabeled documents. Results have been presented in Table 8.

Itera-tion	Sentences added	R	P	FS
0	0	89.97	88.61	89.29
1	129	90.19	88.97	89.58
2	223	90.62	89.14	89.87
3	332	90.89	89.73	90.31
4	416	91.24	90.11	90.67
5	482	91.69	90.65	91.16
6	543	91.88	90.97	91.42
7	633	92.07	91.05	91.56
8	682	92.33	91.31	91.82
9	712	92.52	91.39	91.95
10	723	92.55	91.44	91.99
11	729	92.57	91.45	92.01
12	734	92.58	91.45	92.01

Table 7. Incremental improvement of performance

Model	R	P	FS
ME	90.7	89.78	90.24
CRF	92.02	91.66	91.84
SVM-B	92.34	91.42	91.88
SVM-F	92.58	91.45	92.01

Table 8. Results after unlabeled data selection

5.6 Voting Techniques

In order to obtain higher performance, we have applied weighted voting to the four models. We have used the following weighting methods:

(1). Uniform weights (Majority voting): All the models are assigned the same voting weight. The combined system selects the classifications, which are proposed by the majority of the models. In case of a tie, the output of the SVM-F model is selected. The output of the SVM-F model has been selected due to its highest performance among all the models.

(2). Cross validation *Precision* values: Two different types of weights have been defined depending on the 10-fold cross validation *Precision* on the training data as follows:

(a). Total *Precision*: In this method, the overall average *Precision* of any classifier is assigned as the weight for it.

(b). Tag *Precision*: In this method, the average *Precision* value of the individual tag is assigned as the weight for the corresponding model.

Experimental results of the voted system are presented in Table 9. Evaluation results show that the system achieves the highest performance for the voting scheme 'Tag *Precision*'. Voting shows (Tables 8-9) an overall improvement of **2.74%** over the least performing ME based system and **0.97%** over the best performing SVM-F system. This also shows an improvement of 23.66% *F-Score* over the *baseline* model.

Voting	R	P	FS
Majority	92.59	91.47	92.03
Total *Precision*	93.08	91.79	92.43
Tag *Precision*	93.81	92.18	92.98

Table 9. Results of the voted system

6 Conclusion

In this paper, we have reported a voted system with the use of appropriate unlabeled data. We have also demonstrated how language dependent features can improve the system performance. It has been experimentally verified that effective measures to select relevant documents and useful labeled sentences are important. The system has demonstrated the overall *Recall*, *Precision*, and *F-Score* values of 93.81%, 92.18%, and 92.98%, respectively.

Future works include the development of NER system using other machine learning techniques such as decision tree, AdaBoost etc. We would like to apply the proposed voted technique for the development of NER systems in other Indian languages. Future direction of the work will be to investigate an appropriate clustering technique that can be very effective for the development of NER systems in the resource-constrained Indian language environment. Instead of the words, the cluster of words can be used as the features of the classifiers. It may reduce the cost of training as well as may be helpful to improve the performance. We would like to explore other voting techniques.

References

Anderson, T. W. and Scolve, S. Introduction to the Statistical Analysis of Data. *Houghton Mifflin*, 1978.

Bikel, Daniel M., R. Schwartz, Ralph M. Weischedel. 1999. An Algorithm that Learns What's in Name. *Machine Learning (Special Issue on NLP),* 1-20.

Bothwick, Andrew. 1999. A Maximum Entropy Approach to Named Entity Recognition. *Ph.D. Thesis*, NYU.

Ekbal, Asif, Naskar, Sudip and S. Bandyopadhyay. 2007b. Named Entity Recognition and Transliteration in Bengali. *Named Entities: Recognition, Classification and Use, Special Issue of Lingvisticae Investigationes Journal, 30:1 (2007), 95-114.*

Ekbal, Asif, Haque, R and S. Bandyopadhyay. 2008a. Named Entity Recognition in Bengali: A Conditional Random Field Approach. In *Proceedings of 3rd International Joint Conference on Natural Language Processing* (*IJCNLP-08*), 589-594.

Ekbal, Asif, and S. Bandyopadhyay. 2008b. Bengali Named Entity Recognition using Support Vector Machine. In *Proceedings of the Workshop on Named Entity Recognition on South and South East Asian Languages* (*NERSSEAL*), *IJCNLP-08*, 51-58.

Ekbal, Asif, and S. Bandyopadhyay. 2008c. A Web-based Bengali News Corpus for Named Entity Recognition. *Language Resources and Evaluation Journal*, Volume (40), 173-182.

Ekbal, Asif and S. Bandyopadhyay. 2008d. Web-based Bengali News Corpus for Lexicon Development and POS Tagging. In *POLIBITS, an International Journal,* Volume (37), 20-29, ISSN: 1870-9044.

Ekbal, Asif and S. Bandyopadhyay. 2008e. Appropriate Unlabeled Data, Post-processing and Voting Can Improve the Performance of NER System. In *Proceedings of the 6th International Conference on Natural Language Processing (ICON-08)*, 234-239, India.

Ekbal, Asif and S. Bandyopadhyay. 2009. Improving the Performance of a NER System by Post-processing, Context Patterns and Voting. In *W. Li and D. Molla-Aliod (Eds): ICCPOL 2009, Lecture Notes in Artificial Intelligence (LNAI), Springer Berlin/Heidelberg, Volume* (*5459*), 45-56.

Florian, Radu, Ittycheriah, A., Jing, H. and Zhang, T. 2003. Named Entity Recognition through Classifier Combination. In *Proceedings of CoNLL-2003*.

Lafferty, J., McCallum, A., and Pereira, F. 2001. Conditional Random Fields: Probabilistic Models for Segmenting and Labeling Sequence Data. In *Proceedings of 18th International Conference on Machine Learning (ICML),* 282-289.

Li, Wei and Andrew McCallum. 2003. Rapid Development of Hindi Named Entity Recognition Using Conditional Random Fields and Feature Inductions. *ACM TALIP*, 2(3), (2003), 290-294.

Saha, Sujan, Sarkar, S and Mitra, P. 2008. A Hybrid Feature Set based Maximum Entropy Hindi Named Entity Recognition. In *Proceedings of the 3rd International Joint Conference on Natural Language Processing* (*IJCNLP-08*), 343-349.

Valdimir N., Vapnik 1995. The Nature of Statistical Learning Theory. *Springer*.

Yamada, Hiroyasu, Taku Kudo and Yuji Matsumoto. 2002. Japanese Named Entity Extraction using Support Vector Machine. In *Transactions of IPSJ,* Vol. 43 No. 1, 44-53.

Author Index

Association for Computational Linguistics
209 N. Eighth Street
Stroudsburg, Pennsylvania 18360

CURRAN ASSOCIATES INC
proceedings
.com